Frederick George Lee

The Church Under Queen Elizabeth

An Historical Sketch

Frederick George Lee

The Church Under Queen Elizabeth
An Historical Sketch

ISBN/EAN: 9783337004552

Printed in Europe, USA, Canada, Australia, Japan

Cover: Foto ©Thomas Meinert / pixelio.de

More available books at **www.hansebooks.com**

THE CHURCH

UNDER

QUEEN ELIZABETH

Beati pacifici.

✠

"In the whole carriage of this work I have assumed unto myself the freedom of a just historian; concealing nothing out of fear, nor speaking anything for favour; delivering nothing for a truth without good authority; but so delivering ·that truth as to witness for me that I am neither biassed by love or hatred, nor overswayed by partiality and corrupt affections."
—Peter Heylyn, D.D.

✠

Fide et constantia.

THE CHURCH

UNDER

QUEEN ELIZABETH

An Historical Sketch

By FREDERICK GEORGE LEE, D.D.

VICAR OF ALL SAINTS, LAMBETH

AUTHOR OF "HISTORICAL SKETCHES OF THE REFORMATION," ETC.

A NEW AND REVISED EDITION

WITH AN INTRODUCTION ON

"THE PRESENT POSITION OF THE ESTABLISHED CHURCH"

"That bright Occidental Star, Queen Elizabeth, of most happy memory."
The Epistle Dedicatory of King James's version of the Bible.

LONDON

W. H. ALLEN & CO. LIMITED

13 WATERLOO PLACE, S.W.

1892

"I will say that battered as is that old hull [the Church of England], it is a great breakwater between the raging waves of Infidelity and Catholic truth in this land ; that it has held so long together, under so many disadvantages and difficulties, must be a work of Divine Providence for some great end which remains to be developed."—AUGUSTUS WELBY PUGIN (1853).

"Let only Catholics co-operate with their Anglican brethren, and Anglicans co-operate with Catholics, for the restoration of mutual and corporate unity for the triumph of Catholic truth, not for the destruction of anything that men hold and cling to as the outward and living form of their visible existence ; and the glorious result, which every good man must wish for, and which none but evil men would deprecate, will soon crown our mutual and combined efforts."—AMBROSE L. M. P. DE LISLE (1857).

"Doubtless the National Church has hitherto been a serviceable breakwater against doctrinal errors more fundamental than its own. How long this will last in the years now before us, it is impossible to say ; for the nation drags down its Church to its own level."— H. E. JOHN HENRY CARDINAL NEWMAN (1864).

"Coming nearer home, he said that England had lost the perfection of the unity of faith and the unity of the Church ; but though not a Catholic people it was Christian still. Taken in its millions it was a baptized people. Through the neglect and sin of fathers and mothers, multitudes grew up without baptism ; but the English people still believed in revelation, in the coming of Jesus Christ into the world as the Saviour of men, and in the inspiration of the Holy Scriptures as the Word of God."—H. E. CARDINAL MANNING, Archbishop of Westminster (1879).

TO ALL

WHO ARE PREPARED TO LOOK OUR DIFFICULTIES

AS ENGLISH CHURCHMEN FAIRLY IN THE FACE

AND WHO

HAVING REALISED THEM, ARE ENDEAVOURING

IN A CONSERVATIVE SPIRIT AND BY A REASONABLE METHOD

TO OVERCOME THEM

THE GENEROUS, THE SELF-SACRIFICING, THE ZEALOUS

FRIENDS, KNOWN AND UNKNOWN

ABROAD AND AT HOME

LABOURING

IN THE FAITH AND FEAR OF GOD, AND ON

NO SANDY FOUNDATION

FOR

CORPORATE REUNION

THIS VOLUME

IS RESPECTFULLY DEDICATED

IN THE HOPE, WITH A BLESSING FROM ON HIGH,

OF

RESTORED PEACE AND VISIBLE UNITY

UNDER THE PATERNAL RULE OF

THE CHIEF BISHOP OF CHRISTENDOM

" The Reformation, no doubt, cost much. It broke up the visible unity so dear to Christians who believe our Lord's universal prayer in St. John and the Epistle to the Ephesians to be part of the Word of God. It bred a race of violent experimentalists, who were in their time enemies of faith, of charity, and of order."—Canon Liddon's Sermon at St. Mary's, Oxford, reported in the *Guardian* of 25th June 1879.

"I know of no law, human or divine, which forbids me, or any other free-born Englishman, whilst submitting to every existing ordinance of man for the Lord's sake, to use all constitutional means for the repeal and abrogation of all such laws as I believe to be mischievous and contrary to the revealed and declared will of God. What I, for one, mean, when I say that I will do my utmost to undo the work of the Reformation, is this:—I believe that the chief and most important work which was done at the Reformation was to render the things of God unto Cæsar. I shall always strive, to the best of my humble ability, to give back to God the things of God. And the cuckoo-cry of 'the principles of the Reformation are in danger' certainly will not scare me from my purpose. If the Reformation gentlemen considered themselves justified, as I suppose they did, in upsetting the Settlement of Magna Charta, a settlement brought about and cemented by the martyrdom of our most glorious saint and patron, St. Thomas, why should I have a moment's hesitation in doing my best to strive to alter the Reformation Settlement and go back to that of Magna Charta and St. Thomas? I wait for an answer."—" The Keys of the Kingdom of Heaven:" a Sermon by the Rev. Dr. T. W. Mossman, O.C.R., pp. 14, 15. (London, 1879.)

Introduction.

THE PRESENT POSITION OF THE ESTABLISHED CHURCH.

When, in 1833, the Tractarian movement first arose at Oxford, it is remarkable that its leaders, in their important work of restoration and reparation, commenced with explaining and maintaining the doctrine of the Sacraments, and not that of the true nature and character of the Universal Church. This was like carving the pinnacle before securing the foundation. They assumed, but never once attempted to prove, that the established communion in England was identical, in all essential particulars, with the Old Church of the country, and in communion with the Church throughout the world. They started with the assumption that none of the changes at the "Reformation" had altered its organic life, though the then disorganised religious state of England stared them in the face. Of course this easier method saved them a world of investigation and trouble. Having a solid foundation, as they so obviously believed themselves to possess, they could proceed to build up a superstructure. This, as we know, they did both with system and spirit. In so doing they took for granted that the ordinary historical theories concerning the changes under Henry VIII., Edward VI., and Elizabeth were, in the main, true and to be depended on. But these theories have turned out to be only theories; and, though bolstered up for some years under Burnet's tuition, in the face of historical documents which have been brought to light of late, they now no longer hold their ground. They are exploded; for they were founded only on fraud, fiction, and romance. It is hard to entertain the conviction that, during Queen Elizabeth's reign, the persecutors of the Catholics, men like Grindal, Sandys, Cecil, and Walsingham belonged to the same religious communion as

vii

did those poor souls who, on religious grounds, endured such
virulent persecution at their hands—the Rack, the Scavenger's
Daughter, and the Little Ease. The idea of "the Catholic
Church," as set forth in the Three Creeds, was wholly different,
therefore, in the minds of the persecutors and the persecuted.
With the former "the Church" was a local or national institution recently made by themselves and Parliament, of which the
Queen was the source of all jurisdiction and authority, the lawful
bestower of the chief dignities, the final arbiter of all theological
and ecclesiastical disputes; in fact, the supreme head or
governess. With the latter, as with St. Gregory the Great, it
was "evident to all who knew the gospel, that by the Voice of
the Lord the care of the whole Church was committed to holy
Peter, the prince of all the apostles. . . . For to him it is said,
'Thou art Peter, and upon this rock I will build My Church,
and I will give unto thee the keys of the kingdom of heaven.'
Behold, he receives the keys of the heavenly kingdom; the
power of binding and of loosing is given to him. *To him the
care and government of the whole Church is committed.*"[1]

The Tractarian movement, nevertheless, has done much for
England; for it has given a new phase of character to, and
created a fresh interest in, the Established Church. In external
questions—decency, order, and ornaments—it has brought about
a silent revolution. The slovenly and idle of a previous generation, who moved in a well-defined groove, have given place to
quite another race, much more active no doubt, owning several
meritorious virtues, but distinguished at the same time by greater
narrowness, less solid learning and zeal, and a remarkable tendency on the part of some of its members to rest satisfied with
ephemeral and shallow literature. Art, poetry, and architecture,
however, discreetly made use of, have at the same time each
lent a helping hand in securing the far better reformation than
that which was completed under Queen Elizabeth. Even in
deeper and more important questions much has been likewise
done by the Tractarians. So that if the main bulk of the nation,
the people generally, have only been slightly touched by that
movement; if the Establishment itself has become more comprehensive, a considerable and respectable minority—perhaps a
third of the clergy, their dependents, and their immediate friends

[1] "Cunctis evangelium scientibus liquet, quod voce Dominica sancto et
omnium Apostolorum principi Petro Apostolo totius Ecclesiæ cura commissa
est. . . . Ecce claves Regni Cœlestis accipit, potestas ei ligandi ac solvendi
tribuitur, cura ei totius Ecclesiæ et principatus committitur."—*S. Gregor.
Mag. Epist. ad Maurit. August.*, lib. iv. Epist. 32.

and allies ; certain laymen with ecclesiastical tastes, and many single women of the upper and middle classes—have been largely influenced.[1] Thus, as every one may see, a minority has, both in principle and taste, become more Catholic ; while the Church of England itself, in its corporate capacity, has distinctly grown more latitudinarian and human.

Out of this movement another has recently developed, harmless enough and even beneficial so long as the energies of its more active members were confined to restoring churches introducing Gregorian music and surpliced choirs, putting up stained glass windows, wearing albs and chasubles, and repairing the universal ruin and desolation which the Reformation, the Great Rebellion, and the Revolution of William of Orange—separate acts in one doleful drama—have in turn so efficiently wrought. But anything but harmless, when it inconsistently began to advocate laxity of doctrine, and tolerate "schools of thought" in which Catholicism finds no place ; to enlarge the breach between England and Rome ; to discountenance corporate reunion ; to disparage the English Roman Catholics,[2] who through so long a night of moral darkness have kept the lamp of divine truth burning. These, though persecuted with demoniacal fury, have come forth again to proclaim, without change or variation, the very same faith which Bede and St. Wilfred, St. Thomas the Martyr, Warham, More, Watson, and Cardinal Pole held and taught. They have an admirable organisation ; they cannot be ignored, and on every reasonable Anglican theory, being brethren in Christ, surely should not be abused.

It is, of course, disappointing and melancholy to note that some of the more recent exhibitions of " Ritualism," as it is called, display all the narrowness, virulence, and pettiness of the

---

[1] In this movement it is remarkable, as showing its exceptional characteristics, that individual effort and not corporate action secures success. The Church of England itself, as a corporation, does little or nothing. Even if the ordinary work of Christianity has to be done, a special organisation, like the S. P. G., the Teetotal Society, or the Home Mission Order, has to be started to do it. Moreover, so much depends on the lives of individuals. A certain work may flourish so long as some gifted parson carries it on ; but, if change or death should happen, the work too often altogether collapses.

[2] Mr. Mackonochie, the noted Ritualist, is reported to have declared in a sermon that "separation from the Church of England involved separation from Christ." If to the modern English Establishment had been exclusively entrusted the office of custodian of the faith, it is no exaggeration to say that the faith in England must long ago have perished ; for even now it is impossible for any one to declare for certainty what the Establishment teaches concerning the elementary doctrine of baptism, much less, in regard to others, what it preserves, affirms, or regards with indifference.

most perverse sects.[1] From fair and open argument with
Roman Catholics their self-elected leaders have long ago retired ;
and by a now prolonged silence (except the hebdomadal jabber [2]
of their cheap serials) appear to indicate that, confuted if not
discomfited, they have given up the contest as lost.   Their
influence, consequently, is very much less than they assume it to
be.   It may be, and possibly is, very considerable in certain
private convents, where the Superior, without legitimate authority
or reasonable check of visitor or diocesan, can exercise a moral
tyranny which only old women could practise, and only young
ones put up with.

The reiterated boast, again, that the horny-handed working-
men of London and our great cities care for the ritualistic
movement, is at once confident and loud ; but this appears to be
only based on the daring assertions of unscrupulous wire-pullers ;
who, holding the strings and rings, lie concealed in the background, while their hired puppets caper and threaten, brag and
posturise, reading out what has been written for them to maintain

---

[1] As two recent examples of this, the cases of Mr. E. S. Grindle, the
celebrated " Presbyter Anglicanus," and Mr. Orby Shipley, who disconnected
themselves from the Establishment, will be familiar to all.   The ungenerous,
spiteful, and insolent manner in which some of their old allies at once wrote
of them was pitiful and humiliating to read.

[2] As a specimen of the profane scoffing and infidel-like sneers (worthy of
Voltaire himself) in which some of the Ritualists indulge, the following extract from one of their serials, dated April 19th, 1879, edited by a parson, is
given.   It displays a vicious spirit so thoroughly repulsive and anti-Christian,
that no wonder can arise that God seems to have forsaken the sect it represents, now given up to frivolity, intestine squabbles, and despair :—

"The Romans, I see, have imported miracles into England. France has
no longer a monopoly of our Lady of Lourdes.   She has condescended
to cure the paralytic even in the very midst of 'unorthodox London.'   The
event came off a fortnight ago at a home for poor Roman Catholic boys in the
Harrow Road, and which is supported by sensational advertisements headed
' save the boy.'   Lord Archibald Douglas is about to build a chapel for his
lads, dedicated, of course, to our Lady of Lourdes, and, of course again, some
of the water from the holy fountain was brought to England to be sprinkled
round the foundation-stones.   Two of the lads, who have been unable for
many months to walk, through paralysis, were carried to see the ceremony,
and sprinkled with the precious water.   The story goes that on the morrow
the nurse went to carry the boys as usual, but, *mirabile dictu*, they with one
consent began to walk.   The doctor will, of course, be ready to disclaim all
merit in the earthly drugs which he was giving to them, and the people who
set down the awe to excitement and overwrought expectation will be regarded
as little better than infidels.   And as a miracle is born, if I may so say, at
one's very door, what the miracle will be like when it is full-grown, after all
the witnesses have been scattered and investigation is rendered difficult, those
may guess who have traced the effect of their own imagination in dealing with
the wonderful."   See Appendix, No. III., p. 364.

or assert on some public stage. Disorder and topsy-turvyism must certainly have risen to a perfect climax, and all authority have been repudiated, when compositors, basket-makers, and the owners of cheap newspapers can unblushingly stand forward, without any commission whatsoever from their fellow-workmen, to browbeat, bully, and pretend to instruct the various bishops of the Established Church in their official duties.

But amongst the great mass of Englishmen the general policy of these Ritualists (besides being taken up so much with questions of externals) is altogether too wayward and weak ever to command any but an occasional, and then very often only a contemptuous, consideration.

The old High Church party, or what now remains of it, has still, as is well known, a few great and influential leaders with a small following in the nation, and smaller influence. Unable to resist the Divorce Bill,[1] the infidel School Board system, and Lord Penzance, its members still make weighty speeches and put forth disregarded protests. For promoting union and defending the principles of the Church of England (whatever they may be), they form grand organisations like the English Church Union, which, it is to be feared, only make old separations more patent and fresh divisions more painful. Rome, and all that belongs thereto, they appear fanatically to hate—the language of some being at once ridiculous and profane; while they somewhat ostentatiously profess to be in love with what they call "the *true* principles of the Reformation." Secret societies for special prayer, and for enabling ministerial neophytes to lead a less worldly life than many Church of England parsons live, like the Society of the Holy Cross, are blown down and fall to pieces like a child's card-house, when the breath of public opinion, bearing their condemnation, meets them all of a sudden. Sacred members, forgetting their official dignity, scream at being discovered; and, in fear and trembling which seems perfectly sincere, are soon scattered as sheep without either fold or shepherd.

Archdeacon Palmer of Oxford, in his recent charge (A.D. 1879), has described the position of the Established Church, and stated the case concerning the supreme jurisdiction of the Crown, with

---

[1] "The Divorce Act, so far as it went, *was an act of national apostasy*, and in a marvellously brief space it has succeeded in breaking down the Christian instincts of the community. It gives us a startling view of the degradation of the public morals which has already taken place, to learn from Sir James Hannen that the motive of the suitors who go before him is, in ninety-nine cases out of a hundred, simply to obtain a licence to marry again."—*Church Times*, September 19th, 1879.

great accuracy and singular calmness. Temperate, unambiguous, and plain, he is at the same time frankly and perfectly Erastian ; though apparently ready to sacrifice something, if it can be shown to him that the principle of Erastianism is fatal, as it certainly is, to any efficient Christian work. Moreover, he quite admits the right and reasonableness of endeavouring to remedy the evil in a constitutional method. Here are his words :—

"In my judgment, the cardinal fact is that the final determination of all ecclesiastical causes is vested in the Crown, and is confided to a Court which the Crown has established with the consent of Parliament, and of Parliament alone, and that all other courts ecclesiastical are bound to echo its decisions. This, as I have reminded you, has been the law and use of England for nearly three centures and a half, if we neglect the short reign of Philip and Mary. It has been, in principle, more than once formally recognised, never formally repudiated, by the synods of the Church of England.[1]

"It is our right, as Englishmen, to use all lawful and constitutional means, in order to procure the repeal of the statutes on which this special jurisdiction of the Crown rests, if we think such repeal desirable—as it is our right to use like means in order to procure the repeal of any other statutes now in force. But it is also, I venture to think, our duty, both as Englishmen and as Church-men, to obey these statutes while they are unrepealed, and to submit to the decisions of the court which derives its authority from them. I need not attempt to prove our duty as Englishmen to obey any law of the land ; but I may be asked what further obligation to obedience in this particular lies on us as Churchmen. My answer is twofold. First, we are bound to obey, on the principle of deference to Church authority. Our Church, as I have said already, has more than once synodically affirmed the supreme jurisdiction of the Crown in causes ecclesiastical ; she has never synodically rejected it. Secondly, we are bound to obey, on the principle of regard to the highest interests of the Church. I do not speak of lands, or money, or any civil privileges whatever. I value these things highly. I value highly what men call the establishment of religion in this country. But I value it only as means to an end ; I value it only as a gigantic Home Mission Fund, which enables the Church to carry the message of salvation to the poorest districts of our great towns, and the most secluded nooks in England. Let it all go to-morrow, if it can be shown to be the price of its retention that the Church must deny her Lord, or cease to do His work effectively."

As showing the actual working of this system before our eyes, the following advice by Bishop Moberly, in his recent charge to the clergy of his diocese (A.D. 1879) regarding the use of the

---

[1] This statement of fact and law is mainly identical with that of the Arch-deacon's brother, Lord Selborne, who in his controversies both with " A Sussex Priest," Mr. E. S. Grindle, as to *principle*, and with Mr. James Parker of Oxford as to *fact*, retired in both cases from any attempt to maintain the two untenable positions which his lordship had assumed, and on which, it is to be feared, a Privy Council judgment was in part founded. See *Canon or Statute: A Correspondence on the P. W. R. Act between Lord Selborne and a Sussex Priest*. London, 1875. *Did Queen Elizabeth take Other Order in the Advertisements of* 1566? A Letter to Lord Selborne, with a Postscript. By James Parker, M.A. London, 1879.

mixed chalice and the duty of obedience to Lord Penzance, appears astounding :—

His lordship "was ready to admit, in the abstract, that a secular authority ought not to interpose in matters of sacred doctrine ; but still he thought the wisest course would be to submit to decisions when they had once been pronounced (even when they pressed unduly upon the clergy), instead of permitting them to be pointed at as signs of disunion. The bishop referred to the 'mixed chalice' question, and quoted various authorities to show that the mixed chalice, probably made use of by our Lord Himself at the institution of the Eucharist, was certainly in use in the primitive Church, and that there was nothing to show that it ever gave rise to superstition in the Roman Church before the Reformation. He considered it had never been prohibited by Act of Parliament or canon, but he counselled the clergy, as an adverse judgment had been given, to refrain from the practice in question."

On which it is sufficient to remark that if, in the first stages of the Church, the bishops had shown themselves to have been as amiable, peace-loving, and impressible as Dr Moberly, there would certainly have been no Christianity of any sort or kind left to be squabbled over in the present faithless age. It must surely be rather a stretch of faith—not to write "an act of credulity"—to believe that men like this are divinely-appointed custodians of the Christian deposit of faith.

The key to the spiritual position, as both archdeacon and bishop conclusively show, and as all can now see, was long ago given up, when England was duped into practically repudiating her relations with the universal Christian kingdom, its laws, and its ruler. Cranmer first betrayed the local flock which he was to govern; and so made a similar work easier for those who came after him—Matthew Parker and his immediate allies. The New Church, as finally arranged, formed, and moulded under Queen Elizabeth, was a purely local and national body, neither more nor less ; and has so remained, under a variety of theological and ecclesiastical changes,[1] unto the present day. For no national Parliament can possibly create a divine institution, and the missionary work of a human society ever fails. Parliament may properly give a charter to a gas company, or

[1] Mr. F. H. Dickenson, a frequent correspondent of the *Guardian*, in a letter which appeared in the number for September 10th, 1879, writes most truly and accurately thus:—"Any one who has watched the Church of England during the past forty years must see that *our faith and doctrine have largely altered ; and there is no reason to think that alteration has ceased*,"— one fresh proof, were it needed, of the changeable and human character of the institution in question. Did the *Guardian's* correspondent regard it as divine, he would no doubt instinctively shrink from making proposals to patch, mend, or further "reform" it. As it stands, he merely exercises, with regard to it, the inherent and indisputable right of every free-born Englishman.

authorise a railway board to use a corporate seal; but as for making a "Church" which is not inherently and essentially national and local—this is altogether beyond its great and acknowledged powers.

The sooner, therefore, that members of the established communion admit this, and begin to realise the most primary and elementary detail of God's revelation — and so, by precise thought, recognise respectively the true nature of the Church of Pentecost and the actual character of the Church of England; regarding each of which many have the most confused and inexact ideas)—the better will it be for all of us. By a series of tortuous arguments and historical misrepresentations, confusion has been made worse confounded. For loose expressions, words like "the Church" used in half a dozen different senses, and a mis-bestowal of the marks of the one Catholic body—the ark of salvation,—upon mere local communions, cannot be sufficiently reprehended.[1] Such dialectical ambiguities perplex, confuse, and mislead. The one Church of God is alone divine, all local and national Churches being essentially human.

As a consequence of such unfortunate confusion of thought and expression, certain persons have acted in late years as though the actual laws of the national Church of England ought to be practically revised or modified from time to time by some other external and independent law—some fanciful ideal, some statute of Utopia;—and in so acting have brought much trouble upon themselves and little advantage to their neighbours. How can the Catholic Church — which concerns all nations and peoples, but belongs exclusively to none—which is infallible, for it was created by the Holy Spirit,—how can this divine corporation either revise or reverse the sentences of any parliamentary communion? What actual machinery can be brought into operation to effect such a process? Which of the ancient canons, moreover, ever recognised a woman as capable of being supreme head of a parish—putting aside a diocese or a group

---

[1] I take the following from the current newspapers and serials of September 1879:—"*Our mother, the Church of England.*"—"*Our Church* is far more favoured of God than any other Church."—"Not true members of *Our Church* at all; their hearts are elsewhere, with another Church," etc.— "*Our beloved Church* is founded on the Bible, whereas," etc.—"Where other Churches have secured a vantage-ground *Our Church* should certainly do the same."—"They remain in *Our Church* in order to revile her," etc. etc. etc. *ad nauseam:* all most conclusively proving that in the minds of the loose-thinking scribblers who use such phrases "Our Church" *is* (as without a doubt it most certainly is) something quite different from the Church of the Creeds—the one divine and world-wide corporation set up at Pentecost.

of dioceses? The Catholic Church throughout the whole world is, as we all know, guided by canon law, administered by living and lawful ecclesiastical judges, independent of kings, queens, and all secular rulers, and not amenable to civil courts; while the Church of England is now notoriously governed by Lord Penzance. Thomas Cromwell first ruled it under Henry VIII., Somerset under Edward VI., Cecil under Elizabeth. Ever since its foundation it has been similarly governed, either by commissioners appointed by the monarch, or some local court; and as long as it retains its present position, isolated and local, it will continue to be so governed.

People complain of the English Court of Appeal in spiritual causes,[1] which consists of certain Privy Councillors; but if they are content to remain visibly separated from the rest of Christendom, and not amenable to the great and universal Court of Appeal of the one Catholic Church,—and to this they are certainly *not* amenable, for some positively glory in their isolation,—they must put up with the inconvenience and make the best of it.

The law which this local and peculiar court professes to administer is not the law of God; of that it knows nothing, and cares nothing. Its business is to regulate the public preaching and teaching of the ministers of the Establishment, not according to God's revelation or the canon law of the Church Universal,—with these it has nothing whatsoever to do,—but, as the Reformers first determined, in strict and literal accordance with the statutes of the realm, with the enactments of the British Parliament.

As regards religion, every doctrine of God's revelation is subjected to the decisions of purely State tribunals. Our Blessed Lord is now only permitted to occupy that place which a representation of Him obtained under Alexander Severus, in the

---

[1] "What, I ask," wrote Mr. ex-Chancellor Wagner, "would St. Ambrose have said to the recent trial of 'Jenkins *versus* Cooke'? This unseemly trial proves, beyond all possibility of cavil, that the civil power in England *claims* to decide, in the last resort, not merely '*the temporal accidents of spiritual things*,' but even who shall, or who shall not, be admitted to the Holy Communion, and, *what is infinitely more serious still, that the Primate of all England is quite willing personally to acquiesce in this most fatal claim*, else he would have refused, with horror, to sit in the court at all. It is sadly significant and noteworthy that not one single bishop of the province of Canterbury has, as yet, *publicly* protested against a claim which, if granted, would wholly efface the spiritual authority of a 'bishop in the Church of God,' and make him the mere creature or tool of the civil power, powerless to exert the authority entrusted to him by our Lord Jesus Christ."—*Christ or Cæsar?* part ii. p. 40. London, 1877.

temple of the gods. All religions, it is maintained, are at last alike. The Church is now a "denomination." The crimes of blasphemy, infidelity, sacrilege, and atheism, moreover, are at length no crimes at all. Civil and religious liberty has efficiently changed all that. Images of atheists are set up in the public thoroughfares, and pointed at with pride as representations of great public benefactors. Blasphemers are honoured, and people are thus indirectly enjoined to go and do likewise. Parental rights, moreover, having their roots in natural religion, are, as regards education in England, on the high road to being altogether wiped out and lost. Of this the mob approves. The source of all authority, whether that of kings or priests, is God Almighty; but when legitimate Authority is laughed to scorn and trampled under foot by those who in its place have set up a rival human authority,—always wayward, weak, uncertain, vacillating, and liable to all kinds of error,—those who refuse to believe, fear, and serve their Maker, find that they too soon become slaves, tyrannised over cruelly, and whose backs are in the long run well scourged by scorpions of their own nurturing.

People sometimes remark that our Catholic ancestors must have been very indifferent or greatly wanting in zeal to have allowed such changes as those effected by a few "Reformers" to have been made without resistance. But in answer to this it should be remembered that they *did* resist to the best of their ability. In Yorkshire, Durham, Norfolk, Devonshire, Oxfordshire, and Lincolnshire, at various times, a most noble resistance *was* made by force, as well by poor as by rich. But it failed; and the heavy hand of vengeance, with a sanguinary and cruel grip,[1] came down upon all engaged in that resistance.

But to judge this question more equitably. Let us consider how tamely and quietly the changes effected by the Divorce Court, infidel education, and Lord Penzance's parliamentary authority—certain steps in our downward descent as a nation— are being actually submitted to, before our very eyes, ere we

---

[1] The Catholic Relief Act of 1778, and for Ireland in 1782, which relaxed some of the more ferocious parts of the penal laws and their most cruel grip, was only passed at a time when France and America were in confederation against England, and union at home was sorely needed. Down to that period the penal statutes of Elizabeth, James I., and William of Orange had disgraced our statute-book. In addition to persecution, riots, and violence for Roman Catholics were known under Lord George Gordon; again in 1807, in 1829, and in 1846; and again when the new Roman Catholic Hierarchy was set up. It is highly improbable that this volcano is quite extinct; for, as most of the legal relaxations of late years have been made at times of national trial and political strain, when fears abounded, the real sentiments of the populace may be unknown or inadequately forecast.

judge our ancestors too severely. The disastrous divisions of the Reformation have finally resulted in the anti-Christian system of education now completely in the ascendant. At the universities, in our ancient grammar schools, as well as in the recent national plan for instructing the lower classes—supported by public rates[1]—the Christian religion is quietly and contemptuously set aside,—with evil results which will soon enough be painfully discovered. Such a system of public schools may probably soon result in a corresponding system of public churches, where every sect may perform its orgies ; and where, moreover, every individual may worship whatsoever god or gods may have been set up, or may be tolerated, by the State ; or where the more advanced "philosophers" may worship each other or themselves. Now, it is only a very small minority of the English people who can heartily approve of either of these three dangerous measures, yet they have been each duly carried, and are now the law of the land ; while few, possibly, would dream of agitating for their abolition. The evil is seen, but not the remedy. Patriotism, zeal, and self-sacrifice are all given up in favour of self-seeking, wicked principles, and a false peace— that peace which only too surely heralds national corruption and certain decay.

In our cities and large towns—which are quietly reverting to paganism ; for, of late years, since the infamous "Gorham Judgment," not more than fifteen per cent. of the people are baptized at all[2]—what do we behold? The churches of the

---

[1] Dr. James Fraser, who once occupied the position of a Christian bishop at Manchester, is reported to have quite recently remarked that he looked upon the gradual extinction of all schools save Board schools with calm satisfaction and without any fear. The vicar-general of the diocese of Salford, however, recently pointed out that "the Church of England was gradually surrendering the great principles of religious education and handing her schools over to the School Boards. After a while the Church of England schools would cease altogether to be public elementary schools. When that time came there would remain only the Board schools and the Catholic schools. How long it would be before this change would take place he could not say, but the course followed by the clergy of the National Church left little doubt that a change would one day take place. As for Catholics, they could never surrender their schools to the School Boards or any other authority. With the godless education of the Board schools they could never have anything to do."

[2] At the Swansea Congress, the Rev. G. A. Seymour of Winchester maintained that "there is amongst our people a lamentable neglect of the Sacrament of Baptism, and stated that hardly more than ten per cent. of our people in our large towns are baptized in the Church of England. He considered that amongst Christian nations England was in this particular the lowest in the scale, except perhaps America."—*Guardian*, October 8th, 1879. In the same number, but on another page, of the newspaper from which the above is taken, there appeared a letter signed "A Country Clergy-

Establishment too ill-attended, and in some parts practically empty. Violent changes, from services of a Catholic character to those of a Puritan, and *vice versâ*, have often led to indifference. Zeal in a Catholic direction, having been consistently frowned upon by State authorities, has too often been clean stamped out. The churches on Sundays are thus empty and the streets crowded. What there may we see? A poor, down-looking, stunted race, with hard features and anxious, care-worn faces; out of the effeminate mouths of nine out of every ten stumpy men a burnt and smoking pipe sticking out like a spout or drain—the smouldering narcotic of which is supposed, in some manner, to stimulate their enfeebled and flagging energies. These pitiable forms seem, all of them, at once so self-engrossed and restless, eagerly hurrying on to growl over or gnaw the world's meat which perisheth, that no ray, even the faintest, of the beautiful life to come ever seems to fall upon their thronged and darkened pathway. For faith is dead. They believe only in that which they can handle and clutch. Of the angel-world and the supernatural, of times when the veil around this earth is drawn aside, and glimpses of another world are in mercy momentarily bestowed, they neither know nor care. Their gods and guides are the men of science, falsely so called, or, to rise to a somewhat higher level, it may be

man," which ran thus. The words in italics and within brackets are my own comments :—"Sir,—An unbaptized child died in my parish the other day. Immediately I heard of it I went to the house and offered to show my respect [*for its parents who had studiously despised our Lord's command*] and sympathy [*for them under the stupid charges which believers in the Christian religion might make*] by officiating at the funeral [*contrary to the rules of the Prayer-Book and the law of the land*]. I explained that I would put on my surplice and say the Lord's Prayer at the grave. My offer was most gratefully accepted. I used the following short service, compiled from Bishop How's "Pastor in parochiâ," and from our own services [*and so proved to the parents and the public that baptism is a mere ceremony, and that the unbaptized have quite as much right to Christian burial by the parson as the baptized. Am I not liberal with the trust which has been reposed in me?*] I gave the relatives a copy of the prayer, with which they were much pleased."—In the *Reunian Magazine*, vol. i. pp. 51-73, is an article on "Baptism in the Church of England," from the pen of a layman (as is said), in which some carefully-arranged statistics show that in some parishes just four per cent. of the children born, and no more, are baptized; in others, on an average about nine per cent. On pp. 494-498 are letters which show that Bishop Alford, who has "warned people to be on their guard against the fashionable doctrine of Baptismal Regeneration," openly baptized fourteen adults by once flicking his wetted fingers in the air over all of them, and that in a large Oxfordshire town the font has never been filled for forty years. Cardinal Newman and Mr. Robert Brett long ago pointed out the neglect of baptism, as also did the Rev. W. J. E. Bennett of Frome.

their own bellies. Their dismal gospel is summed up in the popular but dread resolution—"Let us eat and drink, for to-morrow we die." Therefore they all make our nation now stand out as a striking contrast to "Merry England of the olden time."

As to many rural districts, the spirit of indifference, like a dark cloud, has settled on the once happy homes of our country poor. The State religion, on which the Reformation impress is still indelibly stamped,[1] influences them but feebly, if at all. In Lincolnshire, Norfolk, Buckinghamshire, and South Wales many of the village churches, week by week, are practically empty. In towns, dissent still breeds; while unbelief, chilling its thousands to the heart's core, leaves them desolate and sad; restless in the present, hopeless for the future, or quietly indifferent. For, beginning with the elementary doctrine of Baptism, every detail of sacred revelation has long been a topic of controversy, wrangled over by the misbelieving and profane. Faith has at length so melted into opinion or mere sentiment, that even the home of opinion, now swept and garnished, is found to be cold, empty, and desolate. There is neither voice nor language, nor any to answer, nor any to regard. Some few by custom still superstitiously expose their phylactery and quote their favourite texts—like the ancient dame, who, as she asserted, found such personal comfort from mumbling over and over again the con-soling word "Mesopotamia"; but a supernatural law (as it is assumed to be) without a lawful interpreter, a religion without a divine guide, or a so-called "spiritual body" without a spiritual head, can only first lose the confidence, and then deservedly merit the contempt, of those who for generations can trace the dire influence of "reform," and long for a divine peace, for-feited and lost in past centuries; gone perhaps, for those few who most keenly miss it, never to return.

The only persons who have duly surveyed and accurately measured the situation as to profit by it are the modern Latitudinarians or Liberals—the legitimate successors of Socinus,

[1] "I have known the Communion Table used as a writing-desk for Sunday-school children and at vestry meetings."—Rev. W. H. Kelke, *Records of Bucks*, vol. iii. p. 127.—In a small but curious volume, *Odds and Ends* (London, 1872), Mr. William Maskell gives an account of an unique atrocity —the dissection, in the year 1839, of a corpse that had been exhumed, upon the Communion Table of the church of Powderstock, in Dorsetshire. "The church," he writes, "was shut up for three weeks after, on account of the stench which had penetrated through and saturated the entire building. I believe," he continues, "that the Communion Table was then restored to its former sacred purpose."—Pp. 54-73.

Cranmer, Erastus, Tillotson, Hoadley, and Balguy. And, since
the rise of the Oxford movement, the leaders of it, in their
conflicts with Latitudinarians, have, by reason of their losses and
disasters, been again and again compelled to shift their position,
modify their principles,[1] and change their tactics. Persons
professing the Catholic faith, out of communion with the rest
of Christendom, inevitably maintain their difficult position under
the greatest disadvantages. No one could have fought the
battle of Catholic dogma in the Church of England with greater
foresight, discretion, and ability, than did Dr. Newman when at
Oxford. But with all his consummate tact and immense learning, with all his high generosity and notorious zeal, he frankly
and truly confessed himself defeated.[2] The Liberals or Latitudinarians won in almost every conflict. With what result is well
known. Dr. Newman and his friends were driven out; while
Dr. Tait, one of the four tutors who persecuted him, is at
Canterbury, and is still bent on getting rid of the Athanasian
Creed, in which he frankly avows neither he himself nor his

[1] *E.g.* the late Rev. John Keble in the poem on "Gunpowder Treason,"
having relinquished the inexact belief of the Reformers for the teaching of
the Catholic Church, somewhat awkwardly altered his verse. See p. 40,
where the original poem is quoted.—Still more recently, Archdeacon
Denison, who took so prominent a part in the restoration of Convocation,
deplored his mistake in having done so; believing, because of later events,
that Convocation had done more harm than good. The truth is, that until
the question of the relations of England to the rest of Christendom is faced
and settled little can or will be done.

[2] "The most oppressive thought in the whole process of my change of
opinion was the clear anticipation, verified by the event, that it would issue
in the triumph of Liberalism. Against the anti-dogmatic principle I had
thrown my whole mind; yet now I was doing more than any one else could
do to promote it. I was one of those who had kept it at bay in Oxford for
so many years; and thus my very retirement was its triumph. *The men who
had driven me from Oxford were distinctly the Liberals: it was they who had
opened the attack upon Tract 90, and it was they who would gain a second
benefit if I went on to retire from the Anglican Church.* But this was not all.
As I have already said, there are but two alternatives, the way to Rome and
the way to atheism; Anglicanism is the half-way house on the other. How
many men were there, as I knew full well, who would not follow me now in
my advance from Anglicanism to Rome, but would at once leave Anglicanism
and me for the Liberal camp. It is not at all easy (humanly speaking) to
wind up an Englishman to a dogmatic level. I had done so in a good
measure in the case both of young men and of laymen, the Anglican *Via
Media* being the representative of dogma. The dogmatic and the Anglican
principle were one, as I had taught them; but I was breaking the *Via Media*
to pieces, and would not dogmatic faith altogether be broken up, in the minds
of a great number, by the demolition of the *Via Media?* Oh! how unhappy
this made me!"—*History of my Religious Opinions*, by J. H. Newman, D.D.
(original edition), pp. 329, 330. London, 1864.

brother-prelates believe,[1] it being too dogmatic in itself, and too distasteful to the public. Dr. Hampden died Bishop of Hereford. The editor of *Essays and Reviews* is now Bishop of Exeter, welcomed by High Churchmen for his zeal and energy. The present Bishop of Salisbury, who so disliked Dr. Newman's *Essay on Development* that he formerly replied to it, has himself so developed in the Latitudinarian direction that he actually administered the Lord's Supper at Westminster to a Unitarian preacher. Thus the Liberals—aided, of course, by their own political party, and bribed and promoted by the Conservatives —triumph all along the line. And so-called " High Churchmen " have at length condescended to be their faithful armour-bearers and trumpeters.

The spring of these Liberals or Erastians is elastic, and their grasp firm, as when, rising to shake themselves from the temporary dust of any conflict with High Churchmen, they sufficiently realise their own strength, and, with disdain for their discomfited opponents and with considerable self-confidence, march forward to greater victories. They know too well that the power of the English Establishment either to maintain or to enforce the dogmatic principle is as the power of a lifeless and rain-sodden scarecrow, neither more nor less. They perceive most accurately that the authority which first created the Establishment, and, as is reasonable enough, still effectually dominates it, intends to dominate it. This every bishop sees and knows.[2] That power was Parliament ; it is now Parliament, modified, reformed, and extended,—ever influenced in the present enlightened age by public opinion ; but, at best, Parliament.

[1] "We [the archbishop and bishops] do not—there is not a soul in this room who does—take the concluding clauses of the Athanasian Creed in their plain and literal sense."—Speech of Archbishop Tait in Convocation, *Guardian*, February 14th, 1872.

[2] Quite recently the Bishop of Oxford, somewhat misconceiving his position, went in person as a suppliant to the Court of Queen's Bench, asking that he might be allowed to act as a true bishop in his own diocese. But the Court, which of course represents Her Majesty the Queen,—the Supreme Governess of the Church of England, from whom (as Dr. Mackarness on his knees before her duly acknowledged) he received both spiritualties as well as temporalties,—declined to allow him to do anything of the sort. Lord Penzance is now the Chief Ecclesiastical Judge for Her Majesty in every diocese ; in Oxford as elsewhere. He was set up by a recent and special Act, which either all the bishops helped to pass, or now willingly administer ; and therefore Bishop Mackarness' demand was obviously unreasonable. The Act in question, though with art and cunning made specially for the inferior parsons, is thus found to have included the bishops. The Bishop of London has recently admitted, in his " Charge " (1879), that it was both a mistake and a failure.

However, the very boldness of these triumphant Erastians in
high places, their sharply-defined and sweeping policy, carried
out with no regard to the convictions of their opponents, and
with an inconsiderate roughness and rudeness worthy of Thomas
Cromwell or Hugh Latimer, has done more than anything else
to throw many Christian people back on first principles. So
long as some moderation and impartiality were shown at Lambeth; so long as it was possible to believe by a kind of traditional
fiction that the so-called "Church Courts" *were* Church Courts,
people, without inquiring, were content to regard them as such,
and quietly to acquiesce. But the Public Worship Regulation
Act [1] has successfully destroyed all such notions; while the
appointment by the two Primates of an ex-judge of the Divorce
Court to work the Act was a deliberate insult to the Christian
clergy, and an outrage disgraceful to all concerned.[2] It has, at
all events, shown conclusively the true character of the Establishment and its rulers—a singular advantage to those who, like the
late Mr. Keble, have been long doubtful whether it was from
heaven or of men.[3] As long, of course, as people cannot

[1] "It is, in point of fact—at least, so it seems to me—a thoroughly revolutionary measure *in its principle*, having for its main end or consequence the
abolition of all the ancient courts Christian; courts which, however fallen
from their first estate and unsatisfactory in their present condition, have
existed from the very earliest times in this country, and were an integral part
of its Christianity; and the substitution in their stead of a new secular court,
with no Christian instincts or traditions whatever to guide it, and deriving its
authority and jurisdiction in no way whatever from the Church, but entirely
from the new Act of Parliament which created it. Regarded in this light,
which I believe to be the true light, and one, I fear, which the verdict of
posterity will only too fully endorse, the Public Worship Regulation Act of
last year is one of the most mischievous and indefensible measures ever yet
concocted. For it is the virtual triumph of the anti-Christian principle of
Erastianism over ecclesiastical authority and independence; the acknowledgment, in practical effect, by the voice of the nation, that the Established
Church of England is to be regarded from henceforth as little better than a
mere State function or department of the earthly State, instead of (as it must
be if it be Christ's representative) its spiritual ruler and teacher."—*Christ
or Cæsar?* part ii. pp. 6, 7. London, 1877.
[2] "I do not suppose a more galling insult to a body of educated gentlemen,
such as the clergy of England are, is recorded in history than that which has
been practically offered to us by the two archbishops (Tait and Thomson) in
the peculiar character of the appointment they have thought fit to make."—
Christ or Cæsar? by A. D. Wagner, Chancellor of Chichester Cathedral,
part ii. p. 10. London, 1877.
[3] "I suppose, from some part of your letter, that you have been told I am
speaking to friends occasionally as if I was perplexed about continuing where
I am. My perplexity is rather what to say to others who ask my advice,
than how to act myself. Few persons have a stronger feeling than I of the
duty of continuing where one's lot is cast, except where the call to go else-

perceive the evils which exist, so long no remedy can possibly be forthcoming.

In the sixteenth century breach with Rome, the *first* point and position repudiated was that the Pope, either by divine right or of ecclesiastical necessity, had any reason, duty, or call to inter-fere with the concerns of the Church of England. The English Church was affirmed to be, of itself, a perfect and complete spiritual kingdom, wanting neither advice, assistance, nor inter-ference from without. On this point the new Statute of Appeals [1] was very clear. Having thus deliberately removed the key-stone to the perfect arch of truth and unity, other stones, one after the other, some large, some small, were more easily taken out and thrown aside; with what eventual result to that divinely-built arch every one can now too plainly perceive. Many of these stones (to carry on the simile), long lost or lying neglected amongst surrounding rubbish, have been painfully discovered and carefully replaced. For this no Christian patriot can be too heartily grateful. Newman, Pusey, Manning, Keble, Marriott, and Robert Wilberforce, amongst others, did the work. But the last stone to be secured and put up again in the order of time, though the chiefest in importance and most needed (because without it the others are unbonded together, and the spiritual construction remains inherently imperfect), is the key-stone of the completed arch,—the primacy of the father of the faithful, —of him who, in Christ's Name, guides both pastors and sheep, as patriarch of the Church Universal. A visible ruler for a diocese, and a primate for a province, reasonably imply the need of one visible head for the whole family. The day has not yet dawned for this crowning work of the Tractarian movement to be undertaken. But though some for politic reasons, timorous or crotchety, may deny its importance, everything points silently

where is very plain. It may be that I do not see my way clearly in the controversy between us and Rome; but as long as I was in doubt, and perhaps a good deal longer than I might seem to myself in speculation to be so, I should think it my duty to stay where I am."—*Memoir of Rev. John Keble*, by Sir J. T. Coleridge, p. 230. London, 1869.

[1] The words of this innovating statute are:—"The body spiritual whereof having power, when any cause of the law divine happened to come in question, or of spiritual learning, then it was declared, interpreted, and showed by that part of the body politic called the spiritualty, now being usually called the English Church, which always hath been reputed and also found of that sort, that both for knowledge, integrity, and sufficiency of number, it hath been always thought, and is also at this hour sufficient and meet of itself without the intermeddling of any exterior person or persons, to declare and determine all such doubts, and to administer all such duties as to their rooms spiritual doth appertain."

to the certain issue indicated. In the *de*structive Reformation of the sixteenth century the Pope was *first* repudiated, then certain doctrines and practices; in the better and *con*structive movement of the present day, the lost doctrines have already been recovered; an acknowledgment of the traditional and reasonable rights of the See of St. Peter [1] will naturally come *last ;* at all events with those Christians in the Establishment who, by co-operation and reunion, are prepared to resist latitudinarianism, false science, Erastianism, and blank infidelity, so dangerous in these latter days, so potent, so diabolical.

The labour may be painful, the cost considerable, some may be even working against their will, the sacrifices may be great; but for all these the work will be surely and efficiently completed.[2]

And it will be completed from within.[3] Beneficent and practical reformers from all sides, and of all sorts, mainly Liberals, are still at work upon its further "reform"; ever mending, tinkering, and changing it. There is surely room, therefore,

---

[1] The statement that "the Bishop of Rome hath no jurisdiction in this realm of England" (Art. xxvii.) has long ceased to be an accurate proposition. In the present day it is plainly contrary to obvious facts. Under altered circumstances, Parliament ought now to construct another Article, harmonising with parliamentary changes. Again: the 28th Article pronounces a certain doctrine concerning the Sacrament of the Altar to be "repugnant to the plain words of Scripture." Now the plain words are these :—"This is my Body." Consequently when our Lord said, "This *is* My Body," the plain meaning of these words was "This is *not* My Body." By parity of reasoning, had our Lord said, "This is *not* My Body," the plain meaning of His words would have been—transubstantiation. On the same principle, when there came a voice from heaven—"This is My beloved Son," it is "repugnant to the plain words of Scripture" to suppose that the Eternal Father revealed the hypostatic union ; but if the Eternal Father had affirmed, "This is *not* My beloved Son," the plain meaning would have been what in short every good Christian believes—erroneously as it would seem on such "Elizabethan" principles of interpretation—to be true.

[2] About a century and a half ago, this was prophesied as sure to come to pass. Our Blessed Saviour appeared in a vision to a humble Catholic, who was constantly asking at the throne of grace for the restoration of the ancient faith, and He said: "My son, I have heard your prayer so often poured out before Me ; I will have mercy upon England." "When, Lord; oh ! when ?" "Not now," replied our Blessed Saviour, "but when England shall build as many churches as she destroyed at the change of religion ; and when she shall restore and beautify the remainder."—See, for this account at length, *The Future Unity of Christendom*, by A. L. P. de Lisle, p. 68. London, 1857.

[3] The Church of England points out with great clearness how this may be done, by its very distinct directions concerning conditional baptism. What is applicable to the Sacrament of Regeneration is, of course, of equal applicability to confirmation, orders, etc. .

within its wide-embracing fold and comprehensive boundaries, for those few who, having reached a somewhat higher and clearer altitude than that ordinarily attained by their fellows in the fog and mist below, can plainly see that all such destructive "reforms" (judging by past experience) are likely to turn out as profitless and worthless as those of previous centuries; and who long for the religious oneness of old. The English people were promised national unity in religion, but this was never secured to them—poor dupes! even though gibbet and butcher's knife, rack and torture, were enlisted in the enterprising work; and now, instead of the unity of bygone centuries, they are cursed with the active dissensions and noisy screams of a hundred and fifty discordant and repulsive sects.

Who will say, then, that it would be unwise and unreasonable for the National Church, or at all events for those within its broad borders who still believe in the Christian revelation, to admit its failure, and by combination strive to cause its acknowledged isolation and impotence to come to an end?

There are very few members of the Church of England who do not now admit that, whatever its deserts, disestablishment, disendowment, and disruption are not unlikely to be its eventual fate. They only differ as to when these final "reforms," as they term them, are likely to take place. For since the Primate of Christendom has been robbed and disendowed at Rome,—England having stood admiringly by,—local institutions of a similar kind are not likely to survive for long. Why, then, should not such a disastrous issue for our beloved country be duly looked in the face and prepared for? Those who in the National Church still believe in God the Trinity, in the Incarnation of the Eternal Word, and in that divine corporation (baptism being the gate of entrance to it) the One Catholic Church, should on every ground visibly unite, not only amongst themselves, but with all other parts of God's one family (by regeneration). The various recent movements for corporate reunion[1] prove that men's hearts are now, thank God! being, to some extent, turned away from strife and contention towards peace, co-operation, and unity.

Furthermore, as a practical consideration, in the Church of England, the universal liberty which is granted to all cannot be denied only to those who hold the Catholic faith[2] in its

[1] See Appendix, No. II., p. 358.
[2] "Far was it from the purpose of the Church of England to forsake and reject the Churches of Italy, France, Spain, Germany, or any such-like Churches."—Canon, No. xxx. of 1603.

integrity; and who, witnessing the miserable divisions around and about, aim at removing them and healing the breaches. As citizens they have a perfect and unchallenged right, through their natural birth, to all the privileges of membership of the Established Church, just as baptized persons (if baptized) they have an equal right to all the privileges of the Church Universal. These latter privileges, if refused or denied to them in the public edifices of the national communion (in which the national will is dominant), they not only have a similar right, but own a positive duty to secure for themselves in some other way. Furthermore, by argument and reasoning they are free to promote change, so as, without destruction or revolution, to seek out the old ways and return to the ancient paths.

To the few—they are sure to be "Liberals"—who may unfairly deny to others that liberty which they so constantly claim for themselves, and who may urge "patience," love for our stepmother, and "loyalty"; to those likewise who may prate about disloyalty to the Church of England, the author may reply in the forcible words of another :—

"What and where is the Church of England to which I am disloyal? So far as the Church of England is identified with Christian doctrine, Christian worship, Christian discipline, and upholds and maintains these, I am as loyal and as devoted to her now as I ever was, or as any one else can be. But what is meant by the Church of England in connection with the idea of loyalty to the Church of England? Is it the Church of England of the High Church party, or of the Low Church party, or of the Broad Church party? for the members of these three parties seem to me to mean quite different things by the phrase 'Church of England.' Is it a book two hundred years old? or a tradition? or a sentiment? or the will of the nation? or a body corporate—a living organisation? If it be a living organisation, how does it make its voice heard? for a society in which there is 'no voice nor any that answereth' is not the Church of God. As an individual clergyman, I have long been asking myself, 'What is my authority for what I teach and do?' To my mind the responsibility of teaching others in matters affecting their salvation—a responsibility at all times great and overwhelming—becomes absolutely insupportable when there is no living authority to which the individual teacher can refer, and by which he can be guided and fortified."[1]

The author of this volume does not profess that it is a history of the reign of the successful but miserable woman who ruled the nation's destinies for nearly forty-five years, and regarding whom the common herd entertain such loose but glowing ideas. It is only intended to be a sketch of the state of the Church during that period. To write the history of the years between

---

[1] *Do they well to be Angry?* by Presbyter Anglicanus, p. 26. London 1876.

Elizabeth's accession and her death would involve the production of many large volumes. Here the author's aim has been to provide a plain and readable account of what actually occurred, as far as it practically bears on the new ecclesiastical position, upon which recent events have thrown so clear and powerful a light; and, in so doing, neither to keep in the background unpleasant and unwelcome facts—a policy successfully adopted by so many Church of England writers—nor so to lay on heavily the dull colours of a somewhat dark picture as, by finishing-touches, to make it at all darker than it need be. For this there is no necessity whatsoever. The naked acts of certain of those who had secured the upper hand, plainly and faithfully recorded, either from their own words or from authentic documents, are decidedly not pleasant reading for simple-minded folks who reverently believe that what some persons term "the Reformation" was another sacred Pentecost, and had for its Divine Author (may God pardon their delusion!) the Holy Spirit of Truth.

As this book is passing through the press, a friend, who has efficiently aided me, calls my attention to a statement of fact extracted from one of the ritualistic newspapers, concerning the so-called " Reformers," which is here appended :—

" They began by making the Holy Eucharist contemptible in the eyes of the nation, and went on to make it unusual as well as slovenly. The complaint of the people under Edward VI. that the altars had been in many places turned into 'oyster-boards' was not, as has been falsely alleged, a coarsely ribald perversion of facts. It was the literal truth. Wherever the more Zwinglian bishops and clergy had their way, it was no such structure as that which we see to-day in every fairly decent English church, in shape, size, position, and covering—in short, every way except being of wood instead of stone—like the old altars, which served for the celebration of the Sacrament. Common trestles and boards (just like those on which even still street vendors of shell-fish exhibit their wares) carried in and out of church with exactly the same care and quietness as they are now used for a school-room tea, were what the astonished people saw; and the Sacrament dispensed with as much studious irreverence as if the minister had intended nothing save to make it contemptible. Then, besides, whereas up to 1549 there was not a corner of England where there was not at least a weekly mass accessible, and very few where there was not a daily one within easy reach, the first result of the Zwinglian action in 1552 was to sweep away the daily mass[1] everywhere, and the Sunday mass, as it would seem, in a number

[1] The person who could deliberately write of the Elizabethan Reformers' Supper as a "mass" must be either a profound ignoramus or as daring as he is impudent and dishonest. For the celebration of mass was distinctly abolished by Act of Parliament; while those priests who were found celebrating it were drawn, hung, and quartered. Grindal, Pilkington, and Sandys had no more intentions of "saying mass" than they had of restoring circumcision.

of places, at once considerable, and rapidly becoming the great majority.
And in the third place, whereas the mass had been from the earliest days of
Christendom the chief, and for more than a thousand years the most public,
rite of the Church, it was not now merely made infrequent, but was hustled,
as it were, into a corner, just as if a thing to be ashamed of; and the evil
custom sprang up, albeit not justified then or since by any rubric or canon,
of restricting all knowledge of it to the small and steadily dwindling band of
actual communicants on each occasion."—*Church Times*, September 26th,
1879.

As regards English ordinations, concerning which some new
facts are brought to light in the following pages,—putting aside
both historical and theological dissertations, which might apparently be carried on without profit or conviction to either
phalanx of disputants, until the day of doom,—it is self-evident
that the moral argument in favour of their validity is certainly
very strong, perhaps stronger than either the theological or
historical argument. When the frightful state of degradation
into which the National Church during Elizabeth's reign had
been brought is honestly contemplated; and when the striking
contrast between its position then and its altered state now is
duly realised,—the manner in which so much that had been
then cast away as valueless is now sought after and has been
once more secured; the beautiful restoration of cathedrals,
abbeys, and parish churches; the rebuilding of new ones after
Catholic models; the renewed interest in all ecclesiastical
subjects by an earnest and self-denying minority; the restored
worship, the living zeal, the obvious results,—we may reasonably
infer (though there be no exact precedent nor perfect parallel
in past history for the complex character and unique[1] position
of the Established Church of England) that, as divine grace
has never been withdrawn from her crippled rulers, so an inherent and essential distinction between clergy and laity has
been, in the main, consistently and continually remarked and
admitted.

If the author's intention had been to rake up old scandals,
the materials for which are at hand and in abundance, it might
have been done with ease. But this, in the main, has been
carefully and charitably avoided. For such work would have
been in every way distasteful to him. It is only where disagreeable features serve to give an accurate impression of the

---

[1] "The results of the religious movement of the time had taken shape
under the resolute but cautious hand of the Queen [Elizabeth] in *a church
polity which was thought at the time, and has proved to be, unique;* but
which has also proved singularly suited to the character of the English
nation."—*Hooker*, edited by R. W. Church, p. 5, Introduction. Oxford, 1868.

period under description that he has not shrunk from recording bare and obvious facts. This was absolutely necessary in some few cases, for so many historical romancers have shovelled aside all distasteful incidents and events, and have only told their story,—a story in more senses than one, from its sunshiny side, — suppressing, perverting, and misleading, — that it was consequently essential rather, to be fair, honest, and faithful than one-sided, over-picturesque, and false. For until the true nature and virulence of a disease is seen, no adequate remedy can be applied and no cure looked for.

There are a considerable number of footnotes in the following pages, because many of the statements made in the narrative needed to be maintained by careful and exact quotations. These footnotes might have been largely increased from various sources, more especially from the State papers, recent Catholic publications, and private MSS.; but though the author has abundant authority for each and every assertion made by him, he has thought it wise to avoid over-weighting what only professes to be an "Historical Sketch" with too many of such quotations.

The author is considerably indebted to the researches and labours of Brother Henry Foley, S.J., whose *Records of the English Province*, in five handsome volumes, full of authentic and out-of-the-way information, will remain as a monument of his most patient and painstaking labours, and of the noble and charitable deeds of so many eminent and illustrious English members of his great society. The profound treatise by Harpsfield, Archdeacon of Canterbury, on *The Pretended Divorce of Henry VIII.*, so ably edited by the Rev. Nicholas Pocock of Queen's College, Oxford, has been carefully and profitably studied. He has likewise read with interest, and made use of, the three series, entitled *The Troubles of our Catholic Forefathers*, edited by the Rev. John Morris—publications of equal value and interest. Dr. Jessopp's *One Generation of a Norfolk House*, and the *Douay Diary*, have been also studied with interest and profit; for all these recent volumes throw a strong light on the darkened pages of English history in Queen Elizabeth's reign, and are of considerable value.

F. G. L.

ALL SAINTS' VICARAGE, LAMBETH,
November 15th, 1879.

Contents.

CHAPTER I.

CHAPTER II.

CHAPTER III.

CHAPTER IV.

CHAPTER V.

———

CHAPTER VI.

CHAPTER VII.

CHAPTER VIII.

CHAPTER IX.

Excitement, confusion, and disorder rampant.—Insolence of the
preachers.—Matrimonial Inquisitions objected to.—External
religious rites disused. — The churches empty.—Militant disputation at Breachfa.—Parishes destitute.—Bishop Nicholas
Robinson.—Churches like Jews' synagogues.—Representations
of the Queen and Her Royal Arms.—Her Majesty criticised and
prayed for.—Further "reforms" desired.—Some persons Gallio-
like and indifferent.—The gibbet and hangman in requisition.—
Forgers, fabricators, and skulks.—Nine priests and ten laymen
executed. —Hackett, Coppinger, and Arthington.—Dislike of the
she-Supremacy.—More hanging-posts constructed.—Fresh enactments made.—Fresh acts of persecution and cruelty.—Absentees
from church severely punished.—The case of Philip, Earl of

CHAPTER X.

THE CHURCH

UNDER

QUEEN ELIZABETH.

———•———

CHAPTER I.

HENRY VIII. had died, in despair, a dreadful death, terrible to have looked upon, on January 28, 1547; was buried with pomp and ceremony at Windsor, and then speedily forgotten. The prayers and masses which, by his long and elaborate will, he had so earnestly desired might be said for his soul in perpetuity, were never said at all. The desolator of other men's graves, and, worse than this, of God's sanctuaries, was thus himself left desolate and unremembered in a deserted sanctuary where the lamps had been put out, and from which the Adorable Presence had departed.

Then as to his children. Edward VI., a sickly, fanatical, and debilitated youth, — bred in heresy, brought up in schism, flattered by those who ought to have known better,[1] and pampered with cant; until, under such tuition, he had become an offensive and unbearable prig,—was happily removed by Pro-

---

[1] Roger Ascham, when writing to the Duke of Somerset, in 1547, spoke of the king as a juvenile Josiah, a virginal youth, so pure in himself, and so perfect in the new gospel, that he could not be suspected even of the smallest inclination towards, or attachment for, the whore of Babylon. On another occasion (A.D. 1550), Cranmer made himself ridiculous by the following outrageous flattery, which he personally put forth to Cheke, the young king's tutor:—" Ah, Master Cheke, you may be glad all the days of your life that you have such a scholar; for *he hath more divinity in his little finger than all we (the bishops) have in our bodies.*"—Preface to *Foreign Kalendar*, by J. Stevenson, p. 47.

A

vidence to another world, in the midst of his Protestant uncle's disreputable and disastrous rule, and before further and greater evils for the nation had been sealed.

Queen Mary, King Henry's lawful daughter, did a noble work in restoring to the Church tithes and first-fruits; in bringing back certain of the religious orders, such as the Benedictines and Bridgetines, to their old homes; and in vainly endeavouring to stem the tide of innovation, error, and profanity. She duly deposed some of the bishops, who, having been monks, had broken their vows of celibacy and chastity—amongst whom were John Bird and Robert Holgate.[1] More especially does she merit the sincerest admiration from all who believe in one Body, one Spirit, and one Hope of the Christian calling, for having, under lawful authority, visibly reunited desolate England to the rest of Christendom once again. The service of reconciliation in Westminster Abbey on November 30th, 1554, when the Cardinal-Archbishop of Canterbury solemnly absolved the nation from its sin of schism, was the public ratification of a grand deed of Christian charity done in her reign, which, in the great and terrible day when all works are to be tested, shall surely be found to cover a multitude of sins; and which, even in our own national life and history, may yet render her pleasant name— "the sweetest name that ever woman bore,"—so much and so unjustly maligned, sweet to the memory of all who, notwithstanding divisions in the sad origin of which they had no share, still claim the sacred and honoured appellation of Catholic, and are constantly labouring and praying for the gift of visible unity once more upon earth.

Queen Mary at length found that peace which, by experience,

---

[1] "We need not delay long over these two names. Holgate of York and Bird of Chester were respectively a Gilbertine monk and a Carmelite friar, and as such had, amongst other vows, taken the vow of celibacy. Holgate married after he was appointed to York, as he himself alleges, to please the Duke of Somerset. Protestants give him the character of being covetous and worldly-minded; and Burnet admits that though he went along with Cranmer, who got him promoted from Llandaff to York, yet he was no credit to the Reformation. He has left little or nothing by which his opinions may be ascertained, and the principal thing known to his discredit was the claim preferred against him at the council-board of Edward VI., by one, Norman, that he had carried off his wife. The Council that could wink at Poynet's peccadilloes was not likely to be hard upon Holgate. They contented themselves with forbidding him to come to Parliament, and then never troubled their heads any more about the matter. He lived just long enough to be deprived (March 16th, 1554) by Mary, on the same plea with Bird of Chester and the Bishops of St. David's and Bristol, viz. that they had married."—The Reformers of the Reigns of Henry VIII. and Edward VI., *Union Review*, vol. viii. p. 526. London, 1870.

so many discover for themselves the world cannot give, for she died on Thursday, November 17, 1558, on which day Cardinal Reginald Pole went likewise to his blessed and well-earned reward.[1] Of his Eminence, Edwin Sandys, in a letter to Bullinger, dated 20th December of the same year, thus sneeringly wrote :—" That good cardinal, that he might not raise any disturbance or impede the progress of the gospel, departed this life after his friend Mary, 'Maria sua.' Such was the love and harmony between them, that not even death itself could separate them. We have nothing, therefore, to fear from Pole, for 'dead men do not bite.'" [2]

This pious queen has been often severely blamed for her punishment of heretics; and this, not because she caused to be made new and exceptional laws to meet exceptional and unusual difficulties (never the case), but because she could not and did not hinder the lawful authorities from putting into execution very severe laws, long in force and which then existed. A malefactor who, in cold blood, poisons a man or cuts off his head is even now righteously hung. Those decreasing few, who still believe that the spirit of a man is of more importance than his flesh—that the life to come is of more value than the life that now is; that to poison the soul is at least as heinous a crime as to poison the body—may not, after all, be so irrational or eccentric as they are unjustly assumed to be; if, while murder, rebellion, and rapine are still severely punished by modern law, they hold that treason, heresy, and perjury deservedly received, under Queen Mary, equally severe punishments.

When Elizabeth, the king's natural daughter by Anne Boleyn, was in her teens, her bearing towards the other sex had been, to say the least, unusual and remarkable. Various queer and perhaps questionable stories had been afloat regarding her, some of which were possibly false, and others probably exaggerated. But in one notable case this was not so. Her conduct in relation to Lord Seymour of Sudeley, the Lord Admiral, a married man, in the highest degree reprehensible, caused very grave scandal. But perhaps the chief fault lay with his lordship, and not mainly with the young princess. Seymour is believed by many to have contracted a marriage with Katherine Parr, Henry VIII.'s widow, for convenience' sake, and in order to be near

[1] There remains an interesting and well-painted portrait of the cardinal, in his official robes, in the dining-hall of Lambeth Palace, with an older and quainter picture in the State drawing-room, evidently a faithful and excellent likeness.

[2] *Zurich Letters*, vol. i. No. 2.

Elizabeth, who resided with, and was under the care of, her step-mother.   At the period in question, though Elizabeth was barely fifteen years of age, she was as forward and precocious in know-ledge as she appears to have been altogether lacking in feminine delicacy and maidenly modesty.   The familiarities of Lord Seymour which she tolerated were simply disgusting.   Elizabeth actually allowed him to enter her sleeping-chamber in his bed-gown and slippers only, before she was out of bed in the morning, and there to indulge in acts and actions gross in the extreme. He struck her with his palms on the back and other parts of her undraped body, and when she rollickingly rolled about under the disordered sheets; or, hastily slipping out of bed, laughingly hid herself behind the damask curtains, he toyed with her anew both by word and deed, by gross innuendos, scandalous questions of double meaning, and other indelicate words and acts.   Queen Katherine Parr, aroused by jealousy, coming upon them suddenly one day at Seymour Place, found the princess on her husband's knees, with his left arm round her waist.   On this she sent the princess away towards the close of the month of May 1548; but what she had seen and knew, affecting her mind and health, so harassed her, poor lady! that she soon afterwards died in childbirth.   This death happened so opportunely for the Lord Admiral's obvious purpose as regards the princess, that the malice of his enemies at once attributed the timely but sudden decease of his wife, the Lady Katherine, to poison.

During the latter years of Mary's reign several needy and ad-venturous politicians, who, under Edward VI., had already risen by self-assertion, knavery, and craft to positions of some influence, secretly offered their services to Elizabeth.   Most of them were of low birth and origin.   One, Sir William Cecil,[1] was the son of a well-to-do Lincolnshire yeoman, subsequently an inn-holder at Stamford, who, because of his youthful good looks, had been made page to Henry VIII.   This page's only son, a shrewd, cold, and calculating person, knighted in 1551, but better known as Lord Burghley, a title which he subsequently received on February 25, 1571, together with the Order of the Garter, saw exactly how the land lay, and discovered, as he imagined, a fair chance of further temporal advancement.   Educated at Gray's Inn, he had been sometime private secretary to the Duke of Somerset, and was afterwards made that nobleman's "master

---

[1] One writer, the learned and anonymous author of *Responsio ad Edictum Eliz. Reg.*, published at Augsburg in 1592, asserts that Cecil's father held an inferior situation in the office of the Royal Wardrobe; that his grandfather kept an inn at Stamford, and was afterwards one of the Royal Guards.

of requests." At that period he masqueraded as a zealous Reformer, was in confidential communication with the Zwinglian heretics, and ostentatiously declared that he thirsted for what they called "the pure milk of the Word," meaning thereby the blasphemous glosses and odious caricatures of Christianity in which these repulsive and dangerous people delighted. In 1548 he had held a secretaryship of State. On the timely death of Edward, however, like many others, Cecil at once changed his tactics when Mary became queen. Then, dropping the heretics, and having avoided Lady Jane Grey, he appeared as a devout and zealous Catholic. In the silver and velvet gypcyre at his side he carried, and frequently produced, the "Hours of Our Lady," and muttering his devotions, ostentatiously used his large-beaded rosary. But Mary was not to be taken in or duped. Knowing Cecil's antecedents, she never trusted him. To Elizabeth, however, he proved to be welcome. For, passing over her natural and proper advisers, the old nobility of blood and good repute, she at once appointed him Lord Treasurer of her Household and Chief Minister of State. On the very day of her accession, before she started for London, he had presented to her twelve "Minutes of Subjects," needing, as he asserted, Her Grace's instant consideration; while, four days afterwards, he was sworn of her Privy Council. He was thus taken into her confidence. At once he urged her to put away without delay all those who had occupied places of influence under the late queen, some of whom he feared; suggesting that their places be supplied by "men meaner in substance and younger in years"—advice which she certainly took. In order to overawe and compass efficiently the degradation of the Catholic clergy, he suggested that Her Majesty, striking boldly and sharply, should promptly involve them in the disagreeable meshes of a *præmunire;* while, on the other hand, in order to terrify the more rampant and unscrupulous innovators—the communistic Protestants and "Hot Gospellers"—who threatened to become a nuisance and a danger, he recommended the immediate enactment of a sharp law against public assemblies.

Under his advice the kingdom was brought into sore troubles and great straits. Under the plea of serving his royal mistress and benefiting the State, he pursued with art so tortuous a policy that bribes to secure supporters of it, and acts of corruption and venality were again and again repeated. He carefully enriched himself,[1] ruined his enemies, and rewarded his

---

[1] He contrived to secure for himself the greater part of the endowments of the Abbey of Peterborough, which formed an adequate estate with which to

friends. By his instrumentality true liberty was banished. There was no fear of God before his eyes; for, more than any other man then living, he deliberately sealed the irreligious division between England and the rest of Christendom, and left our distracted nation a prey to every kind of ambitious and crooked-minded adventurer who thought fit to set up as a reformer of religion or a self-appointed concocter of new phases of mischief. In fine, he was one of those keen-sighted worthies, condemned rather than commended by an apostle, who think that gain is godliness.[1]

Another State official of almost equal influence to that wielded by Cecil was his fellow Secretary of State, Sir Francis Walsingham. For art in corrupting others, and skill in elevating treachery to the dignity of a science; for ability in planning and carrying out forgery, as well as in arranging for the assassination of inconvenient allies or open enemies, he was vastly superior to Cecil, as will ere long be discovered; for while his hypocrisy was consummate, his ability and dexterity were obviously greater, and his general success consequently very considerable. He was of an exceedingly savage nature. It was evidently a pleasure to him, however strange, to inflict personal cruelty upon any supposed enemy who might chance to be in his power. When prisoners of the old faith, later on, were brought before him in his judicial capacity, or for due and careful examination, he would sometimes kick and cuff them in a passion, or strike them heavily with his staff; while, if they hesitated to convict themselves, the numerous rude epithets he made use of were frequently disgusting, and his oaths equalled in coarseness, though in repulsiveness rarely surpassed, those which so frequently glided glibly off the compressed and pursed-up lips of his royal mistress.

Such tools, tactics, and events served once more and anew to point out to the educated and more thoughtful how true was Plato's expressive saying of old,[2] that free nations have seldom lost their liberties by conquest, but chiefly at the hands of low-born and unscrupulous men who have ridden into power upon the tumultuous waves of popular passion.

The queen, being present at the Bishop of Carlisle's mass,

support his new dignity of a peer, which later on he received. But he was not content with these, for, as Dr. Peter Heylyn wrote—"During the vacancy of the See of Norwich, and during his (Dr. Scambler's) incumbency, Sir William Cecil, Principal Secretary of State, possessed himself of the best manors in the Soke, which belonged to it; and for his (the bishop's) readiness to confirm them to him, he preferred him to the See of Norwich."

[1] I Tim. vi. 5.
[2] Plato's *Republic*, viii. 562 ; sec. 99.

soon after her accession,—on Christmas morning, as some assert, and while the cantors of her chapel were singing the *Gloria in excelsis* at their lectern,—sent a messenger to his lordship within the sanctuary peremptorily forbidding him to elevate the Host.[1] But Oglethorpe replied that, as it was the unvarying rule of the Catholic Church for all priests to do so, he must ask Her Majesty's permission to allow him to conform. Upon this, before the gospel, and at once, without further parley, she rose from her fald-stool, biting her thin lips in anger, and, motioning her attendants to follow, re-clasped her book of devotions, stamped vigorously on the floor, and thus hastily departed. This incident, obviously pre-arranged, was much discussed and commented upon by many. The bishops duly noted it.

On the 27th of December, at Cecil's instigation, exercising her assumed office of Supreme Spiritual Head of the Church of England, she issued a proclamation throughout both the provinces of Canterbury and York, formally and distinctly forbidding any elevation of the Blessed Sacrament by any of her priests. Her chaplain, Minter, saying mass in her presence on the morning of the same day, duly and dutifully observed his sovereign's commands.[2] In the same proclamation—as a temporary makeshift, until the old and sacred rites brought back under Queen Mary were again abolished by parliamentary authority—the Supreme Governess graciously permitted the Creed, the Lord's Prayer, and the Ten Commandments, as well as the Litany, to be said or sung in the vulgar tongue.

At Sandwich, Dover, and Canterbury the Protestant exiles, having realised the new situation, arrived in force and high spirits, and were noisy and triumphant in their bearing. If Jewell may be trusted, the queen was extremely gratified by their return, and expressed her satisfaction.[3] Afterwards, however, Her Highness had some reason for somewhat changing

---

[1] " Nothing, however, has yet been publicly determined with respect to the abolishing popish superstition, and the re-establishment of the Christian religion. There is, however, a general expectation that all rites and ceremonies will shortly be reformed by our faithful citizens and other godly men in the afore-mentioned Parliament, either after the pattern which was lately in use in the time of King Edward the Sixth, or which is set forth by the Protestant princes of Germany in the above-named Confession of Augsburg." —Richard Hilles to Bullinger, dated February 28, 1559, *Zurich Letters*, 2nd series, No. 7.

[2] *Laderchius*, iii. p. 204, and Tierney's edition of Dod's *Church History*, vol. ii. p. 124.

[3] " We hear that their return was very acceptable to the queen, and that she openly declared her satisfaction."—Letter from John Jewell to Peter Martyr, dated January 26, 1559, *Zurich Letters*, vol. i. No. 3.

her mind concerning the value of their presence and labours.
Some of them, in their enthusiasm at her accession, made a
disturbance during mass in the parish church of Dover, hurling
a missal[1] during the elevation at the head of the celebrant,
whom they termed "a cursed popish dog," "a shaveling," "an
antichrist," and an "idol-smacker."[2]

Without authority, the Zwinglian service-book of Edward VI.
was again brought into requisition in several places. Legally-
instituted clergy were hooted at, spat upon, and persecuted;
so that in some places they were unable to minister in public.
Several images of our Divine Lord, His Blessed Mother, and
the Saints were violently wrenched down from the rood screens
and treated with obscene indignities. At Canterbury, as a
deliberate act of contempt, a holy-oil stock was emptied of its
sacred contents, in order to grease the creaking wheels of a
wainman's cart, which had come in from the adjacent village of
Harbledown. At Brentford, at the same time, an indignity too
disgusting for words was perpetrated in the font of the parish
church by one of the new gospellers, as a practical protest against
the religion of Bede, St. Anselm, and Sir Thomas More. The
Babel voices of noisy controversialists,[3] young as well as old,
everywhere rose anew; while furious preachers, with screaming
voices and deep maledictions for their opponents, went so far
in creating serious riots,[4] at Oxford, Newark, and Chichester, as
that the existing authorities of those places had to step in and
keep the peace by armed force, amongst these energetic evangelists
of "another gospel which is not another."

During Edward's reign, or possibly later, Jonn Knox, the so-

---

[1] Some writers say it was a breviary. But as it was taken off the cushion
on a side altar, it was most probably a missal.

[2] "Ape of antichrist," "mass-monger," "Balaamite," "abbey-lubber,"
were some of the other choice names given to those who clung to the ancient
faith. I have gathered both these and those in the text above from the MS.
correspondence and Protestant literature of the day.

[3] "They held arguments also among themselves about the meaning of
various Scripture texts, all of them, men and women, girls and boys, labourers,
workmen, and simpletons; and these discussions were often wont, as it was
said, to produce quarrels and fights."—*Life of William Weston*," p. 241.
London, 1875.

[4] "On the other (the Protestant) side many were raised to great preferments, who, having spent their time of exile in such foreign Churches as
followed the platform of Geneva, returned so disaffected to episcopal
government with the rites and ceremonies here by law established, as not
long after filled the Church with most sad disorders; not only to the
breaking of the bond of peace, but to the grieving and extinguishing the
spirit of unity."—*The History of Queen Elizabeth*, by Peter Heylyn, p. 115.
London, 1671.

called "Reformer," had written a treatise[1] in his vigorous but coarse and illogical style, indirectly aimed at Mary Tudor, directly at Mary Stuart, maintaining that the rule of a woman was "repugnant to nature, a contumely to God, a thing most contrarious to His revealed will and approved ordinances, and finally the subversion of all equity and justice." Elizabeth, of course, knew of this treatise, which is a wonderful production for its sanctimonious language, but did not at all appreciate either its logic or rhetoric. John Knox, when brought into communication with her, overcame the difficulty not by giving up his principle, but by boldly maintaining that the queen was a remarkable and obvious exception to the general rule. Her whole life, he pointed out in writing, had been so blessed and favoured by God Almighty, she was so overflowing with grace, she had been so evidently elected by Him, and specially preserved for His chosen people, that what was unlawful and unnatural in all other women was perfectly lawful and even desirable in her. This appeared to satisfy her temporarily, though it is more than probable, as Sir William Throckmorton pointed out, that the political services of Knox were still required, and therefore that his printed insults should be overlooked:—
"Considering what Knockes is hable to doo in Scotlande, which is verie muche, all this turmoil there being stirred up as it is, it shuld stande your Majestie instead (if) his former faultes were forgotten."

Before determining the exact day for her coronation, the queen sent her favourite, Robert Dudley, to consult the well-known and notorious necromancer and astrologer, Dr. Dee,[2] to

---

[1] *A First Blaste of the Trumpett against the Monstrous Regmen of women,* by John Knox.

[2] *Vide* Godwin's *Life of Dr. Dee, in loco.* This also is clear from the actual entries in Dr. Dee's Diary and writings, from which the following is taken:—"Her Majestie refused to come in; but willed to fetch my glass so famous, and to show her some of the properties of it, which I did: her Majestie being taken down from her horse by the Earle of Leicester, Master of the Horse, at the church wall of Mortlake, did see some of the properties of that glasse, to Her Majestie's great contentment and delight."—Dr. Dee's *Compendious Memorial,* p. 516. When Lord Leicester and Lord Laskey dined with Dee (A.D. 1583), he was not sufficiently well off to provide a suitable repast, so the queen, who was at Sion House, hearing of it, sent him "forty angels of gold." In 1592 Mr. Thomas George brought him "an hundred marks from Her Majestie." "1577. Nov. 22nd, I rod to Windsor to the Q. Majestie. Nov. 25th, I spake with the Quene *hora quinta.* Nov. 28th, I spake with the Quene *hora quinta.* I spake with Mr. Secretary Walsingham" (Ashmole asserts that this person was one of Dee's greatest patrons). . . . "1578. Oct. 8th, the Quene's Majesty had conference with me at Richemond inter 9 et 11. . . . 1580. The Quene's Majestie, to my

whom Her Majesty, having privately renounced the sacrament of penance and its competent ministers, often went for advice, and with whom she held close conversations,—a notable case of degeneracy; proving that, when the Christian faith in its integrity is mutilated by choice or cast aside, gross superstition often takes its place.   Dr. Dee then dwelt at a small house, close to the water side and no great distance from the parish church of Mortlake.[1]   On her personal application, through Dudley, Dr. Dee informed her that Sunday, the 15th of January, was undoubtedly a lucky day; and so, with the sanction of her Council, the ceremony was appointed to be then performed.

On Thursday, the 12th, Her Majesty consequently proceeded from Westminster to the Tower preparatory to the grand and customary "procession of recognition."

On the 14th of January, leaving the Tower about two o'clock in the afternoon, the queen passed through the city back to Westminster, according to ancient precedent.   Her coach, covered with crimson velvet, and richly caparisoned horses, was surrounded by a well-ordered cavalcade of State officers and attendants, all magnificently attired.   Eight knights bore a broad canopy of cloth of gold over her.   She was almost everywhere greeted with acclamations by the curious and interested crowds which thronged Cheapside and Fleet Street, or ranged themselves in front of the mansions of the nobility in the Strand. Before she started, her ladies-in-waiting heard her piously and complacently compare herself to Daniel delivered from the den of lions, and thank God out loud for His providential care of her.[2]

The rich decorations in Fenchurch and Gracechurch Streets were continuous.   Triumphal arches with complimentary allegorical representations, which were supposed to be explained by the recitation of wordy verses, were the scenes of much applause from dense crowds.   In Cheapside, a stage had been erected and adorned, where eight little children personified the Beatitudes, and expressed a hope, in rugged but honest verse, that God would make the queen strong and bestow upon her His blessing.

This part of the city was decorated with sumptuousness and taste.   Here the rich mercers dwelt in quaint and picturesque

great comfort (*hora quinta*), came with her trayn from the court, and at my dore graciously calling me to her on horseback."—*Dr. John Dee's Diary.* Camden Society.   London, 1842.
[1] MSS. Ashmol. No. 1788. fol. 149.
[2] Holinshed's *Chronicles*, vol. ii. p. 1787, etc.

gabled houses, one storey overhanging another; all the walls
and windows of which were tastefully adorned with carpets,
costly hangings, streamers, banners, and tapestries; and from
which crowds in holiday attire looked down with smiles and
greetings upon the moving pageant.   Here, too, the city
authorities, who had been efficiently stirred up to do their duty
by Cecil, had gathered in their picturesque and effective official
dresses—before vulgarity was rampant and good taste had quite
decayed—headed by the Recorder, Sir Ranulph Cholmely, who,
in the name of the Lord Mayor and citizens, offered Her
Majesty as their gift a crimson satin purse containing a thousand
marks in gold.   This was graciously accepted, and Elizabeth
then promised to be a good queen to all her people—a promise
that was certainly not kept for any length of time.

A halt was made, by previous appointment, at a triumphal
arch near St. Paul's, where in the cold January air a female
child, [half-draped, in accordance with the revived paganism of
that day, and let down by silken cords from above, came forward
with rehearsed grimaces and exaggerated genuflections to present
Her Majesty with a large early copy of the mistranslated Geneva
Bible with its wordy preface and Calvinistic notes.

This questionable present she graciously received with bows
and other acknowledgments; and then, ostentatiously placing
it to her heart, acknowledged, with condescending smiles, the
boisterous applause of Cecil's creatures—placed there to close
this impressive incident in a prearranged drama.

As the procession took its way along the Strand westwards,
the Tower guns were heard booming in the distance.   Darkness
soon overspread the city, and the stars came out.   Her Majesty
rested that night in the palace at Whitehall, and prepared herself
for the solemnities of the morrow.

The queen, as will be seen, was crowned at Westminster by
Oglethorpe, Bishop of Carlisle.   It seems more than probable
that up to the latest hours of the previous Saturday evening,
though several prelates had been tampered with and tested, no
bishop[1] could be thoroughly relied upon to perform the act;
for, early on Sunday morning, it became necessary to hastily
borrow from Bonner, the Bishop of London, suitable episcopal
vestments for the officiating prelate.   This necessary part of the
solemnity, therefore, could hardly have been finally arranged

---

[1] In an existing record of the coronation in the Ashmolean MSS. now in
the Bodleian Library at Oxford, other bishops are mentioned as being present.
If so, these were no doubt those guilty of treasonable acts and heresy, who
had gone abroad in Mary's reign, and had now hastily returned.

until the small hours of the night.   Oglethorpe, after great persuasion, had consented; but he stood alone, and very soon repented him of his act and deed.   In the Abbey there remained, as there still remains, an old literary treasure, the *Liber Regalis*, possibly used at the coronation of Richard II. and his queen, containing *Ordo consecrandi reginam solam*, which, after it had been inspected by Sir William Cecil,—five of whose MS. notes may still be read on its thick vellum folios—was by him approved and made use of by Oglethorpe in the ceremony.[1]   This book, the copy of an office of the fourteenth century, with special rubrics applicable to the coronation of kings and queens in the Benedictine Abbey of Westminster, was no doubt prepared for the actual use of the officiating prelate on such occasions.

The Abbey Church, where most the Catholic *ornamenta* remained, had been arranged for the ceremony in accordance with recognised tradition ; though, on account of the exhausted state of the Treasury, the ceremonial was shorn of some of its ancient splendour.   Early in the morning the queen came in the royal barge from Whitehall to Westminster, where the populace, and specially the Protestant and Reforming part of it, had gathered to greet her with acclamations and applause.

She was met in Westminster Hall by the Bishop of Carlisle, vested in cope and mitre, and bearing a pastoral staff; while other inferior clergy, in surplices and copes, were in attendance. But none of the diocesan bishops, who were in canonical and lawful possession of their Sees, were present.   One and all, save Oglethorpe, deliberately and intentionally stayed away.   The choristers and clerks of the Royal Chapel, in scarlet cassocks and lawn rochets, were there to do their part, and a large cross of silver-gilt was carried at the head of the procession.   All the high officers of State were in attendance, while a canopy of cloth of gold was borne over the queen as she walked with state and dignity from Westminster Hall to the Abbey, along an appointed pathway railed in and spread with blue cloth powdered with conventional roses.

Within the Abbey, which was crowded, some of the Benedictine monks looking down upon the gay scene from the southern triforium of the choir, as Father Seigebert Bulkeley mentioned, all the detailed rites of the *Liber Regalis* were duly observed— the Recognition, the Proclamation, the customary Offerings, the

---

[1] "Liber Regalis, seu Ordo consecrandi Regem solum : Ordo consecrandi reginam cum Rege: Ordo consecrandi reginam solam.   Rubrica de Regiis exequiis, è codice West-monasteriensi Editus."—Printed for the Roxburgh Club (at the cost of Frederick, Earl Beauchamp).   London, 1870.

Oath, and the Unction.[1] Every step was duly taken in accordance with precedent, as Cecil had enjoined should be the case, and nothing essential or important seems to have been omitted.

The Oath, the Unction, and the actual rite of Consecration were, of course, details in the sacred service of the most essential and important public character—and were seen and acknowledged so to be, as well by those who favoured the old, as by those who were secretly promoting the advance of the new, religion.

On this occasion, by the advice of Cecil and her new councillors, and in order to secure to herself the crown without danger of subsequent question or dispute, the queen had been carefully advised to dissemble falsely, in God's own house and presence, to swear and forswear, to appear to be what she certainly was not, and to seem to believe in that which she had privately resolved to set aside. Within a few feet of the shrine and sacred relics of St. Edward, our saintly confessor, she openly took the usual solemn and sacred oath of Christian kings,[2] when it was tendered her, kissing thereupon the precious text of the Holy Gospels, and, in sight of peers and people, promising thereby to defend the Catholic religion, and to guard faithfully the rights and immunities of God's Holy Church, as all the previous monarchs from the days of St. Edward had each done. The bystanding peers heard her repeat the solemn words, and saw her do the appointed acts. Any honest "Reformers," so called—and some were certainly present—must surely have been ashamed of the oath she then took, for they well enough knew that she had no intention of keeping it, though not one of them is known to have publicly protested against such an immoral method.

At the appointed time Elizabeth withdrew with her ladies-in-waiting to be prepared for the act of anointing. This was done on forehead, breast, and hands, as usual; though the queen

---

[1] "In Nomine Patris," etc. "Prosit tibi hæc unctio olei in honorem et confirmationem æternam in sæcula sæculorum. Amen."—*Liber Regalis, in loco.*

[2] Miss Strickland thus attempts to defend this act :—"It is our duty to our subject to suggest, as her defence from the horrid appearance of wilful perjury, that it is possible she meant at that time to model the Reformed Church she. projected, and for which she challenged the appellation of Catholic, as near as possible to the Anglo-Saxon Church."—*Lives of the Queens of England,* vol. vi. p. 164. London, 1884. Upon which defence the only remark that need be made is, that, as far as ordinary research has enlightened us, perjury is not known to have been an authorised practice of the Anglo-Saxon Church.

does not appear to have much liked the ceremony, for, on retiring again for a few moments afterwards, she, with unpardonable levity, observed to one of her personal attendants that the oil was stinking,[1] and that she had " much misliked the greasing."

When she returned to the space before the high altar, she was found arrayed in a mantle of cloth of gold and ermine: she was then ceremonially girt with a sword, endued with the *armillum* and solemnly crowned. The coronation ring was put on the accustomed finger:[2] in her right hand was placed the sceptre, in her left the orb. After this the officiating prelate first did homage, followed in order by the peers,[3] and then solemn high mass was continued. All the ancient rites of the Salisbury missal were scrupulously observed, save that the Epistle and Gospel were sung in English as well as in Latin, and there was no elevation of the Sacred Host.[4] At the offertory the three State swords were offered, with other customary oblations. Her Majesty, kneeling at her fald-stool, communicated under one kind, received the *pax* with apparent devotion ; and so, in due course, the sacrifice was ended, and the coronation service completed.

It had long been a custom for English monarchs on the occasion of their coronation to release certain prisoners. Elizabeth, on the morning afterwards, making no exception to the rule, did the same, in the presence of her Court. At the close of the proceedings, one of the courtiers, who had duly rehearsed the farce beforehand, came forward, with the accustomed genuflections and bows, and in a loud voice, but keeping his countenance effectually, implored the queen that four or five more prisoners might be graciously released. Her Majesty inquired their names.

[1] " She was also anointed, but she disliked the ceremony and ridiculed it ; for when she withdrew, according to the custom, to put on the royal garments, it is reported that she said to the noble ladies in attendance upon her, 'Away with you, the oil is stinking.'"—Edward Rishton's *Continuation of Sander's History*, edited by David Lewis, M.A., p. 243. London, 1877. *Good News from London*, pp. 65, 66. Printed at the Sign of the Swan. London, 1675.

[2] *Vide Liber Regalis*, pp. 33-35. Ed. London, 1870.

[3] Miss Strickland, in her *Life of Queen Elizabeth* (vol. vi. p. 168), remarks that the issue of the Bull of Pope Paul IV., dated 12th January 1558-9, "declaring heretical sovereigns incapable of reigning . . . did not deprive her of the allegiance of her Catholic peers, all of whom paid their liege homage to her," failed to note that as the coronation took place only three days after the time of its promulgation, the Bull could not possibly have reached England or become known to the peers in question.

[4] Opinions and accounts differ on this point, though testimony for the statement in the text predominates.

"Matthew, Mark, Luke, and John, the four Evangelists, and the Apostle Paul," was the immediate retort. "These men, most dread sovereign, have been, as it were, so closely shut up in the prison of an unknown tongue, that until released they cannot converse with the Lord's people."

As Bacon has recorded, the queen answered gravely: "It is first best to inquire of them whether they themselves approve of being released or not."

This incident was spoken of in public and commented on by the preachers from the Continent.

On the 13th January 1558–1559, five new peers were created, viz. William Parr, a Lancashire nobleman, restored to his title of Marquis of Northampton; Edward Seymour, made Earl of Hertford; Thomas Howard, son of the late Duke of Norfolk, made Viscount Howard of Bindon, in Dorsetshire; Sir Oliver St. John, made Lord St. John of Bletsoe; and the Lady Mary Boleyn's son, Sir Henry Carey, created Baron Hunsdon. All these belonged to the innovating, or, as some term it, the "Reforming" party. The Court, under Cecil's advice, resolved at the same time to influence the elections to the House of Commons; so five candidates were previously named for each of the counties and three for each of the boroughs, from amongst whom the members were chosen.

Ten days after the coronation the Houses of Parliament met. The first act taken by the Commons was to vote and present a "humble but earnest Address to the Queen, that she would vouchsafe to accept some match capable of supplying heirs to Her Majesty's royal virtues and dominions." The queen, who evidently did not like interference on this subject, told the Speaker and other members that she might long ago have married if she had so willed, but that for herself she should be heartily content to have it inscribed on her tomb after death that she had lived and died a virgin queen. She added, for their future guidance, amongst some involved sentences of studied ambiguity, that it was obviously neither their duty to prescribe to nor to bind her, but to petition, if they so willed, and then humbly to obey.

Other important work was at once taken in hand. Thus :—

Queen Mary, King Henry's lawful daughter by his queen the Lady Katherine, and Elizabeth, the illegitimate daughter of the King by Anne Boleyn, had both been expressly declared illegitimate by statute under Henry VIII.[1] When Mary succeeded to the throne, however, an Act had been at once passed[2] declaring

[1] 28 Henry VIII. c. 7. [2] 1 Mary, Session ii. c. 1.

that she had been born "in a most just and lawful matrimony," and thus the unstained honour of her mother was dutifully and properly vindicated. Elizabeth at the present time, who, of course, stood on another platform, acted in quite a different manner; possibly under the influence of her advisers, who saw the complex and complicated difficulties before them, and who in the new Act passed were consequently vague and ambiguous in the language they selected. This Act at once claimed for Elizabeth regular and due royal descent, and at the same time conferred upon her the right to reign by the authority of Parliament; two features obviously inconsistent and self-destructive.

In due course, after some discussion, but at no long interval after assembling, the two Houses passed some most momentous laws, the full force and importance of which upon the National Church are even now scarcely realised.

By these new laws what was not over-exactly termed the "ancient jurisdiction of the Crown over the estate ecclesiastical and spiritual" was said to be "restored," while all "foreign jurisdiction repugnant to the same" abolished. By this Act, the general repeal under Queen Mary of the "reforming" statutes of Henry VIII. and Edward VI. was directly abrogated: all spiritual and ecclesiastical jurisdiction of every sort and kind, without any exception, being thus vested in the Crown, though now worn by a woman, in virtue of which enactment special Royal Commissions, composed of clerks and laymen, were at once appointed, their powers from time to time being renewed and extended; while the "Court of High Commission," as it was termed, was subsequently established on the same parliamentary authority in 1583.

Furthermore, and at once, all ministers and officers whatsoever, whether temporal or spiritual, whether bishops or judges, canons or magistrates, parish clerks or pikemen, were bound to take an oath acknowledging the queen to be "the only supreme governor of the realm as well in spiritual or ecclesiastical things or causes as temporal ";[1] and renouncing "all foreign jurisdictions, powers,

---

[1] That this tradition, now all but exploded, has come down to the present time is abundantly evident from the following Protest of the Dean and Chapter of Westminster, read, prior to the consecration of the Bishop of Durham (A.D. 1879), by the Dean in the Jerusalem Chamber :—

"I, the Very Reverend Arthur Penrhyn Stanley, Doctor in Divinity, Dean of the collegiate church of St. Peter, Westminster, *immediately subject to the Queen's Majesty and no other*, do hereby, on behalf of the Dean and Chapter of the said church, declare and protest that by compliance with licence of the Lord Archbishop of Canterbury to the Lord Archbishop of York to conse-

superiorities, or authorities," under pain of forfeiture of present
office, and disability to hold any other.

It was further enjoined that the oath in question should be
formally and duly tendered to every such person throughout the
realm within thirty days of the prorogation of Parliament at
the end of its session.[1] All persons about to take orders, or to
receive degrees in the universities; all clergymen about to be
promoted to any spiritual livings, or already in possession of
benefices; as well as all laymen in office, such as judges,
magistrates, or persons receiving wages of the Crown, or suing
out livery of their lands, were to take the oath. It was specially
enacted, moreover, as a leading and crucial principle, that the
authority needful for the visitation of all spiritual persons, and
the correction of errors, heresies, and abuses, should be annexed
to the Crown; and that the power of exercising this authority by
delegates to be appointed by Letters Patent under the Great
Seal should remain with the queen and her successors for ever.

Against this revolutionary and ridiculous act John Feckenham,
Abbot of Westminster, made a powerfully-argumentative and
even brilliant speech in the House of Lords, in which he thus
dwelt on the deeds of disorder, disobedience, and destruction
then being perpetrated :—

"In her late Majesty's reign, your lordships may remember
how quiet and governable the people were. ˙ It was not then
their custom to prescribe to authority, to run before the laws,
nor disobey the proclamations of their sovereign. There was
then no sacrilegious rapine, no plundering of churches, no
blasphemous outrage and trampling the holy sacraments under
their feet. It was none of their way to tear down the pix, and
hang up the knave of clubs in its place. They did not hack and

crate the Rev. Joseph Barber Lightfoot, Doctor in Divinity, to be Bishop
and Pastor of the cathedral church of Durham, we do not intend to acknowledge any jurisdiction or authority of the Lord Archbishop of Canterbury
over us, the said Dean and Chapter, or over our said collegiate church;
*but do claim and assert that we are immediately subject to the Queen's Majesty
and no other ecclesiastical authority whatsoever;* and that we have granted the
use of our said collegiate church to the Lord Archbishop of York for the said
consecration, in pursuance of the mandate of Her Majesty the Queen, dated
at Westminster the 29th day of March last, in the forty-second year of Her
Majesty's reign.

"Dated the 25th day of April 1879.
"(Signed)   ARTHUR PENRHYN STANLEY."

[1] In this enactment Temporal Peers were excepted by a special clause;
just as in recent times the English bishops succeeded in getting the Public
Worship Regulation Act passed for the clergy generally, while they duly and
carefully secured themselves from either or any of its operations.

B

hew the crucifix in those times. They were better observers of
discipline than to eat flesh openly, and fill their shambles with
butchers' meat in the holy solemnity of Lent.   In the late reign
the generality of the people, and particularly the nobility and
those of the Privy Council, were exemplary for their public
devotion ; it being the custom to go to a church or chapel, to
beg the protection of God, before they entered upon the business
of the day.   But now the face of things is quite otherwise."[1]

This supremacy in things spiritual, as the whole tenor of the
new Act most clearly shows, was not held to be inherent in the
Crown,—such an idea would have been absurd,—but was regarded
as a special grant,[2] expressly made by the power and authority
of Parliament.   Here, then, was a portentous and complete
revolution.

Those, therefore, who should be found to maintain, "by
express words, deed, or act," the authority of any foreign prince
or prelate, were, by this new enactment, to forfeit their goods :
or if these did not amount to the value of £20, such persons
were, for the first offence, to be put into prison for twelve
months ; to incur the penalties of *præmunire* for the second ;
and to be regarded as guilty of high treason, and to be put to
death as traitors—*i.e.* drawn, hung, dismembered, disembowelled,
beheaded, and quartered—for the third offence.

This Act, be it noted, directly revived all the most obnoxious
and atrocious of the enactments of Henry VIII. and Edward VI.,
as has been already pointed out.   The substitution, however, of
the term "Supreme Governor"[3] for "Supreme Head" of the
English Establishment[4] was a mere distinction without a difference, as subsequent events too truly proved.

---

[1] Abbot Feckenham's speech against the Act of Uniformity.—*Bib. Cott.
Vesp. D.*, xviii. fol. 8, *et seq.*

[2] No person nor assembly of persons can give or grant that which he himself or such assembly does not possess nor own.   So was it in the case of
Elizabeth's Parliament.

[3] Calvin, in his *Commentary on the Book of Amos* (ch. vii. v. 13), had
written thus :—"Erant enim blasphemi qui vocarent eum (Henricum VIII.)
Summum Caput Ecclesiæ sub Christo" ; so those Protestant theologians who
valued this heresiarch's opinions had the craft and wisdom to change the term
without changing the thing.

[4] No special provision was made in case the monarch became a Brownist, a
Lutheran, or Presbyterian, an omission which might have caused difficulties
in recent times had not the "supremacy of public opinion" been gradually
allowed to take the place of the Tudor supremacy, which, as all except the
modern Erastians admit, has long lost both its moral and political value and
importance.   Originally introduced by the application of the rack, the halter,
and irons, it is now bereft of its power, and has completely collapsed. The
"supremacy of public opinion," however, as administered and enforced in

It must not be supposed that such a revolution was brought about without both expostulation and protest on the part of some. The whole of the Episcopate to a man voted against the third reading ; while two bishops, on behalf of their brethren in spiritual authority, made efficient speeches against it. These were Archbishop Heath of York, and Bishop Scott of Chester.

The archbishop most forcibly pointed out that, as the queen's sovereignty descended by hereditary right, the grant of such special supremacy in spiritual matters was quite beyond the power of Parliament to bestow, and altogether so great a novelty, and unprecedented, as to be both dangerous and wrong. His Grace further maintained that all women, of what sort soever they might be, were entirely unqualified for spiritual functions. They could neither preach nor administer the Sacraments nor exercise spiritual censures—acts which belonged exclusively to the clergy and the hierarchy.

Bishop Scott of Chester then argued that without a chief pastor the visible Church would be weakened. Such a guide was practically necessary for receiving appeals from, and determining controversies within, the boundaries of all local or national churches. Taking notice that the Pope's authority had been disclaimed by an English provincial council, he announced that the resolutions of such an assembly were of no force whatsoever against the decrees of the Universal Church.[1] England, he

parliamentary law courts, has efficiently taken its place, and, of course, will remain in power in the State Establishment so long as it is the will of the majority of the electors that a State Establishment shall be maintained.

[1] As a recent author has so forcibly and ably written :—" When England embraced the Christian faith, she became a part of Christ's spiritual kingdom or empire. She did not become the whole of that kingdom. It was an absolute impossibility for her to do so. Until, therefore, one part of anything can be equal to the thing itself, so long is it impossible that a part of Christ's kingdom can be His whole kingdom. In other words, England is not an empire, speaking spiritually. And if England is not a spiritual empire, but one mere province of a spiritual empire, then appeals cannot have their final determination without the assent and consent of the other provinces of the universal kingdom. If such a thing were possible, then might one province claim to decide a spiritual question in one way, and another province in another way. Thus direct conflict would arise. There would be instead of one spiritual kingdom or empire of Christ, as many spiritual kingdoms as there are Christian nations in the world, all absolutely independent one of another, and every one possibly divided against every other, and fighting against every other. And thus the Catholic Church would have long since been brought to desolation, and have had an end. This was not the way, beloved, that the Divine Wisdom built His house, and hewed out His seven mystic pillars. It is the Statute of Appeals, and the assertion that England is, spiritually speaking, an empire, and that the Church of England as a part is equal to the whole ; and that this part of the one kingdom of Christ

maintained, was only one part of Christ's universal kingdom ; and, furthermore, that no man nor body of men can bestow that which they themselves do not already possess. These speeches were carefully heard and warmly applauded.

About this period a document of "Questions and Advices," drawn up, no doubt, by Sir Thomas Smith, one of King Edward's advisers, was submitted to Cecil, as a guide in the work of so-called "Reformation." A new Service-Book was at once needed, so the queen by Letters Patent appointed Drs. Bill, Parker, Cocks, and May, together with Mr. Grindal, Mr. Whitehead, and Mr. Pilkington, to prepare it. The lawful bishops of the Church of England were in this work wholly ignored in favour of men owning no spiritual authority whatsoever, and deeply tainted, moreover, with dangerous heresies. Cecil, desiring moderation and comprehensiveness, gave these persons very express orders both what to do and what to avoid.[1] The Lord Keeper Bacon, in his speech at the opening of Parliament, pointed out that "nothing should be advised or done which anyway in continuance of time was likely to breed or nourish any kind of idolatry or superstition." In these particulars, his lordship's timely and valuable advice was certainly not ignored.

With a few trifling alterations, what is known as the "Second Prayer-Book of Edward VI."[2] was now, by the Act of Uniformity, restored to use, having been thus recommended. That devotional volume was the baldest and barest that could have been compiled. Its scrappy service for the Holy Communion, into which the Ten Commandments had been introduced,[3] for the sake of the second

is competent to decide spiritual questions apart from the other provinces of Christ's kingdom, and independently of them ; in other words, without the consent of the rest of Christendom, which is in direct and irreconcilable antagonism to the revealed word of God, and a bold and daring contradiction to the express will of the Incarnate Son of God."—*The Keys of the Kingdom of Heaven*, by the Rev. Dr. T. W. Mossman, O.C.R., p. 8. London, 1879.

[1] A frightful passage from the Litany, which harmonised well enough with the maniacal notion of most of the "Reformers," that the Bishop of the See of St. Peter is "*the* antichrist "—"From the tyranny of the Bishop of Rome and all his detestable enormities "—was, at Cecil's suggestion, but after considerable opposition, omitted.

[2] On July 19, 1559, a Commission was issued by the queen, constituting Parker, Archbishop-elect of Canterbury, Grindal, Bishop-elect of London, and others, Commissioners for carrying into execution the Acts for the uniformity of Common Prayer, and for restoring to the Crown the ancient jurisdiction of the State ecclesiastical.—*Domestic Papers, Elizabeth*, vol. v. No. 18.

[3] A long and wearisome dissertation by Pollanus, delivered at Strasburg, pointing out how the Second Commandment forbids the worship of the Host, and how desirable it is that this "law of God" should be kept before the

(believed by the narrow-minded fanatics who had first compiled the new production to be a protest against what has been in recent times called *Eucharistic Adoration*[1]), was supposed to have been founded on an English version of the Sarum Mass; hacked about and mutilated, however, in every portion. All the old introits, many of the proper prefaces, all the secret prayers, and collects after Communion, were abolished by a few rude strokes of the pen. Those sacred parts of the ancient Canon not cast aside as idolatrous, or rejected because the venerated saints of Christendom were thereby had in memory, were mistranslated, detached from their contexts, broken up, interpolated with novel phrases of ambiguous meaning, separated either from other; and without an ancient parallel formed into a new service which remains as a monument of the deliberate craft, skilful double-dealing,[2] and heretical tendencies of those who compiled it.

At what is known as the "Consecration Prayer," no directions whatsoever were given to the presiding minister for blessing the bread and wine, or for touching either of those elements while the prayer was being said—a crucial omission. For church ministers to have done so from the time of Elizabeth to the period of revision under Charles II. would have been to have broken the statute law of the land. It is open to question, therefore, if, notwithstanding the profound special pleading of

eyes of the populace, was no doubt the origin of the introduction of the Ten Commandments both into the Liturgy and on to the east wall of our English churches.

[1] The doctrine of the Reformers concerning what they called "the Lord's Supper," was truly and faithfully taught by the late Rev. John Keble, in his well-known unrevised verse in *The Christian Year:*—

> "O come to our Communion Feast:
>   There present in the heart.
> Not in the hands, th' eternal Priest
>   Will His true self impart."

"The minister gives what is in his power, namely, the bread and wine, and *not the Body of Christ;* nor is it exhibited by the minister and eaten by the communicant, otherwise than in the word preached, read, or meditated upon. And to eat the Body of Christ is nothing more than to believe, as He Himself teaches in the sixth (chapter) of John."—Letter of Hooper to Bucer, *Original Letters*, p. 47. Parker Society's Works.

[2] The saying that "the Church of England owns an Arminian Prayer-Book and Calvinistic Articles," though perhaps strictly inexact, is a testimony to the intentional vagueness and studied ambiguity of those formularies. At the present day, none of her authorities can declare what she teaches even with regard to Baptism. All "views" (as they are called) are tolerated, from the doctrine of Catholics to the heresy of Calvinists. Anything and everything is allowed, little is forbidden, but nothing definite or precise is authoritatively and universally taught.

several modern writers in its favour, such a form for celebrating the Holy Eucharist in use for exactly a hundred years, could have been valid.   If there be intentionally no act of blessing, of course no benediction is given.   If there be no express deed of consecration (as both theology and common sense declare), no consecration is by consequence effected.

The well-known "rule of contraries" was duly applied by those who made these changes.   For example, in the mass there was always an altar of stone used : in the new Service of the Supper, a table of wood.   At the former, the priest was enjoined to stand before the altar; at the latter, by way of contrast, the minister was directed to go to the north end of the table.   In the mass the priest invariably began the service on the Epistle side, and the *Gloria in excelsis* was said or sung at its commencement; in the Supper the minister began on the Gospel side, while in this new service the *Gloria in excelsis* was placed at its close.

Moreover, the mixed chalice, the invocation of the Holy Ghost, and the sign of the cross were all omitted.   At the delivery of the bread and wine, instead of the old form, the offensive words "Take and eat this in remembrance that Christ died for thee," etc.,[1] were substituted.   A table consisting of a pair of rude trestles and a horizontal wooden board,[2] now

---

[1] In the mass, as the words spoken on giving communion indicated, the Body and Blood of Christ were bestowed ; whereas, in the Supper, the minister distributed "bread and wine" to a seated congregation in remembrance of our Saviour's death upon Calvary.   No greater contrast, than that so manifest between the new and the old, could be conceived.

As Jewell, a bishop and an authority, thus wrote :—" Spiritually and with the mouth of our faith we eat the Body of Christ and drink His Blood. . . . The bread that we receive with our bodily mouths is an earthly thing, and therefore a figure, as the water in baptism is likewise a figure."—*John Jewell, Bishop of Sarum, in Controversy with Harding*, p. 448.

And Bishop Grindal—" Whoso will be relieved by the Body of Christ must receive Him as He will be received, with the instrument of faith appointed thereunto, not with his teeth or mouth."—Grindal's *Remains*, p. 46.

[2] " Twain trestlys and a boord of joyner's work for the Supper."—Churchwardens' Accounts, A.D. 1559, for St. Mary's, Ipswich.

"*Item* (paid) to John ye carpenter for ye mackyng of treystles for ye Communyon, iijs. 4d."—Churchwardens' Book, Thame, Oxon, A.D. 1560.

Mr. J. H. Parker, C.B. (A.D. 1879) thus kindly writes to me :—" Some thirty years ago a friend of mine, who was a brother archæologist, published a pamphlet to explain that all the Communion Tables of the time of Elizabeth and James I. had the table itself—that is, the wooden slab, *tabula*, or board—detached from the framework, on which it is placed, but many of them still remained undetached.   He printed a list of these, and I verified many of them.   Others had been attached to the framework in quite recent times with modern iron screws.   In some cases, instead of a framework, tressels were used, and this, I believe, is still the case in the Isle of Jersey, at least when I was there.   The table, or wooden slab, was brought out of the

occupied the place of the ancient consecrated stone altar. Sometimes it was placed in the middle of the choir, and occasionally in the nave.   Cross and candlesticks were swept away. Instead of the old "massing cups," the "chalices of antichrist," "cups of the sorceress," as they were profanely called,—most of which had disappeared,[1] having been too affectionately grasped and retained by the Edwardian "Reformers" and their energetic agents,—newly-made domestic and secular-looking vessels for the Communion Table, of quite a different shape, with covers, seem to have been almost universally adopted.   Thus a Supper of bread and wine, given once a quarter at mid-day, in remembrance of an act done long ago, Christ's death, was once again intentionally substituted for the adorable sacrifice of the Christian dispensation, enjoined by our Divine Master to be offered continually—a sacrifice true, proper, and propitiatory, as well for the departed as for the living.

Furthermore in our Baptismal Service the exorcisms, the unction, the trine immersion, and the putting on of the chrisom-cloth were all omitted.   The Service for Confirmation[2] was so altered and disfigured, both in its form and matter (for here likewise the use of unction and the sign of the cross were dropped), that many doubt whether it can be valid ; it being thus reduced to a mere episcopal or paternal blessing which might be again and again repeated without any danger of sacrilege.   In the Service for the Visitation of the Sick, all mention of the Sacrament of Extreme Unction was cast out, and reservation of the Holy Eucharist omitted.   In the Burial of the Dead, all the touching and beautiful prayers for the departed were dropped, while the Eucharist at funerals was disallowed.   Neither alb, vestment, nor cope was henceforth to be used ; but only a surplice for a priest or deacon, and a rochet for a bishop.

The solemn and expressive services for Holy Week ; the various episcopal rites peculiar to Maundy Thursday and Easter

chancel and placed in the nave on tressels by the side of the reading-desk for the Communion Service.   I was told this was always the case in that island."

[1] It seems very doubtful if so many as twenty old English chalices and patens remain throughout the whole of the two provinces.   I know of old examples at Trinity and Corpus Christi Colleges, Oxford ; Wymondham, Norfolk ; Nettlecombe and Pilton, Somersetshire ; Brancaster, Norfolk ; West Drayton, Middlesex ; St. Sampson's, Guernsey ; Great Waltham, Essex ; Combe Pyne, Devonshire ; Cliffe, Kent ; Walmer, Kent ; Leominster, Herefordshire ; Shernbourne, Norfolk ; and a few in private keeping. The Rev. E. J. Phipps owned a good specimen.

[2] See a short, but learned and vigorous, article on this subject—" Confirmation in the Church of England"—on p. 271 *et seq.* of *The Reunion Magazine*, vol. i.   London : Nutt, 1879.

Even; the special hallowing and beneficent solemnities of Good Friday; as, for example, the consecration of the holy oils, the service of the Præ-sanctified, the creeping to the cross, the benediction of new fire, of the Paschal taper and of the font,—ancient and hallowed rites which so efficiently taught people through the eye,—were all swept away. So that, in our own day, as a consequence of such changes, the Christian feasts having, many of them, been long disused, Parliament has thought it desirable and necessary to appoint four secular days of recreation; while Good Friday, the death-day of the world's Redeemer, has been practically made a festival; and Ascension Day, a feast of obligation, has been almost entirely forgotten.[1]

The magnificent and appropriate services common to days on which prelates, martyrs, confessors, virgins, and holy women had been for centuries commemorated were totally and completely abolished. Portuaries, manuals, missals of the various national rites, books of the hours of our Lady, the offices for the dead, pontificals, ceremonials, antiphonals and jewelled books of the Gospels, were each and all utterly cast out and burnt—save, of course, the acceptable gold and jewels which adorned them. Severe punishment followed even the possession of such volumes. A restless desire for change, combined with a repulsive fanaticism, thus led those who in the struggle had now secured the whip-handle of usurped power, to destroy and sweep away whatever seemed to be at variance with their newly-formed tastes or personal ambition.

In the early part of the month of May, a Bill for annexing to the Crown all abbeys, priories, nunneries, chantries, and hospitals passed through both Houses of Parliament. In the Upper House every one of the Lords Spiritual voted against it, and when passed, dissented from it by a formal act. It will thus be seen that the legal spiritual authorities of the Church of England, as bound by oath and office, declined, as by every principle of morality they were bound, to take any part in this fresh act of sacrilege and robbery.

While Parliament sat considering the new propositions, the clergy as of old were assembled in Convocation. To these the queen sent a somewhat arrogant message of warning, indicating with sufficient clearness to those who had already watched the course of recent events, what her royal will, as Supreme Governess

---

[1] As the Church of England in its corporate capacity takes little heed for this loss, and its authorities adopt no measures to restore the due observance of the day, a new and special society has been set up to compass and effect this object, so much required, and so excellent in itself.

of the Established Church, was in reference to those propositions.   On being informed of the opposition of all the prelates,[1]
she had stamped her foot violently and sworn her usual expressive oath.   But the fearless bishops, nobly and bravely doing
their duty as guardians of the faith and their flocks,—neither
hirelings, wolves, nor robbers come into the fold "some other
way,"—drew up a profession of faith, and presented it to the
House of Lords,[2] asserting, firstly, the true and undoubted
doctrine of the Holy Sacrifice and the Real Presence, in opposition to a sentimental presence in the heart or mind of the
receiver, which the innovators maintained ; secondly, the lawful
and generally-recognised power and privileges of the Holy See ;
and, thirdly, the exclusive right of the spiritual rulers of the
Church Universal, and not of the laity or a lay assembly, to
define, declare and decide upon, its doctrine and discipline.
    In consequence of this, and as one mode of blunting the
power and destroying the influence of the bishops, a lawful disputation was appointed to be held in Westminster Abbey on
March 31st, by which clever expedient the critical spirit of the
period was fostered, public attention aroused, and time for more
consideration of the grave circumstances which had arisen
efficiently secured.   The Lord Keeper Bacon, delegated to
represent the Supreme Governess, presided, and the sittings of
the Houses of Parliament were suspended, in order that idle,
curious, or interested members might attend and witness the
exciting dialectical contest in question.   Numerous languid
loungers,[3] accustomed to the fashionable delights of the rat-pit

---

[1] Bishop Tunstall wrote to Cecil from London on August 19, 1559,
who declared that he could not consent to the visitation of his diocese, if
it extended to the pulling down of altars, the defacing of churches, and the
taking away crucifixes.—*State Papers, Domestic, Elizabeth*, vol. vi. p. 137.
  [2] The chief points of their profession stand thus :—
  " Primò, quod in sacramento altaris, virtute verbi Christi à sacerdote debitè
prolati existentis, præsens est realitèr, sub speciebus panis et vini, naturale
Corpus Christi, conceptum de Virgine Maria ; item naturalis ejus sanguis.
  "Item, quod, post consecrationem, non remanet substantia panis et vini,
neque ulla alia substantia, nisi substantia Dei et hominis.
  "Item, quod in missa offertur verum Christi Corpus, et verus ejusdem
sanguis, sacrificium propitiatorium pro vivis et defunctis.
  "Item, quod Petro apostolo, et ejus legitimis successoribus in Sede
apostolica, tanquam Christi vicariis, data est suprema potestas pascendi et
regendi Ecclesiam Christi militantem, et fratres suos confirmandi.
  " Item, quod authoritas tractandi et definiendi de iis, quæ spectant ad fidem,
sacramenta, et disciplinam ecclesiasticam, hactenus semper spectavit, et
spectare debet, tantum ad pastores Ecclesiæ, quos Spiritus Sanctus ad hoc in
Ecclesiâ Dei posuit, et non ad laicos."—Wilkins' *Concilia*, vol. iv. p. 179.
  [3] Thomas Cecil wrote to his father, Sir William, on July 25, 1561, to say

and bear-baiting, gathered for the anticipated entertainment. Protestant ballad-singers and buffoons, stationed near the west door of St. Margaret's Church, amused the lower classes by caricaturing religion. Various controversial subjects were discussed within the Abbey ; *e.g.* whether prayers in Latin were to be henceforth permitted ; whether local churches have the right and power to set themselves up against the decisions and decrees of the whole Church of God ; and whether the Eucharist be a propitiatory sacrifice for the quick and the dead. On the side of the ancient faith were Archbishop Heath, Bishops White, Bayne, Scott, and Watson ; with Dr. Cole, Dean of St. Paul's ; Dr. Nicholas Harpsfield, Archdeacon of Canterbury and Judge of the Court of Arches ; and Dr. Langdale, Archdeacon of Lewes. On the side of the innovating party were Bishop Scory, Dr. Cocks, Mr. Horne, Mr. Aylmer, Mr. Whitehead, Mr. Grindal, Mr. Ghest, and Mr. Jewell. The prelates in rochets and violet mantles assembled in the choir, where a long and narrow table down its pathway had been placed for their use, and were seated on the Gospel side. The other party, in gowns, putting their trust in the queen's delegate, and on the look-out for some of the good things of this world,[1] took their places on the south. The monks' stalls were filled with certain peers and others interested in the dispute. A gathering of exiled preachers and foreign divines in black cassocks and stiff white ruffs, armed with large tomes, from which to prompt and aid their friends, were grouped near the choir doors. The public, wherever a sight and hearing could be had, assembled in numbers. The whole dispute, conducted with singular one-sidedness, but anxiously listened to, was so unfair to the legal representatives of the Ancient Church, that the Catholic party, perceiving this, after vain remonstrances, and being wholly in the hands of Bacon who presided, wisely and resolutely retired on the second day. Upon this Bishops White and Watson were at once, without notice, process, or trial, committed to prison in the Tower—a gross piece of high-handed tyranny.[2] Nothing, of course, could have

that he had been present at the Court at Paris at a fight between a lion and three dogs, in which the dogs were victorious.—*State Papers, Elizabeth*, 1547–1580.

[1] Edmund Ghest, on August 31, 1559, wrote to inform Cecil that " Mr. Seth Holland will not renounce the Pope," and then solicits that he (Ghest) may succeed him in the deanery.—*Domestic Papers, Elizabeth*, vol. vi. p. 137.

[2] Some writers assert that these two bishops' true offence was that they had already privately and solemnly threatened the queen with excommunication if she continued to intrude in matters inherently and essentially spiritual.

been more effective in overcoming the force of their telling arguments, or in preventing their incisive logic and solemn appeals from having reasonable and just weight with the listeners. It was asserted in justification that they were thus punished for disobedience to the queen's delegate, who sat and acted in Her Most Sacred Highness's place, and who had enjoined them to proceed and not to retire ; but the real object of this bold action was to overawe others and overbear all legitimate opposition to the proposed parliamentary legislation.

The Bill enjoining the new Prayer-Book soon afterwards became law, it having been carried in the Upper House by a narrow majority of three in a large assembly—a tolerably clear indication of the feeling against innovation and change which existed, and proving that such an act of tyranny as that just recorded· was absolutely essential for the success of the innovators.

The Act of Uniformity enjoining the use of the revised Service Book, indirectly decreed that on and after the Feast of St. John the Baptist, 1559, any one who said mass according to those rites of the Church of England which had been followed essentially for nearly a thousand years, as well as any and every one who heard mass, or administered baptism or any of the sacraments according to the old directions and services, or who used any but the new, should, for the first offence, be fined one hundred marks ; for the second, four hundred marks ; and if these respective fines were not promptly paid, imprisonment for twelve months followed ; with imprisonment for life and the forfeiture of all goods and chattels if a third offence were proved. Jewell, though a severe and sour writer of bad theology, sometimes became witty, and occasionally postured as a buffoon ; as, for instance, when he wrote to Peter Martyr, some months later, telling him the welcome news that the Catholics had no right to complain of the queen, for that mass had never before been so highly valued or expensive as then ; for, by God's gospel, it cost every spectator of it no less than two hundred crowns.

On the day appointed, therefore, the public celebration of mass ceased. Those who elected to range themselves in opposition to the innovators soon found what was involved in such a choice.[1] As the records of this reign are examined step by step, and the harrowing tale of persecution is told, it will be seen with

---

[1] On June 30, 1559, the Marquis of Winchester wrote to Cecil to inform him that the Dean and Canons of Winchester Cathedral, the Warden and Fellows of New College, and the Master of St. Cross' Hospital "left their services, and will enter no new service, being against their consciences."

what a high hand those carried affairs who by the use of might over right had secured influence, authority, and power. All the varied "beggars-on-horseback" rode a random and rapid race to their due and proper goal.

But to proceed step by step, and with due care, and to state exactly only that which can be surely and conclusively proved to be true.

With the single exception of Anthony Kitchin, Bishop of Llandaff, who had been consecrated by Cranmer on May 3, 1545, without approval by, or authorisation from, Rome, the whole body of bishops, one and all, firmly resolved to refuse assent to this new legislation. Involving as it did both a fresh separation from the Chief Bishop of Christendom, whose saintly predecessor, Pope St. Gregory the Great, had sent St. Augustine to become a light to our country; and being likely, as they believed, to augment all the complex evils of new and needless divisions, they declined to be participators in that which was obviously wrong. In their noble opposition—being unable to render to a woman, a female Cæsar, the things of God—they were all firm and determined. They could not in conscience maintain that the queen was the Supreme Governor or Governess of the Church under Christ, and, therefore, repudiated the action and legislation of the civil authority as beyond its due and proper powers, and by the law of God altogether illegal.

Amongst these are several names of men of high virtue and repute, names which because of their action at the crisis in question deserve to be had in everlasting remembrance. The first is that of Nicholas Heath. He had been consecrated Bishop of Rochester by Bonner of London, and others, in the chapel of London House, in the spring of 1540. Translated three years afterwards by Henry VIII. to the See of Worcester, he was thrown into prison and treated with great harshness under Edward VI.; but on Queen Mary's accession, confessing his previous failings, and the aid he had given to the innovators, he was reconciled to the Church and made Archbishop of York and Lord High Chancellor. In his province he laboured assiduously, and was venerated and respected both by high and low.

Edmund Bonner was another. A Worcestershire and Oxford man, he had for some years been one of Henry VIII.'s courtly chaplains, and had certainly made himself notorious enough by his mistaken zeal in promoting that king's divorce. When in Rome, in so doing (as he himself admits), he had behaved with great personal rudeness and insolence to the Pope. At home he had gone a considerable way on the "Reforming" road, and

had even accepted many of the violent changes under Edward
VI.; but the fanaticism, heresy, and blasphemies then in favour
at Court—working on all sides so many evils—were more than,
by any strain of conscience, he could approve of or adopt.   So
the civil authorities deprived him of his See, which was given
to Nicholas Ridley; and Bonner likewise was cast into prison.
Under Queen Mary, having been duly restored to his former
episcopal seat, he did a great work in stemming the tide of
irreligious revolution; in restraining misbelievers; and in building anew the waste and desolate places of his important diocese.
He was certainly unpopular with some; his acts in administering
a harsh and cruel law have been considerably misrepresented,
while his name has been cast out as evil by certain historical
romancers or one-sided partisans.   But when, after experiencing
the evils of innovation, a man of resolute and settled principles,
owning authority, acts with decision and boldness on the side
of truth, he must expect opposition, and scorn the unjust condemnation of petty and misinformed scribes, too often the
trumpeters and apologists of error and falsehood.

Cuthbert Tonstall, Bishop of Durham, old and afflicted, and
Thomas Thirlby, Bishop of Ely, were committed to the care of
Matthew Parker, the queen's new archbishop, and his lady, at
Lambeth Palace.   The former, Tonstall, soon died, some said
of a broken heart, in November of the same year, and was buried
in the parish church;[1] the latter lived through eleven stirring
years, and witnessed more changes and greater violence, passing
to his rest in August of the year 1570.

John White, born at Farnham, in Surrey, was educated at
Winchester and New College, of which latter he was made a
fellow in 1527.   Successively head master and warden of
Winchester College, he was consecrated Bishop of Lincoln
by Bonner and others at St. Saviour's, Southwark, on April 1st,
1554.   Two years afterwards he was translated to Winchester,
where his reputation for sweetness of disposition and sanctity
was great.   He preached the funeral sermon of Queen Mary,
and was so affected at the loss which Her Majesty's death had
occasioned,[2] that for some time he stood in the pulpit overwhelmed with sincere grief, and speechless.

Even as these resisted the innovations, so did others.   James
Turberville, Bishop of Exeter, so consecrated on the Feast of

[1] "November (1570).   The xxix day Cuthbret Tunstall a popish bishop was
buried."—MS. List of Baptisms, Marriages, and Burials at St. Mary's, Lambeth.
[2] He "fell into such an unfeigned weeping that for a long space he could
not speak."—*Brief View*, etc., by Sir John Harington.

the Nativity of Our Lady in 1555, was faithful and true even unto death.   Gilbert Browne, sometime Archdeacon of London, but subsequently Bishop of Bath and Wells, deprived by Queen Elizabeth for disallowing her spiritual supremacy, was then consigned to the custody of Gregory Dodds,[1] Dean of Exeter, and so died in 1569.   David Pole, sometime Dean of the Arches Court, and subsequently Bishop of Peterborough, was deprived, because he likewise similarly resisted, and departed this life in June 1568.   Ralph Baynes, a Yorkshireman and a great Hebrew scholar, consecrated Bishop of Lichfield in 1554, was deprived in June 1559, and died five months afterwards.   Queen Elizabeth sent Cuthbert Scott, Bishop of Chester, having first deprived him, to the Fleet Prison; but he soon afterwards escaped, and died most devoutly at Louvain.   Owen Oglethorpe, Bishop of Carlisle, was also deprived in 1559—on the last day of which momentous year he slept his last sleep in peace.   Thomas Watson, Bishop of Lincoln,[2] was likewise turned out of his bishopric at the same time, as were also Thomas Goldwell, Bishop of St. Asaph, and John Feckenham, Benedictine Abbot of Westminster.   Of these three, the first and the last were carefully imprisoned, first in the Marshalsea, and subsequently in the unwholesome dungeons of Wisbeach Castle, situated in the flat and unhealthy fen country of the east, and after much suffering died there in 1585.   Goldwell escaped to the city of Rome, living there for more than a quarter of a century in great sanctity and full of years, when he too slept sweetly in Christ.   Richard Pate, sometime Bishop of Worcester, who had been officially present at the Council of Trent in 1552, happily escaped to the Continent, and there died in peace.

On the 9th of September 1559, Letters Patent were issued appointing a Royal Commission to confirm the election of Matthew Parker, who had been irregularly elected by a minority of the Chapter of Canterbury on the 1st of August, and to give him episcopal consecration.   At this time, ten of the English Sees were vacant by death; for many of the bishops had been thus called away from a scene of much anxiety and trouble, by a strange and fatal malady, some called it "the Plague," which wrought great havoc amongst all classes.   Shortly afterwards,

---

[1] Some writers give another name to this dean who had the custody of this Bishop of Bath.

[2] For a most interesting account of Bishop Watson, the reader should consult *Sermons on the Sacraments* by that prelate, edited by the Rev. T. E. Bridgett, who has prefixed thereto an admirable "Biographical Notice" of the bishop, and has edited the book with conspicuous care and ability. London : Burns & Oates, 1876.

fifteen other bishops either resigned voluntarily, on marking what additional changes were about to take place, or were formally deprived by certain Royal Commissioners, to whom, for this purpose, Her Majesty had duly delegated that supreme spiritual authority which had been vested in her by Parliament.

The Letters Patent concerning Parker's promotion had been addressed to Tonstall, Bishop of Durham ; to Bourne, Bishop of Bath ; to Poole, Bishop of Peterborough ; to Kitchin, Bishop of Llandaff, all occupying Sees, and to William Barlow and John Scory, bishops without Sees.   By an unusual and unexplained inadvertence, however, no clause enabling a bare majority, or a certain number without the rest, to act, was inserted in the document.   So that if any individual, or more, declined the honour, the work of the Royal Commissioners could not be carried out. This Commission, therefore, remained unfulfilled, to the great vexation of the queen, and to the deep annoyance of Sir William Cecil, who found himself in a considerable difficulty.

For, as it soon turned out, none of the prelates occupying the old Sees, and possessing due and recognised canonical jurisdiction, could by any possible means be induced to act.   Neither public arguments nor private threats could move them from their resolution of abstention from participating in any way in what they believed to be the irregular and uncanonical act resolved on.

Besides the prelates who thus stood aloof (all, in truth, except Anthony Kitchin), there were several suffragan bishops alive, whose orders were undoubted, but who were, of course, without jurisdiction, some of whom had gone into retirement ; others had received benefices and were still hale and strong, but much disinclined for further change.   Amongst these were Thomas Sparke, Bishop of Berwick, who lived until 1571, and Robert Pursglove,[1] Bishop of Hull, who only died in 1579. William Finch, Bishop of Taunton, went to his rest in the very year in which Parker was consecrated.   Of Thomas Morley, Bishop of Marlborough, John Bradley, Bishop of Shaftesbury, and Thomas Manning, Bishop of Ipswich, all most probably alive at Elizabeth's accession, there are no existing records known.   None of these suffragans, however, were sought out.

[1] At Tideswell, in Derbyshire, where this bishop, Robert Pursglove was born, and educated under his uncle, William Bradshawe, Prior of Gisburne, in Yorkshire, he was also buried in 1575, and a memorial brass representing him in full pontifical vestments, with a series of verses in Latin and English still remains.   He was Bishop-Suffragan of Hull, Archdeacon of Nottingham and Provost of the College of Rotherham.—See *The Gentleman's Magazine*, vol. lxiv. part ii. p. 1101.   London, 1794.

In consequence of the *fiasco* referred to, therefore, several learned clerks and canon lawyers, who either had a leaning to the Protestant party or were avowed members of it, viz. Drs. May, Weston, Leeds, Harvey, Yale, and Bullingham, were immediately consulted by Cecil, in order not only to suggest some remedy, but likewise to remove two very practical impediments to legal security and actual success. For just then Cecil could not move. His existing letters and MSS. show that he was truly and completely puzzled.[1] These two leading practical difficulties stood thus: first, the law of the land unquestionably required the metropolitan and three provincials, or at least four bishops holding Sees, to confirm the election of a new Primate, but, as Cecil wrote, "*There is no Archb. nor iiij bishopps now to be had;*" and, secondly, the revised Ordinal, legalised under Edward VI.,[2] had by Act of Parliament been formally and regularly abolished at the commencement of Queen Mary's reign. "*This booke is not established by Parlement,*" continued the Secretary of State; while the ancient Pontifical of Salisbury,—*Liber Regalis,*—used then once again, had in its turn been just formally set aside by Elizabeth. There was, therefore, no legal form for consecration in existence, or available at all. Here, then, was a grave dilemma.

The canon lawyers in question, however, came to the conclusion that under the difficult and pressing circumstances—for necessity notoriously has no law—a new Commission might be issued to Anthony Kitchin of Llandaff and to certain unattached prelates, bishops without Sees, authorising them to confirm and consecrate[3] Matthew Parker. This advice was taken.

Accordingly on December 6th, 1559, a fresh Commission by Letters Patent was appointed and issued, addressed to the occupant of the See of Llandaff; to Barlow, sometime Bishop of Bath, a prelate of very fly-blown character; to Hodgkins, sometime Suffragan of Bedford; to Scory and Coverdale, bishops; to John Salisbury, Suffragan Bishop of Thetford; and

---

[1] *State Papers, Domestic, Queen Elizabeth,* vol. v., July 1559. London, 1856.

[2] "They have invented a new way to make bishops and priests and a manner of service and ministration that St. Augustine never knew, St. Edmund, Lanfranc, St. Anselm, nor never one Bishop of Canterbury, saving only Cranmer, who forsook his profession as *apostata;* so that they must needs condemn all the bishops in Canterbury, but Cranmer and he that now is."—"The Addition concerning the Burning of St. Paul's" (a sixteenth century fly-leaf).

[3] It should be particularly noticed that this course of action would only touch the regularity, canonicity, and due legality of the consecration in question; not its validity.

to John Bale, Bishop, by Letters Patent, of Ossory, in Ireland, a boisterous and alarming fanatic,—enjoining them, or any four of them, to proceed to the confirmation of the election, and so to the consecration of the archbishop-elect.

Kitchin, the only bishop with a See, save Bale, the coarse and foul-mouthed Protestant from Ireland, when he thus found himself utterly isolated from the rest of his episcopal brethren, deliberately and firmly declined to act. Reasoning and threats were again both made use of, but to no avail. He would not and did not appear.

Accordingly, Parker's election was confirmed on the 7th of September 1559, and he subsequently received episcopal con-secration in the Chapel of Lambeth Palace on Sunday the 17th day of the same month and year, very early in the morning, at the hands of Barlow, Scory, Hodgkins, and Coverdale.[1]

As the records which chronicle this important act inform us, with unusual and almost unaccountable minuteness, the east end of the sanctuary on that occasion was hung with tapestry, and its floor laid with crimson cloth. In lieu of the abolished altar, a table had been placed at the east end, covered with a carpet, and having on it a cushion. To the north was set a seat for the archbishop-elect; to the south, fald-stools for the consecrating

---

[1] An able writer in the eighth volume of *The Union Review* for 1870, pp. 532, 533, believed to be one of our leading historical critics, thus refers to this inauguration of the new rulers, and to some of those who took a leading official part in it:—"That the ceremony was gone through admits of no more doubt than does the contempt of three at least of the four consecrators for the rite which they were called upon to perform. But it will be re-membered that Scory has been accused of performing a jesting ceremony in imitation of a consecration at the Nag's Head Tavern, where the consecrators met on the day of the confirmation of the new Primate after the work of the morning was done, and dined together. It is certain that Scory was quite capable of going through a mock ceremony of consecration, and, considering the character of the man, we think it is very likely he did. Neither of his colleagues would have been at all shocked at such a piece of profaneness; and probably Parker himself would have made light of it. Parker himself was at least externally a decent character, but we do not find that he at all shrunk from intercourse with such rascals as Barlow and Scory were. We have already alluded to Barlow, but Scory was the worst of the two. His course very much resembled Barlow's, with the additional scandal that he abjured his faith and dismissed his wife, and served under Bonner, in Queen Mary's reign. That he was chaplain to Archbishop Cranmer can add no infamy to Cranmer's name; but it must be admitted to be a blot on Ridley's fair fame, that he also made Scory his chaplain. When we have added to this, that he preached at the burning of Joan Bocher for heresy, and that amongst other Protestant notions held by him, he was notoriously opposed to the consecration of churches, we have said all that is necessary to secure him from being quoted with approbation by Anglican divines."

C

bishops were arranged. These persons, as already pointed out, were Barlow, Scory, Hodgkins, and Coverdale. They came in long before it was light, accompanied by Parker, and preceded by four torchmen, by choir, chaplains, and legal officials. Edmund Grindal, Richard Cocks, and Edwin Sandys—all subsequently bishops—were also present, together with two registrars and two public notaries. Morning prayer was said by Pearson, a minister, and a sermon was preached by Scory; after which the archbishop-elect and the other bishops went out into the vestry, prepared themselves for the actual consecration, and again returned. Barlow took the chief part in the consecration, and with his attendants, Edmund Ghest, Archdeacon of Canterbury, and Nicholas Bullingham, Archdeacon of Lincoln, was vested in surplice and cope. Scory and Hodgkins appeared simply in surplices or rochets. Coverdale, who shunned what he termed such "heathen and Babylonish garments," appeared in something less ornate, a simple woollen gown. In the rite the new and bald Ordinal of 1549 seems to have been almost exactly followed (though it had been legally set aside under Queen Mary, and never restored), save that, as the chief consecrator was not an archbishop, all the four bishops, when laying their hands upon Parker's head, *each* said: "Take the Holy Ghost, and remember that thou stir up the grace of God which is in thee by the imposition of hands, for God hath not given us the spirit of fear, but of power and love and soberness." In these words there was no specification whatsoever of the office proposed to be conferred. There was no unction either, nor was there any delivery of a pastoral staff, though this last-named rite was formally and expressly enjoined in the Edwardian service presumed to have been used.

Here then, and in this manner, the new succession began;[1] and some persons maintain that its validity depended exclusively

[1] On the subject of the Nag's Head Fable, out of which uninformed controversialists have endeavoured to make capital, Dr. Lingard wrote as follows:—"Of this tale concerning which so much has been written, *I can find no trace in any author or document of the reign of Elizabeth*. It is not improbable that the Commissioners, having confirmed the election, dined together at the Nag's Head, the inn chiefly frequented by the clergy at that period, and that this circumstance may have given rise to the story."—*History of England*, by John Lingard, D.D., p. 380, vol. vii. London, 1838. "It may be admitted as proved," writes Canon Estcourt, in his learned, able, and temperate treatise, entitled *The Question of Anglican Ordinations Discussed*, "that *the Nag's Head story is a legend without foundation in fact*, and that the charge sometimes made of Parker and the first Elizabethan bishops assuming their place and discharging their functions without consecration of any kind is also unfounded"—p. 115. London, 1873.

upon William Barlow. Hodgkins, however, had been certainly consecrated by John Stokesley, Bishop of London, and two others, as early as 1537, and Scory and Coverdale by Cranmer in 1551; so there is something of importance and consideration to be said in favour of the validity, though little for the canonical regularity, of this unprecedented official act.

The objection to Barlow that he was possibly unconsecrated, because the actual register of his consecration is wanting, seems unreasonable and groundless; for, during more than twenty years he publicly and continually acted as a bishop, and specially took a chief part in the mortuary masses for the soul of Henry VIII.; and this in the presence of other prelates who notoriously disliked change and dreaded innovation, and must have known well enough that, as regards his episcopal character, he was truly and actually what he was generally supposed to be.

This consecration having been effected, Parker in turn confirmed the election of Barlow to Chichester, and of Scory to Hereford; and then with their aid soon afterwards, in due course, proceeded to consecrate the other persons who at the command of the Supreme Head had been elected to the various vacant bishopricks.

CHAPTER II.

PRIOR to the later events recorded in the last chapter, a proclamation had been issued in the spring of the year, of which Grindal, writing from London to Hubert the Reformer, about the end of May, thus gave his opinion :—

" Now at last, by the blessing of God, during the prorogation of Parliament, there has been published a proclamation to banish the Pope and his jurisdiction altogether, and to restore religion to that form which we had in the time of Edward VI. If any bishops or any beneficed persons shall decline to take the oath of abjuration of the authority of the See of Rome, they are to be deprived of every ecclesiastical function and deposed. No one after the Feast of St. John the Baptist next ensuing may celebrate mass without subjecting himself to a most heavy penalty." [1]

This proclamation produced immediate fruit. The innovators, who had been expecting it for some weeks, were, upon its receipt, at once prepared to act with boldness and determination. The carrying out of its decrees was, of course, left to local authorities. To such, considerable latitude was given. These authorities, beforehand and from headquarters, had been privately but duly instructed. There was to be an immediate contemporaneous raid on everything valuable in the churches, more especially on all ecclesiastical articles wrought in precious metal, while the Church lands were to be revalued and possibly, as regards ownership, rearranged. [2] Those country gentlemen, therefore, who were at once doubtful on their own part of what to do, and were doubted as to their zeal and competence by the agents of Cecil throughout the kingdom, were to be discreetly and confidentially sounded as to whether a substantial share in

[1] Grindal to Conrad Hubert, *Zurich Letters* (Parker Society), vol. ii. No. 8.

[2] An information made to Queen Elizabeth of the several abuses and frauds, etc., done unto the State, etc.—Harl. MSS. quoted in p. 124 of Weaver's *Funeral Monuments*.

the anticipated pickings and stealings might not probably quicken their interest and stir up their dormant energies to accomplish what the Council so earnestly desired should be immediately done.

In order to rouse public opinion, therefore, scurrilous publications from the pens of the returned exiles, or foreign Protestants, had been simultaneously circulated by thousands. Some of these were gross in their language, filthy in their suggestions, revolutionary in their proposals, and, though garnished with numerous texts of Scripture, blasphemous in their teaching.[1] Such appear to have been sent for distribution to those laymen and apostate clergy who were known to be favourable to the tactics of the innovators. They were likewise freely distributed throughout the various Inns of Law, and especially amongst the students of Oxford and Cambridge. The authorised Commissioners for continuing and completing the changes resolved upon, found that the various parishes which had been selected for their special visitation had been duly prepared for their advent by the receipt, no one knew how or from what quarter, of the inflammatory, infamous, and obscene literature in question.[2] The language applied therein to the Pope was frightful, far worse than that which had recently been eliminated from the Litany; but it will be found more than equalled by the ribald trash and rancorous letters and homilies which have been reprinted and issued of late years in portly volumes by modern Puritans.[3] In the afore-mentioned literature, the sacraments were disparaged, the priesthood ridiculed, the act of ordination written of as "a magical incanting," extreme unction styled "a corrupt following of the apostles" and the "dirty greasing of antichrist"; while the Blessed Sacrament of the Altar, hitherto reserved in a silvern or golden pix, was profanely called "Little Jack-in-the-box, "John in captivity," and treated with deliberate and artfully-designed indignities too fearful to describe.

All over the kingdom, in fact, wherever the innovators were

---

[1] In the 51st of the Injunctions of Queen Elizabeth in 1559, this crying evil was seen and acknowledged thus:—"Because there is a great abuse in the Printers of Books, which from covetousness chiefly regard not what they print, so they may have gain, whereby ariseth the great disorder by publication of unfruitful, vain, and infamous books and papers," etc.—*Sparrow's Collections*, p. 80. London, 1671.

[2] The natural descendants of these unpleasant scribes, judging by modern literature of the same type, may possibly be found amongst the modern Soupers of Connemara.

[3] Publications of the Parker Society.

sufficiently numerous, daring, and profane, this kind of controversial blasphemy was current, and often became fashionable
and popular; while some of the deeds done, by no means unlike in character to that about to be recorded, are in truth too
frightful for any detailed description of them to be put into words.

One record of such, with the swift punishments which
followed, will for the present suffice. It has come down to us
on good and sufficient authority,—a priest of the Church of God,
—and affords, it is to be feared, too graphic and accurate a
picture of similar dark deeds then perpetrated :—

"After that the Holy Mass was, by public proclamation of
the late queen,[1] commanded to surcease immediately in all
places of England by Midsummer Day immediately following,
four men of Dover, in the county of Kent, besides others which
assisted at the same action, went into the church of the same
town and took forth the copes, vestments, and other priestly
ornaments belonging thereto, giving forth and boasting abroad
that they would go fetch the Pope from Canterbury; and the
very next day after Midsummer Day, these companions came to
Canterbury, put on the said copes, and other ornaments upon
their backs, and in a pix, made to reserve the Blessed Sacrament
of the Body of our Saviour Jesus, they put a dog's [excrement];
and then beginning at St. George's Gate, rode in form of procession quite through the city, till they came to Westgate,
which done, the very same night they posted back again to
Dover.

"One of these four was Captain Roberts, who presently after
carried all the copes, vestments, and other ornaments over the
seas to Dunkirk, where he sold them. His miserable and
wretched end was, that there leaping out of one small boat into
another, to go to his ship, the boat he was in slipping away, he
stepped short of the other, and so falling into the water, pitched
his unhappy head upon an anchor, where he beat out his brains.

"The second, shortly after running mad, cast himself off from
Dover Pier into the sea, and so was drowned.

"The third died of John Calvin's disease ; that is to say, he
was eaten up with lice, being yet alive.

"The fourth, who afterwards became minister of Maidstone,
falling grievously sick, endured God's terrible judgments, for he
stunk so abominably that none, no, not his own wife, could
endure to come near him ; so that when they gave him meat to
eat, they were forced to put it upon the end of a long pole, and
so to reach it unto him through a window. For confirmation

[1] The book was not published until the reign of King James the First.

whereof they are right credible and worshipful persons yet alive who can testify the same for a certain truth." [1]

It is sometimes asserted, by interested or ignorant writers, that such acts as these never took place at all until the frightful and unhappy period of the Great Rebellion. Oliver Cromwell and Lord Brooke they condemn; for Thomas Cromwell, Nicholas Ridley, Grindal, and Aylmer, they have only apologies or praise. The picture drawn by such writers of the days of Queen Elizabeth is consequently rose-tinted, peaceful, and pleasant to look upon. But it is a picture of pastoral beauty, peace, and repose, drawn rather from heated imagination than from stern facts. Horrible, in truth, as were the deeds of Dowsing and Prynne sixty years later, none of them equalled in atrocity those just related; while these last-named unhappy Puritans, who had sucked in the principles of Protestantism and the rejection of all authority with their mother's milk, must have well known by tradition hundreds of dismal precedents for their own sacrilegious iniquities and destructive acts, which may have spurred them on to overturn, murder, upheave, commit outrages, and destroy, as they did to their hearts' content.

It has been also asserted by recent writers, some evidently in good faith, that the Oath of Homage as at present taken by the bishops of the Church of England is a modern invention,[2] unknown until quite recent years, or at all events of no earlier antiquity than the disordered days of the revolutionary William of Orange, and of no formal authority. These writers, however, have only unintentionally helped to darken knowledge by bold assertions which, alas! most efficiently exemplify their own ignorance and blundering. That oath, in the actual terms still made use of, came into existence when the new Church was originally set up, and it was certainly and dutifully taken by the first Protestant Archbishop of Canterbury on his knees before the queen. Sir William Cecil, no doubt, was its author, and possibly Dr. Matthew Parker himself had a hand in its revision;

---

[1] From the preface to *A Devout Exposition of the Holy Mass*, by John Heigham, A.D. 1622.

[2] "Can any of your readers tell us something about the history of this secret oath? Who was the first bishop who ventured to swear that he held his spiritualties from the Crown? Has any bishop denied this, or protested against its apparent meaning? Or will any one give an explanation of the term which will relieve consciences, and effectually meet the charges our enemies are sure to bring against us—that here is proof positive of the unmitigated Erastianism of the whole English Episcopate?"—Rev. Charles Gutch, B.D., on the *Oath of Homage*.

for he not only took it himself,[1] but thus created a precedent for all his suffragans, without any single exception, the most remote as well as the more proximate.

No long period after her accession, the Lord Treasurer was directed by the queen, under the advice of Aylmer, an exile for his Protestantism, to assign the grand and effective church of the Austin Friars in the city of London—a church, be it noted, which in Edward the Sixth's time had already been thoroughly cleared out of all its ancient furniture and valuable ornaments, and left as bare and bald as possible—to the use of French, Flemish, and other foreign Protestants. Upon this Grindal, in full communion with the continental sectaries, applied to Calvin for a pastor, who in response despatched Monsieur Nicholas de Gallars, a French preacher, to undertake the office of superintendent there, and who received the bishop's "authority." The service, exactly modelled after those of the foreign conventicle, consisted of long prayers and longer sermons. But the disputes about free will and justification,[2] original sin and prevenient

---

[1] The following is the Oath of Homage, taken on February 23, 1560 (See *Domestic State Papers, Elizabeth*, vol. xi.):—"I, Matthew Parker, Doctor of Divinity, now elect Archbishop of Canterbury, do utterly testify and declare in my conscience, that Your Majesty is the only Supreme Governor of this Realm, and of all other Your Highness's dominions and countries, as well in all spiritual or ecclesiastical things or causes, as temporal, and no foreign prince, person, prelate, power, superiority, pre-eminence, or authority, ecclesiastical or spiritual, within this Realm; and therefore I do utterly renounce and forsake all foreign jurisdictions, powers, superiorities, and authorities; and do promise that from henceforth I shall bear faith and true allegiance unto Your Majesty, Your heirs and lawful successors, and to my power shall assist and defend all jurisdictions, privileges, pre-eminences, and authorities granted or belonging to Your Highness, Your heirs and successors, or united and annexed to the Imperial Crown of this Realm. And further, *I knowledge and confess to have and to hold the said archbishopric of Canterbury, and the possessions of the same entirely, as well the spiritualties as temporalties thereof, only of Your Majesty and the Crown Royal of this Your Realms.* And as for the said possessions, I do my homage presently unto Your Highness, and to the same, and Your heirs and lawful successors, shall be faithful and true. So help me God, and the contents of this book."

"We also, whose names be underwritten, being bishops of the several bishoprics within Your Majesty's Realm, do testify, declare, and acknowledge all and every part of the premises in like manner as the right reverend father in God, the Archbishop of Canterbury, has done."

[2] "If any preacher or parson, vicar or curate, so licensed shall fortune to preach any matter tending to dissension, or to the derogation of the religion and doctrine received, that the hearers denounce the same to the Ordinaries, or to the next bishop of the same place; but no man openly to contrary or to impugne the same speech so disorderly uttered, whereby may grow offence and disquiet of the people, but shall be convinced and reproved by the Ordinary."—*Articles for Doctrine and Preaching*, issued by Queen Elizabeth, 1564.

grace, became so fierce and furious—for the preacher was constantly answered on the spot by his hearers—that the civil authorities were often called in to settle biblical controversies, which had ended in a free fight and a riot, by turning out both preacher and hearers by force, and then locking the doors.

Moreover, some of the foreign reformers who had arrived here, in order to stir up the sluggish nature of English Protestants, were persons who had so offended against the laws of their own country, that their presence in London was not particularly desired. We all know that justification by faith rather than by good works—for "good works are but filthy rags," as the preachers of this new gospel maintained—was their chief and favourite dogma ; a dogma not conducive either to sound morals or sober conduct. So that in the course of a very few years, *i.e.* in 1568, the queen issued a proclamation,[1] requiring all such intruding Protestants to be examined, as many of them were credibly believed to have been guilty of "rebellion, murders, robberies, or such like," and to have only come over here to preach their blasphemous gospel in order to avoid the reasonable consequences of notorious transgressions in their own country.

Eventually, when their extravagances became dangerous and unendurable,[2] for it is always far easier to open the flood-gates of heresy and rebellion than to close them again—these foreign Protestants, on pain of imprisonment and loss of goods, were ordered to leave the kingdom within twenty-one days.

Such a strong measure, of course, excited them greatly ; and their preachers were fierce in its denunciation and furious with Cecil. Many of these openly maintained, as Knox and Calvin had done long ago, that the rule of women in the Lord's fold was a monstrous anomaly and a sin ; and dealt out covert maledictions at the queen and her secret love affairs most unsparingly, using language rather forcible than either choice or clean.

Soon after the queen's accession, Giovanni Angelo de Medicis, Pope Pius IV., wrote a beautiful and even touching letter to Her

---

[1] Wilkins' *Concilia*, vol. iv. pp. 204 and 254.

[2] " Here under the shelter of the reformed religion, they maintained several gross errors and heresies. Some of these were German Anabaptists ; and others propagated opinions of a very dangerous tendency ; and thus misbelief gained ground, and some of the ignorant natives were miserably misled. To stop the spreading of this infection, the queen, by a proclamation, ordered these hereticks, both aliens and natural-born English, to depart the kingdom within one-and-twenty days. The penalty of staying longer was imprisonment and forfeiting their goods."—*An Ecclesiastical History of Great Britain,* by Jeremy Collier, vol. vi. p. 322. London, 1846.

Majesty, sending it by a nuncio, the Abbot Vincent Parpaglia,[1] who was directed to travel through Lower Germany towards England.   But the queen, learning the purport of his coming, and having consulted her Council, who feared any change of purpose on her part, declined to allow him to land in her kingdom.   He had reached Calais, but was thus compelled to return.

The paternal action of His Holiness has been so often misrepresented that the actual words of this fatherly communication ought to be carefully studied :—

"Very dear daughter in Christ, We send you greeting, health, and the apostolical benediction.   How greatly We desire (Our pastoral charge so requiring it) to procure the salvation of your soul, and to provide likewise for your honour, and the security of your kingdom withal, God, Who is the Searcher of all hearts, knoweth; and you yourself may understand by what We have given in charge to this Our beloved son Vincentius Parpaglia, Abbot of St. Saviour's, a man well known to you, and well approved by Us.   Wherefore, We do again and again exhort and admonish your Highness, most dear daughter, that, rejecting evil counsellors, which love not you but themselves, and serve their own lusts, you would take the fear of God into council with you, and, acknowledging the time of your visitation, would show yourself obedient to Our fatherly persuasions and wholesome counsels, and promise to yourself from Us all things that may make not only to the salvation of your soul, but also whatsoever you shall desire from Us, for the establishing and confirming of your princely dignity, according to the authority, place, and office committed unto Us by God.   And if so be (as We desire and hope), that you shall return into the bosom of the Church, We shall be ready to receive you with the same love, honour, and rejoicing, that the father in the gospel did his son returning to him; although Our joy is like to be the greater, in that he was

[1] Some writers have asserted, but with little or no evidence of the fact, that Parpaglia bore a message from the Pope volunteering to reverse his predecessor's sentence against the so-called "marriage" of Henry VIII. with Anne Boleyn, and to sanction the revolutionary changes which had been made anew in the divine office, on condition that the queen acknowledged His Holiness's supremacy; but from the days of Camden down to those of Chancellor Harington of Exeter, no sufficient and conclusive proofs of this proposition have been forthcoming.—See Camden's *Annals*, p. 46.   London, 1688.   Tierney's edition of *Dodd's Church History*, vol. ii. p. 147.   London, 1839.   *Collier's History*, vol. vi. p. 395.   London, 1840.   Ware's *Foxes and Firebrands*, part iii. p. 15 ; and *Pope Pius IV. and the Book of Common Prayer*, by E. C. Harrington.   London, 1856.

joyful for the safety of one son, but you, drawing along with you all the people of England, shall hear Us and the whole company of Our brethren (who are shortly, God willing, to be assembled in a General Council, for the taking away of heresies, and so for the salvation of yourself and your whole nation), fill the Church Universal with rejoicing and gladness. Yea, you shall make glad Heaven itself with such a memorable fact, and achieve admirable renown to your name, much more glorious than the crown you wear. But concerning this matter, the same Vincentius shall deal with you more largely, and shall declare Our fatherly affection toward you; and We entreat your Majesty to receive him lovingly, to hear him diligently, and to give the same credit to his speeches, which you would to Ourself.

"Given at Rome, at St. Peter's, under the Fisherman's Ring, May 5th, 1560, in the first year of our Pontificate."[1]

But to proceed. Edmund Grindal, who, after a fashion, but with considerable canonical irregularities, had been elected Bishop of London, was by Parker and others consecrated at Lambeth on St. Thomas' Day, 1559, at the same time that Richard Cocks, Rowland Meyrick, and Edwin Sandys were likewise consecrated for the Sees of Ely, Bangor, and Worcester.

The first and most striking fact which was brought home to the new bishops, after they had secured possession of their temporalties, was the extremely small amount of money which the episcopal lands and manors actually produced. Many had been already sold or alienated; of those remaining, long leases had already been granted by the Crown during vacancies; while all the lands had sorely deteriorated by want of due attention and proper cultivation. The prelates, therefore, made formal complaint to Sir William Cecil; but on the part of the Supreme Governess he delicately rebuked them for their importunity,[2] pointing out with grim satire that spiritual persons should learn to be satisfied with spiritual things, and not look too anxiously after things temporal.

Preparations also were about this time made for filling up the many other Sees vacant, a work in which Sir William Cecil took a leading and prominent part. Even at this period he foresaw clearly enough that the "foreign gospel" and its strange preachers

---

[1] MS. "Vatican," 2896, n. 214. MS. "Titus," C. vii., n. 11. Brit. Museum.

[2] "When the bishops sued to the Lord Treasurer for revenue, they were merely answered that spiritual things be meetest for spiritual men."—R——ny to Challoner, *Foreign Papers, Elizabeth*, p. 137, No. 323, Nov. 23, 1559.

might cause him considerable inconvenience. He was extremely careful, therefore, not to commit himself absolutely to their policy. And though he occasionally condescended to employ them and secure their help, he was shrewd enough to keep them all at arm's length.

The new bishops found themselves likewise terribly embarrassed by the pressing want of clergy,[1] and had no means to their hands with which to supply it. Many of the parish churches, having lost their chief endowments and been completely cleared out of everything of value in metal,—in some nothing but a tin or latten vessel remaining for the Communion board,[2] the windows of the choir broken, the lead from the roofs stripped off, and side chapels or chantries often destroyed for the sake of the stones of which they had been built,—even the exiles from Geneva and elsewhere declined to serve them. Numerous cures were vacant, and several hundreds of chapelries unserved; students for the ministry at Oxford and Cambridge had been so reduced in numbers that they might be now counted rather by tens than, as of old, by hundreds, or even by thousands.[3] Those of the cast-out monks who were in any way competent for the office had been duly promoted to the priesthood six years previously in Queen Mary's reign; others, however, had long ago taken to secular callings and married;[4] some, again, had become parish

---

[1] "Many of our parishes have no clergymen, and some dioceses are without a bishop. And out of that very small number who administer the sacraments throughout this great country, there is hardly one in a hundred who is both able and willing to preach the Word of God."—*Zurich Letters*, 1st series, No. 35, From Thomas Lever to Bullinger, dated 10th July 1560. "In the diocese of Durham the ministry is destitute of a sufficiency of worthy men, there and in other places."—Robert Horne, Dean of Durham, to Cecil, Nov. 13, 1560, *Foreign Papers, Elizabeth.* London, 1865.
"Where is there any learned number to supply their rooms? There be few schools abroad to bring up youth; but so many benefices so small that no men will take them; and so the parishes be unserved, and the people wax without fear of God."—*Bishop Pilkington's Works* (Parker Society), p. 593. London, 1842.

[2] "That the parish provide a decent table, standing on a frame, for the Communion Table."—*Queen Elizabeth's Articles for Doctrine and Preaching,* 1564.

[3] In the year 1561, as Anthony à Wood has put on record, so frightful was the emptiness and depression at Oxford, that throughout the whole year there were no degrees given "in Divinity, and but one in the Civil Law, three in Physic, and eight in Arts," and, in the Act of the same year, "not one in Divinity, Law, or Physic." The students also were so poor and beggarly that many of them were forced this and the year following to obtain licence under the Commissary Seal, to require the alms of well-disposed people.—*Annals of the University,* by Anthony à Wood. *Sub anno* 1561.

[4] *E.g.* Hugh Wren (son of Geoffrey Wren, Confessor to Henry VII.),

clerks and sextons; some had been charged on suspicion, captured, and allowed to rot and die in prison; others had gone
abroad in their extremity; a few, in despair of securing anything
more suitable, had undertaken the office of steward to noblemen
and gentlemen who had obtained possession of the monastic
lands; while many of the monks had found, what had been
denied to them throughout the last years of their chequered
lives, peace and rest in death.

Amongst the more fanatical innovators, preaching, and the
desire to attend it, had at this time become such a rage—the
Communion Table, as well actually as metaphorically, being now
wholly overshadowed by the pulpit—that unless a divine could
expound a crabbed text with art, skilfully analyse its various parts
in detail, compare it with twenty other texts dealing with the
same or a somewhat similar subject, and then adroitly branch off
with perplexing dissertations in half-a-dozen unexpected directions,
he was fearlessly written down as at once incompetent and godless,
lacking spiritual gifts and free grace, a mere dumb dog, unworthy
of hire or notice.

Such human treasures as those who could thus preach popu-
larly for two hours or so without any break or mishap were
still few and far between. Though fully appreciated, they could
not be secured every day or anywhere. Their homiletic gifts
were choice, rare, and superfine. The demand for them, consequently, was very greatly in excess of the supply. But even
these when handling Scripture—often casting pearls before swine
—were properly shunned, with a shudder, by those who at heart
clung to the ancient faith.

Inferior officers of the Establishment, the illiterate and ill-
mannered, the "sundry artificers" and those of "base occupation," to whom Parker and Grindal had, it may be supposed,
given some kind of new ordination, and a special commission to
preach,[1] were required, instead of "holding forth out of their

chanting priest of Hanslope, Bucks, at the dissolution in 1547, was sixty years
of age. In 1549 a pension of 6s. 5d. a year, together with the Chanting
Lands, were granted to him for twenty-one years. He had a son of the same
name, whose wife was Margaret, by whom he had four daughters. This son
was buried at Hanslope, 29th August 1585. He belonged to the race of
Matthew Wren, Bishop of Ely, and Sir Christopher Wren, the architect of
St. Paul's Cathedral; and his will, proved at Oxford, was dated 28th August
1585.

[1] "The supply of clergy was insufficient, and even the withdrawal or removal of what but for this would have been so considerable a portion as one
in fifty-three of the beneficed clergy in England, seriously embarrassed the
new bishops. As in other times, men unqualified by learning, and by the
possession of clerical gravity, or deficient in regard to our ideal moral

own heads"—as the phrase then stood, and so remained almost
to our own day—were required to deliver over and over again
the "godly" but somewhat coarse-languaged homilies which the
innovators had authoritatively put forth for the practical use of
their ill-instructed,[1] ignorant, and vulgar allies. If these homilies
in question were those which satisfied the not over-refined tastes
of the new prelates, we need not stay to contemplate what was
the kind of taste then popular with these new and too truly
"inferior" clergy.

The dearth of spiritual privileges and the desolation consequent
thereupon became by consequence truly awful. Churches were
closed, for there were none to serve them. Infants remained
unbaptized, women were not churched, children were uninstructed. In some places the dead were buried, like dogs,
without either rite or ceremony; save that poor and pious
neighbours gathered near to tell their beads and recite the *De
profundis*, and this often at the risk of condign punishment.

Even in cathedrals the Communion was administered but
once a quarter, though ordered once a month. Sometimes the
authorities tolerated the ministerial acts of persons who had not
received any but Presbyterian ordination, and possibly not even
that. The "Lord's board," as it was called, was brought down
with its tressels from the east end of the chancel,[2] and placed, as
for a domestic meal, with benches round, in the middle of the choir.
It was covered with an ample table-napkin of Damascus cloth. A
large leathern bottle of wine,[3] some loaves of bread, and a knife,
sometimes a pewter plate and flagon, or occasionally a wooden

---

standard, however truly they conformed to the naturally low standard of
general morality, were ordained and beneficed to supply the deficiency of the
first years of the reign of Elizabeth.—*The English Episcopate at the Accession
of Elizabeth*, p. 289. *Union Review*. London, 1875.

[1] "We are only wanting in preachers, and of these there is a great and
alarming scarcity. The schools also are entirely deserted."—*Zurich Letters*,
John Jewell to Peter Martyr, 1st series, No. 38. Parker Society.

[2] The table is ordered to be "set in the place where the altar stood . . .
*saving when the Communion of the Sacrament is to be distributed, at which
time the same shall be so placed in good sort within the chancel. . . . After
the Communion is done, from time to time, the same holy table to be placed
where it stood before*."—Queen Elizabeth's Injunctions, 1559.

[3] "A bottyl of leather and a flagon of white metall for wine for the
Supper."—Churchwardens' Accounts of St. Mary Magdalene's, Oxford,
1551-2. "*Item*, whether you have a faire potte or two of pewter for the
sweet keeping of the wine?"—William Chaderton's Visitation Articles for
the Diocese of Lincoln, A.D. 1603. "The bread delivered to the communicants be such as is usual to be eaten at the table with other meats. . . . No
other bread to be used by the minister."—William Overton's Visitation
Articles, 1584.

platter and a tin cup, were by the sexton then placed upon it.
A cushion and a Prayer-Book of the latest revision completed the
ornamenta. The proceedings began by the singing of a hymn.[1]
Round the table the people sat or stood. The minister, though
ordered to go to its north end by the direction of the rubric,
often stood at the eastern [2] part, or seated himself in an arm-
chair, where he alternately preached and prayed. When the
service was over, what remained of the bread and wine [3] was
passed round again to the congregation, who helped themselves,
and so were communicated, after a fashion, twice over. The
bottles and flagons were then taken away, the cloth removed, and
the table often lifted back again to its place under the east wall.

Such was the ordinary rule and custom with reference to what
was termed "the Supper."

Some of the more fanatical and mad of the innovating party,
however, adopting the Protestant method of interpretation of
Scripture, maintained that even such practices were wrong and
without biblical authority, and that the Lord's Supper ought to
be something very different—a well-prepared and substantial
meal, at which the faithful could satisfy the cravings of hunger
with "a variety and abundance of meat and drink."[4] Ever
since the days of St. Paul, the Catholic Church, as they so
modestly maintained, had been in blind error. As some persons
imagined, it was thus reserved to certain infallible innovators of
the sixteenth century, madmen, fanatics, and demon-possessed,
to redeliver the lost truth. One fool often makes many. There
were several who enthusiastically embraced this new and remarkable idea.

[1] "There may be sung a hymn or such-like song to the praise of Almighty
God in the best sort of melody and music that may be conveniently devised,
having respect that the sentence [Qy. sense] of the hymn may be under-
standed and perceived."—Injunctions of Queen Elizabeth, 1559.

[2] "The minister, when there is no communion, useth a surplice only,
standing on the east side of the table, with his face towards the people."—
Strype's *Life of Parker*, vol. i. p. 365.

[3] No less than ten "rundletts of wine" were used at Amersham, Bucks,
during the year 1603, for the Lord's Supper; thus showing anew that " the
mystery had become a meal."—See remains of a *MS. Volume of Church
Accounts* of that town, A.D. 1541–1684, still in the vestry-room.

[4] Robert Cooke, one of the gentlemen of the Queen's Chapel, wrote:—
" My remarks relate to the Last Supper of Christ, in the administration of
which a mistake is made nowadays, and ever has been almost from the
time of St. Paul: since he placed before the Corinthians a supper to be
eaten; we only a morsel of bread in mockery of a supper. They used a
variety and abundance of meat and drink, so as to depart satisfied; we return
hungry."—Robert Cooke to Rodolph Gualter, *Zurich Letters*, 2nd series,
Letter 95.

When such services as that just described were calmly contrasted with the ancient and familiar mass,[1] no wonder that the
dazed and staggered people felt disposed to leave the despoiled
and empty churches to the owls and bats; no wonder that, as
was so often the case, they refused under any circumstances to
enter them. Except with those who were on the look-out for
their own advancement, the changes effected were most unpopular.
Some of the new bishops, in their exuberant piety, scolded like
angry fishwomen, or swore like their Royal Mistress;[2] but neither
bad language nor coarse oaths served the cause of the new
gospel, which in many parts sorely languished. The novel title
of Supreme Governess, the new-fangled supremacy itself, with
all its complex consequences, as well as the newly-revised Prayer-
Book, were each and all disliked. Nothing in the recent proclamation had commended itself to the great body of the people,
—whether ancient nobility, lawful clergy, or gentlemen of blood
and estate be comprehended in that wide but ambiguous term,—
so that a large and influential majority refused to acquiesce in
the changes.

What, therefore, the upholders of might against right were
compelled to attempt could only be effected by a tortuous and
astute policy, not by direct but by crooked courses; and these
were taken artfully and warily, according to varying circumstances
and by the aid of means ready to hand. The work was done
by degrees, and in the manner and by a method now to be
described.

The Oath of Supremacy was duly tendered to all the clergy
in accordance with the recent enactment. Many important
offices were vacant. By almost the whole of the leading digni-

---

[1] "For their continual massing afore noon, we praise God that hath
delivered us from it, as a thing contrary to His holy will and ordinance. St.
Paul says that when they came together to eat the Lord's Supper they should
tarry one for another; but those shorn, shaveling, shameless priests would
neither remain together one with another, nor yet let the people have any
part with them. Every one would creep into a corner to an altar alone,
there lift up on high, eat and drink up all alone, sell good pennyworths, and
bless them with the empty chalice."—*Bishop Pilkington's Works*, Parker
Society, p. 528. London, 1842.

[2] "The cholerick oaths and manifold rare upbraidings" [of my Lord of
Hereford] "be of no avail with the bastards of Antichrist, though spoken in
the Quene's Majestie's name." — Again: John Best, Bishop of Carlisle,
writing to Cecil, reports the state of his diocese. "The priestes are wicked
impes of Antichrist, for the most part very ignorant and stubborn; past
measure false and subtle."—*Domestic State Papers, Elizabeth*, vol. xvii.

For a due account of Her Majesty's ability and proficiency in profane
swearing, the reader should consult her godson Sir John Harington's *Nugæ
Antiquæ.*

taries of the Church it was firmly and resolutely refused. More than twelve of the deans of cathedral and collegiate churches deliberately declined to take it, and, as some avowed, were quite prepared for the consequences of their refusal. Numbers of the archdeacons, canons, and prebendaries did the same,[1] as was the case also with numerous heads of colleges and influential members of the two universities. Amongst the parochial clergy, an important rather than a considerable minority were likewise equally true to the faith of their fathers; declining with firmness and resolution to acknowledge an illegitimate woman as, in any form or shape, or because of any legislation, the Supreme Governess of the Church of England. In this they were sometimes supported by the public.[2] Many of them, however, were passive and obedient, waiting for another change, and hoping earnestly for better and brighter times. One reaction had happily taken place; others, they assumed, might possibly follow.

As a consequence of their refusal, certain of the dignitaries in question were either cast into prison and loaded with chains, or promptly banished the realm. No favour was shown to any who resisted the enactment, except, for personal reasons, to a few feeble and worn-out clergy who were cruelly denied the consolations of religion, confined to special localities, and not permitted to go beyond well-defined limits. But the old priests[3] retained their well-deserved popularity. The Friars Observant at Greenwich, some of the Benedictines from Westminster, the Carthusian Fathers in Richmond, as well as the Bridgetine Nuns of Sion House, one and all, marking the signs of the times, left their desolated country, and for ever turned their backs upon their former sacred homes. Persons of blood and rank, noblemen and gentlemen, and sometimes, indeed, noble and delicate

---

[1] "The whole of the clergy deprived at this time stands thus: fourteen bishops, already mentioned; three bishops-elect, one abbot, four priors, and one abbess; twelve deans, fourteen archdeacons, sixty canons or prebendaries, one hundred priests, well preferred; fifteen heads of colleges in Oxford and Cambridge, to which may be added about twenty doctors in several faculties."—*Ecclesiastical History of Great Britain*, by Jeremy Collier, vol. vi. p. 242. London, 1846.

[2] On the inauguration of Dr. Francis as the new Protestant Provost of Queen's College, Oxford, there was a serious riot.—Letter of Scholars of Oxford to Cecil, May 11, 1561, *Domestic State Papers, Elizabeth*, No. 7, vol. xvii.

[3] Some old priests, Brigg, Blaxton, Arden, Gregory, and others, though driven out of Exeter, were received in Bishop Scory's diocese (Hereford) with acclamation, and feasted in the streets by torchlight—of which he wrote and made complaint.—*Domestic State Papers*, 1547-1580, August 17, 1561.

ladies likewise, cheerfully left their pleasant mansions and ancient possessions, suffering any spoiling of their goods and destitution rather than give up their faith. The most respected and best learned of the universities, becoming exiles, were scattered throughout foreign lands, weeping by strange waters because of the religious desolation of their native homes. Some found a refuge and home in Flanders, others in France, some in Italy. As regards the latter country, it is interesting to remember that the saintly Archbishop of Milan, Charles Borromeo, received the English exiles in that beautiful city with cordial kindness. He truly bound up their spiritual wounds, pouring in oil and wine. For several years, indeed, His Grace's own confessor was a Welsh canon, Dr. Griffith Roberts, and his last grand vicar was another Welshman, Dr. Owen Lewis.

For the inferior clergy these days were indeed days of trial. Many of them obviously conformed to the new order of things for fear of poverty, others because they preferred the licence and freedom which an acceptance of the new doctrines practically ensured. Step by step, those who would not take the Oath of Supremacy[1] were "weeded out," as one of the new prelates phrased it ; but though the Visitors and Commissioners appointed by the queen went about their work with a will, the practical difficulties which met them at every turn were considerable. Though the innovators were a small minority, they were perfectly united and determined, while the great body of the people were against the changes ; and the hearty resolutions of such were constantly met with by those violent and foul-mouthed officials who had been sent forth to continue and complete the revolution.[2] By degrees, however, because of the constant and continual fines imposed for nonconformity, many who clung to the ancient faith did not altogether decline to attend the new service, and even to receive the bread and wine distributed at what was called "the Supper of the Lord."

The exact state of affairs at this melancholy period was graphically described by a competent judge and author, Edward Rishton, a watchful and observant priest, who followed a con-

---

[1] Those who resigned their appointments rather than do so were possibly under two hundred and fifty in number ; but of those who remained, hoping for another change and better days, several hundreds, possibly some thousands, heartily disliked the new religion and its founders.

[2] John Scory, Bishop of Hereford, writes to Cecil, June 21, 1561, to say that there are great disorders in the cathedral church of his diocese, which, he charitably remarks, is "a very nurserye of blasphemy, whordom, pryde, superstition, and ignorance."—*Domestic State Papers, Elizabeth*, vol. xvii. No. 32.

siderable number of the clergy of the ancient faith, in a total
denial of the validity and value of the new ordinations. Some
moderns may have desired, and yet desire, that a different
contemporary judgment might have been given at the time when
the new rites and regulations were first set forth and adopted;
but from the days of Thomas Goldwell, Bishop of St. Asaph,[1]
to those of Canon Edgar Estcourt of St. Chad's Cathedral, in
Birmingham, one uniform opinion and tradition appears to have
been held. The limited number of exceptions only serve to
prove the rule.

"It may be confidently asserted," writes Canon Estcourt,
"that there is an unbroken tradition from the year 1554 to the
present time, confirmed by constant practice in France and
Rome, as well as in this country, in accordance with which
Anglican ordinations are looked upon as absolutely null and
void; and Anglican ministers are treated simply as laymen, so
that those who wish to become priests have to be ordained un-
conditionally. Not a single instance to the contrary can be
alleged."[2]

There are certain difficulties which, it must be frankly allowed,
have been always felt by learned Roman Catholics and Orientals
with regard to the fact of Parker's consecration, and which must
be duly faced and removed before any recognition of the validity
of English ordinations can be reasonably expected either from
the Eastern or Western Churches. Anglicans must not remain
contented with assertions which appear to satisfy themselves, but
be prepared with arguments and conclusions which will serve to
convince their opponents.

The modern Easterns, though personally civil and polite
enough, frequently repudiate our ordinations with scorn.[3] Such,

[1] A contemporary inquiry was made at Rome in the spring of the year
1570, as well concerning the character of the new orders as of the assumed
prelatial dignities held by those who had not been previously ordained priests.
Goldwell, Bishop of St. Asaph, gave his opinion, as did also Dr. Nicholas
Morton, of the diocese of York; Henry Henshaw, of the diocese of Lincoln;
Edmund Daniel, Dean of Hereford; Thomas Kinton, of the diocese of Sarum,
and others. All the opinions of these persons were against the validity of the
new rites and ordinations.—See, for the document itself, the continuation of
the *Annals of Baronius*, by Laderchius, vol. iii. pp. 197 *et seq.*

[2] *The Question of Anglican Ordinations Discussed*, by E. E. Estcourt,
M.A., pp. 145–6. London, 1873.

[3] The late Archbishop of Syra and Tenos, even more civil than some of
his brethren, reordained absolutely the Rev. James Chrystal, an American
clergyman of the Protestant Episcopal Church; while the Servian Archi-
mandrite, who once gave the Holy Communion to a London clergyman, the
Rev. William Denton, who had rendered good service to the Servian Church,
was most severely reprimanded by authority, and made to give a promise in

in their judgment, are on a level with the ministries of Lutherans, Calvinists, and continental Protestants. At Rome every care is taken to arrive at the truth, so that the inadequate defences regarded as sufficient and satisfactory by some at home, will never pass muster in the presence of the skilled theologians of the Eternal City.[1] A huge assumption, as the majority of Roman Catholic theologians maintain, that all was right in Parker's case, is, of course, easily enough made; but detailed proofs of facts and satisfactory replies to objectors often give trouble, entail research, and yet remain insufficient for the purpose.

As regards the *fact* of Parker's consecration at Lambeth on the 17th of December 1559, it must be admitted that the following difficulties appear to exist :—

1. The Lambeth Register was not publicly produced—in fact, no reference of any sort or kind, either in attack or defence, was made to it—until 1613, fifty-three years after the date of Parker's consecration; though the new bishops had been constantly pressed to show some written proofs of their consecration by Nicholas Sander, William Allen, Stapleton, Bristow, Reynolds, and more especially by Harding in his *Confutation of Jewell's Apologie*, first published only six years after Parker's consecration, *i.e.* in 1565. Why it was not produced is, to say the least, singular, if not mysterious.

2. Stowe, the chronicler, though he, as any reader may see, was often exact and circumstantial in recording the most trivial matters, and duly put on record the consecration of Reginald Pole and others, omitted by some strange oversight any account whatsoever of Parker's consecration, or any reference to it, though he was very intimate with this new prelate, and was frequently a guest at Lambeth Palace.

3. Holinshed and Stowe both make the remarkable statement that *Archbishop* Parker, and Grindal, *Bishop* of London, were present at the obsequies of Henry II., King of France, performed in St. Paul's Cathedral on the 8th and 9th of September 1559;[2]

---

writing that he would never repeat that his canonical offence ; and this in a formal document which described the Church of England as "unorthodox" and "Protestant," and the clergyman in question as "without the priest-hood."

[1] The author had hoped (if he may be pardoned for writing thus) that his book maintaining the *Validity of the Ordinations of the Church of England*, in which he made the best defence in his power, might have called our bishops' attention to a subject of the gravest moment, which touches the organic life of the Established Church ; but at present these have made no sign.

[2] Parker had been elected on August 1st. In a letter to the Privy Council,

yet the first-named, Parker, was certainly not consecrated until December 19th, and Grindal not until the 21st of that same month. The terms "archbishop" and "bishop," therefore, were consequently most inexact; unless, indeed, the Queen's Letters Patent enjoining the respective chapters to elect these persons, were regarded by Stowe as of more importance than any other previous or subsequent rite.

4. From an original document in the State Paper Office,[1] it is clear that Matthew Parker, who then styled himself "elect Archbishop of Canterbury," did homage for his temporalties before the queen at Westminster, in February 1559. At that period he certainly was neither elected nor consecrated, and it is equally certain that bishops did not usually do such homage until their consecration had been effected. Here it may be remarked by some that February 1559 may possibly mean February 1560; but if so, then the Lambeth Register, in which his consecration is recorded as having taken place in December 1559, is altogether wrong; for Parker, in February 1560, could never have then wittingly termed himself merely "elect archbishop," when, according to the said register, he had been actually consecrated two months previously.

5. Again. There is in the State Paper Office[2] a Commission from the queen, constituting Parker, who is termed "Archbishop-elect of Canterbury," Grindal, who is styled "Bishop-elect of London," and others, Commissioners for carrying into execution the Acts for the Uniformity of Common Prayer, and for restoring to the Crown the ancient jurisdiction of the State Ecclesiastical. This document is dated the 19th of July 1559, nearly a fortnight before the election of Parker to the See of Canterbury, which took place on the 1st of August; consequently the use of the term "bishop-elect" is inexact, or else the dates of the Lambeth Register, as regards these events, are wrong. At all events, this State Paper is distinctly and remarkably out of harmony with them.

dated the 27th of that month, he signed it "Matth. C[antaur.]" And it appears, as Canon Estcourt points out (on p. 83 of his *Question of Anglican Ordinations*), that he is addressed in the same style in official documents. Another remarkable error is that, in an Order of the Queen, dated 26th October, it is asserted that, amongst others, the elect-bishop of Chichester, Dr. William Barlow, "remains unconsecrated."—*State Papers, Elizabeth*, vol. vii. p. 19.

[1] It is referred to in the *State Papers of Elizabeth, Domestic*, vol. xi., under the date 23rd February 1560, and is printed at length in Collier's *Ecclesiastical History of Great Britain*, vol. ix. pp. 331-2.   London, 1846.

[2] *Domestic State Papers, Elizabeth*, vol. v. No. 18.   London, 1856.

Whether these various difficulties, either apparent or real, are not removed by the knowledge that certain independent documents exist, plainly proving that the ceremony took place on December 17th, 1559, is, of course, quite another question, which each investigator must determine for himself after duly weighing the harmonious or conflicting evidence on both sides. But that the evidence is conflicting, and that difficulties do exist, cannot be doubted.

There are some persons, it should here be noted, who go further, and maintain that the whole of the first and earlier parts of Parker's Register, including the heraldic title-page, are in one handwriting; and that this is of a later date than 1559, possibly of the subsequent reign of James I., when, in the new Church of England, different and less questionable opinions concerning the subject began to prevail. But this, of course, is a subject for impartial Catholic theologians and skilled paleographers satisfactorily to decide.

But to return to the course of public events. Immediately the clergy found themselves at liberty to enter the honourable estate of matrimony, most of the reforming party took to themselves wives. Some had already done so secretly. Archbishop Cranmer's distinguished precedent of having had two[1] was in many cases dutifully followed by the new bishops, though of course, these wives were procured one after the other, and not both at the same time. But these married prelates, and, indeed, the married clergy likewise, were looked upon with intense dislike, and often with contempt, by the people in general; while the terms which were sometimes applied both to their wives and children were much more plain and impressive than complimentary.[2]   Even the Queen's Highness disliked the wives of prelates. As a rule, the reforming clergy, when waxing amorous, could only secure helpmeets from the lowest of the people—almost all others turned away with disgust at the proposal;[3] while many of those thus secured owned questionable or fly-blown characters, had been waiting-women, ale-house attendants, or publicly disreputable.   The gravest scandals by consequence arose in several places,[4] to which from time to time the attention of

---

[1] "The husband of *one* wife."—Titus i. 6.

[2] See *Briefe Confutation of a Godlie Warning*, p. 47. London, 1572.

[3] "No knight's daughter, nor esquire's, could be so certified to accept of him."—*Briefe Confutation, etc.*, p. 50.

[4] "Because there hath grown offence, and some slander to the Church, by lack of discreet and sober behaviour in many ministers of the Church, both in choosing of their wives and indiscreet living with them, the remedy whereof

the Queen's Privy Councillors was officially drawn. On two occasions Sir William Cecil wrote contemptuously of those whose matrimonial acts had been called into question, to the great annoyance of Parker. The subject was new, and certainly difficult. Sir John Mason informed Cecil that " in sundry particular churches at this present [there is] such fleshly demeanour in appearance, as small difference is to be seen in any point between them and lay-houses, wherewith the world taketh occasion of offence, and God, I think, is not much pleased."[1] Some other instances of wantonness and demoralisation in the houses of the ministers cannot be further alluded to.

The Queen's Injunctions had laid down some excellent and practical rules on the subject ; but these appear to have been too generally disregarded. When a minister or deacon had made choice of some buxom woman or country lass, and she was certified to be ready, or at least not unwilling, to accept him, the bishop of the diocese and two neighbouring justices of the peace on some holiday, and in church in presence of the congregation, were to examine her personally, " behind and before, in mind and in body, by inspection and by report," to see that she was whole and sound, healthy, and of good repute, free from either moral or physical blemish,[2] and, in order to find this out, her parents, or, if they were dead, two of her nearest kinsfolk, or " her master or mistress whom she serveth," being summoned to appear, " shall make a good and certain proof thereof " both to the minister of the parish and to the assembled congregation. Such was usually known as a " matrimonial inquisition " : profane or over-witty persons sometimes gave it a less pleasant name. Having passed through this disagreeable but perhaps necessary ordeal, the bishop and the magistrates, if satisfied, gave permission, under their hands and seals, to the two persons more particularly interested, to gratify their praiseworthy intentions " with all due and convenient speed."

A similar process was also necessary and enjoined by the queen in the case of bishops. Only here special commissioners of rank—not mere justices of the peace—were appointed to undertake the needful examination, and with these were associ-

is necessary to be sought."—Queen Elizabeth's Injunctions to the Clergy, A.D. 1559.

[1] *State Papers*, August 11, 1561, Sir John Mason to Secretary Cecil.

[2] A transcript of the minutes of such an examination—*Inquisitio Matrimonialis, etc.*—is before me as I write. It took place in an Oxfordshire Peculiar of the ancient diocese of Lincoln, before its rearrangement ; and, though faithfully paraphrased in the text above is, in some of its details, far too coarse to be verbally quoted.

ated the venerable metropolitan, himself a married man. For
such an exalted ecclesiastical officer this was certainly a new,
as no doubt it must have been an interesting, duty.

Deans of cathedrals and heads of houses, fired with matrimonial
ambitions, when proposing to wed, were to apply to the official
visitor of their respective institutions, whose duty it was, as the
Supreme Governess enjoined, to make a similar personal examination of the wife-designate, and to see that the proposed union
"tend not to the hindrance of their house."

Archbishop Parker was terribly mortified at the queen's formal
edict about the marriage of the clergy, and horrified at her
unscriptural and unfeeling language. He wrote to Sir William
Cecil [1] to explain his manifold grievances, and evidently looked
for some word of consolation from him. He went so far as to
lament that under such conditions he had ever accepted the See
of Canterbury. If the bishops' inferior servants might have
their wives within the precincts of the cathedrals, and in the
useful outhouses of the episcopal palaces—if these respectable
officers might rock their offspring's cradles, why might not the
lady of the most reverend and loyal Primate of all England do
the same? Parker was evidently very sore at what he termed
these "rebukeful separations."

Bishop Cocks of Ely likewise on his own part complained
loudly to Archbishop Parker that the "women of the bishops
and prebendaries" were by the Queen's Majesty's edict turned
out of the colleges and precincts of the cathedrals. He wrote,
"forasmuch as it is not needful, but at this time very miserable,
and sounding contrary to the ordinance of the Holy Ghost in
the Scriptures of God," he hoped that the edict might be withdrawn. He went on to inform his afflicted metropolitan that
there was then but "one prebendary dwelling with his family in
Ely Church," and "if the wife and children were turned out, the
prebendary himself would go." "'Turn him out," wrote the
bishop plaintively, "doves and owls may dwell there for any

---

[1] Parker, in this letter, asserts of the queen that he was "in an horror to
hear such words to come from her mild nature and Christianly learned
conscience, as she spake concerning God's holy ordinance and institution of
matrimony." And again: "To tarry in cathedral churches with such open
and rebukeful separations, what modest nature can abide it? Or tarry where
they be discredited. Horsekeepers' wives, porters', pantlers', and butlers'
wives may have their cradles going; and honest learned men expulsed with
open note, who only keep the hospitality, who only be students and preachers,
who only be unfeigned orators in open prayers for the Queen's Majesty's
prosperity and continuance, where others say their back paternosters for her
in corners."—Parker to Cecil, Petyt MSS., No. 47, folio 374.

continual housekeeping.   It is miserable that the poor man's
family should be turned out, and miserable that such a number
of houses should be left desolate."[1]   Expressive sentences like
this sufficiently set forth the awful havoc which had been made
in the garden of God by these "wild boars" of the Reformation.
They had indeed rooted up the garden, for, where flowers of
grace erewhile grew in abundance, now only sterility and desolation reigned.

As regards the practical action of those who resisted the
innovators, we may learn much from the following interesting
and pregnant words :—

At the same time, they had mass said secretly in their own
houses by those very priests who in church publicly celebrated
the spurious liturgy, and sometimes by others who had not
defiled themselves with heresy; yea, and very often in those
disastrous times were on one and the same day partakers of the
Table of our Lord and of the table of devils; that is, of the
Blessed Eucharist and of the Calvinistic Supper.   Yea, what is
still more marvellous and more sad, sometimes the priest saying
mass at home, for the sake of those Catholics whom he knew
to be desirous of them, carried about him Hosts consecrated
according to the rite of the Church, with which he communicated
them at the very time in which he was giving to other Catholics
more careless about the faith the bread prepared for them
according to the heretical rite."[2]

At the same time, Elizabeth maintained her unprecedented
dignity.   When, for example, the queen visited Canterbury, she
was received pontifically, as the Head of the Church of England.
On one occasion Parker, supported by the Bishops of Lincoln
and Rochester, met her outside the west door.   There a
"grammarian" made a long-winded oration in her praise, in
which the words *Ave Eliza!* and numerous exaggerated epithets
were used.   Then, alighting from her palfrey, she entered the
cathedral, where the psalm *Deus misereatur* and some collects
were said.   The choir men and boys, with the dean and prebendaries, stood in order on either side, and "brought Her
Majesty up with a square song, she going under a canopy, borne
by four of her temporal knights, to the traverse, placed by the
Communion board, where she heard evensong."[3]

[1] Petyt MSS., No. 47, folio 378, in the Inner Temple.
[2] Continuation of the *History* by Rev. Edward Rishton, B.A., B.N.C.,
Oxon. ; edited by David Lewis, M.A. ; p. 267.   London, 1877.
[3] This is Parker's own description of the event.   See Petyt MSS., No. 47,
folio 22.   "The Communion board" is what contemporary writers of the

In 1560 the Geneva Bible was printed and circulated. Both in its preface and notes the false doctrines of Calvin were studiously inculcated; and these being popular with the now extending Puritan party, it had a considerable circulation, exercising much influence. Some of its notes were obviously directed against prelacy; while others were so grossly heretical, that, in the then excited state of public opinion, their evil teaching was avowedly feared by the bishops. These superintending officials, though much divided both in faith and opinion, were mainly desirous of doing what the queen enjoined upon them, and of subserviently following Her Highness's spiritual directions, however such might change or vary; yet at the same time feared altogether to offend their foreign allies and puritanical supporters. Archbishop Parker, therefore, arranged that Cranmer's English version of the Scriptures should be at once revised and reissued—a work which was accomplished about eight years afterwards, and is the foundation of our present English version of the Bible.

Early in the year 1563, Parliament met and considered more important measures concerning religion (or irreligion, as some might phrase it) and the New Church. The wheels of the Establishmentarian machine often creaked and groaned, and continually stuck in the progress of ordinary motion; for the concern being lumbering, unwieldy, ill-planned, and rudely constructed, made extremely little way onwards.

To drop a simile. The confusion which reigned when Puritans, Catholics, and State-religionists were in constant and active conflict was steadily increasing. In many places disorders of a gross character were abounding. The laxest doctrines of common morality were proclaimed by the new preachers, who were at once venal and "godly." Vapid and vain sentiments were highly valued, more especially by the foolish persons who uttered them; while good works, looked upon by some as external tokens of predestined reprobation, seem to have been altogether at a discount.

At the same time, these self-constituted prophets pushed themselves and their wares to the forefront; and in scriptural phraseology, interlarded often with highly scurrilous assertions, condemned all those who would not promote, or abhorred, the new gospel; proclaiming for such temporal ruin here and everlasting misery hereafter. Sometimes, with the solemn deliverance of prophecies, they combined the practices of palmistry, necro-

old religion termed "the Protestant oyster-board," which it no doubt greatly resembled.

mancy,[1] and astrology. Others again, called up, or professed
to call up, familiar spirits whom they consulted; or peered
into a crystal globe either to watch distant events therein
revealed, or to obtain special guidance in seeking for hidden
treasures. When it was known that the queen and some of her
new nobility consulted such professors, it need not cause surprise
that the common people followed their example. By a fanciful
study of the armorial bearings granted to some new peer or
recently-made knight, some of these necromancers of the new
gospel professed to forecast the certain future of those who bore
the arms, and to unfold for such the mysteries and marvels of
coming years. In the royal coat the proximity of the lilies of
France with the lions of England led some of the prophets—
why, is not on record—to predict either sudden death or a
disagreeable future for the queen; reports of which reaching
Her Highness's ears caused her to fume, fret, and even to swear
right royally. Many members of the old and noble families, as
well as the "new men,"—who had pushed themselves forward,
and, because of their greed and rapacity, were not over-popular,
—became the subjects of such-like necromantic inspiration.
Those who were superstitious, and many of them were this,
gravely feared the prophets in question, and trembled when they
heard their predicted doom. In alliance with the prophets came
the perambulating conjurors who, on a slightly different platform,
undertook to prove by ocular demonstration, to the shallow or
to those who thought themselves wise, the impossibility of the
reality or value of the Sacrament of the Altar; and who, clothed
in disused or imitation sacerdotal vestments, and by the aid of tin
cups and thin pellets of bone, on which were engraved representations of the enemy of souls, or some inferior demon, most

---

[1] A certain William Wycherley practised necromancy, from whose formal
depositions the following is taken:—"23rd August. *Item*, he saith that
about ten years past he used a circule called *Circulus Salamonis* at a place
called Pembsam [Qy. Pepplesham], in Sussex, to call up *Baro*, whom he
taketh [to be] an Orientalle or septentrialle spirit. Where was also one
Robert Bayly, the scriere of the cristalle stone; Syr John Anderson, the
magister operator; Syr John Hickley, and Thomas Goslyng, in the which their
practice they had sword, ring, and holly water; where they were frustrated, for
Baro did not appere, nor other vision of spirit, but there was a terrible wind and
tempest for the time of the circulation. *Per me* Wylliam Wycherley. . . .
Maier, a preest, and now lay-master of the Mynt at Durham House, hath
conjured for treasure and their stolen goods. Sir John Lloyd, a preest that
sometime dwelt at Godstone, besides Croydon, hath used it likewise. Thomas
Owldring of Yarmouth is a conjuror, and hath very good books of conjuring,
and that a great number."—Lansdowne MSS., British Museum, vol. ii.
art. 26.

profanely caricatured the mass and its manual actions, with utterances of "*Mumpsimus*" and "*Sumpsimus*," and the still perpetuated phrase of modern conjurors, "*Hocus-pocus.*"[1]

The work of destroying the ancient faith of a nation is, of course, never so difficult as the work of building it up. Hence, when in the interests of Cecil, Bacon, and Walsingham, the ballad-singers, the self-constituted prophets, and the wandering conjurors were openly allied with the Establishmentarian preachers and diocesan superintendents (while the representatives of the old system were thumb-screwed, hung, or banished), the work of corruption and destruction, of course, went on apace.

But the prophets and conjurors were so personally distasteful to the queen and her Council, having caused them so much annoyance, that in 1563 Parliament promptly passed an Act[2] against "fond and fantastical prophecies," in which the punishments were most severe. Persons convicted of excogitating or spreading prophecies founded on the armorial bearings of any nobleman, knight, or gentleman, or upon the days of the month or year on which they had been born or ennobled, were rendered punishable with a year's imprisonment and a fine of ten pounds for the first offence; and to the forfeiture of all their goods and chattels and imprisonment for life for the second. By the same severe enactment, any persons practising "conjurations, enchantments, and witchcraft" were declared felons, and ordered to be punished as such without the benefit of clergy. If, however, the witchcraft was not directed against the life of any one, perpetual imprisonment was the extremest punishment permitted.

But all such measures were impotent to do the work intended. The flood-gates of impiety, superstition, and disorder had been deliberately opened by those who had assumed power; but it was seen to be no easy task to close them again.

As to the bishops of the new sort, they found themselves hampered and hindered on all sides. For not a tenth part of the people, even in the towns and cathedral cities, went with the Reformers,[3] while scarcely a fifth of those in rural villages and

---

[1] Originally a horrible travestie of the divine words of consecration in the Canon of the Mass, "*Hoc est Corpus Meum.*"

[2] 5 Elizabeth, c. 15, 16.

[3] On January 12th, 1562, in a letter to Cecil, Bishop Horne gave a deplorable account of the Protestant cause at Winchester: "Having many ways endeavored and travailed to bring and reduce the inhabitants of the City of Winchester to good uniformity in religion, and namely to have the cures there served, as the Common Prayer might be frequented, which hath not been done sithence the massing-time; and also that good and sound

hamlets were prepared to accept the new religion. But those who had grasped the whip-handle of authority or might declined to slacken their hold upon it; while any dutiful return of the nation to faith and obedience was held to be simply out of the question.

A study of the "Visitation Articles" and "Injunctions" of the bishops show evidently enough the true state of their dioceses. As to the old churches, most of them had been thoroughly cleared out of all their sacred ornaments.[1] Rood-lofts and their crucifixes [2] had been hewn down; pictures, paintings, and banners, looked upon as tokens of "impietic," had followed the vessels of silver and gold. Almost everything, including screens, woodwork, roofs, and walls, had been painfully whitewashed. As to the new ministers, disorder and confusion, irregularities and example of self-will were everywhere apparent, and the bishops could do little or nothing to mend matters.

doctrine might be taught amongst them, which they as yet do not so well like and allow, I could not by any means hitherto bring the same to pass. . . . The said inhabitants are very stubborn, whose reformation would help the greatest part of the shire bent that way, and I would the rather have this brought to pass, for that some of them have boasted and vaunted that do what I can I shall not have my purpose. . . . Sundry there are in the shire, which have borne great countenance in late times, which hinder as much as they can the proceedings in religion."—Original MS. in State Paper Office, A.D. 1562.

[1] For example, in John Parkhurst's *Visitation Articles for the Diocese of Norwich*, A.D. 1561, the following inquiry is made of the various church-wardens:—"Whether all aulters, images, holi-water stones, pictures, paintings, as of Th'assumption of the Blessed Virgin, of the descending of Christ into the Virgin in the fourme of a little boy at Th'annunciation of the Aungell, and al other superstitious and dangerous monuments, especiallie paintings and imagies in walle, boke, cope, banner, or els where, of the Blessed Trinitie, or of the Father (of whom there can be no image made), be defaced and removed out of the churche and other places, and are destroyed, and the places wheie such impietie was, so made up as if there had been no suche thing there." And, again, Grindal inquired "Whether in your churches and chappels all aulters be utterly taken down and cleane removed, even unto the foundation; and the place where they stood paved, and the wall whereunto they joined whited over and made uniform with the rest, so as no breach or rupture appear. And whether your rood-lofts be taken downe, and altered, so that the upper partes thereof with the soller or loft be quite taken down unto the crosse-beame, and that the said beame have some convenient creast put uppon the same."—*Articles to be Enquired of, etc.*, by Edmond Grindall, Archbishop of York, A.D. 1571. London, William Serres.

[2] In the vestry of St. Anthony's Chapel, Cartwell Fell, was found a wooden figure of our Saviour, part of the ancient rood. It is of oak, has been covered with some composition and then gilded. The arms are gone, the feet, which seem to have been crossed, are burnt off. It has the usual cloth about the loins, and the ribs show distinctly. It is said to have been used to poke the vestry fire.—*Transactions of the Cumberland and Westmoreland Antiquarian and Archæological Society*, vol. ii. p. 398.

These poor perplexed officials of the Supreme Governess, not having learnt to obey, were in no case competent to rule. Certain of the principles which they had imbibed abroad were at once heretical and revolutionary; so no wonder that disorder reigned throughout the land, and that self-pleasing was the leading principle which guided men's minds. When once the principle of "Reform" had been duly and practically admitted, every one had his own nostrum for the existing national sickness; while no one exactly approved of that change which his neighbour had endeavoured to effect or had effected. The "reforms" which the mushroom peers had daringly carried out, and by which they themselves had so considerably benefited in things temporal, were, by other people who wished to try their hands at a like game, voted to be totally inadequate to the grave necessities of the times; so that fresh and wider changes were by consequence ruthlessly inaugurated. Faith and stability had vanished, though sentiment and opinion sometimes secured a hearing amid the disputes of controversialists and the profane and ponderous cant of hysterical preachers. But peace and unity, twin sisters of a divine corporation endued with God's Holy Spirit, had been duly and efficiently banished from the realm. In their place the confusion of Babel and an excruciating discord as of combative demoniacs rose on all sides.

Some of these hysterical preachers—"gospellers," as they were now called, or "ministers" (though the fact has too often been ignored)—were mere tinkers; some were tailors, who believed themselves to be "inspired; others farm labourers, such as ditchers, hedgers, or ploughmen, who thought themselves "called"; a few had probably been admitted, in some mode or another, to the office of *Lector* or reader; on which authority, as it appears, they presumed to baptize, to celebrate the Lord's Supper, and to marry couples. Discipline had long been flung to the winds. As such ministers only received a miserable pittance for their "labours in the gospel," and as most of them were married, they took to trading—buying and selling—in order to keep body and soul together, to feed their wives and children, and thus to keep the wolf from the door. The bishops, who were better housed, fed, and paid, did not approve of all this; but by their lordships' Injunctions and Visitation Articles[1] condemned the traders; and though they hated and persecuted "the greased

[1] "Whether your minister ordereth the course of his life answerable to his vocation, or useth buying and selling or trading or tinkering or tailoring, or to hedge, ditch, or go to plough; or hath sollicited other men's visits for gaine, or hath employed himself about other such business not beseeming or

varlets of Antichrist,"[1] as they termed the old priests, they could scarcely sanction the ministrations of vulgar and unordained adventurers from "the lowest of the people."

During the whole of the reign of Queen Elizabeth, it may be here properly pointed out, the loosest notions regarding the importance and value of ordinations almost universally prevailed. The old Catholic doctrine, with the ancient Ordinals, having been abolished, the necessity of imposition of hands with corresponding "form"[2] gave place to a notion that what alone was truly necessary to the making either of an overseer or a minister was a call from the congregation whose servant he was then to become. Hence, in the tractates published and in the discussions which arose, this "call" became the leading feature in the making of ministers. Superadded ceremonies were held to be ornamental and perhaps politic, but not in any way essential. In fact, no Church of England controversialist whatsoever of that reign can be found who maintained plainly and categorically the present doctrine of the Established Church on the subject; nor was it until the year 1597, when Richard Bancroft was "called" to be Bishop of London, that any practical attempt was made to reach any higher theological level than that which most of the Zwinglians, Calvinists, and Establishmentarians regarded as perfectly scriptural, secure, and true. When this prelate was in 1604 elevated to the See of Canterbury, he succeeded in stemming the further progress of such lax teaching; for, pressed as the Establishmentarians had been by so many able defenders of the ancient faith, it was found that no defence of the polity of the New Church could be efficiently made in which the necessity of valid ordination, independent of any "call," or supposed "call," was not plainly and systematically asserted as essential to validity and value.

As regards the character of divine service, it was universally meagre in the extreme. The Reformation advocates were sorely offended at what little of ancient order and decency had been deliberately retained—the surplice, organs, and the observance of holy days; so that several of them, and some of these in high

---

fitting his calling?"—*Articles of Enquiry*, of Cocks, Bishop of Ely, A.D. 1566. "*Item*, whether that any reader being admitted but to reade, taketh upon him to baptize, to marry, to celebrate the Lord's Supper, or to distribute the Lord's cup."—*Injunctions of Parkhurst, Bishop of Norwich*. London: John Day, 1561.

[1] Arnoldus Raissius, quoted by Austin Allfield in his *Answer to Justitia Britannica*, cap. iii. p. 103.

[2] This word is, of course, here used in its technical and theological sense. The "form" and "matter" of ordination own a special meaning.

positions, declined to participate in services at which such practices were adopted. For example, Peter Martyr, Canon of Christ Church, Oxford, declared : "As to myself, when I was at Oxford, I would never wear the surplice in the choir, although I was a canon ; and I had my own reasons for doing so."[1] John Jewell,—who was never more fitly or aptly described than when the late Richard Hurrell Froude[2] termed him "an irreverent Dissenter,"—when writing to this said Protestant Canon of Oxford, remarked that "the scenic apparatus of divine worship is now under agitation ; and those very things which you and I have so often laughed at are now seriously and solemnly entertained by certain persons (for we are not consulted); as if the Christian religion could not exist without something tawdry."[3] It was this person, subsequently made a bishop, who put himself forward, or was put forward by others, to defend by his pen the new National Church which had been set up by Parliament; and a laboured, tortuous, and poor apology and defence he made of it, as the numerous and forcible replies to his treatise sufficiently prove. The language of Richard Cocks, Bishop of Ely, still further shows the true character of certain of these miserable innovators:—"We are only constrained," he writes, "to our great distress of mind, to tolerate in our churches the image of the cross, and Him Who was crucified : the Lord must be entreated that this stumbling-block may at length be removed."[4] In 1563, Edwin Sandys, then Bishop of Worcester, petitioned the Convocation of Canterbury "to supplicate the Head of the Church," by which he meant the queen, "that all curious singing and playing of the organs may be removed;" while two other prelates, Grindal and Robert Horne, in a letter to their foreign ally, Bullinger, who appears to have been greatly exercised in his mind that such eminent English gospellers should appear to tolerate these superstitions, thus plainly declared their private convictions : "We do not assert that the chanting in churches, together with the organ, is to be retained." Nothing of the sort was their real wish. They desired that the prayers, if said at all, should be preached or pronounced to the people ; while, as to popish chanting, they write : "We disapprove of it, as we ought to do."[5] This same person, Edmund Sandys, proposed in Convocation, "That all saints' feasts and holy days

[1] *Zurich Letters*, 2nd series, No. 14.   Parker Society's Publications.
[2] The well-known early Tractarian leader.
[3] *Zurich Letters*, 1st series, No. 9.   Parker Society's Publications.
[4] *Zurich Letters*, 1st series, No. 28.
[5] *Zurich Letters*, 1st series, No. 75.

bearing the name of a creature may, as tending to superstition, . . . be clearly abrogated."[1] On the other hand, certain of these cringing fanatics and heretical preachers having abolished the chief feasts of the Mother of God—though some of them were restored, for very shame's sake, about a hundred years later—had no scruple whatsoever in profanely making Queen Elizabeth's birthday a new feast of the first importance, equal to those of Christmas or Ascension Day ; of singing invocations of Her Majesty, commencing *Ave Eliza !* in St. Paul's Cathedral, instead of the ancient and beautiful *Angelus Domini*, or the antiphons which often followed evensong ; or of placing her portrait and coat-of-arms over the chancel arch of certain churches. The Erastianism and wickedness of such innovations will be now frankly acknowledged by all Christian people.[2]

What they had produced throughout the country may be readily enough gathered from the books and tracts of the day, copies of which can still be studied. Irreligion and indifference, twin giants of evil, stalked unopposed throughout the land. Even some of the highest officials were startled at the sharp and striking results of their own deplorable handiwork, occasionally standing aghast at the existing desolation and demoralisation. They had succeeded in overturning one religion, that which St. Augustine brought from the sacred city of Rome ten centuries before, and hundreds of thousands deplored its overthrow. They had set up another, recently made by the queen and Parliament, which the people, knowing its origin and authorship, looked upon both with aversion and contempt.

To suppose that the main body of the baptized desired any such change as was effected under Elizabeth is a fond and false notion, without historical sanction, and in the teeth of numerous batches of evidence to the direct contrary. The churches, bare and barn-like, were, in fact, almost deserted.[3] The preachers often addressed only their own families and the whitewashed

---

[1] Wilkins' *Concilia*, vol. iv. p. 239.

[2] See Wilkins' *Concilia*, vol. iv. p. 239 ; Edward Rishton's continuation of *Sander's History*, Book iv. chap. vi. ; a paper by Dr. Rimbault on " Music of the Reformation Period ; " Grindal's *Remains*, Parker Society's edition, *in loco ;* and Nichol's *Progresses of Queen Elizabeth*. At Rycot Chapel, Oxford-shire, there was anciently a portrait of this queen placed exactly over the Communion Table ; but when the adjoining mansion, Rycot House, was pulled down, this picture is said to have been taken to Wytham, near Oxford, the present seat of the Earl of Abingdon. "In St. Peter's Church in ye East Oxon, on the North Wall, is painted Queen Eliz. lying at full length in her Royal Robes, wth a Crown on Her Head," etc.—Hearne's *Collections*, August and September 1706.

[3] "Come into a church on the Sabbath day, and ye shall see but few,

walls.   The old religion the poor could understand; but they
pardonably preferred the quiet pleasures of the ale-house to the
dismal doctrines of John Calvin and the noise of his disciples.

Let a writer on behalf of the ancient faith state his position
and judgment of what had been done :—"This manner of
ministration of sacraments set forth in the Book of Common
Prayers was never allowed nor agreed upon by the Universal
Church of Christ in any General Council or Sacred Synod; no,
not by the clergy of England at the last Parliament; but only it
was agreed upon by the laity, which have nothing ado with
spiritual matters or causes of religion, but ought to stand to the
decrees, judgment, and determination of the clergy in causes of
faith and religion."[1]

Again, let the same writer point out what was the impression
in his own day as to the substitution of a table for an altar, and
as to the intentional absence—for, to use a modern phrase and
phantasy, "omission was prohibition"—of any act of consecration
in the new and chopped-up Service of the Supper :—

"The Catholic Church, which we professed at our baptism to
believe [in] and obey, teacheth us to receive Christ's Body consecrate at Holy Mass with prayers, invocations, and benediction
with the sign of the holy cross; and not bare bread and wine
without consecration and benediction as is used in this Communion, being against the decrees and ordinance of Christ's
Catholic Church.   Almighty God does command us to separate
ourselves from such as take in hand a ministration of sacraments
against the ordinance of Christ's Church, and that ye touch
nothing pertaining to them, lest ye be lapped in their sin."[2]

These statements are clear enough.   The writer honestly
urged all his readers not to participate in the heresies[3] and

though there be a sermon; but the ale-house is ever full. . . . A popish
summoner, spy or promoter, will drive more to the church with a word to
hear a Latin mass, than seven preachers will bring in a week's preaching to
hear a godly sermon."—Bishop James Pilkington's preface to his *Commentary on the Prophet Aggeus.—Works*, p. 6.   Parker Society.   London, 1842.

[1] *Certain Questions Propounded, etc.*   London, 1564.

[2] *Certain Questions Propounded, etc.*   London, 1564.

[3] The following is a specimen of the anti-religious poetry of the Elizabethan
era :—

> " O presumptious undertaker,
> Never cake could make a baker,
> Yet a Preist would make his Maker.
> What's become of all ye Christs ye preists have made?
> Do those hosts of Hosts abide, or do they fade?
> One Christ binds, ye rest doe flie;
> One's a truth, the rest's a lie."

MS., in quarto, in the library of the Rev. E. Higgins of Bosbury House,
Herefordshire,—the Commonplace Book of the Lady Elizabeth Cope.

blasphemy of the innovators. Whatever else such charitable warnings serve to show, they certainly prove that some at least were true to the faith of their forefathers.

On the other side, let the varied words of an eminent innovator and Protestant Prince Palatine, Bishop Pilkington of Durham, be studied. He spoke with authority, even the authority of his Supreme Mistress, Queen Elizabeth, whom he obsequiously maintained[1] had rightly all spiritual pre-eminence, even over patriarchs and popes:—"In the restoring of the gospel many weep when they see not the churches so well decked and furnished as before. The Pope's church hath all things pleasant in it to delight the people withal; as for the eyes, their God hangs on a rope [*i.e.* in the pix or *ciborium*], images gilded, painted, carved most finely, copes, chalices, crosses of gold and silver, banners, etc., with relics and altars; for the ears, singing, ringing, and organs piping; for the nose, frankincense sweet; to wash away sins (as they say), holy water of their own hallowing and making; priests an infinite sort; masses, trentals, diriges, and pardons, etc. But where the gospel is preached, they knowing that God is not pleased but only with a pure heart, they are content with an honest place appointed to resort together in, though it were never hallowed by bishop at all; but have only a pulpit, a preacher to the people, a deacon for the poor, a table for the Communion, with bare walls, or else written with Scriptures, having God's eternal word sounding always amongst them in their sight and ears."[2]

Again,[3] as regards the contrast between the Old and the New:—

" For when thou comest to Communion with the Papists, and according to St. Paul would 'eat of that bread and drink of that cup,' they will neither give thee bread nor wine according to Christ's institution (for they say the substance is changed, and there remaineth no bread); but they will give thee an idol of their own making, which they call their God. They come not

---

[1] " As I noted before, so it is not to be lightly considered, that, where so often the prophet here rehearseth the names of Zerubbabel and Joshua, the two chiefest rulers; yet he evermore setteth in order the Civil Magistrate and Power before the Chief Priest, to signify the pre-eminence and preferment that he hath in the commonwealth and other matters, more than the Chief Priest (by what name soever he be called), whether it be the pope, archbishop, or metropolitan."—*Aggeus and Abdias*, by James Pilkington, chap. i. London: W. Serres, 1562.

[2] Bishop Pilkington's *Aggeus and Abdias.* London: W. Serres, 1562.

[3] Bishop Pilkington's *Exposition upon the Prophets, etc.*, pp. 171, 172. Parker Society. London, 1842.

together, according unto Christ's rule, to break the bread; but they creep into a corner, as the Pope teaches them, to sacrifice for the quick and the dead, to sell heaven, to harrow [*i.e.* to plunder] hell, and sweep purgatory of all such as will pay. They come not to communicate with the people, but to eat up all alone."

No words could possibly set forth the actual position of the innovators more exactly and correctly. Yet, it is clear that the people cared not for the recent inventions in religion; on the contrary, being earnestly and heartily attached to the one true faith, they disliked them.

Pilkington, by consequence, goes on to grumble because the desecrated and deserted churches were despised and neglected by the populace, as they deserved to be; and to complain of the people because they did not appreciate the alternate preaching and reading, reading and preaching, so wordy, tedious, and uninteresting, of the restless innovators. Then, as now, many affirmed that they themselves could read quite as profitably, if not more so, at home :—

"Let us be ashamed, then, of those lewd sayings, 'What should I do at the church? I may not have my beads; the church is like a waste barn; there is (*sic*) no images nor saints to worship and make curtsey unto; little God-in-the-box is gone (! !); there is nothing but a little reading and preaching, that I cannot tell what it means. I had as lief keep me at home.'"[1]

About this period, the Bible and the newly-revised Prayer-Book, already altered three times since 1549, were ordered to be translated into Welsh, for use in the Principality of Wales, where the people knew little or nothing of English; though they could follow well enough, and join in, the ancient Latin services of the Western Church. The Rosary they knew, and the Litany of the Saints, and the *Angelus*, which they recited three times a day. But these new translations being strange to them effected little good.

As we all know, the Established Church in Wales has turned out a complete failure. Foes assert it, friends admit it. What religion still remains is of a dissenting type. Englishmen not knowing the language and customs of the Welsh people have been too often appointed to the highest offices in that communion. Both deans and bishops have frequently been merely commonplace aliens. So that prelates, rewarded for political services, or younger sons of impoverished noblemen, have been chiefly distinguished—and it is no mean worldly advantage—for

[1] *Aggeus and Abdias.* London : W. Serres, 1562.

the fruitfulness of their wives, the size of their families, the excellence of their wine, and the large sums of money left to their English survivors by testamentary bequests at their unmourned decease.

The cathedrals, until quite lately, had long lain in partial ruin. The snows of winter and the sunshine of summer alternately fell on the floors of unroofed chantries and desecrated chapels, where a few chipped and cast-down altars and battered monuments, slowly crumbling to decay, told of a worship that had been long ago cast out, and of Catholic families long gone to their rest or become extinct. The cathedral choir—musty in its atmosphere, and gloomy in its aspect, with no scrap of colour throughout it from floor to roof, except maybe the crimson stair-carpet of its lofty pulpit, or the velvet cushion for the dean's elbows—may have been used as a preaching-place once a week ; and perhaps for the Lord's Supper, travestied by some ministerial sloven, once a quarter. Otherwise it stood only as an impressive monument of a cast-out faith ; and as an actual reminder to the more thoughtful of the impotence of reforms and revolutions to benefit a Christian population. In the chief Welsh towns at the present day, the Establishment can scarcely hold its own ; while in the villages too many of the antique barn-like churches, so cold, desolate, and unused, green with damp and rot, and sometimes not even paved, are not unfrequently practically empty. In the disastrous principles of reform and change there was obviously no finality. If one set of men might mend, mar, and muddle—why not the restless, the self-seeking, and the revolutionary of every succeeding generation ?

So great was the confusion existing, so perplexing were the discords of controversialists ; while cross-purposes, the sowing of political discord in foreign nations, and an universal upheaving of opinion, popular with self-seekers and reformers, were so common that the wisest were most anxious for the close and consequences of the Council of Trent.

Here it may be incidentally, but not inappropriately, noticed, with regard to General Councils, that the sublime doctrines of the Christian religion have been duly developed in a certain historical sequence, parallel to the order in which they are set forth in the Creeds. Thus the true doctrine of the adorable Trinity chiefly occupied the two first Œcumenical Councils ; the four next—those of Ephesus, Chalcedon, the Second and Third of Constantinople—were engaged in expressing with unerring exactness the faith concerning the Incarnation ; while the first indirect definition regarding the Holy Eucharist was made by

the seventh Œcumenical Council, the Second of Nicæa. The
subjects of grace and of the sacraments in general, of man's free-
will and justification, were treated and settled, once for all, by
the Council of Trent. Later questions, mainly rationalistic,
relating to the true nature of the Church, the office and work of
the Holy Ghost, His Divine indwelling, and the infallibility and
indefectibility of the kingdom of the world's Redeemer, have
been treated more recently. The rationalism of the present
day, in which the very existence of God has been denied, and
the evils which flow from such rationalism—Erastianism, godless
education, and nationalism in religion—are the great subjects
which quite recently have been authoritatively condemned.

On the 3rd and 4th of December 1563, the last session of the
sacred Council of Trent was held. It had been in abeyance for
the greater part of the time since its first assembling on the
13th of December 1545. Pope Paul III. and Pope Julius III.
had in due course guided its decisions and decrees, but during
its sessions had passed to their reward. Its work, from beginning
to end, was one of true, honest, and legitimate reform. The
lawful rulers of the Western Church—duly and painfully considering all heresies, schisms, defects, innovations, and errors,
and more especially those modern "reforms" which had become
so disastrously current amongst the Northern races—carefully
amended whatever needed amendment, and this in no ambiguous
terms. Its Catechism, Canons, Decrees, and Confession of
Faith remain consequently as monuments of the consummate
wisdom of its members, and as certain tokens of the guiding
presence of the Divine Paraclete, with the Chief Bishop of
Christendom, the cardinals and prelates.

The close of the Council was impressive indeed. First, all
things that had been duly done for the progress of Holy Church
and the benefit of the faithful were solemnly confirmed by those
present in the presence of the Blessed and Adorable Sacrament.
To the then Pontiff, Pius IV., the members of the Council
wished many years and eternal memory. Peace from the Lord
God, everlasting glory and eternal happiness in the sight of the
Saints, were asked for on behalf of the two departed Popes who
had reigned during the Council's previous sessions. For the
Emperors Charles V. and Ferdinand, and for all Christian kings,
"preservers of the right faith," the members of the Council prayed
God to bestow many years of life. Prayers went up to the
Almighty, likewise, for the legates, the cardinals, and the
bishops. The faith of the Church, as newly explained, was
confessed by all, and promises openly made to keep the Council's

Decrees. "We all thus believe," they affirmed. "We all think the very same thing; we all, consenting and embracing both Creed and Decrees, voluntarily subscribe thereto. This," they went on to declare, "is the faith of blessed Peter and of the Apostles; this is the faith of our fathers, this we believe, this we hold, to this we adhibit our names."

Then the Cardinal of Lorraine, arising uncovered, declared as follows :—"Adhering to these Decrees, may we be rendered worthy of the grace and mercy of the first and Great High Priest, Jesus Christ, Our Lord and God; Our Immaculate Lady, the Holy Mother of God, and all the Saints interceding for us."

"Amen; so be it!" was the unanimous and universal response.

"To all heretics," continued His Eminence, "be anathema."

"Amen!" was the like hearty and unanimous answer.

Then, after having sung *Te Deum*, the members dispersed. Such was the Council's impressive and solemn close.

In England what had been effected was at once seen to be of the gravest and greatest importance. Independent of the discussions concerning doctrines, the very practical point of occasional conformity with the new religion and worship, which certain Englishmen had followed, was fearlessly dealt with; while those who had occasionally frequented the churches were distinctly forbidden to do so any longer.

Immediately this decision was formally proclaimed, a change came over those who clung to the ancient faith. Reports of the terms in which the decision had been given reached England in due course, some months before the formal decree. An authority hitherto recognised by all the Christian nations of the West, the Chief Bishop of the Church of God, now spoke. His words were reverently listened to; the old law of Christianity, newly applied, was at once dutifully heard and duly obeyed.

Much suffering followed upon obedience; but it sanctified the sufferers, and abundantly blessed them all, during the anxious and trying time of their earthly probation.

CHAPTER III.

THIS decision of the Council of Trent, as will soon be discovered, exercised great and direct influence on the course of events in England. But these must not be forestalled. The exact point and purport of that decision were not publicly made known by the issue of any formal document; but the duty of those who retained the old faith soon became perfectly well understood.

Hence, more completely and generally than ever, the churches in England, and especially the more remote and village churches, became deserted.[1] This fact is on record again and again in the writings of the Fathers of the so-called "Reformation." The new prelates deplored the emptiness of the sacred edifices in writing to each other. Some of them, furthermore, grumblingly complained to Sir William Cecil; but if the existing fines for absence and for non-participation in the new "rites of the Supper" would not aid in filling the desecrated sanctuaries, that statesman, as he responded, was unable as yet to suggest any more efficient practical remedy. The bishops should more painfully and piously give themselves to preaching and prayer. They should be "less with your women and children, and more with your flocks,"[2] as an anonymous writer forcibly remarked.

The division, therefore, between the ancient Catholics and the upholders of the new religion became still further marked and manifest; while the State authorities thus confessed themselves impotent either to bridge over the newly-made chasm, or to prevent further rents and fissures being deliberately made by those standing on its brink.

Ere we pass on to the deeds of later years, it is necessary to deal here with a few particular events and positions of some importance.

---

[1] In some of the towns, pre-arranged theological controversies and squabbles over the meaning of Scripture enlivened the ordinary dulness, when bull or badger baiting was out of season.

[2] "*A Modest Cure, together with a Cry from the Wilderness, etc.*, pp. 35, 36. London, 1566.

The state of ecclesiastical affairs, about the year 1564, more especially the frightful confusion everywhere practically existing, and in some places rampant, is sufficiently proved from a record still remaining in Sir William Cecil's own handwriting.[1]   It was evidently made after due and careful inquiry on the part of that influential State official.   As regards the performance of 'divine service and the administration of those sacraments which were retained,—Cecil's own expressive sentences are scarcely altered in what is about to be reproduced, and, where altered, only paraphrased in what follows :—

Some of the ministers say the service and prayers in the chancel, others in the body of the church.   Some say the same in a seat made in the church, others in the pulpit, with their faces to the people.   Some keep precisely the order of the new Prayer-Book, others introduce metrical psalms ; some use a surplice at prayers, while others minister in their secular and ordinary attire—hat, doublet, and hose.   As regards the position of the Communion Table, in certain places it stands in the body of the church, in others in the choir.   Within the latter it is sometimes placed altar-wise about a yard from the east wall ; in other cases it stands in the midst of the chancel, north and south. In a few places it consists of a table duly constructed in joiner's work, in others it is a mere rough board placed upon common trestles.   By some of the new ministers it is covered with a carpet or an old vestment ; by others the bare oak table is intentionally left perfectly exposed and uncovered.   In the actual administration of the Communion, ordered to take place once a month, some of the cathedral clergy and the Queen's chaplains ministered the ordinance in a surplice with a cope over it ; others were clad in a surplice only ; others, again, with no official dress of any sort or kind.   Uniformity was thus out of the question, as those discovered, who, with unbridled self-pleasing and licence, having altered the ancient services to suit their own tastes and opinions, found it exceedingly hard to induce others to adopt exactly the same standard of ecclesiastical taste, though prescribed by injunction or proclamation.   So it was, likewise, as regards details.   Some used an ancient chalice and paten at the table, others a Communion cup of the new sort, others a common cup.   The bread, either leavened or un-leavened, was received by some kneeling, by others standing, by some walking round the table,[2] by others sitting, by many with

---

[1] See vol. iii., No. 7, of the Lansdowne MSS. in the British Museum.
[2] " They used to begin with three or four sermons, preached one after the other.   They then went to Communion, not receiving it either on their knees

their heads covered.   All thus pleased themselves, while discord reigned.   Again: at baptism some ministers administered the sacrament at the font, others in a basin; some with a surplice, others without; some drew the sign of the cross on the child's brow, others, with an honest shudder at the very notion, deliberately omitted it as the acknowledged "mark of the Apocalyptic Beast."

This new religion, so eminently selfish, which Cecil and Elizabeth had set up, had given point to the well-known foreign Protestant maxim "every one for himself, and God for us all.". The poor, therefore (now so haggard and famishing), whom the Divine Author of Christianity had declared that His followers should always have with them, were voted an eyesore and a nuisance.   When, consequently, the queen, in her royal progresses, passed through different districts of this once-favoured land, she could not fail to observe the miserable condition of the lean and famishing peasantry, who came out from their hovels to stare sullenly at her as she was borne along on her velvet-dressed litter.   Ill-fed, half-clothed, lantern-jawed, and wolf-like, with scarcely any rights left, with no protectors against tyranny from above or grinding cruelty from below (for the new nobles and the local constables equally oppressed them), those few who were old enough to remember a former state of things may have been pardoned if they felt disposed to curse the day upon which they had been born.

During the whole of her reign, in truth, the state of the lower classes was appallingly sad, and their destitution deplorable.   The monasteries having been already destroyed, or put to secular purposes, and their ample revenues given away to worthless adventurers as bribes; and these revenues too often lost, squandered, and dissipated by those who had by law sacrilegiously taken possession of such sacred possessions and their corresponding treasures,—the country poor suffered severely. Often no moral consideration could induce the new owners of the monastic estates to aid in relieving or maintaining the indigent and aged people, who bore in patience their poverty and woes. No doubt such estates were grievously impoverished, and produced but little; for, as a rule (the times being times of change), they were neither cultivated so well, nor looked after so carefully, as when the monks owned only a life interest in them.   Too often the new secular proprietors—men of low birth and breeding— were tyrants, oppressive usurers, cold-hearted, and godless.

or standing, but moving by, so that it might be called a Passover in very truth."—*Life of William Weston*, p. 241.   London, 1875.

Our Divine Redeemer, as all Christians know, has left here upon earth the poor, the unfortunate, and the miserable—a beautiful necessity—to become objects of the love and care of those who have received temporal blessings and the riches of this world.   Like a refreshing shower during sunshine, He has caused to descend upon them a double portion of His divine charity— the graces of Calvary and the glories of Tabor.   Withdrawing Himself awhile during man's time of probation, He has thus bequeathed the poverty-stricken to us.   They are at once His liveliest image and His best-loved inheritance.   But under Queen Elizabeth they were neglected, despised, and passed by.   For faith was cold and charity was not.

On the occasion of the queen's visit to Cambridge, she went in State, on a Sunday morning in August 1564, to King's College Chapel, to hear a Latin sermon by Dr. Perne, prefaced by the new Bidding-Prayer.   Prior to this, the Litany in English was sung, during which she entered with a combination of regal and pontifical splendour.   Four Doctors of Divinity carried a canopy of cloth of gold over the Supreme Governess—the same canopy which, in the fourth year of her sister's reign, had been borne over the Blessed Sacrament by four knights in the same chapel ; and she was attended by her ladies-in-waiting and high officers of State,—some of whom carried those external symbols of Her Highness's spiritual and ecclesiastical authority which she had assumed, and desired never should be wanting on such occasions. The queen approved of the sermon ; and "liked the singing of the choir so well," that she attended evensong in the afternoon, on which occasion some lyrical verses in her honour, parodying one of the ancient antiphons of Our Lady with which the Sunday Vespers had been formerly concluded, were sung.

It had been arranged that one of the plays of Plautus—the "Aularia"—should be represented in the hall of King's College on Sunday evening ; but as the space of that refectory was limited, and there was not sufficient room to erect a suitable state-throne and canopy for the queen, Her Majesty gave orders that a stage should be put up and that the play should be acted in the chapel, which was done, and the performance was not concluded until midnight.   The queen was so pleased with the acting, but more particularly with the good looks, of a handsome youth who had very cleverly personified Dido, that on that sultry autumn midnight she at once sent for him to her apartments at King's College, "to speak to him and to commend him to his face ;" and, when she left the university, graciously bestowed an annual benefaction of twenty pounds per annum for life upon

this favoured and lucky performer.[1]   It will thus be seen that
the revived taste for pagan literature had at this time become
so rampant, as that a chapel dedicated to the solemn worship
of God the Trinity was, by royal command, thus deliberately
profaned.

By the queen's numerous love affairs—for she was always in
love, ever making plans for matrimony—she contrived to render
herself the scandal of England and the laughing-stock of the
European Courts.   Details of her personal behaviour when her
favourites were concerned, often so unwomanly and disgusting,.
of her coarse words and questionable sayings, were, in open
letters or by occult cypher, transmitted by the clever ambassadors
from abroad to their various royal and imperial masters; who
were thus kept well and truly informed of what was actually
going on, and who, on reading them, grinned over such records
of her amorous antics.

The first of her lovers was a knight of a respectable family,
Sir William Pickering, of whom John Jewell informed Bullinger
that he was "both a prudent and pious man."   Sir William had
been sent on a mission to one of the petty princes of Germany,
and on his return the queen, suddenly smitten, heaped such
favours on him, and paid him such unusual attention, both at
proper and improper times, that the courtiers quite believed that
a marriage would (or at all events, after what had happened,
that it *should*) take place.   Pickering was undoubtedly handsome, with a fine brow, regular features, and small hands and
feet; his address, moreover, was courtly, his tastes were refined.
Whether, on discovering the amatory peculiarities of the Supreme
Governess, and her expectations, he became both alarmed and
disgusted, or not, may never be accurately known.   Anyhow,.
the affair all at once collapsed—no one knew why or wherefore.
—and this as suddenly as it had been initiated.

Her next lover was Henry, Earl of Arundel, K.G., born in
1512, at heart a staunch supporter of the ancient faith, a brave
soldier,[2] and one who on several occasions had done good
service to the State.   In Edward VI.'s reign he had been unjustly

---

[1] The authorities at Cambridge seem to have been exceedingly annoyed, if
not greatly disgusted, at her parsimony and favouritism.   On leaving, she
simply thanked them for their hospitality, and gave some of the Heads of
Houses her right hand to kiss.   A "Copie of verses" then penned and printed;
—commenting on her gift to the youthful actor, and hinting that the said
gift was a reward for questionable favours,—too coarse to transcribe, is preserved there.

[2] He had distinguished himself greatly by his bravery at the siege of
Boulogne.

and heavily fined upon frivolous pretences; but his noblest achievement was to have peaceably secured the throne to the late pious and religious Queen Mary. He it was who proclaimed her in the city and then rode down to Suffolk to receive her commands and serve her faithfully. But this unhappy nobleman, in order to please the new queen, had voted in the House of Lords, against the convictions of his conscience, in favour of the so-called "Reformation" and the new laws, and kept up an appearance of maintaining it. A member of the old nobility, for he was the eighteenth earl of his house and name, he was munificent and even regal in his choice offerings and rich gifts to his sovereign, often entertaining her with masques, banquets, and balls. In fact, his vast fortune had proved wholly inadequate to pay for the expenses thus incurred, and he greatly impoverished his estates by so doing. At length, irritated by the queen's behaviour, he haughtily returned his staff of office as Lord Steward, with some over-plain and too homely words of warning and expostulation. Later on, however, he opposed the Court party (disliking the queen's projected marriage with the Duke of Anjou), and, being by them feared, was soon persecuted. When he could no longer minister to the queen's amusement, evinced independence, and was growing old and gouty,[1] she speedily turned her attention to younger and livelier favourites; and not only treated the earl with contempt, but with great harshness. He died in 1580.[2]

The person who made the deepest impression on her heart was a worthless fellow of neither family nor blood, Lord Robert Dudley. He, with his father the Duke of Northumberland, the low-born son of the rapacious usurer of Henry VIII.'s reign, had been attainted for the attempt to remove both Mary and Elizabeth from the succession to the Crown. But he had recently been restored in blood, received several official appointments and grants, and met with great favour from the queen herself.[3] He

---

[1] In 1565 he went to try the effects of the baths at Padua for relief from the gout in his feet, but with no great success. "He had been made her tool in politics and her sport in secret," writes Miss Strickland.

[2] "In him," wrote Camden, "was extinct the surname of this most noble family, which had flourished with great honour for three hundred years and more; from the time of Richard Fitz-alan, who, being descended from the Albinis, ancient Earls of Arundel and Sussex, in the reign of Edward I. received the title of earl without any creation, in regard of his being possessed of the castle and honour of Arundel."

[3] In the fifth year of her reign she granted Robert Dudley the castle and manor of Kenilworth and Astel Grove, the lordships and manors of Denbigh and Chirk, with other lands and possessions, together with a special licence for transporting cloth, which he disposed of to John Mark and others,

was appointed Master of the Horse, with a fee of one hundred marks a year, and, to the astonishment both of the peers and the public, made a Knight of the Garter, and soon afterwards Constable of Windsor Castle.   On September 29th, 1563, he was created Baron of Denbigh and Earl of Leicester.   This took place with great state at Westminster, as Sir James Melville, who was present, has left on record.   The queen, in her chair of state, personally invested Robert Dudley with the new robes of his dignities as he knelt before her.   During the trying process, many eyes being upon him, he bore himself with due gravity and discretion ; for several peers, officers of State, and foreign ambassadors were present. Before the new peer arose, however, the amorous queen had the execrable taste to tickle him in the neck underneath his linen shirt, at which he crimsoned deeply ; and afterwards, with smirks and smiles of satisfaction, to ask Melville, the Scotch ambassador, what he thought of the earl's person and bearing.[1]

Elizabeth had evidently pressed a marriage between Mary, Queen of Scots, and Lord Leicester, in order that when the former refused him, as was sure to be the case, the way might be more easily opened for the completion of her own matrimonial arrangements with the new nobleman.   Should Mary accept him, which was highly improbable, it would not be difficult for Elizabeth to bring the proposal to nought, and then secure the man for herself.

There was at one time a coolness between the queen and Leicester, which the latter cleverly turned to his own account, and made use of in the following manner.   Holding that a temporary absence might serve his purpose, and whet Her Highness's appetite for his return and company, he resolved to ask to be sent to France on some diplomatic mission, and induced De Foys, the French ambassador, to make this request in person of the queen.   On hearing it she flew into a passion, swore her usual impressive oath, and at once ordered Leicester into her presence to offer some explanation of his unexpected desire.

The earl came in due course, when she immediately asked him if it were possible that he truly wished to go to France.   " I

---

merchant adventurers.—See *The Sidney Papers, in loco*, and the grant of the peerage for life to Alice Dudley (wife of Sir Robert Dudley, son of the Earl of Leicester), as Duchess of Dudley, by King Charles I.

[1] A very fine miniature of this nobleman, from the pencil of Isaac Oliver (1556–1617), is in the possession of the Duke of Buccleuch, K.G.   It is inscribed with the name of Leicester and with the date of his death, 1588.

will have it," she said, "from thine own lips, if so it be." He replied, with unusual calmness, "With your Highness's permission and favour, it is one of the several things I most desire."

The queen was so nettled by this quiet response that she told him, with bitterness, that it would be no great honour to send a groom (this was a sarcastic allusion to his office of Master of the Horse) to so great and puissant a prince as the French king.

He is said to have been made intensely indignant by this studied insult, and to have changed colour greatly. But he kept his temper, and wisely restrained his speech.

When he had retired from her presence, which he did at once, she laughingly observed to the ambassador—"I cannot live, believe me, I cannot live without a sight of that man daily. He is like my lap-dog. When that is seen running forward, they who see it say that I, his mistress, am nigh. And so it is. Where my Lord of Leicester is, there too am I: there, good De Foys, must I be likewise."

Soon afterwards fresh warmth, not to write heat, took the place of the temporary coolness which had existed between the queen and her favourite; while, as a consequence of their becoming inseparable companions, once more the case, fresh scandalous reports were current at home, while abroad it was openly asserted that they lived in adulterous intercourse.[1]

On one occasion Elizabeth had condescended to discuss these reports with Quadra, the Spanish ambassador. In so doing, the poor lady surely forgot both her dignity as a queen and her delicacy as a woman, in personally and argumentatively pointing out the *à priori* improbability of what was asserted by her enemies, by a joint inspection of her own and her favourite's sleeping-chambers, and their due geographical relation to each other. This unpleasant incident, which, it is to be feared, altogether failed of its purpose, was discussed by some of the other ambassadors, and, as usual, also talked about abroad.

Subsequently the queen, finding that her favourite's health was likely to suffer from the alleged dampness of the room in which he had hitherto slept, had the daring indelicacy to assign him a chamber in close proximity to the royal sleeping apartment.[2] The boldness of this act quite astonished some of the

---

[1] A gentleman in Norfolk was put upon his trial for having asserted that "my Lord of Leicester had two children by the queen," and for this plain-speaking was compelled to lose both his ears or else to pay a fine of £100. —See *Lodge* vol. ii. p. 47.

[2] Testimony of Quadra, Bishop of Aquila, in original despatches at Simancas.

more refined amongst the courtiers; while certain of the old
nobility, though silent, shook their heads gravely at the mention
of it.   But no one publicly criticised or protested.   Fortune in
this, as in other cases, favoured the brave.   Elizabeth, in these
amorous contrivances, was truly as brave as she was bold,
and, it may be added, as daring as she was indelicate and un-
blushing.

But more of this hereafter.   Almost to the day of her death
she was always seeking for the admiration of the other sex.   As
she grew in years, so she grew in vanity, selfishness, and cruelty
—cruelty such as in a woman the world has seldom been called
upon to contemplate and turn from in aversion.

Her treatment of the venerable Archbishop of York, Dr.
Nicholas Heath, for example, was simply inhuman and scandalous.   She had been deeply indebted to him, seven years
previously, at a sore crisis in her life, the death of her half-sister
Queen Mary, but seems to have speedily enough forgotten her
obligation.   He it was who, when her title to the throne was so
doubtful, served by boldness and prompt action to establish her
questionable position; for, like an apt statesman and loyal
subject, he secured the sanction of both Houses of Parliament
to the proclamation by which her reign was peacefully and duly
inaugurated.   Yet because, being "a Churchman of the true
ancient sort," he was conscientiously unable to accept the ridiculous figment of her so-called "supremacy," and, as in duty
bound, resisted, both in the Houses of Lords and Convocation,
the imposition of such a fraudulent novelty upon Englishmen,
by every lawful means at hand, she had the archbishop privately
conveyed to the Tower, without charge or trial, and there for
five weary years confined in a dark and unwholesome dungeon,
to his great sorrow and pain.

When in ordinary conversation the Venetian Ambassador so
properly put before the queen the strong judgment entertained
abroad of such unjustifiable acts of persecution and iniquity,—
for, as he remarked in regard to the imprisoned archbishop,
"no man in a civilised State should be condemned to punishment without a hearing,"—she enjoined that Archbishop Heath
was to be "less straitened."   At that time, Thomas Young, an
intruder, neither canonically elected nor duly confirmed, had
usurped the place and revenues of the ancient archiepiscopal See,
legally belonging to Heath, and was doing his best to serve the
cause of Cecil and the innovators in a loyal and beautiful county
—the people of which were almost unanimously in favour of the
ancient faith.   Heath was, therefore, permitted to retire to the

Manor House in York,[1] formerly the residence of the Abbot of St. Mary's and subsequently one of the official houses of the See in question; and, though kept under a close watch, was allowed to walk abroad within a certain distance of his place of confinement. But even this moderate liberty was looked upon by some with dislike and jealousy. The suspicions regarding this venerable prelate were, however, suspicions and nothing more; possibly the consequence of malice, or probably of mere gossip. In the meantime Lord Scrope[2] applied to the Council for advice and directions in the case of the archbishop's suspected peregrinations. The question was discussed, in the queen's presence, on the 22nd of June 1565, with the assistance of the Lord Keeper Bacon, the Marquis of Northampton, the Earl of Leicester, Mr. Secretary Cecil, Mr. Cave, Mr. Petre, and Mr. Sackville; when it was determined that Lord Scrope should deal sharply and promptly with the old man of eighty, "to the end that he should declare the full truth why he wandereth abroad, and if he will not be plain in his declaration,"—the queen, just turned thirty years of age, goes on to have "fully determined" and recorded on the Council Register that he must be tortured, pinched, or thumbscrewed,—"to use some kind of torture to him, so as to be without any great bodily hurt, and to advertise his (Lord Scrope's) doings herein,"[3] are the exact words of the Privy Council Order.

About this time, i.e. 1566, another controversy arose, not from maintainers of the old order of affairs, but from certain of the more advanced innovators. And it arose as follows :—

For the new bishops a lawn rochet and black chimere, with silk scarf, and neckband of sable or other furs, was customarily adopted or enjoined to be worn. In existing pictures of them they are thus represented.[4] This was the ancient domestic dress

[1] Canon Raine of York thus most courteously writes to me :— "If the place is described as 'the Manor House in York,' it is the large building formerly the residence of the Abbot of St. Mary's and now the Yorkshire School for the Blind. It was generally called 'the Manor House' or 'the King's Manor,' as the Stuart kings resided there."

[2] This was Henry, ninth Lord Scrope of Bolton, K.G., summoned to Parliament from 21st October 1555 to 4th of February 1589. In the fifth year of Queen Elizabeth he was appointed Governor of the Castle of Carlisle and Warden of the West Marches. He married, first, Eleanor, daughter of Edward, Lord North, by whom he had an only daughter; and, secondly, the Lady Margaret Howard, sister of the Duke of Norfolk, by whom he had an only son Thomas, who became tenth Lord Scrope.

[3] See, for the documents and authorities relating to this act of iniquitous cruelty, *Memorials of the Howards*, edited by Mr. Howard of Corby Castle.

[4] See a contemporary portrait of Matthew Parker in the dining-hall of Lambeth Palace.

F

of a Western Catholic prelate—not a dress for public ministrations, but for hall or study—which he always used in private. But as it seemed to mark off the chief superintendents from ordinary ministers, it gave great offence to the latter and their followers, more especially when these were violent Calvinists or rampant Zwinglians.   Equality in the House of God was what was wanted by the innovators, with a complete banishment of all external signs, symbols, or "vestures of superstition," as they were termed.

Anything more than the ordinary dress of the preachers was consequently held in horror.   The same was the case with the use of the surplice and silken hood enjoined upon the inferior clergy. From the outset the foreign Protestants had rudely characterised the surplice as "the whore of Babylon's chemise," "the Romish ragge," " Antichrist's shyrte," and by other equally choice terms. As early as 1550, however, John Hooper, an apostate Cistercian monk, who had been duly infected with the heresies of Geneva, had firmly refused to wear any such vestments, and had carried on a furious and angry controversy with Dr. Nicholas Ridley against them ; while Miles Coverdale, a rough Yorkshireman, who had once been an Augustinian friar, but repudiated the faith and had become first a Lutheran and subsequently a Calvinistic heretic, was heartily at-one with Hooper in his practice ; and was even obstinately vigorous and foul-mouthed in his anti-vestment frenzy.   The extravagant violence of this old man's language, glanced at now, only raises a smile or a sincere feeling of pity.

This controversy, which obviously covered theological differences of a true and deep nature, grew rapidly in fierceness and fury.[1]   The anti-vestment agitators pleaded for a " pure and plain " service, which, judging from contemporary statements on the subject, it might not unreasonably be presumed, from their own standing-point, they had already secured—for the churches had been largely emptied of their ornaments, wrecked of all that was valuable, and whitewashed.   Still the innovators declined to

---

[1] To add a few details as to facts :—The Puritans objected to the pre-eminence and authority of the bishops, and the jurisdiction of the episcopal courts.   They disliked the repetition of the Lord's Prayer, as savouring of vain repetitions on popish beads ; they would not use the versicles and responses, which were, they maintained, too much like the "ancient idolatrie." The reading of the Apocrypha, the sign of the cross in baptism, the ring in marriage, and the terms of the marriage-contract were equally distasteful. Chanting the psalms, the use of organs or musical instruments, and more especially the enjoined dresses of the clergy, were all signs or marks of the Beast.

attend any worship where surplice, rochet, or hood appeared on the backs of the ministers; and expressed this their settled determination in scurrilous pamphlets and the most violent speeches, as well as in action. Many of these tractates were printed at private presses, some had been prepared abroad, others were issued without any publisher's name, so that no one could be held responsible for what they contained. All of them were wildly anti-episcopal, and full of abuse of the new Protestant bishops, who were characterised as "turncoats," "anti-gospellers," and "traitors." The Master and Wardens of the Stationers' Company consequently were formally enjoined to search for and seize all such works. Their authors were to be dealt with by the arbitrary Court of High Commission, which, managing by a side-wind to make laws as they seemed to be required, came down upon all Puritan offenders with sledge-hammer force. The recent "reforms" were asserted to be at once "godly" and "sufficient"; anything further was ruthlessly condemned. Furthermore, any book-dealer selling a copy of the offensive pamphlets in question was to be fined twenty shillings for each offence. The printer was to be imprisoned, while both printer and bookseller was each henceforward forbidden to follow his respective calling on any plea, at any time, in any case, or under any circumstances.

These tyrannical and contemptible enactments—which came fresh from the soiled hands of the daring rebels who, without any authority, had pretended to "reform" the Church of God, and which enactments, it may be remarked, were quite worthy of their authors—utterly failed of their purpose. The Puritans continued to read, write, and publish most violent and obnoxious tractates; and, as a party, soon became distasteful, and a source of grave danger, to the Government.

These energetic persons who on principle, however false, objected to the "prelatial" and "popish" character of the new religion, soon secured for themselves the title of "Noncon-formists." According to their consciences (or what may have done duty for the same) they could not and would not adhere to the system recently set up. They deliberately dissented from it; they could not conform to it, even though enjoined thereto by so high an authority as the Queen's Highness herself. Of course, it was quite reasonable that any of the preaching-ministers who adopted this policy should retire from work in the new state organisation or religious institution—leave the pulpit and close the Book of Homilies. But this was not enough. Her Majesty's advisers went much further in their dealings with these unhappy

people.[1]   All Englishmen, as the teaching then stood, must
acknowledge the Queen's Supreme Headship, and worship exactly
as she worshipped, bow when she bowed, pray as she prayed,
sing as she sang, and in no other way.   The ponderous preach-
ments and dreary services of Geneva, which some miserable
fanatics, stricken with self-delusion, looked upon as the highest
types of evangelical purity, were consequently as much forbidden
as the Hereford or Salisbury rite for Holy Mass.   The so-called
"prophesyings" of the Puritans were quite as odious to the
queen as the Catholic Sacraments of Confirmation and Extreme
Unction, the Rosary or the Angelus.   Such a practical policy
scarcely befitted those who so loudly condemned the proceedings
of the previous reign.   And this point was more than once ably
but unavailingly pressed upon the queen by some of the official
representatives of foreign Courts.   Yet, let the truth be told, it
was only by persecution, fines, imprisonment, and the gallows
that the new system of nationalism in religion could be maintained at all.

About this time an ecclesiastical case of great importance—of
such importance indeed as that special legislation immediately
took place because of it—was heard in the secular courts.
Robert Horne, Bishop of Winchester, a Puritan gentleman of
some zeal, indicted Dr. Bonner, the *de jure* but not *de facto*
Bishop of London (for Edmund Grindal by royal authority had
usurped that important position), for refusing to take the recent
Oath of Supremacy.   Bonner had been for years a close prisoner
in the Marshalsea, and this place of confinement was in the
diocese of Winchester.   The plea which Bonner put in was a
plain and bold one, viz. that Horne, falsely calling himself
"Bishop of Winchester," had never been duly, regularly, and
legally consecrated according to the laws of the Church of
England; and consequently that he could not be, and was not,
bishop of the diocese in which Bonner was confined, and therefore had no legal authority whatsoever to tender him the oath
in question.   It was a bold move on the part of the closely-
imprisoned and ill-treated prelate; but, being founded on fact
and law, turned out to be a due, proper, and valid plea.   The
judges who heard the case were much annoyed and sorely

---

[1] In June of the year 1567 a congregation of more than a hundred Puritans
was surprised and seized at Plumbers' Hall, in the city of London, of which
fifteen were marched off to prison without either charge, trial, or condemnation.   After they had thus been treated they were examined by Grindal,
the Bishop of London, who rated them fiercely, but failed to secure their
conformity.

puzzled by the position into which Bonner, a learned canonist, had thus so adroitly placed Horne. They resolved, therefore, to give no decision whatsoever; for otherwise it must have been clearly and unquestionably against Horne, and in favour of Bonner. So the proceedings were most irregularly and unjustly stayed and quashed. Bonner was sent back to the unhealthy cells of the Marshalsea. Horne did not venture to tender him the oath again; while the result of this lawsuit sorely vexed and dismayed the new prelates, and annoyed the Queen's Council greatly.

Throughout the whole country the issue of this suit gradually became known, and it was largely discussed. It had effectually served to test the question whether the new bishops and ministers were "true and lawful" or not. The old clergy, who compared the novel form of ordination with the old, looked upon the New Church officers with both suspicion and aversion, the more vigorous amongst them with contempt. They were unnoticed by the rich and learned,[1] and despised by the poor and unlettered; so much so indeed that the Supreme Governess had to invoke the aid of Parliament to fill up what was so obviously wanting, and to strengthen that which was so notoriously weak.

An Act of Parliament was therefore passed declaring that the method of making and consecrating the archbishops and bishops of this realm, notwithstanding all objections, was "good, lawful, and perfect." The tedious terminology and numerous redundancies of expression in the Act are remarkable; but inasmuch as, under the circumstances, such was obviously the only method available for settling, once for all, the various disputes[2] which had arisen on the subject, it is necessary to put a part of it, at all events, on record.

Its preamble asserted that "divers questions by overmuch boldness of speech and talk of the common sort of people, being unlearned, having lately grown," concerning the new kind of ordinations, whether the same be done according to law or not, "which is much tending to the slander of all the state of the clergy"; therefore, for avoiding such slanderous speech and for enabling Parliament to settle the question, this Act is passed.

---

[1] Grindal, when Archbishop of York, writing from Cawood to Cecil, on August 29, 1570, tells him plaintively that he has not been well received; the greater part of the gentlemen of the county being not well affected towards godly religion, and among the common people many superstitious practices remain.—*Domestic State Papers, Elizabeth,* vol. lxxiii. p. 390.

[2] The writers who during Elizabeth's reign dealt with this subject, and who had occasioned such "various disputes," were Harpesfield, Hoskins, Sander, Harding, Stapleton, Allen, Reynolds, and others—all of whom, it should be remembered, were English Churchmen vigorously resisting the innovators.

No reference is made to any rites older than those of King Henry's reign, and whatever has been or is wanting is duly supplied "by the authority of Parliament"—of course, a high authority in things temporal, but nothing more. Parliament, of course, can compass many deeds and effect much, but it is utterly powerless to make either a priest or a bishop, and no declaration, resolution, or statute can render valid and certain any ordination or consecration already invalid or doubtful.

The most important part of the new enactment is now verbally quoted :—

"And further, for the avoiding of all ambiguities and questions that might be objected against the lawful confirmations, investings, and consecrations of the said archbishops and bishops, Her Highness, in her Letters Patent, under the Great Seal of England, directed to any archbishop, bishop, or others, for confirming, investing, and consecrating of any person elected to the office or dignity of any archbishop or bishop, hath not only used such words and sentences as were accustomed to be used by the said late King Henry, and King Edward, Her Majesty's father, and brother, in their like Letters Patents, made for such causes, but also hath used, and put in Her Majesty's said Letters Patents divers other general words and sentences, whereby Her Highness, by her supreme power and authority, hath dispensed with all causes or doubts of any imperfections, or disability, that can or may in anywise be objected against the same, as by Her Majesty's said Letters Patents remaining of record more plainly will appear ; so that to all those that will well consider of the effect and true intent of the said laws and statutes, and of the supreme and absolute authority of the Queen's Highness, and which she, by Her Majesty's said Letters Patents, hath used, and put in use, in and about the making and consecrating of the said archbishops and bishops, it is, and may be, very evident and apparent that no cause of scruple, ambiguity, or doubt can or may justly be objected against the said elections, confirmations, or consecrations, or any other material thing meet to be used, or had, in or about the same; but that everything requisite and material for that purpose hath been made and done as precisely, and with as great a care and diligence, or rather more, as ever the like was done before Her Majesty's time, as the records of Her Majesty's said father's and brother's time, and also of her own time, will more plainly testify and declare.

"Wherefore, for the plain declaration of all the premises, and to the intent that the same may the better be known to every of the Queen's Majesty's subjects, whereby such evil speech, as heretofore hath been used against the high state of prelacy, may hereafter cease, be it now declared and enacted, by the authority of this present Parliament, that the said act and statute made in the first year of our said sovereign lady, the Queen's Majesty, whereby the said Book of Common Prayer, and the administration of sacraments, with other rites and ceremonies, is authorised and allowed to be used, shall stand and remain good and perfect, to all intents and purposes; and that such order and form for the consecrating of archbishops and bishops, and for the making of priests, deacons, and ministers, as was set forth in the time of the late King Edward VI., and added to the said Book of Common Prayer, and authorised by Parliament in the fifth and sixth years of the said late king, shall stand, and be in full force and effect, and shall, from henceforth, be used and observed in all places within this realm, and other the Queen's Majesty's dominions and countries:

"And that all acts and things heretofore had, made, or done, by any person or persons, in or about any consecrations, confirmation, or investing of any person or persons elected to the office or dignity of any archbishop or bishop within this realm, or within any other the Queen's Majesty's dominions or countries, by virtue of the Queen's Majesty's Letters Patents or commissions, since the beginning of her reign, be, and shall be, by authority of this present Parliament, declared, judged, and deemed, at and from every of the several times of the doing thereof, good and perfect, to all respects and purposes, any matter or thing that can or may be objected to the contrary thereof, in any wise, notwithstanding:

"And that all persons that have been, or shall be, made, ordered, or consecrated archbishops, bishops, priests, ministers of God's Holy Word and Sacraments, or deacons, after the form and order prescribed in the said order and form how archbishops, bishops, priests, deacons, and ministers should be consecrated, made, and ordered, be in very deed, and also by authority hereof declared and enacted to be, and shall be, archbishops, bishops, priests, ministers, and deacons, and rightly made, ordained, and consecrated; any statute, law, canon, or other thing to the contrary notwithstanding."

Some may say that the deed done, or pretended to be done, by this wordy and unprecedented Act, was, in truth, a large stretch of the new supremacy. But surely the same national authority which had created that power could equally define its limits, supply its existing deficiencies, and furthermore extend its operation.

The queen herself, however, did not in the least believe, though officially she was bound to do so, in her so-called "supremacy." She was not so theoretically uninstructed in the Christian religion as to conceive for a moment that a woman could either own or exercise such spiritual power, or that any other warrant for her having assumed such a title as Supreme Governess could be found beyond the bare yet bold decree of the English Parliament. She more than once distinctly admitted as much.[1] To Lausac, an envoy from France, sent hither on certain special business, she frankly owned her sure conviction that the supremacy of the Church of England, and indeed of the whole family of God, did not belong to her, but to the successor of St. Peter; but she apologetically added that circumstances had created a breach with the Pope, and that the English Parliament and people, having resolved to make a new Church for themselves, she was thus obliged to assume and exercise the office of Supreme Governess of it; in which, for the sake both of convenience and necessity, she was officially compelled to feign her belief.

At the same time that much persecution was being carried on against two parties—the anti-innovating and the non-conforming—certain foreign princes endeavoured so to influence the queen that she might be induced to repudiate the wicked and dangerous policy of her advisers, more especially this newly-invented spiritual supremacy. The Emperor Ferdinand, in a holograph letter, implored Her Majesty not to forsake the religious fellowship of all the Christian princes of Europe, or of a long line of illustrious Catholic ancestors at home; nor to set her own fallible opinion, and that of the "new men of yesterday"—themselves so notoriously unsettled and changeable—in opposition to, and above that of, the Universal Church of our Redeemer, the Church of fifteen centuries and more. He also entreated her to refrain from imprisoning and persecuting the suffering remnant of true Catholic prelates, whose only fault was that they were loyal and faithful to the almost universal religion of Christendom and its chief bishop. Moreover, His Majesty suggested that, for those of her subjects whom no fines could

[1] This can be seen on record from a perusal of *An Answer to Sir Edward Coke's Reports* (p. 365), the author of which also points out that Lord Montagu and the Earl of Southampton had heard similar expressions of the queen's mind. So, too, had the Duke of Feria, who, after talking with the queen on the inherent absurdity of a woman ruling a Church, wrote to his master, King Philip, to inform him that she did not in her innermost heart believe in any such notion, but only took the title and office because Cecil and Bacon had assured her of the urgent necessity of so doing.   .

make apostates, no bribes serve to pervert, and no persecution alter, some few desecrated and empty churches here and there might be given up for the ancient rites and religion as heretofore.[1]

But these wise and timely proposals fell upon a heart that was being alternately excited by the lusts of the flesh and chilled by the pride of life, and upon a conscience dulled to the voice both of truth and of justice. Nothing whatsoever was gained by the emperor's well-intended and charitable letter. Affairs steadily and surely went from bad to worse.

For practical action the ancient Church of England men were at this time led by a very able and remarkable ecclesiastical statesman,—a leader of experience, learning, and prudence,—who rendered good service to their cause. William Allen, a Lancashire man, educated at Oxford, Fellow of Oriel in due course, and for some years the Principal of St. Mary's Hall in that university, had ever set his face as a rock against the innovators and their innovations. On the death of Queen Mary he had withdrawn to Louvaine, but on his return to England, about this period, became foremost in condemning any participation whatsoever in the mutilated rites or public services of the new religion.[2] All true Catholics, he asserted, were absolutely bound to abstain from taking any part in the worship set up by Act of Parliament,[3] and patiently to suffer the consequences of non-compliance. Since the decision at Trent, no controversy on the subject could even be entertained. This was Dr. Allen's opinion, stated with lucidity and frankness; and it was largely followed.

When, therefore, this pious and learned Churchman (afterwards Cardinal Allen) defended the position of those who sought a remedy for the existing spiritual desolation in England by the establishment of a theological college abroad, he thus beautifully and powerfully wrote, describing the situation exactly :—

" The universal lack, then, of the sovereign sacrifice and sacraments catholicly ministered, without which the soul of man dieth, as the body doth without corporal food ; this constraint

[1] The queen had already given up the Church of the Austin Friars and the crypt of Canterbury Cathedral to certain foreign heretics ; while the nave of the Abbey of Glastonbury had been actually turned into a workshop for Protestant weavers from Flanders.

[2] It seems a little doubtful when Dr. Allen was in England. Possibly he may have come over for awhile with Dr. Morton and others to consult the old bishops and the ancient Catholic nobility on his proposition, and soon gone abroad again.

[3] " In Lancashire," as Richard Barnes, Bishop of Carlisle, wrote to Cecil, " the people fall from religion, revolt to Popery, and refuse to come to church."—Carlisle, October 27, 1570, *Domestic State Papers, Elizabeth*, vol. lxxiv. p. 395.

to the contrary services, whereby men perish everlastingly; this intolerable oath, repugnant to God, the Church, Her Majesty's honour, and all men's consciences; and the daily dangers, disgraces, vexations, fears, imprisonments, impoverishments, despites, which they must suffer; and the railings and blasphemies against God's sacraments, saints, ministers, and all holies, which they are forced to hear in our country, are the only causes, most dear sirs, or (if we may be so bold, and if Our Lord permit this declaration to come to Her Majesty's reading) Most Gracious Sovereign, why so many of us are departed out of our natural country, and do absent ourselves so long from that place, where we had our being, birth, and bringing-up, through God; and which we desire to serve with all the offices of our life and death, only craving correspondence of the same, as true and natural children of their parents."[1]

In the year 1569, it seemed to many of those who still remained faithful to the old religion, that, as a consequence of the action of the Fathers of Trent, they were being verily driven to desperation by the cruel severity of the penal enactments; by the gross persecution which, over and above the law, was notoriously connived at and tolerated; and by their own utter inability, as mere isolated units, to defend themselves, to stem the tide of social ruin, or to oppose the policy of those who were in authority.   Amongst the new ministers, controversy and squabbles appeared interminable.[2]   The old clergy had either been silenced or compelled to adopt the new religion, its regulations and worship.   Numbers of the most learned who had refused to do so—dignitaries of the highest rank—had been deprived, imprisoned, or sent abroad.   Many more, the very flower of the learned clergy, had become voluntary exiles.   Protests and expostulations to the harsh makers of cruel laws were useless.   Such had been made in abundance, in various forms and shapes, by various persons; but, as already pointed out, were always made in vain.   For nobody heeded them.   Obedience to the new laws was carefully exacted from all.   The dictates of

---

[1] *Apologie and True Declaration of the Institution of the English Colleges, etc.*, pp. 12, 13.

[2] "Our people (the innovators and so-called 'Reformers') are carried away with every wind of doctrine.   If you know what their belief is to-day, you cannot tell what it will be to-morrow.   Is there one article of religion in which these communities, which are at war with the Pope, agree together? If you run over all the articles, from the first to the last, you will not find one which is not held by some of them to be an article of faith, and rejected by others as an impiety."—"Letter of Dudith to Capitonius," amongst the *Epistolæ Bezæ.*

conscience, like the ancient faith and its rites, were laughed to scorn.   Men who clung to the old religion were harassed to death by persecution, fines, and imprisonment.   The many sores in the body politic were deliberately and carefully kept open. Rich and poor, ignorant and learned, alike suffered.   So deep was the feeling of irritation in the Northern Counties that, under the guidance of the Earls of Northumberland and Westmore-land, the people eventually rose as one man to throw off the unbearable burdens by which they were being thus oppressed. Her Majesty, it was maintained, was surrounded " by divers new set-upp nobles, who not only go about to overthrow and put downe the ancient nobilite of the realme, but also have misused the Quene's Majestie's own personne,[1] and also have by the space of twelve years nowe past sett upp and mayntained a new-found religion and heresie contrarie to God's Word."[2]   In York-shire, Durham, and Northumberland, there had long been a stir amongst all classes.   Dr. Nicholas Morton, sometime a Prebendary of York, who had gone to Rome for counsel and advice, came back again with the rank and office of Apostolical Penitentiary ; in order to bestow afresh upon the ancient clergy who so deliberately rejected the innovations, those special faculties required, and that needful jurisdiction desired, which so many believed to have lapsed altogether.   He was a near relation of the old Yorkshire families of Markenfeld and Norton, owned considerable influence, and had long done his best to band together the leading representatives of the ancient nobility in resisting the innovators.   He received sympathy and support from the families of Dacres, Ratcliffe, Swinbourne, and Tempest —names to be had in renown.   During the summer and autumn he visited these and other families at their pleasant homes, where his welcome was hearty and sincere ; and pointed out plainly the only practical remedy for discord and disunion.   His words were acceptable.   But when he treated of passive obedience, his advice was not taken by all.   Some were for action rather than words.   Words and expostulations were useless.   Strength must now be met by strength : the brute force of unbelief and revolu-tion by the chivalry of faith and self-sacrifice..

As Sir Ralph Sadler was careful to inform the Court, there were not at that time "in all this country ten gentlemen that do favor and allow of Her Majesty's proceedings in the cause of

---

[1] This was evidently a direct allusion to Robert Dudley, who elsewhere was characterised, with regard to his relations with the queen, in terms which cannot be decently quoted.

[2] Author's excerpts and MSS.

religion."[1]   When forced by fine and confiscation to attend the
now dreary services and dreadful sermons of the new Calvinistic
religionists—in which damnation was sternly dealt out to all
doubters of their own and their partisans' election—and this
entirely against their consciences, they were only the more
exasperated by such enforced attendance, and made the more
discontented.   On this point sentiment, both amongst rich and
poor, was almost unanimous.   The Countess of Westmoreland,
and several members of the Markenfeld and Norton[2] families
were for open and active resistance.   Some asserted that Dr.
Allen favoured this policy.   In the middle of November, therefore, the banners of another Pilgrimage of Grace were unfurled,
and many prayers went up to heaven for success and victory.

At Durham, which was immediately occupied by the armed
retainers of the two earls, High Mass was once more celebrated
in the cathedral, in the presence of several thousand earnest and
excited worshippers.   Whittingham, the pseudo-dean,[3] who had
never received any ordination whatsoever by a bishop, and therefore was a mere layman, with a great show of practical wisdom,
took himself out of harm's way with more than convenient speed.
In the cathedral the "tressells of bordes" for the Lord's Supper
were ignominiously kicked out of the choir and broken into
splinters; the English Bible and the Zwinglian Service-Books
were enthusiastically torn into fragments.   Nobody desired that
the Word of God should be doctored by mistranslations,
omissions, and false human glosses.   A portable altar was set up
at the east end of the deep choir, flanked by velvet hangings;
and a processional crucifix with taper-bearers on either side was
uplifted once again at the head of the procession in that sacred
sanctuary.   The old vestments were brought out from the
sacristy; the wax tapers were once more lit; a chalice and
ciborium of precious metal, with a York missal, were sought out
anew and used; while the voices of those who sang the *Gloria
in excelsis*, *Credo*, *Sanctus*, and *Benedictus* of the sacred mass—
an united crowd, which filled the Norman nave from northern
side to southern, and from the sanctuary steps to the western
Galilee—rose grandly like the sound of many waters.

From Durham the "Pilgrims of Grace" marched southwards,
in strict order and with some confidence, issuing appeals to the

---

[1] Sir Ralph Sadler's *State Papers*, vol. ii. p. 55.
[2] See Pedigree of "Norton *alias* Conyers," pp. 244, etc., of *The Visitation
of Yorkshire*, edited by Joseph Foster. London, 1875.
[3] William Whittingham, a layman, installed October 8th, 1563, died 10th
June 1579.

afflicted populace westward and eastward to rise in defence of the religion of their forefathers. The watchwords, " God, Our Lady, and the Catholic Faith," were passed from lip to lip, and from village to village. Bells from the church towers welcomed the Pilgrims with merry peals. The old clergy came out of their retreats and seclusion to offer a silent prayer for success, or to bestow a coveted blessing, as the army with banners passed down the northern lanes. The innovators, on the other hand, cowardly and terrified, offered no resistance. Some few stared with astonishment, but did nothing more. At Darlington and Stain-drop the mass was restored amidst the acclamations and thanks-giving of thousands. People, congratulating each other, flocked in from the villages around to worship and rejoice. The banner of our Divine Redeemer, representing His blessed Passion and sacred wounds was upborne by an old esquire, Richard Norton, whose Christian character and high social position had, for many years, secured the respect and affection of the populace. At Richmond and at Ripon the Pilgrims were also welcomed and strengthened, and there likewise the old rites were restored : so that the Court, on learning from Sir Ralph Sadler of what was taking place, became thoroughly alarmed ; while the Supreme Governess, after her impressive but unhallowed custom, swore like an excited fishwife.

But the royal plans in opposition to this movement had been well made. The Earl of Warwick was steadily advancing north-wards with twelve thousand soldiers. Lord Hunsdon, likewise, was on the march thither. Troops under the command of the Earl of Sussex, who had made York his headquarters, soon after-wards came up to and faced the Pilgrims. Amongst these, spies and agents had already misreported the advance of many other forces of the Crown ; so that the insurgents, losing heart, and being divided in counsels, ill-fed and dispirited, at length dis-persed and fled. The Earl of Westmoreland succeeded in making his escape to Flanders ; but the Earl of Northumberland, crossing the Scottish border, was soon confined as a prisoner by the Regent Murray in Lochleven Castle. Many of the northern gentry also escaped to Scotland, and obtained protection from the heads of the southern clans.

At home the work of vengeance, which more than rivalled the cruelties of William the Conqueror, began with no delay. Martial law .was everywhere proclaimed. Of the nobility and gentlefolk there were no less than fifty-seven persons promptly attainted of treason. The legal machinery speedily did its work. Their confiscated lands, goods, and chattels served both to pay the expenses of the royal troops and to reward those who had condescended to do the queen's dreadful work at the same time. No less than three hundred villages were at once wasted with fire and sword. People who had heard mass, as well as priests who had said mass, were specially singled out for severity. Any one who confessed to having carried a cross, worn a surplice, or borne a banner stood self-convicted of treason, and was decreed to be "strung up" without mercy or delay. An old widow woman named Alice Wilkinson, who had been seen to use her beads and pray for Esquire Norton and the Pilgrims, found her cottage in flames over her head, and herself homeless and penniless, as a fitting punishment. Most persons will think this too severe. Moreover, homesteads and farm produce in general were ruthlessly burnt, and cottages destroyed; while in every town and village the gibbets were hung with the carcases of those who had been killed. Many were turned out to die in the cold of a severe winter. Sir William Cecil had personally given strict orders that the chief inhabitants of each township should be at once summoned before the soldiery, and compelled by imprisonment or starvation—if need be "by lack of food" was his exact phrase—to disclose the names of those of their neighbours who had joined in the rebellion. Lord Sussex, naturally harsh, appears, in doing this, to have shown no mercy whatsoever. Three hundred people, in the county palatine of Durham, at once suffered death; but, in writing to Cecil, on the 28th of December, the Earl of Sussex informs him that the number of those hung was at present uncertain; but "I guess," he continues, "that it will not be under six or seven hundred at the least that shall be executed of the common sort, besides the prisoners taken in the field," who appear to have been at once cruelly butchered in cold blood. Subsequent to this, Lord Sussex, using again a favourite and expressive Elizabethan phrase, ordered eighty to be "strung up" without benefit of clergy—that is, unconfessed, unabsolved, and uncommunicated — at Durham, forty-one at Darlington, twenty at Barnard Castle, and no less than one hundred and seventy-two in the other towns and villages of that county. To each and all, religious consolations were peremptorily refused. The poor creatures were forced to die without either prayers, houseling, or unction. Numbers more were imprisoned, half-starved, tortured in various modes, beaten, hung up by the wrists to a beam, and otherwise grossly maltreated; but several of those who survived were subsequently pardoned, on the sole and express condition that they took the Oaths of Allegiance and Supremacy. Those who declined to allow that the queen was Supreme Governess of the Church were compelled to linger on for years, and finally to rot and die in prison.

During the perpetration of these Nero-like atrocities, it appears that even the stern Lord Sussex was not sufficiently prompt in his harshness, nor savage in his cruelty, to satisfy the requirements of his most religious and gracious queen.   What he had done was good and politic as far as it went, she intimated ; but Her Sacred Majesty was evidently anxious to hear of the perpetration of yet further and greater severities.[1]   "The Queen's Majesty," as he informed his lieutenants, "doth much marvel that the executions are not yet ended, and she disburdened of the charges which are considered for that respect ; wherefore I pray you heartily to use expedition [in torturing, starving, and hanging], for I fear this lingering will breed displeasure to us both." [2]

The stern calamities which befell the old nobility of the north and their faithful retainers, on this and on other occasions, are not forgotten even at the present day.   Their chivalric deeds of unselfish daring, having inspired some of the most musical ballad writers of former days, when they penned their touching songs ; noble aspirations and lofty thoughts being thus scattered like good seed, which bore good fruit for many an after generation. Through times of moral darkness and heresy, in the esquire's hall, and round the cottage hearth, of the Northern Counties,—the land of the Percies, the Nortons, and the Nevilles,—touching records of faithfulness to conscience, fidelity to God, and of noble self-sacrifice were, with tearful eye and faltering voice, told to those who came after,—by which for generations many a sanctified heart was silently edified, and many a strong arm nerved for the doing of good and great deeds.

Early in the spring of the year 1570, the saintly and self-denying [3] Pontiff, Pope Pius V., at last issued his solemn Bull of Excommunication against Queen Elizabeth.   Some assert that

[1] See *Memorials of the Northern Rebellion*, by Sir Cuthbert Sharp, from which interesting and valuable compilation the main facts of the text have been thankfully taken.

[2] Later on, it appears that even Lord Sussex was thoroughly weary of his bloody work and brutal butcheries ; for he wrote complainingly to Cecil : " I was first a lieutenant ; I was after little better than a marshal ; I had then nothing left to me but hanging matters."   For further evidence regarding the putting down of this rebellion, the original letters of Sir George Bowes, quoted by Sir Cuthbert Sharp, furnish most reliable but melancholy information.

[3] " Pius V.," wrote Lord Macaulay, " under his gorgeous vestments, wore day and night the hair-shirt of a simple friar ; walked barefoot in the streets at the head of processions ; found, in the midst of his most pressing avoca-

the absence of any authority from Rome to defend their righteous
cause by force of arms had powerfully influenced several of the
old nobility in their action with reference to the recent Pilgrimage
of Grace, and induced them to desist altogether from active
co-operation with those who, as a last resort, had been driven to
take up arms in defence of God, the Church, and their country.
Henceforth such a doubt could not exist.   The terms of the Bull
are luminous, concise, and full of vigour.   Warnings from one
who certainly had the right to make them, the Chief Bishop of
Christendom, had remained unnoticed; friendly expostulations
were wholly unheeded; his patience had been taken undue
advantage of; it was now the obvious duty of the Father of the
Faithful to act.   Of the world's Redeemer and King it had been
foretold by David, long previously to the Incarnation—" He
shall call Me, Thou art My Father, My God and My strong
salvation : and I will make Him My first-born, higher than the
kings of the earth.   My mercy will I keep for Him for evermore ;
and My covenant shall stand fast with Him. . . . But if His
children forsake My law, and walk not in My judgment; if they
break My statutes and keep not My commandments, I will visit
their offences with the rod and their sin with scourges." [1]   The
divine and eternal kingdom, thus prophesied of, then existed.
Christ ruled everywhere by delegation.   Parish priest, bishop.
metropolitan, archbishop, and patriarch, each and all, in due
order and subordination, and with their legitimate authority
acknowledged, in their degree represented our ascended Lord.
But the Bishop of the See of St. Peter represented Him in one
eminent and special manner, claiming jurisdiction over the
whole family of God.   Most confused and inexact notions exist
regarding this jurisdiction of the Roman Pontiff.   All that was
claimed for him was an acknowledgment that, as Chief Bishop
of Christendom, he had everywhere authority to reform and
redress heresies, errors, and abuses within the Church, which
was not confined to any place or nation, but was Catholic or
Universal.   Furthermore, so as to avoid discord and disputes,
and to preserve the visible and actual unity of the Episcopate, it
belonged to the Holy Father to confirm the election of bishops
and to approve of and sanction their institution.   He also

tions, time for private prayer ; often regretted that the public duties of his
station were unfavourable to growth in holiness ; and edified his flock by
innumerable instances of humility, charity, and forgiveness of injuries ; while
at the same time he upheld the authority of his See with all the stubbornness
and vehemence of Hildebrand."—Essays, Ranke's *History of the Popes, in
loco.*

[1] Psalm lxxxix. 26 32.

claimed to grant to the clergy licences of non-residence, and permission to hold more than one benefice with cure of souls, as also to dispense by act and deed with the canonical impediments to matrimony ; and, finally, he received appeals from the highest spiritual courts throughout the whole Christian world. In England the lawful successor of him who had sent St. Austin to Kent, and by whose authority he had placed his chair as archbishop at Canterbury, by whose own graces and miracles the beautiful tree of the Church had taken root downward, and borne fruit upward,—now so weightily spoke, not with the stuttering accents of usurping and pitiful heretics, but with the due and delegated authority of the First-born of the Most Highest.

Here follows an English version of this important Latin instrument :—

"Sentence declaratory of our Sovereign Lord, the Pope Pius V., against Elizabeth, pretended Queen of England, and the heretics who abet her, whereby all subjects are declared released from the Oath of Allegiance, and every other bond, and those who hereafter shall obey her, are bound by the bond of anathema.

" Pius, Bishop, servant of the servants of God, in memorial of the matter.

"The sovereign jurisdiction of the One Holy Catholic and Apostolic Church (outside of which there is no salvation), has been given by Him, unto Whom all power in heaven and on earth is given, the King Who reigns on high, to but one person on the face of the earth, even to Peter, Prince of the Apostles, and to the successor of Peter, the Bishop of Rome. Him He has set up over all nations, and over all kingdoms, to root up and destroy, to waste and to scatter, to plant and to build; to the end that he may maintain in the unity of the spirit the faithful people bound together by the bond of charity, and present them unto Him their Saviour perfect and without loss.

"In the discharge of this duty, We, whom God of His goodness has called to the Government of His Church, shrink from no labour, striving with all Our might to preserve in their integrity that very unity and the Catholic religion which are now assailed by so many storms, by His permission from Whom they come, for Our correction, and for the trial of the faith of His children. But the wicked are so many, and are growing so strong, that there is no part of the world which they have not attempted to corrupt by their evil doctrines ; among others labouring for this end is the servant of iniquity Elizabeth, the pretended Queen of England, with whom, as in a safe refuge, the worst of these men have found a secure retreat.

G

"This woman having taken possession of the kingdom, unnaturally claims for herself the place, the great authority and
jurisdiction of the sovereign head of the Church throughout all
England, and has involved in miserable ruin that kingdom so
lately recovered to the Catholic faith and piety.

"She has forbidden by the strong hand of power the observance of the true religion, overturned by the apostate Henry
VIII., and by the help of the Holy See restored by Mary, the
lawful queen, of illustrious memory. She has followed after and
accepted the errors of heretics. She has driven the English
nobles out of the Royal Council, and filled their places with
obscure heretics. She has been the ruin of those who profess
the Catholic faith, and has brought back again the wicked
preachers and ministers of impieties. She has done away with
the Sacrifice of the Mass, the Divine Office, fasting, the distinction
of meats, celibacy, and the Catholic rites. She has ordered the
use of books, containing manifest heresy, throughout the realm,
and the observance by her subjects of impious mysteries and
ordinances, according to the rule of Calvin, accepted and practised
by herself.

"She has dared to take away their churches and benefices
from the bishops, the parish priests, and other Catholic ecclesi-
astics, and has given them with other ecclesiastical goods to
heretics. She has made herself a judge in ecclesiastical causes.
She has forbidden the prelates, clergy, and people to acknowledge the Church of Rome, or to obey its mandates and the
Catholic constitutions. She has compelled many to take an oath
to observe her wicked laws, to renounce the authority of the
Roman Pontiff, to refuse to obey him, and to accept her as the
sole ruler in temporal and spiritual matters. She has decreed
pains and penalties against those who do not submit to her, and
has inflicted them upon those who continue in the unity of the
faith and obedience.

"She has thrown Catholic prelates and parish priests into
prison, where many, worn out by sorrows and their protracted
sufferings, have ended their days in misery.

"All this being notorious and known unto all nations, and so
confirmed by very many grave witnesses, as to leave no room for
palliation, defence, or concealment, sin being added to sin, and
iniquity to iniquity, the persecution of the faithful, and the ruin
of religion daily growing more and more at the suggestion and
under the direction of Elizabeth aforesaid, whose will is so
obstinate and whose heart is so hardened that she has set at
nought not only the charitable prayers and counsels of Catholic

princes entreating her to return to a better mind and be converted, but also Our own, by her refusal to allow the Nuncios of the Holy See to enter the realm. We, having recourse, by necessity compelled, to the weapons of justice, are unable to control Our grief that We must proceed against one whose predecessors have rendered signal services to Christendom.

"Relying, then, on His authority Who has placed Us on this sovereign throne of justice, though unequal to the bearing of so great a burden, We declare, in the fulness of the Apostolic power, the aforesaid Elizabeth a heretic, and an encourager of heretics, together with those who abet her, under the sentence of excommunication, cut off from the unity of the Body of Christ.

"Moreover, We declare that she has forfeited her pretended title to the aforesaid kingdom, to all and every right, dignity, and privilege; We also declare that the nobles, the subjects, and the people of the kingdom aforesaid, who have taken any oath to her, are for ever released from that oath, and from every obligation of allegiance, fealty, and obedience, as We now by these Letters release them, and deprive the said Elizabeth of her pretended right to the throne, and every other right whatsoever aforesaid: We command all and singular the nobles, the people subject to her, and others aforesaid, never to venture to obey her monitions, mandates, and laws.

"If any shall contravene this Our decree, We bind them with the same bond of anathema.

"Seeing that it would be a work of too much difficulty to send these Letters to every place where it is necessary to send them, Our will is that a copy thereof by a public notary, sealed with the seal of an ecclesiastical prelate, or with the seal of his court, shall have the same force in courts of law and everywhere throughout the world that these Letters themselves have if they be produced and shown.

"Given at St. Peter's, in Rome, in the year of the Incarnation of our Lord One thousand five hundred and sixty-nine, on the fifth of the calends of March,[1] in the fifth year of Our Pontificate.

" CÆ. GLORIERIUS.
" H. CUMYN."

What resulted from this instrument will be apparent from the events of later years, to be recorded and commented upon in due course.

In the spring of the year 1571, there was a severe, sharp, and

---

[1] February 27, 1570, according to the present computation. Anciently the year began on the 25th of March.

carefully-organised raid upon the beggars. In the north the distress, of course, was most severe. Hundreds in the past winter had died of starvation. Poverty, even then, as may be noted, was a sin for which, by order of the autocratic authorities, there was to be no absolution and no forgiveness. Charity was dead. Selfishness reigned.[1] The poor and miserable were hateful to look upon and expensive to feed. The old were far too long-lived. Somehow or another they must be put out of the way, or confined to their miserable habitations. (When the queen took her journeys through the country, therefore, the lean, the famished, the wolf-like, and the repulsive-looking were now, by special Privy Council order, to be carefully kept out of her royal sight; for she disliked their aspect and dreaded their cries of hunger.) Thirty years ago and more, the monasteries had all been destroyed, and with them had been lost any adequate realisation of the duty of practising the corporal works of mercy; for good deeds were regarded by the new gospellers as "filthy rags." Most of the older monks and friars had found their only rest in death. But of the younger who had been professed, some still lived; a few had passively accepted the new state of affairs; while many of the lay brothers had no doubt become mendicants —reasonably dissatisfied with having lost their only homes, and having no apparent chance of obtaining work in the present, and less hope of being able to keep body and soul together in the future.

These and such as these, their name was "legion," seemed to fill the land—for field after field remained untilled; acre after acre now lay fallow—they infested the towns and villages, the wild bye-ways and out-of-the-way hamlets, asking alms of esquire and yeoman, hind and peasant, at the portal of the hall and at the thatched porch of the cottage; living often during autumn on wild fruit, uncooked roots, and during winter upon the barley-bread of alms. In the frost and cold they frequently herded with

---

[1] As Bishop Sandys himself wrote:—"But we are fallen into these evil times, wherein iniquity aboundeth, and charity waxeth cold. Hearty love is turned into hearty hatred: our hands are bloody, and our hearts malicious. He liveth not that loveth his neighbour as himself. If we did love our neighbours as ourselves, we would not oppress them with extortion and usury: we would not undermine them, and wring them in bargaining: we would not so proudly contemn them, so spitefully envy them, so impudently slander them, or so greedily practise for their infamy and discredit: we would not speak them fair, and mind them evil: fawn on them, and betray them; seek our credit by their reproach, our gain by their loss: when we see their necessities, we would relieve and succour them, bind up their wounds with the good Samaritan, and charitably provide for them."—*Sandys' Works*, pp. 206, 207. Parker Society. London, 1842.

the cattle at night, or in summer went to rest under hedges and trees. With no apparent means of subsistence, and always practically witnessing against the success of the new religion, —for they constantly deplored the destruction of the religious houses,—and often, when lingering near village cross or way-side hostel, in language frequently bold and sometimes possibly seditious, they forcibly contrasted the past with the present, to the grave disparagement of the latter, and to the annoyance of the powers that were.

Such dangerous wanderers, therefore, as the Privy Council determined,[1] must now be everywhere persecuted ; hunted from pillar to post ; examined by justices of the peace to find out if they used the rosary or sympathised with the old religion ; flogged on their naked backs, without regard either to age or sex, for being poor and having no home ; put into the stocks on a starvation allowance for several days ; whipped afresh when they were taken out, until the purple wale-marks on their shoulders became bloody wounds, from which the gore trickled downwards to the earth ; while sometimes the poor creatures, being so weak with want of food, and feeble and shrunken because of their poverty, suddenly sunk senseless towards the ground, straining the cords round their wrists, and so were literally flogged to death.

It was an awful sight and a horrible ; worthy of the reign of a woman falsely called "glorious" and "good,"—a sight to have made angels weep and Englishmen shudder and sicken) and a national sin well meriting all the various and heavy punishments which one after another descended, sixty years afterwards, upon our distracted nation, during those fearful twenty winters and more of the miseries of the Great Rebellion and the dire slaughter of the Civil War.

[1] It was required by the Privy Council that "certificates of all the vaga-bonds, rogues, and mighty valiant beggars, men and women," who had been "examined, whipped, stocked, and punished according to law," should be duly made out and sent up.—*Domestic State Papers, Elizabeth*, vol. lxxx., August 20, 1571. In Gloucestershire, William Wynter, justice of the peace, and others, have made search for vagabonds, but have found none but such poor beggarly persons as are not thought fit to trouble their lordships with. —August 27, 1571. At Aylesford, on August 28, the justices of Kent apprehended "thirteen men and women, stout and valiant vagabonds, all of whom have been stocked and whipped severely."—Vol. lxxx. At Thame, in Oxfordshire, some "proper stoute abbey-men" were convicted and punished as vagabonds. Of these it is stated that on September 8th, 1571, "they took their stocking and whipping verie ill. So they were sore bloodied, and one thereafter died, no long while thereupon."—Author's MSS., from Churchwardens' and Parish Accounts of Thame.

CHAPTER IV.

THE two events recently recorded, viz. the formal condemnation of the queen by Pope Pius V., and the strong determination to persecute even unto death, and so extirpate, those of the English poor who still adhered to the old religion, by taking care that all obstinate persons of that class could be summarily and easily dealt with and disposed of by the new laws, effectively cleared the way for the queen's advisers, and enabled them to act with still greater decision than they had hitherto shown. The recent enactment against beggars would enable the authorities to worry, starve, brand with a hot iron, flog and put in the stocks and pillory, any persons of the lower or migratory class supposed to be dangerous. The possession of a string of prayer-beads, a crucifix, an *Agnus Dei*, or any foreign book of devotions, served to secure for the poverty-stricken possessor of it, the title of "Italianate atheist."[1] A poor, friendless man who was found saying his prayers on a rosary, at the steps of a wayside cross, was held to be a certain ally of the Pope and a possible assassin of the queen. As regards the Bull of Pius V., Cecil and Walsingham could never henceforth mistake the attitude of the Primate of Christendom. Exercising his acknowledged powers, he had at length drawn the spiritual sword from its scabbard, as all the European nations then saw, and had spoken out in a cause in which, as the Father of the Faithful, he believed himself to have both an official and personal interest. His Holiness had not acted in haste, nor without a perfect knowledge of the degraded state of England, nor without exact information of what the new prelates preached and taught;[2] nor without

---

[1] "The number of obdurate Papists and Italianate atheists is great at this time, both desperate, and grown, as it evidently appeareth, to the nature of assassins."—Grindal to Lord Treasurer Burghley, 29th January 1572, Grindal's *Remains*, p. 333. Parker Society's Works.

[2] Sandys had written thus:—"Our Gracious Governor (*i.e.* Elizabeth) . . . hath caused all rubbish and whatsoever was hurtful to be removed ; the den of thieves to be dispersed ; buyers and sellers of popish trash, monks, friars, mass-mongers, with like miscreants, to be hurled and whipped out,

constant consultation with those exiles for their faith at Rome,[1] who knew the exact situation accurately, and were able to afford him the most complete information as to what was needed. Queen Elizabeth's bishops were obviously and notoriously of a new and unprecedented kind and make.[2] Her "ministers," whatever they were, were certainly not of the same order as the parish clergy of old. The "ancient priests" altogether repudiated the new; while the new in turn caricatured and condemned the old as worshippers of the blessed Sacrament, which they so profanely termed "Jack-in-the-box," and of idols. A strong measure would evidently not have been adopted, if one less vigorous and decisive would have been likely to have wrought a cure.

It was not, however, the queen's dealings with her own religious subjects alone which brought about the Holy Father's action. At the instigation of her ministers she had again and

the stumbling-stones of superstition, the baggage of man's traditions, with all monuments of idolatry, vanity, and Popery, to be cast out of the house of God and vineyard of the Lord."—*Sandys' Works*, p. 59. Parker Society. London, 1842.

"The Popish Church hath neither the true foundation, nor yet the right marks of the Church of God; her foundation is man; her 'marks' are blasphemy, idolatry, superstition. Christ is 'the Head of His Body the Church;' this Head cannot err. The head of the Church anti-Christian is the Pope, that man of sin, a liar; yea, a very father of lies."—*Ibid.* p. 67.

[1] These were Goldwell, Bishop of St. Asaph; Glennock, Bishop-elect of Bangor; Nicholas Morton, Prebendary of York; Henshaw, Rector of Lincoln College, Oxford; Daniel, Dean of Hereford; Bromborough, Hall, and Kirton, Doctors of Divinity, and some other priests of experience and good reputation.

[2] "The position of bishops in the Church of England has been from the first anomalous. The Episcopate was violently separated from the Papacy, to which it would have preferred to remain attached, and, to secure its obedience, it was made dependent on the Crown. The method of episcopal appointments, instituted by Henry VIII. as a temporary expedient, and abolished under Edward as an unreality, was re-established by Elizabeth, not certainly because she believed that the invocation of the Holy Ghost was required for the completeness of an election which her own choice had already determined, not because the bishops obtained any gifts or grace in their consecration which she herself respected, but because the shadowy form of an election, with a religious ceremony following it, gave them the semblance of spiritual independence, the semblance without the substance, which qualified them to be the instruments of the system which she desired to enforce. They were tempted to presume on their phantom dignity, till the sword of a second Cromwell taught them the true value of their apostolic descent; and we have a right to regret that the original theory of Cranmer was departed from—that being officers of the Crown, as much appointed by the sovereign as the Lord Chancellor, the bishops should not have worn openly their real character and received their appointments immediately by letters patent without further ceremony."—Froude's *History of England*, vol. vi. pp. 552, 553. London, 1870.

again proclaimed herself the determined opponent everywhere of the cause of Catholic Christianity abroad. Secretly yet efficiently, by the aid of spies, secret agents, and bribes, she had co-operated with the fanatical rebels of several neighbouring states in opposing their sovereigns; and this not unfrequently when she herself professed to be at peace with the latter, and actually had accredited ministers at their respective Courts. Her treatment of Mary, Queen of Scots, likewise, was marked by gross injustice, and by indecency without a parallel. This treatment ensued because of Queen Mary's religion; for she was the last hope of those who looked for another restoration of the ancient faith. The persecution which she endured,—and which, as will be seen, terminated in her murder,—she endured because she was true to that faith, from which in no single *iota* did she intentionally swerve.

Here, therefore, it will be convenient to set forth with certain detail and at some considerable length, in a record ranging over several years, the true state of ecclesiastical affairs, both as concerns the kingdom in general, and certain parts of it in particular. A private letter, an official document, a public trial, or a personal squabble between officials, may often comprise much of interest and point, as will be shown. The changes which had now taken place had been brought about, not by unauthorised private individuals acting on their own responsibility, but by exalted officials, the archbishops and chief bishops of the National Church, who had been clothed with all such temporal authority as Parliament could authorise the queen to bestow upon them; and who had indeed worked with a will and system both in the overthrow of the old, and the consolidation of the new, religion. Some readers, in that which follows, may think that out-of-the-way and valueless details of information have been gathered together without object; but surely any record of facts which serves to bring out points of historical interest may well be rescued from oblivion and be made to serve its purpose.

Throughout the whole of the queen's reign, there had been constant complaints from all quarters of the difficulty in getting the existing cures served by persons who could read sufficiently well to recite the morning and evening prayers. Early in Parker's episcopate, in addition to the "readers" everywhere set apart, he had ordained more than a hundred and twenty "ministers" in one week; and many of these were reported to have been schoolmasters, "scribes," "most ignorant persons,"[1]

---

[1] What must we say, when most of them are popish priests, consecrated to perform mass, and *the far greater part of the remainder are most ignorant*

tradesmen who had failed to get their living, and even husbandmen. When these persons, in their ordinary secular habits,[1]
appeared in the pulpits, they made such a deplorable exhibition
of fanaticism and ignorance, that the congregation was sometimes
moved to laughter and ribaldry, the new service was brought
into contempt, and the people declined to go to church at all.
This kind of irreverent exhibition became so common at one
period, that disputes and brawls constantly occurred, even at the
font and Communion board. The consequence was that fresh
legislation took place, by which all criticism of these distressing
ministers during divine service was forbidden under pains and
penalties,[2] though the practice was not by any means stopped.
It has been calculated that out of the nine thousand benefices,
including chapelries attached to mother churches, which about
the year 1570 required pastors, at least half were unoccupied
and unserved during the greater part of this queen's reign. The
work of destruction had not been so difficult as was anticipated :
the work of reparation and restoration would possibly remain
uncommenced, most certainly uncrowned, for generations.

persons, appointed at the will of the people, not to the ministry of the Word?"
—George Withers to the Elector Palatine, Letter lxii., *Zurich Letters*, 2nd
series, Parker Society. Parker's admissions may be thus read in his own
words :—" Whereas occasioned by the great want of ministers, we and you,
brother, for tolerable supply thereof, have heretofore admitted into the
ministry sundry artificers and others not traded and brought up in learning,
and as it happened in a multitude some that were of base occupation ; forasmuch as now by experience it is seen that such manner of men, partly by
reason of their previous profane acts, partly by their light behaviour otherwise and trade of life, are very offensive unto the people, yea, and to the
wise of the realm [*i.e.* to Bacon and Cecil], are thought to do great deal more
hurt than good, the gospel there sustaining slander ; these shall be to desire
and require you hereafter to be very circumspect in admitting any to the
ministry, and only to allow such as having good testimony of their honest
conversation, have been traded and exercised in learning, or at the least have
spent their time with teaching of children, excluding all others which have
been brought up and sustained themselves either by occupation or other kinds of
life alienated from learning."—*Archbishop Matthew Parker's Correspondence*,
vol. i. p. 121.
   [1] So averse was Dr. Turner, holding the important position of Dean of
Wells, to sacerdotal habits, that acting in his official capacity in 1565 he
caused a common adulterer to do public penance in a priest's square cap.—
See Dr. W. Turner to H. Bullinger, Letter li., July 23rd, 1566, *Zurich
Letters*, 2nd series, Parker Society.
   [2] One of the bishops thus inquired :—" Whether there be any that hath
unreverently abused or given any evill and unseemly terms of any minister of
God's Word and Sacraments . . . either in the time of his celebration of
Divine Service, or Sermon, or in the time of the administration of the sacra-
ments in the Church?"—*Visitation Articles of Thornborough, Bishop of
Bristol*, 1603.

In some cases the lay leaders and allies of the innovators, needy gentlefolks, succeeded in getting themselves appointed to vacant cures, more especially to those impoverished. Benefices which had thus remained unfilled for several years (such were numerous) were often granted to the new nobles, to knights,[1] and to Protestant yeomen who asked for them. Sometimes one person would secure as many as four or five cures within a given radius. He thus became the "farmer" of the various benefices, and was known as such; and then proceeded to seek out some "abbey-man," "old schoolmaster," or "cunning scribe and reader," who would be prepared to minister alternately at the various churches for some pitiable and paltry pittance. Many of these persons were unordained.[2] By increasing the rents of the church lands; by inducing the reader to curtail the appointed services, and so get through four or five in one day; by private arrangements with the diocesan officials who winked at such pro-ceedings (if paid to close their eyes or purposely look in another direction); these "benefice-farmers" were thus enabled to squeeze a little more out of the impoverished cures. Giving as little as they could and getting as much, the last thought that

[1] In Edward VI.'s reign, William Cecil, a layman (eventually Lord Burghley), had been made Rector of Wimbledon, and occupied the rectory house. At the same period the Princess Elizabeth secured, through Cecil himself, the parsonage of Harptree, in Somersetshire, for "Master John Kenyon," who had been yeoman of her robes—of course, only a layman. He was, however, duly instituted, and then hired a "reader" to supply his place and do the work while he received the revenues. Sir Thomas Smith, Dean of Carlisle, was only a deacon, while Sir John Woollery, who enjoyed that dignity from A.D. 1577 to 1596, and Sir Christopher Perkins, who suc-ceeded him, living until 1622, were laymen. Examples of this kind of jobbery are constantly met with in the official correspondence of the Reformation bishops.

[2] Of a certain Lowth, a minister of Carlisle side, Grindal, after some inquiry as to the fact, wrote to Parker on the 4th March 1575 : " I think it will fall forth that *he was never ordered priest or minister; and yet hath he these fifteen or sixteen years exercised that function.*"—Grindal's *Remains*, p. 353, Parker Society. Eleven years afterwards, Bishop Aylmer, in the diocese of London, officially inquired "whether any ministers appointed *without orders taken of the bishops* do baptize, minister the Communion, or deal in any function ecclesiastical?"—Aylmer's *Articles of Enquiry*, 1586. In the queen's letter to the bishops, for suppressing "prophesyings," she asserts that " in sundry parts of Our realm there are no small number of persons presuming to be teachers and preachers of the Church (*though neither lawfully thereunto called, nor yet fit for the same*)."—Cotton MS., British Museum ; Cleopatra, F. 2, folio 287. "January 4th, 1572: William Bele, M.A., was presented to the Prebend of Schalford, *alias* Scarford, at the queen's presentation by lapse ; because one Alwood, the pretended Canon and Prebendary was, *mere laicus*, as it is set down in the Register."—Strype's *Annals*, vol. ii. part i. p. 277. Oxford, 1824.

ever entered the heads of such reforming gentry was any consideration for the neglected population. "Greed of gain," as
Archbishop Parker admitted and deplored, " be, together with
self-seeking, eating up of all charity to God and one's neighbour."
The archbishop's opinions concerning ordination, its true nature,
importance, and value, may not inaccurately be gathered, though
but indirectly, from a very important letter written to him by
Jewell,[1] Bishop of Salisbury, dated April 26th, 1568, as follows:—

"Whereas I wrote of late under Your Grace touching the
bearer M. Lancaster, now elect of Armagh,[2] that it might please
Your Grace to stay him from further ordering of ministers, it
may now like the same to understand that I have sithence com-
muned with the same M. Lancaster concerning the same, and
find by his own confession that he hath already ordered divers
(although not so many as it was reported): Howbeit among the
same he hath admitted and ordered one whom by the space of
these eight years I, for many good and just causes me moving,
evermore have refused. Your Grace may further advertise him
hereof, as unto your wisdom shall seem good ; certainly in such
cases his discretion is very small."

Now when the date of this letter is carefully noted, it is found
that Lancaster was not consecrated for nearly two months after
wards, i.e. until the 13th of June. Yet, as a mere minister or
priest, he had already been ordaining others ; and Jewell takes
it for granted, that, like himself, Parker will regard all such
ordinations, if a previous call has been made, as perfectly good
and valid, though somewhat irregular ; and he does not for a
moment declare them to be utterly null and void, as they
certainly were. Does it not follow, therefore, as an obvious consequence, that the opinions then current in the New Church, and
the lax practices then tolerated by its chief officers, prove that
some at least of the leading "reformed" prelates practically
repudiated altogether the Catholic doctrine of ordination ? If it
had been otherwise, if the law on the subject had been then
what the law now is, such a case as that of which Jewell makes
mention would have been properly and severely dealt with.
Yet how stands the question? This very man Lancaster, a Protestant, who had notoriously assumed episcopal duties without

---

[1] For this letter, at length, see *Jewell's Works*, Parker Society, vol. iii.
part ii. p. 1274. London, 1850.
[2] Thomas Lancaster had been Treasurer of Salisbury, and was consecrated
Archbishop of Armagh, June 13th, 1568. A person of the same names had
been consecrated, eighteen years previously, to the See of Kildare.—Loftus
MSS., Marsh's Library, Dublin.

episcopal consecration, was not only not even reprimanded, but was soon afterwards consecrated Archbishop of Armagh, as if, in the case in question, nothing worthy of complaint or reprimand had occurred, or nothing out of the way happened. Election by the people, from a Lutheran point of view, was regarded as an essential in the "making of ministers"; the imposition of hands was held to be an ornamental but useless addition.[1] In this conviction the above facts show that Archbishop Parker and Bishop Jewell were perfectly agreed.

Many of the bishops, it is evident, were adventurous self-seekers, sometimes taken from the lowest of the people; or needy and impecunious gentlefolks, who, together with their property and old position, had lost their self-respect; and who, when their willingness to aid the innovators had been authoritatively made clear to the Council, were put into places of trust and importance to continue and consolidate the policy of change. They were too often keen and successful money-hunters, and willing tools of the Court. A large majority of these Reformation prelates, though constantly prating about the "gospel" (as they termed their own immoral principles), were always sharply on the look-out for something more solid and less transcendental than the Calvinistic calculations and phantasies in which they themselves professed to believe. There is scarcely one who is free from the charge of peculation, double-dealing, and self-aggrandisement.[2] Their whole energies seem to have been set on securing for themselves, their wives and families, every temporal advantage which could be had from their official positions, or squeezed out of the estates connected with them. From the days of William Barlow, "the calamity of his See,"[3] as he was termed, to those

---

[1] Luther taught that there were two kinds of calling to the office and work of the ministry—one, internal, from God, such as that of prophets, apostles, and holy teachers; the second, external, by the free election of the people, or by the selection and nomination of persons having authority, such as rulers and magistrates. The imposition of hands, with prayer, by some presiding minister, was a public indication to the congregation gathered together that the person had already been selected, and it was at the same time a ratification of the choice made. But it was not held to be a means of grace. The essential act was the selection, not the imposition of hands.

[2] Camden's *Annals, in loco.*

[3] For an account of the disagreements between Sandys and Parker, see Petyt MS., No. 47, folio 376, in which the former writes at length to the latter. Again: of the ruin wrought under William Barlow at Bath, Sir John Harington gives the following graphic account from personal knowledge:—"I speak now only of the spoil made under this bishop, scarce were five years past after Bath's ruins; but as fast went the axes and hammers to work at Wells. The goodly hall covered with lead (because the roof might seem too low for so large a room) was uncovered, and now this roof reaches to the

of Bishop Pilkington, who robbed the diocese of Durham right royally, the same unchanging policy was pursued. Sometimes, as in the case of Aylmer, Bishop of London, and his immediate predecessor, they openly quarrelled amongst themselves over the temporalties, and so drew public attention to their selfish proceedings.

We may learn from what Strype and others have put on record, that the queen was highly incensed on hearing that James Pilkington, Bishop Palatine of Durham,[1] had so managed to manipulate the revenues of that See, which he held for seventeen years, as to have been enabled to give a marriage portion of no less than ten thousand pounds to his daughter—an enormous sum in those days, equal, in fact, to that which the queen herself had received from King Henry VIII. her father. "If the revenues be so mighty," remarked Her Highness, "and the Crown be so poor, my lord of Durham [2] can surely spare Us a little. We will charitably lighten his heavy burden for him somewhat." So, without process or further ado, she henceforth took one thousand pounds a year from the bishop's income, and devoted it to maintaining her garrison at Berwick.

Sandys and Grindal disagreed fiercely about dilapidations, for which neither cared to pay, while the forcible words and strong adjectives they both used in controversy on the subject were very remarkable. In a fierce dispute about a leasehold house at Battersea, which the Archbishops of York had frequently used when in London, the language uttered and written was both unprelatic and violent. Aylmer, too, was not a whit behindhand either in the vigour of his words or in the grasping spirit he displayed. He and Sandys had so furious a public quarrel regarding the revenues due to either from the See of London

sky. The Chapel of Our Lady late repaired by Stillington, a place of great reverence and antiquity, was likewise defaced, and such was their thirst after lead (I would they had drunk it scalding) that they took the dead bodies of bishops out of their leaden coffins, and cast abroad the carcases scarce thoroughly putrified."—*Brief View of the State of the Church of England*, p. 110.

[1] When this Puritan was a poor exile at Frankfort, he is said to have consoled his afflicted and complaining fellows with "the heavenly promises of riches hereafter," asserting that "few men were predestined to celestial joys who owned much money."

[2] James Pilkington, born at Rivington, county Lancaster, in 1520, was third son of Richard Pilkington. He graduated B.A., Cantab., 1539; became Fellow of St. John's, Cambridge, 26th of March 1539; M.A., 1542; B.D., 1550. He married Alice, daughter of Sir John Kingsmill, and died 23rd of January 1575, aged fifty-five, leaving his wife and two daughters as survivors. He was buried at Bishops Auckland, but afterwards removed to Durham.

upon Sandys' translation to York, that the Lord Treasurer, for decency's sake, was called in to appease it, but in vain. The two prelates wrangled and snarled for some hours. Cecil as arbiter offended both, and satisfied neither. The prelates continued to dispute for several years, and died engaged in tortuous lawsuits. In these, and in other particulars, their characters were certainly not a little fly-blown.

The first wife of this man Edwin Sandys, sometime Bishop of Worcester, is said to have been his own niece or great-niece, the young and attractive widow of one of the keepers of the Marshalsea prison, where, at the outset of his career, Sandys had been for some weeks confined. She was formally described as the daughter of "Master Sandys of Essex," and "a right buxom woman." But she died shortly after their illicit and uncanonical union; and he soon married another—thus piously consoling himself—Cecilia, daughter of Sir Thomas Wilford.

In Worcestershire, Sandys acted with a very high hand. For example: On a visitation tour, his attention was called to an old stone altar still standing in the parish church of Battenhall,[1] where the chief proprietor was Sir John Bourne, who had been Secretary of State under Queen Mary. Sandys ordered it to be "removed, defaced, and at once put to some common use." But Sir John and his allies resisted this injunction by force, so far as that when the altar-stone was pulled down he had it taken to his own mansion. Hearing of this, Sandys became impressively violent, and ordered another visitation of the same village church to be held without delay. But when an appeal was made to Archbishop Parker, as metropolitan, as to the need for such a step, Sandys was advised to be quiet and not push matters to further extremities—advice which he appears reluctantly and not very good-temperedly to have taken.

Sir John Bourne, on the other hand, made a series of grave and disagreeable accusations against Sandys, some of which were certainly true enough;[2] but, on an appeal to the Privy Council

---

[1] Some assert that this occurred at a parish in the city of Worcester.

[2] Amongst Sir John Bourne's charges against Bishop Sandys are the following, given by Strype:—" That the manor house of Northwike (built in the beginning of Henry VII. his reign) he had already pulled down and razed from the bottom of the foundation; and having sold the hall, and the most part of the matter and stuff unto his friends, making thereof a great piece of money; with some part of the rest had raised at his palace a pretty building, which he called his *nursery:* to which it was also put, his wife being of good fecundity, and a very fruitful woman. And that for the furniture and finishing of the said nursery, he had likewise razed and pulled down a fair long vaulted chapel of stone, standing within his said palace. That his wife being thus fruitful, he had for one of his children procured, in

(all of whom were disposed to defend and uphold the innovators at any cost, and who certainly had the power to do so), Bourne was condemned for having spoken disparagingly of Mistress Sandys and urged his retainers to do likewise, and committed to the Marshalsea.   Subsequently, on retracting his sayings, he was released.   But when invited to spend Christmas with the bishop, who in this case appears as a peace-maker, he threw the letter of invitation into the fire.[1]   He continued to criticise the Protestant prelate and his lady very sharply, until the former was translated to London.   At Worcester, Sandys was likewise accused of granting long leases of farms and lands belonging to the See to various poor Protestant relations, who had secured them for very low and inadequate rents.   But adequate inquiry on the subject was suppressed.   When he went to London, with a like benevolent intention of doing good to the household of faith, more particularly his own, he attempted a similar policy ; but the Court, hearing of his contemplated proceedings, warned him in time that such tactics were not to be again attempted with impunity ; while the Lord Treasurer, in the name of the Chief Governess, rebuked him in very strong and vigorous Scripture phrases.   In London, Sandys was good enough to take under his special protection the Dutch Protestants in Austin-friars ; and, on the other hand, suppressed for awhile the mass celebrated at the Portuguese ambassador's mansion in Tower

his brother's name, one lease of the parsonage of Flodbury : which benefice was yearly worth four hundred marks, and better, being one of his own patronage, having a goodly mansion, and a goodly demean : whereof was wont to be kept great hospitality."—Strype's *Annals*, vol. i. part ii. pp. 38, 39. Oxford, 1824. Sir John Bourne likewise asserted that the pipes of a great pair of organs, which had cost two hundred pounds, had been melted down to make the prebendaries' wives dishes for their kitchens, and the organ-case had made them bedsteads ; that the silver plate of the sacristy had been divided amongst the prebendaries, and that it was intended to divide the copes and other ornaments. The bishop, though evidently much annoyed that these and such-like reports should get abroad, admitted of his accuser that "none love him for himself, but for his religion many like him." —Strype's *Annals*, vol. i. part ii. pp. 39-42.

[1] Bourne treated Sandys with contempt, as the bishop maintained. When after many contentions the latter invited Sir John and his lady to spend Christmas with him, he not only refused to come, but threw the letter into the fire. Sir John's eldest son had a special aversion to priests' and bishops' wives, which at that period was shared by many, and applied a term to them which certainly was strong and not over polite. Sir John himself in this particular had equally offended, as the bishop averred, "three women going through his park, wherein was a path for footmen, he, supposing they had been priests' wives, called unto them, ' Ye shall not come through my park, and no such priests' w——s.' "—Strype's *Annals*, vol. i. part ii. pp. 24 and 30. Oxford, 1824.

Street, to which crowds had for some time resorted. He was translated to York on the 8th of March 1576; but, as he complained to the Lord Treasurer, was most coldly received[1] by the nobility and gentlepeople on his arrival.

In May 1581, Sandys was holding a visitation at Doncaster; and, contrary to the canons, went to an inn in the town, where he remained for some days for rest and refreshment. One midnight the wife of the innkeeper was found in His Grace's bedchamber by her own husband.[2] The latter had returned home, as it appears, somewhat unexpectedly, and, seeking his spouse in vain in her own room, thus discovered her elsewhere. Such a discovery, of course, required an explanation. It certainly had an awkward appearance. The noise which ensued disturbed other inmates of the hostel, amongst whom was a shrewd and popular Yorkshire knight, Sir Robert Stapleton of Wighill,[3] who, at once taking in the situation, and for the honour of the archbishop's cloth and dignity, is said to have endeavoured to prevent unnecessary scandal. The excited host of the inn had gone so far as to threaten the exalted prelate with a taste of his unsheathed dagger, which he brandished again and again. But Stapleton interposed with earnestness and temporary success; for the archbishop, who, if innocent, committed an unpardonable error of judgment, consented at once to give the innkeeper a considerable bag of golden angels to purchase his forgiveness and silence.[4] Subsequently other demands were made upon the unfortunate prelate under a threat of exposure, to which both

[1] Sandys could scarcely have looked for a very cordial greeting from the nobility and gentry of the ancient faith in Yorkshire, as he had thus described the ecclesiastical position in a sermon at York Minster: "As Christ hath delivered all His out of the captivity of Satan and sin, so hath He also us, after a more special and peculiar manner, out of that den of thieves, out of that prison of Romish servitude, out of the bloody claws of that cruel and proud antichrist."—*Sandys' Works*, p. 180. Parker Society. London, 1842. Grindal, on going to York to take up his new office seven years previously, had written to Sir W. Cecil to the same effect: "I was not received with such concourse of gentlemen, at my first coming into this shire, as I looked for." It is evident, therefore, that the "new cause" had not gained many adherents.

[2] For detailed particulars of this case, see Strype's *Annals*, vol. iii. Book i. chap. ix., and Appendices Nos. 20 and 21. Also, *Biographical Notice of Sandys*, by the Rev. John Ayre. Parker Society's Works. London, 1842.

[3] Sir Robert Stapleton of Wighill, of an old Yorkshire family, was a connection of the ancient Catholic houses of Neville and Constable. For pedigree, see p. 333 of Foster's *Pedigrees of Yorkshire*. London, 1875.

[4] Sir John Harington asserts that the hostess had previously been Mistress Sandys' waiting-maid, and that on taking a candle to the bishop in bed, she "slipped into my lord's bed in her smock." Parsons, a contemporary writer, asserts that "this prelate had in his younger days been too familiar with this

Stapleton and the injured husband, whether rightly or wrongly, are reported to have been parties. Such an incident in the case of so dignified a prelate, who had a wife of his own, of course afforded food for conversation and criticism in a very loose and dissolute Court when the news reached Richmond and White-hall. The queen and Leicester, evidently sympathising with the archbishop, had the innkeeper brought up to the Star Chamber for examination; and the evidence in detail was written out for Her Majesty's perusal and edification, Leicester directing Her Grace's attention to its more salient and striking points. The result was that the judges condemned the inn-keeper to acknowledge the archbishop's innocence at the York Assizes, which was formally done; but only amidst the jeers and contemptuous laughter of those who filled the court-house. For many months the archbishop shut himself up at home. Several coarse squibs in prose and verse on this topic were secretly printed and hawked about the castle-yard and cathedral-close; while copies of two were affixed to the chief entrance of Bishops-thorpe Church, His Grace's parish, to the interest and amusement of the shrewd and observant Yorkshire rustics. Subsequently, Sir Robert Stapleton, when found to be an adherent of the old religion, was confined in the Tower for nearly two years, because he declined either to vary from his original statement or to express regret for the charitable part which he had taken in a very questionable and unpleasant affair. Archbishop Sandys never recovered this blow.[1] According to his monument, he was soon afterwards translated to a better world.[2]

A few pages must now be devoted to Dr. John Bale,[3] one of

woman, which is said to pass as a veniall sin with those of his profession."—
Brief View of the State of the Church of England, pp. 177-179.

[1] On his monument in Southwell Minster this disagreeable event is un-necessarily commemorated. The archbishop is said to have "suffered, from what the innocent mind can least of all endure, atrocious slanders."

[2] The following, though vigorous and plain-spoken, is true:—"The 'Reformers' differed from each other, as widely as the colours of the rainbow, in most other things; but they all agreed in this, that good works were unnecessary to salvation, and that *the 'saints,' as they had the modesty to call themselves, could not forfeit their right to heaven by any sins however numerous and enormous.* By those, amongst whom plunder, sacrilege, adultery, poly-gamy, incest, perjury, and murder were almost as habitual as sleeping and waking; by those who taught that the way to everlasting bliss could not be obstructed by any of these, nor by all of them put together; by such persons, charity, besides that it was so well-known a Catholic commodity, would be, as a matter of course, set wholly at nought."—*History of the Protestant Reformation*, by W. Cobbett, p. 189. Dublin, 1868.

[3] John Bale, a Suffolk man, first a Carmelite friar, was perverted to Protestantism, and then married a woman whose Christian name was

the chief bishops of the Reformation era, and certainly one of
the most outspoken and plain spoken.   His name occurs in the
commission for Dr. Parker's consecration; and although, for
some reason or another, he was not present on the occasion, it
is evident that he was well known to the authorities, and held in
high estimation by them.   He had been for some time Bishop
of Ossory, in Ireland; but found himself extremely unpopular in
that Catholic land, where the unattractive gospel of which he
was a minister was wholly repudiated.   So, as the income of the
Irish See in question was very small, and his followers corre-
spondingly so, Dr. Bale thought it prudent to turn his steps
homewards, more especially when his family increased and his
wife anxiously desired preferment for him in England.

His language was often unusually coarse, as will be seen from
the specimens of it now to be given.   He deals with the most
sacred subjects in a spirit of virulence [1] and buffoonery—a spirit
perfectly in harmony with certain of the doings of his allies and
himself, but very much out of place in a minister of religion.
He writes of the Catholic sacraments and sacred rites of the
Universal Church in language so frightful, that many will find it
difficult to believe that the profane author of such sentiments
was in his right mind; while modern Anglicans may feel a little
ashamed of owning him as a successor of the apostles.   His
contemporaries, however, were well enough pleased with him,
and his writings do not appear to be out of harmony with the
official "Homilies" which had been recently issued.   For
Parker secured him the place of a prebendary at Canterbury;
consulted him on several occasions, and sometimes used his
services in preaching, confirming, and visiting certain churches
in the diocese.

The following are his sentiments concerning priestly ordination and the Sacrament of the Eucharist:—

Dorothy.   As regards his perversion, Bishop Nicholson remarks that "his
wife seems to have had a great hand in that happy work."   He was
patronised by Cromwell and Cranmer, and subsequently by Queen Elizabeth
and Matthew Parker.   Bale died, under Parker's rule and patronage, Prebendary of Canterbury, and was buried there in 1563.   Though more coarse
in his language than some others of the Reformers, he was a fair and faithful
specimen of an outspoken and consistent Reformation prelate.   It is only
just to the late Rev. Henry Christmas, D.C.L., to note that, when re-editing
Bale's Works for the Parker Society, he left his conviction on record that
certain of them "could not with propriety be presented to the public."

[1] Pilkington of Durham was sometimes equally virulent:—"I will show
you what is written in the life and history of Thomas Becket, Bishop of
Canterbury, their stinking martyr and traitor to his prince."—Pilkington's
Works, p. 589, Parker Society's Works.   London, 1842.

THE NEW AND DANGEROUS OPINIONS.

"As touching the priests' consecration, which is such a charm of enchant-
ment which may not be done but by an oiled officer of the Pope's generation ;
. . . for in all the Bible it is not that any man can make a dry wafer-cake a
new Saviour, a new Redeemer, a new Christ, or a new God : no, though he
should utter all the words and Scriptures therein."[1]

Of the same adorable sacrament this impious "Reformer"
likewise writes—

The mass "serveth all witches in their witchery, all sorcerers, charmers,
enchanters, dreamers, soothsayers, necromancers, conjurors, cross-diggers,
devil-raisers, miracle-doers, dog-leeches, and bawds ; for without a mass
they cannot well work their feats."[2]

The old clergy, legitimate successors of Saint Augustine, Saint
Anselm, and William of Wykeham, he calls, "puffed-up porklings
of the Pope ;"[3] and again writes—

"These were the idle priests at London and their beastly ignorant broods,
with old superstitious bawds and brothels, the Pope's blind cattle."

Of preaching clergy of the old order of things he is equally
abusive—

"Let beastly blind babblers and bawds, with their charming chaplains,
then, prate at large out of their malicious spirit and idle brains."[4]

The Church Universal is—

"The madam of mischief and proud synagogue of Satan."

And the Catholic bishops are—

"Those two-horned whoremongers, those conjurors of Egypt, and lecherous
locusts, leaping out of the smoke of the pit bottomless."[5]

The "communion of saints," according to this apostate
Carmelite, is the—

"Proud synagogue of Satan, with gold, silver, pearl, precious stones,
velvets, silks, mitres, copes, crosses, cruets, ceremonies, censurings, blessings,
babblings, brawlings, processions, puppets, and such other mad masteries
(whereof the Church that Christ left here behind Him knew not one jot), to
provoke the carnal idiots to her whoredom in the spirit."[6]

---

[1] *Works of Bishop Bale*, pp. 232, 233, Parker Society's Publications.
London, 1849.
[2] *Ibid.* p. 236.   [3] *Ibid.* pp. 242 and 249.   [4] *Ibid.* p. 245.
[5] *Ibid.* p. 259.   He may be fairly matched by Dr. Walter Haddon, in his
reply to Jerome Osorius, a Portuguese, who wrote thus of the outcast English
monks and nuns—"It was provided by laws that the sows should not again
wallow in such filthy mire."—Strype's *Annals*, vol. i. part ii. p. 74.   Oxford,
1824.
[6] *Ibid.* pp. 259, 260.

No fanatic who ever put pen to paper could possibly outstrip in coarseness the following episcopal blasphemy; never repudiated by any authority in the new Church, and recently republished for the edification of those who are charmed with, and attracted towards, Bale's religion.

"Who ever heard of so great a wonder that a dry cake should become a God to be worshipped? . . . they will take upon them to create (Him) every day afresh, and when their old God stinketh in the box, remove Him out of the way, and put a new in His room." [1]

Finally, for it is impossible to quote much which he wrote, and which his modern admirers have thought it decent to reproduce, he declares, in language borrowed from the Apocalypse and most blasphemously misapplied, that the Catholic Church is a "great whore," "a stinking strumpet." [2]   "She is," he goes on to maintain, "in like case flourishingly decked with gold, precious stones, and pearls, not only in her manifold kinds of ornaments, as in her copes, corporasses, [3] chasubles, tunicles, stoles, fanons, and mitres, but also in mystery of counterfeit godliness."   "Their shavelings of prodigious beastliness in lecherous living [live], under the colour of chastity." [4]

The bishops, as cannot fail to be remarked, were all most obsequious and obedient to the queen; [5] and at all times dutifully and faithfully regarded the Crown as the source of all their authority and the fountain of their jurisdiction, as Parliament had decreed.   They thus most thoroughly understood their true position, frankly accepted it, and do not appear to have ever desired any change; save, of course, that all of them looked to become archbishops (it was only in human nature to do so), while the Archbishop of York for the time being, no

---

[1] *Bale's Works*, p. 283.

[2] *Ibid.* p. 494.

[3] The Reformers had always much disliked these.   Bishop Hooper had asked, Anno 1552, "whether the Communion be used in such place and after such sort, as most varieth from, and is most distant from the popish mass, and whether they use any *corporas cloth* in the Communion?"—Hooper's *Interrogatories*.

[4] *Bale's Works*, p. 497.

[5] Bishop Sandys was particularly laudatory of Elizabeth.   Here are his words:—"Did God ever bless the throne of any man as He hath done the royal seat of His anointed this day?   Hath the like ever been heard of in any nation to that which in ours is seen?   Our Deborah hath mightily repressed the rebel Jaben; our Judith hath beheaded Holofernes, the sworn enemy of Christianity; our Hester hath hanged up that Haman which sought to bring both us and our children into miserable servitude."—*Sandys' Works*, p. 81.   Parker Society.   London, 1842.

doubt, expected in due course to be translated to Canterbury. Their new Oath of Homage, taken by each one and every one on his knees before Her Highness, has already been referred to. It behoved them, therefore, never to forget her to whom they owed all that they were, or might be, in dignity, rank, office, and state—the queen. On the whole, it must be ungrudgingly admitted that their memories were tolerably faithful, and did not often fail.

As examples of their profound subservience to the Supreme Governess, it may be here recorded that Parker and Grindal, in 1561, humbly approached the queen, for letters " to authorise the now Bishop of Hereford to visit the same church from time to time as occasion shall serve." [1]

Thus none of them presumed to do anything whatsoever which involved the exercise of jurisdiction, without having first sought permission from the only person in whom it was now supposed to be vested.

Three years later, that is, in March 1564, the queen issued a dispensation,[2] on the humble petition of the Warden of Winchester College, abolishing Wednesday as a fast day in that venerable institution; for with Her Majesty it now lay to undertake all which the Chief Bishop of Christendom, since the days of St. Augustine, had by right of his office and dignity hitherto done for this island. She could grant licences, dispensations, and graces; for, to quote the Bidding-Prayer, she was "in all causes, and over all persons, both civil and ecclesiastical, in these her dominions, supreme."

When, therefore, some years afterwards, Grindal, who had so faithfully proclaimed the "principles of the Reformation," resigned his archbishoprick, A.D. 1583, he probably resigned it into the hands of the queen, the fountain of spiritual authority in the New Church, as the following extract from his formal instrument declares:—"Purè, spontè, simpliciter, et absolutè, in manus excellentissimæ ac illustrissimæ in Christo principis et Dominæ, Elizabethæ, Dei gratiâ Angliæ, Franciæ et Hiberniæ Reginæ, etc., cujus singulari favore et benignitate dictum archiepiscopatum consecutus sum, resigno." Between himself and his spiritual Master, Jesus Christ, there only stood one person, and that person was Queen Elizabeth.

Some idea in detail of the state of the various dioceses of England at different periods during Elizabeth's reign [3] must now

---

[1] 13th March 1561.—State Paper Office.
[2] Parker MSS., C.C.C. Camb., No. cxiv. p. 547.
[3] In 1571 there was a Communion only once a quarter in every parish church,

be given from the words of her new prelates themselves, and others, otherwise the Pope's action might appear too severe.   As regards that of Durham, in the north, let Dr. Pilkington in a plain-spoken letter to the Archbishop of Canterbury first tell his own story :—

"It is too lamentable," he writes, concerning one of his chief towns, Blackburn, "to see and hear how negligently they say any service there, and how seldom. . . . The old Vicar of Blackburn, Roger Linney, resigned for a pension, and now, A.D. 1564, Whalley has as evil a vicar as the worst ; and there is one come thither that has been deprived, and changes his name, and now teaches school there, of evil to make them worse." [1]

Archbishop Parker, in writing to Lord Burghley, gave a terrible account of the state of Norwich Cathedral, in the east of England.   The diocese appears to have been equally bad ; [2] and the same is supported by local records.   The choir was an utter desolation.   It had long ago been cleared of everything valuable — ornaments, service-books, lamps, vestments, and tapestry.   The rain came in from the roof, partly stripped of its lead, and the walls were sodden ; the pictured glass of the windows broken, so that the wind whistled round transepts, ambulatory, and chapels ; the font was thrown down ; the monuments in the various chantries were in course of destruction. "The church is miserable," are the archbishop's exact words. It "hath but six prebendaries ; and but one of them at home, both needy and poor, of which some of those six I know to be Puritans.   Chapman of late displaced by the Bishop of Lincoln ; Johnson cocking abroad, with his four several prebends (as they say) in new-erected churches, both against statute and his oath.'

with a sermon an hour long.   For servants and officers it began at five o'clock in the morning, and ended at eight ; for masters, gentry, and dames, another commenced at nine, with a like sermon to end at twelve.   "The people," as may be read, "do orderly arise from their pews, and so pass to the Communion Table, where they receive the Sacrament ; and from thence in like order to their place ; having all this time a minister in the pulpit, reading unto them comfortable Scriptures of the Passion or other pertaining to the matter in hand."—Strype's *Annals*, vol. ii. part i. pp. 134, 135. Oxford, 1834.

[1] Parker MSS., C. C. Coll., Camb., No. cxiv. p. 519.

[2] One Mr. Nesse, of the diocese of Norwich, caused his bishop some vexation.   He was reported to be of "troublesome and disordered behaviour." So the bishop rebuked him in a letter dated February 25th, 1572, and threatened him with legal process if he did not mend his manners.   He had been for some time a great preacher of the new evangel, but now the bishop looks upon him as "slanderous" ; because he would not marry, but "frequented a suspected house."

There was no daily service, either in cathedral or parochial church : a mere "reader" read out matins and evensong once a week, and kept the parish registers.[1] Communion was celebrated only three times a year; no sermon at the period of Parker's complaint had been preached in the cathedral for nine months previously, and none of the people of the city apparently cared to attend [2] for "the common prayer sayd only on the Sundaies." The prebendaries, with a single exception, were away, their houses dilapidated; the deanery of Norwich was vacant.   Of the late dean of the cathedral and of the bishop of the diocese, Parker indirectly and vaguely, but forcibly remarked : " I have been of late shamefully deceived by some young men, and so have I been by some older men." [3]

At St. Saviour's Church in that city, all organs and singing having been abolished, and the minister having taken to reading the Sunday prayers from a new pulpit in the nave,—as Parkhurst had enjoined,—some of the parishioners were exceedingly displeased.   One, Thomas Lynn,[4] so far resented this innovation, that he appeared in the church with some "cunning queristers," as some say—or with "three or four lewd boys, set on by some lewder persons," as they were described by others ; and when the parson facing the people preached the *Magnificat* like a sermon, they, on their part, "chaunted it out loudlie, after the auncient mode."

The bishop, John Parkhurst, was a strong and irreverent Puritan ; and seems to have been always on the side of the Protestant innovators.   Anything approaching to what he impiously called "the clouted popish mass" his unrighteous soul abhorred.   When the tressels and Communion board were brought down for "the Lord's Supper," he forbade its being decked like an altar ; or the retention of any rites by the presiding minister, which might in any way recall the ancient

---

[1] The readers, formally set apart, in some way or another, but by no public, authorised, and legal form, " were not to preach, administer the Sacrament of the Lord's Supper, nor baptize; but to read the Common Prayers and keep the registers.   They were taken out of the laity, tradesmen or others ; any that was of sober conversation and honest behaviour, and that could read and write."—Strype's *Annals*, vol. i. p. 516.   Oxford, 1824.

[2] The cathedral was not singular in this respect, for it is on record that " many were now departed from the communion of the church, and came no more to hear divine service in the parish churches, nor received the Holy Sacrament according to the law of the realm.   This was especially taken notice of in the diocese of Norwich."—Strype's *Annals*, vol. ii. part i. p. 161. Oxford, 1824.

[3] Lansdowne MSS., British Museum, No. xvii. folio 58.

[4] Strype's *Annals*, vol. ii. part i. p. 328.   Oxford, 1824.

Sacrifice.[1] The sign of the cross he also forbade, as well as any washing of the Communion cup after its use. If any minister went forth for a perambulation at Rogation-tide, he was to go without surplice, and not to stop at any wayside cross. Nor was any banner to be carried. On taking possession of his episcopal seat, he apparently allowed any one who, in his own estimation, could preach and proclaim the new gospel — though "not bred to learning," a trader, or even a husbandman—to officiate in the parish churches of his diocese. Fanaticism, ignorance, and presumption were, with him, sure tokens of election and grace. At Cotessey, near Norwich, a "love-feast" was held in the chancel, the Communion board of which served as the table for the profane entertainment, round which the elect sat—an entertainment which ended in scandals too shocking for any detailed description.[2]

In the city of Norwich the Calvinists and Zwinglians from Flanders had a church apportioned to them, and Parkhurst took them under his protection. The three ministers were named Anthonius, Theophilus, and Isbrandus. Neither was superior to the other two, yet in controversy each wanted to have the first word, the last retort, and the final triumph. They quarrelled violently, and their respective adherents came to blows. "Falling in their sermons upon particular doctrines controverted amongst themselves [they] preached so earnestly in answers and confutations one of another, that the congregation was all in confusion, and the peace of the church broken up."[3] When the bishop interfered they would not obey, laughing him to scorn, and openly defying his authority.

It will cause no surprise, therefore, that Sir William Cecil, when writing to Parker on the 12th of August 1561, declared that "the Bishop of Norwich is blamed even of the best sort for his remissness in ordering his clergy. He winketh at schismatics and Anabaptists, as I am informed. Surely I see great

---

[1] These were the bishop's express and formal directions:—"*Item*, that they neither suffer the Lorde's Table to be hanged and decked like an aulter, neyther use any gestures of the popish masse in the time of ministracion of the Communion, as shifting of the booke, washing, breathing, crossing, or such-like."—Injunctions of John Parkhurst, Bishop of Norwich, A.D. 1561. And, again, eight years later:—"At such times as ye shall use the perambulation in the *Rogation* dayes for the boundes of your parish, you shall not use any surplas uppon you, or stay at any crosse, or suffer any banners to be carried, or other superstition to be used."—Injunctions of Bishop John Parkhurst. A.D. 1569. London, John Walley.

[2] MS. letter in the possession of the author from the collections of the Very Rev. F. C. Husenbeth, D.D.

[3] Strype's *Annals*, vol. ii. part ii. p. 174. Oxford, 1824.

variety in ministration. A surplice may not be borne here. And the ministers follow the folly of the people, calling it charity to feed their fond humour. Oh! my Lord, what shall become of this time?"[1]

With all such laxity of discipline, however, some hundreds of parishes in the eastern portion of the country remained wholly unserved.

In the year 1563, in the Archdeaconry of Norwich, for example, there were no less than eighty vacant benefices; in the Archdeaconry of Norfolk, one hundred and eighty-two; in the Archdeaconry of Suffolk, one hundred and thirty; in the Archdeaconry of Sudbury, forty-two. In addition to these, there had been a large number of chapels "standing so ruinous a long time, that now they were quite taken down."[2]

In the diocese of Carlisle, to go back again northwards, a similar state of affairs existed. The destroyers had done their work only two well. Every rapacious "reformer" had gained his point. The altars had been overthrown and broken down, the chalices and pixes stolen, either legally or otherwise, and the old religion utterly cast out. No one could be obtained, however, judging from Archbishop Grindal's complaint to Sir William Cecil, to preach the new gospel :—

"The Bishop of Carlisle (John Best) hath often complained to me for want of preachers for his diocese, having no help at all of his cathedral church. Sir Thomas Smith is his dean, occupied in the Queen's Majesty's affairs, as ye know. All his prebendaries . . . are ignorant priests, or old, unlearned monks."[3]

Again, about the year 1565, in the diocese of Bangor, then presided over by Dr. Rowland Meyrick, the new gospel was evidently making but little, if any, progress, and the salutary practice of good works even less. "Many of the churches be utterly closed." "Therein there be neither Word nor Sacraments." The bishop, though a Welshman, was very unpopular, except with the laxest and most immoral of the preachers, for

---

[1] Petyt MSS., No. 47, folio 372, in the Inner Temple. In Parkhurst's Visitation Articles for 1561, under the head of "The People and theyr Duetie," he seems active enough against the innovators, and asks "whether any man is known to have said or heard masse, sithens it was abrogate by lawe; and whether any man maketh any singing cakes to say masse withal, reserveth vestments, superaltaries, masse-bookes, or other instruments of this supersticion?"—*Injunctions.* Printed by John Day, 1561.

[2] Strype's *Annals,* vol. i. p. 539. Oxford, 1824.

[3] Lansdowne MSS., British Museum, No. vi. folio 86. Grindal to Cecil, 27th December 1563.

he seems to have been sorely intent on both contemplating and grasping things temporal. For spiritual concerns he showed but little interest. He is reported to have been cringing and abject to his superiors, always lazy and indolent in himself, and most pompous, overbearing, and tyrannical to those beneath him. His lordship was evidently more indebted to the new religion than the new religion was to him. This diocese, it is put on record, is "much out of order," "having no preaching there, and pensionary concubinage openly continued." [1]

Nor was the extensive diocese of Lichfield apparently more favoured. It suffered, as the bishop himself admitted, "lamentable inconveniences growing to the Church of God by the insufficient ministry." [2] The new gospel, which the old clergy secretly hated and despised, had not as yet shed many blessings upon the cruelly-robbed people in that part of the queen's dominion, nor could the religious state of the diocese compare with what it had been in the previous century.

On June 11, 1581, Dr. William Overton, Bishop of that See, had, he asserted in writing, the stubbornest diocese in all this land, and a clergy the most unwilling to show themselves ready and dutiful in any good service, specially if it touched their purse. [3]

The chief church of Coventry had been long ago efficiently "reformed." The "robbers of churches" had gathered in bands and flocks, and had there left little worth taking. Some writers have laid this and similar acts of destruction to the charge of those who, in the succeeding century, sided with the usurping ruffian Oliver Cromwell. But it was certainly effected under Edward VI. and Elizabeth. Everything of great value in the shape of gold or silver plate, jewels, MSS., and rich vestments, had long ago vanished under the rule of Protector Somerset. The vessels of latten, brass, and white metal—all savouring of superstition—had already been devoutly stolen, so that no one might henceforth sin by using them. Several of the bells and much of the lead had been removed. The rafters and roof-boards of aisles and chantries had rotted; rain sometimes poured in on to the pavements; in the spring, birds built their nests above the wall-plates; in the winter, the aisles and side chapel-floors were flooded with water; while green lichen and weeds

---

[1] Lansdowne MSS. British Museum, No. viii. folio 78.

[2] "To help the lamentable inconveniences growing to the Church of God by the insufficient ministry, they are not only to be sifted which are already made ministers, but also a diligent care and foresight is to be used that only sufficient men be admitted to that function hereafter."—Certain "Advertisements," by William Overton, Bishop of Coventry, A.D. 1584.

[3] *Vide State Papers, Domestic, Elizabeth,* vol. cxlix. p. 18.

soon grew luxuriantly on their walls. Certain of the chapels were thus partially roofless. Yet even then some adventurous gospeller with a sham commission, a mere poor gleaner in a harvest-field once rich, came and stole all the remaining brass.[1]

A few words may now be written as to the diocese of Oxford, one of the new Sees. Henry VIII. had intended to have had it styled the "Bishoprick of Osney and Thame," after two important religious houses in Oxfordshire which had been suppressed. But the abbey churches of Osney and Thame were soon both destroyed; while the parish church of Thame, though of prebendal rank, and a cruciform and dignified building of considerable size for its purpose, was inadequate. So, in 1546, the bishoprick had a seat appointed to it in the priory church of St. Frideswide, now Christ Church, Oxford. From the death of Robert King, who for some time had been Abbot of Thame, with the title of Bishop of Rheon, and was one of the suffragans of the Bishop of Lincoln, a death which had taken place in the last year of Queen Mary's reign, until the year 1567, the See of Oxford had been kept vacant; so that its revenues might be utilised in serving the queen's friends or bribing her enemies. On the 14th of October of the last-named year, Dr. Hugh Curwen, sometime Archbishop of Dublin, who, like other of the Protestant prelates, had not been at all appreciated in Ireland, was appointed to the See of Oxford; but he died within a year of his enthronisation. It then remained unfilled for the long period of nearly twenty-one years, when Dr. John Underhill was consecrated on the 14th of December 1589. The poverty of this See of Oxford; the actual difficulty of living; the misery of many of the burdened clergy; the notable fact that more than one hundred and ninety benefices had been unserved for nearly a quarter of a century, and that the country people, some not baptized, were untaught, unfed, and often buried without Christian rites, depressed his lordship so seriously that, within two years and a half, in a state of incurable melancholy, he took to his bed, and passed to his final account. So that the episcopal seat in this new cathedral of Our Blessed Lady and St. Frideswide was filled for little more than three out of forty-six years. The Spiritual Governess had given its lands and

---

[1] "The pavement of Coventry Church is almost all tombstones, and some very ancient. But there came in a zealous fellow, with a counterfeit commission, that, for avoiding of superstition, hath not left one pennyworth, nor one pennybreadth, of brass upon the tombs of all the inscriptions, which had been many and costly."—*Brief View of the State of the Church*, by Sir John Harington, p. 85. London, 1653.

revenues to her favourite, the Earl of Leicester; after whose death, Lord Essex, another favourite secured them for himself. Both these noblemen so spoiled and wasted them, that there was nothing left to later bishops but impropriations and a dilapidated mansion in St. Aldate's, at Oxford.   So devastated was this and other new Sees, in truth, that the bishops were actually obliged to solicit pecuniary aid from the rectors and vicars of their respective dioceses to enable them to furnish their episcopal residences.

Within a single century of Queen Elizabeth's death, those who admire her vigorous policy will learn with satisfaction and thankfulness that, whether true or false, good or bad, the old religion had been thereabouts almost entirely rooted and stamped out. Judging from a "Return of the Popish Recusants for the County and City of Oxford" made in 1706,[1] they might then be easily numbered.   A mere handful, no one could pretend to fear them. Mr. Nathaniel Bevan, Vicar of North Aston, officially reported that one Sutton, "supposed to be the priest," "reads mass in my parish most Sundays and holidays."   At Somerton, twenty-seven persons remained, of whom the vicar wrote: "We have probable grounds to believe that they meet sometimes for their service in a house in the parish; but they are civil, quiet, and peaceable."   At Whitchurch there was only one—Esquire Hyde. At another parish there were "two old women only."   At North Leigh, near Blenheim Park, "Mary Morris, wife of a day labourer," was the sole representative of the religion of William of Wykeham.   At Burford, "Elizabeth Haines, a poor sojourner; no other."   At Checkendon, there was a family of the name of Grimsditch who were Catholics.   At Sandford, Esquire Powell and his dependents likewise clung to the ancient faith, as did the Earl and Countess of Kildare at Caversham, together with the knightly family of the Curzons of Waterperry, and a few more.   However persons may shrink from approving the policy of Elizabeth's advisers, they cannot deny that, by the aid of fine, imprisonment, knife, halter, and torture-chamber, it thus turned out a complete and triumphant success; for the solitude had been made, the peace was secured.   With some persons, the selfish and the shallow, success is a certain test of truth.

The actual state of affairs in the diocese of St. David's likewise may be tolerably well gleaned from certain "Injunctions to be observed and kept,"[2] issued to the clergy of his diocese by

[1] To be seen in the Diocesan Registry at Oxford.
[2] The original of these, printed in 1583, can be seen in a large and curious collection of such documents in the Bodleian Library at Oxford.

Middleton, Bishop of that See, in 1583. Judging them from a Christian stand-point, it is not easy to determine whether their heresy or profanity be their most notable feature.

This man, Marmaduke Middleton, a person remarkable for nothing in particular, had been made Bishop of Waterford, in Ireland, in 1579, by Letters Patent. No canonical election had ever taken place, and there seems to be some doubt whether he had ever received episcopal consecration of any sort or kind.[1] Four years afterwards, like other Protestant prelates, who had laboured in vain, if they had laboured at all, he found that Ireland was no fitting place for him, as the "gospel" he proclaimed was there repudiated with scorn; so, after the death of Richard Davies, Bishop of St. David's, on November 7, 1581, he begged for that vacated See, and in the following year, with Burghley's sanction, was appointed to it. Within twelve months he issued a large series of Visitation Articles, or Injunctions, from which much exact information may be gained as to his actual goings-on. He persecuted with vigour those who clung to the old faith; he was a profound, intelligent, and obsequious Erastian; he destroyed several churches and built none; and at the end of ten years was called to his account.

These "Injunctions" are worthy of careful study. They contain his lordship's sage and mature directions, and as must be allowed, are quite free from any taint of superstition. In the administration of the Sacrament of Baptism, trine immersion and trine affusion were each distinctly forbidden by them. No chrisom-cloth was to be used; the godfathers were not allowed to touch the child's head as heretofore; for Bishop Middleton, as he was careful to explain, discountenanced the ancient but erroneous idea that there was any "virtue or hidden mystery" in baptism; and desired, as a godly exercise, in the new method of baptizing, that all young sponsors should "saie the whole Catechisme," and "make an open confession at the font of the articles of their faith," before assuming that office and duty. Lay baptism he distinctly disallowed.

All the old ceremonies of the mass, and especially consecration, were likewise deliberately forbidden. The minister was neither to handle, bless, lift up, consecrate, nor show to the people, the bread and wine, but to "let it lie upon the table until the distribution thereof." He was to act exactly "accord-

---

[1] It is only fair to the late Archdeacon Cotton to state that he believed himself to be in possession of indirect evidence of Middleton's consecration. See also on the other side, *The Episcopal Succession, etc.*, by Dr. Maziere Brady, vol. i. p. 351. Rome, 1876.

ing to the orders of the Book [of Common Prayer] without any
addition or detraction." In this, of course, the manual actions
had been deliberately omitted.[1]   No one was under any circumstances to remain either in church or chancel unless an actual
communicant, prepared then and there to communicate ; for this
likewise savoured of the "abominable and vain" custom of
hearing mass ; and if any stubborn or obstinate person kneeling
on his knees, knocking his breast, or devoutly saying his prayers,
proposed to remain, and would not depart when quietly ordered
out of church, the presiding minister was, with no consideration for
the expectant or the hungry, to stop the whole proceedings at once
without further ado, and then summon the "troubler of God's
divine service"—the ignorant person who, believing in the efficacy
of prayer, prayed—before the judge of the local Consistory Court.

The officiating parson himself was enjoined to stand always in
the "bodie of the church, or in the lower end of the chancel,
with his face invariably turned unto the people." Turnings
about were solemnly discountenanced. The use of a low voice
or mumbling, as it was contemptuously called, was expressly
forbidden. The "mass-mongers" had mumbled ; so by way of
contrast the minister was expected to bellow or bawl. He was
to use a loud voice, or as loud as he could make it,—for "faith
cometh by hearing,"[2] and never to go near the Communion
board unless there was an actual Communion ; for such custom,
to use the bishop's own profane language, "doth retain a
memorie of the idolatrous masse."[3]   To avoid even the appearance of anything so heinous during the ante-Communion service,
he was to stand in his own seat or pulpit and nowhere else,
"with his face turned down towards the people ;" and he was,
moreover, to take special care that the board and tressels
remained wholly unadorned, in their plain and severe simplicity.
No linen cloth[4] was to be laid upon the Communion Table, and
no other covering ordinarily ; and, when the tressels and board
were done with, when the ante-Communion prayers were ended,

---

[1] This omission, perfectly intentional, was entirely in harmony with the
opinions of Elizabeth's bishops, who had adopted the Second Prayer-Book.

[2] This text was actually quoted as a justification for shouting out the
prayers.

[3] This custom was almost universal throughout England up to the period
of the commencement of the Oxford movement, except perhaps in cathedrals
and colleges. Thus chancels, when large and long, often stood disused and
deserted.

[4] "No linen cloths called altar cloths, and before used about masses, be
laid upon the Communion Table, but that new be provided."—Grindal's
Register, *sub anno* 1572.

or when the sacred meal was over, they were to be removed "to the upper end of the raised chauncell."

Again, when any woman gave thanks to God for her safe delivery, neither she, when making her offering, nor the midwife who accompanied her, were "to kiss the Communion boarde," a very old Catholic custom, common in many parts of England, of old; and almost universal abroad.

As regards ceremonials at funerals, those expressive rites which the Church of God had ever made so solemn and hallowing, blessing and benefiting all who took part in them, no hand-bell was henceforth to be rung throughout the diocese of St. David, no oblations were to be offered, "no prayers for the dead were to be made"—the exact words of this episcopal heretic are quoted—"either in the house or upon the way, or elsewhere": practices which, it appears, had been too frequently and universally tolerated by the clergy of this diocese up to the time of Middleton's unwelcome arrival. Month's-minds or year's-minds were absolutely prohibited. All "popish superstition" was to be given up. A practice of the communion of saints was thus authoritatively forbidden and cast out. Again, if strange ministers came to pay their respects to the memory of any departed Welshman, they were not to array themselves in rochets or surplices, nor to carry lighted candles or torches, nor to place any wax tapers on or near the corpse whilst it was in the church. If they prayed at all, they were to pray not for the person departed but for themselves, a form of selfishness peculiarly repulsive on such an occasion. A short peal was to be rung both before and after the funeral; and then the people were to depart without adding any ancient Catholic prayers of their own, or anything which resembled them. Wooden crosses were not to be erected, as had been so long the custom, and was common, where the corpse had rested on its way to its last earthly home; while the putting-up of "crosses of wood" in the churchyard "upon or about the grave" was also distinctly forbidden. Hence, until quite recent times, no cross was ever found placed at the head of a grave. Almost all churchyard crosses were broken, though sometimes the shaft remained.

Moreover (and here the actual words are quoted), "Images, pictures, and al monuments of fained miracles, as well in walles, as in glasse windowes [shall] be defaced; and namely [*i.e.* particularly] the Image of the Crucifixe[1] and the two Maries in the

---

[1] It has always seemed to the author quite an incomprehensible mystery why these "Reformers" displayed so satanic a hatred of the crucifix and of representations of the crucifixion.

chauncell windowes." Pictures of the queen herself, together with gorgeous representations of Her Majesty's heraldric achievement, were alone allowed by way of internal decorations. Later on, when Christian sacraments had been dragged down to the level of Jewish types of the same, representations of Moses and Aaron were admitted. All rood-screens likewise were to be pulled down.

With regard to questions of living, morals, and theological duties, it was enjoined that those ministers who had previously kept inns, taverns, or "victuallying houses" were to give them up, learn to read better and more intelligibly, and stick to the study of Bullinger's "Decades" or the published "Homilies," which were so plain spoken, spirited, and impressive. Nor were these ministerial worthies, who, never having themselves learnt, were now commissioned to teach, ever to play at dice, cards, tables, or bowls. Four times a year, with a loud voice and in an impressive manner, they were to read out in church the "Queen's Majestie's Injunctions." They were, furthermore, to possess no books of divinity except such as had been specially recommended and approved by their bishop; nor was any man to have two wives, or any woman to have two husbands—one of his lordship's most practical and important provisions—for gross looseness of morals had too speedily followed upon misbelief and grave laxity of doctrine.

From Wales let us now pass to Lincolnshire, the chief part of one of the most important dioceses of England.

The old diocese of Lincoln, then as now, embraced more than one county and a large tract of land, perhaps but sparsely populated. It took in the whole of the central part of eastern England, from Barton-upon-Humber and Great Grimsby in the north, to Crowland and Market Deeping in the south, with the Isle of Axholme and the county of Nottingham. As early as the reign of William Rufus, St. Remigius, the devoted Bishop of Dorchester-upon-Thame, in Oxfordshire, had, for good and sufficient reasons, removed his See from a sacred spot, well wooded and watered, where the junction of two ancient rivers is made, to a fortified place in the north-east—the present ancient and interesting city of Lincoln. St. Hugh the Carthusian, and Alexander the Munificent, by their charitable labours, had each left their impress upon the devout and reverent people under them; while those parts of Oxfordshire and Buckinghamshire which in previous generations had perhaps owned Dorchester as their mother Church henceforth turned to the important See of Lincoln, as a child turns to its parent, for guidance and aid.

The city itself must have been once fair and beautiful in the sight of God and the holy angels; for there, independent of the glorious and richly-furnished cathedral of Our Lady and St. Hugh, which towered over weald and wold, no less than fifty-two parish churches,[1] with all their efficient machinery,—their rich altars and lighted lamps, their means of grace for the unregenerate, and their angel's food for the pious wayfarer,—stood around and about that majestic sanctuary, calling people by open door and pleasant chime to worship and prayer, and silently reminding them ever of the unseen world, its beauty and its peace.

Throughout the shire, all around, northward, eastward, and westward,—dotted here and there amid clumps of trees, or where willows marked out the tortuous way of some sluggish stream, or nestling under some green slope,—rose spire or tower or stunted bell-cote of many a village fane.   Throughout Lincolnshire, prior to the sixteenth-century changes, no less than a hundred and eight religious houses had long been centres of light and life to a people who appreciated and valued them.   Of these the more celebrated were the abbeys of Barlings and Bardney, Swineshead and Croyland, with the notable priory of Sempringham, where St. Gilbert had so often prayed.

The Knights Templars had owned five houses, which were suppressed and destroyed; while no less than fourteen hospitals, where the corporal works of mercy had long been charitably practised to the great benefit of the poor, shared a similar fate. Those persons who had been subservient to King Henry VIII., those who in the succeeding reign had actively supported Protector Somerset and his policy, and those who later on were secret and sure allies of Cecil and Walsingham, had secured a considerable share of the various spoils.   Such gained a few things here, if they lost more hereafter.   Many ancient families, impoverished by the disastrous Wars of the Roses, to their eternal shame, consented to acquiesce in the unhappy changes carried out, on condition of being allowed to participate in the lands and manors stolen from the religious communities.

Under Edward VI., as is well known, much had been done in many parts of England to strip the parish churches of their ornaments and treasures.   On the 15th of February 1549, Commissioners had been despatched in all directions to find out exactly what still existed of value, and to take inventories of the same.   Two years afterwards, other commissions were issued to do a similar work; and, again, two years later, in May 1553,

---

[1] Now there are but fifteen.

I

a fresh set of inquisitors was sent about to different dioceses
on a like errand.   These Commissioners were even then most
unpopular.

The people in general were Catholic, and saw with horror and
dismay the churches of the Most High plundered, desecrated,
and rendered utterly destitute of any kind of religious worship or
service.[1]   The bells of the churches were never rung; the doors
seldom opened.   Parsonages were in ruins.   It was in vain,
however, at that time that Humphrey Arundell, the valiant
Cornish soldier, rose in defence of the faith, in his wild western
country, and in the name of some hundreds petitioned for an
immediate restoration of the abolished mass; for the ancient
rites and the old religion.   In Berks, Hants, and Oxfordshire[2]
the people likewise rose in a fury to defend their parish churches;
so that the Commissioners on several occasions slunk away in
fear and dismay, terrified at the intensifying opposition.   But a
recent Act against unlawful and rebellious assemblies[3] was
speedily put into operation; and men were thus warned that the
king, their sovereign lord, charged and commanded them to
disperse themselves, and peaceably depart to their habitations
and to their lawful business, under the pains and perils of the
Act.   If more than twelve persons assembled they were liable

---

[1] "Great endeavours were also made in this Synod for the mending the
poor and bare condition of vicarages, many of which were of so small
revenue, that abundance of parishes were utterly destitute of ministers, to
assist the people in their serving of God, and to instruct them in spiritual
knowledge for the edification of their souls. So that there was no small
apprehension that in time a great part of the nation would become pagans.
Besides, to render the condition of small livings more deplorable, the
pensions that were due to religious persons, and allowed them for their lives
when their houses were dissolved, seemed to have been by patrons charged
upon their livings, when themselves ought to have paid them. And
commonly poor ministers, when they came into livings, were burdened with
payment of divers years' tenths and subsidies that were payable by former
incumbents.   There seemed now also to be some that put the queen upon
taking a new survey of all ecclesiastical livings, pretending that thereby the
values of first-fruits and tenths would be considerably advanced to her, to the
further oppression of the needy clergy."—Strype's *Annals*, vol. i. pp. 512, 513.
Oxford, 1824.

[2] In this county the old families of Simeon of Brightwell, Dormer of
Thame and Ascot, Davey of Dorchester, Wolfe of Haseley, Browne (afterwards) baronets of Kiddington, Curzon of Waterperry, Phillips of Thame
and Ickford (Bucks), and many others were warm defenders of the ancient
faith.   At the close of Elizabeth's reign three distinguished priests, Francis
Harcourt, Anthony Greenaway, and Roger Lee, all belonging to knightly
families of Oxfordshire, and all connections of each other, were in the
forefront as regards their prayers and labours for Catholic Christianity.

[3] 3 and 4 Edward VI., cap. 5.

to punishment. Though they demanded a restoration of the old religion of their forefathers, and the rites and ceremonies of bygone times, of which they reasonably enough felt the loss, their demands were not only contemptuously disregarded, but they were at once tried as rebels, soon found guilty, and speedily enough "strung up,"—as the brief and expressive phrase stood,—as a punishment for their inconvenient and fanatical attachment to the ancient faith; and as a warning to others who might be secretly attached to it, that if they ventured actively to resist the innovators in authority they would similarly and sharply suffer.

All this, of course, was well and accurately enough remembered on all sides. The issue was quite evident. Those who lifted up their voices for God and His truth knew plainly enough what they had to expect. The least resistance to constituted authority would at once merit the strictest and severest punishment. Judges and bishops prated about "the law"; while justice was dethroned and true religion was being strangled. And though news travelled slowly in those days, when conveyances were lumbering, bridges few, and roads impassable; yet the Lincolnshire gentlepeople and the sturdy yeoman of the wolds knew too well what lay in store for them, if they should dare to oppose the triumphant policy of Elizabeth's chief advisers. The dark doom of the Abbot of Barlings, in the days of the first pilgrimage of grace, had not been forgotten; for, by the side of many a Lincolnshire hearth, when the days were drawing in, had been frequently recited the vigorous and stirring ballads which so properly commemorated that prelate's strong faith and noble self-sacrifice.

When, therefore, the high-principled adherents of the old religion had been silenced, either by imprisonment, fines, persecution, or expatriation; and when, for the sake of peace and quietness, the weak-kneed and cowardly were quite known to be unlikely to make any resistance; the work of destruction, carefully planned, was most efficiently carried out in the diocese of Lincoln. All the ancient clergy of any note or influence had been put out of the way. Bishop Watson, the chief pastor of that flock, could do little or nothing but pray, and hope for better days; for he was safe and secure in prison. Nicholas Bullingham, one of the ministers who had been present at the inauguration of the new hierarchy, when Matthew Parker was consecrated, had been himself subsequently elevated to the episcopate in the month of January 1560, by Parker and others; and, having by the queen's authority usurped the place of his betters,—come into the fold in fact by some other way,—now ruled at Lincoln, with the sanction and under the special and direct patronage of the Supreme Governess.   If heresy be opposition to the Catholic faith, and sacrilege be sinful, then Bullingham's words and tactics certainly merit an application of those terms to him.   It would be a distasteful word of super-erogation, condemned by the Thirty-nine Articles,[1] to set forth in detail the theological propositions by which Bishop Bulling-ham recommended his new gospel to the acceptance of the Lincolnshire peasantry.   He and Jewell and Bale and Pilking-ton, with Sandys and Grindal, were the burning and shining lights of the new system, and the coarse-languaged evangelists of another gospel.   What took place under his rule in the work of what was styled " Reform " — comprised in a duly-recorded document of melancholy interest—will best be shown and more accurately apprehended than by any study of the " Decades," or by any perusal of his existing manuscript letters.   No more frightful record of deliberate sacrilege and savage profanity could be found, either on parchment or paper, amongst the records of any civilised country.

This work of destruction had been begun in 1566, under the special direction of Dr. John Aylmer, then Archdeacon of Lincoln, but eleven years afterwards, *i.e.* in 1577, Bishop of London.   The various acts performed were not the result of a sudden burst of maniacal fury, on the part of an ignorant and brutalised populace, maddened by previous sufferings, or spurred on to violence and reprisals by unjust persecution ; but they were deeds done calmly and coolly[2] at the express direction of those who perhaps may have believed themselves in a special manner to have been the living agents of the incarnate Son of God ; and who certainly were the appointed officers of a royal lady who, at

---

[1] See Article xiv. *Of Works of Supererogation.*

[2] Mr. Edward Peacock thus thoughtfully writes :—" It requires an effort to place ourselves, in imagination even, in the same position of affectionate reverence for mere articles of furniture—silk and gold, brass and stone—as our forefathers ; but let us remember that the vestments thus wantonly cut up into hosen and cushions, or made into costumes for strolling players, were the solemnly blessed garments in which they had seen their priests celebrate the Great Sacrifice of the Catholic Church ; that the altar slabs thus used as fire-backs and bridges had been dedicated by episcopal unction and the relics of the saints, and had received the far higher consecration of being the appointed place whereon that same sacrifice was consummated ; that the rood was to them the visible representation of their God—of Him who had died for them on Calvary, and who, with hands, feet, and side pierced as they saw Him there, would, as they believed, come ere long in glory and terror to judge the universe.   The bells that profane persons hung to the

her coronation, had openly professed the Catholic religion, received the Sacrament of the Altar under one kind, and who had then solemnly pledged herself in the face of the nation to maintain the ancient faith.

The destruction and desolation thus caused by authority, carried out in cold blood, with preparation, resolution, and success, can now scarcely be imagined; nor, from a religious point of view, can the dead and miserable state of affairs, which speedily ensued be easily conceived. What had taken place in the diocese of Lincoln, so far as regards about a hundred and fifty parish churches, can still, however, be tolerably well realised from the careful study of a volume[1] edited with care and judgment by a very competent hand, and which is mainly the reprint of an original "Inventory of the Monuments of Superstition," the document referred to, preserved amongst the miscellaneous papers of the Episcopal Registry at Lincoln,—with interesting and copious footnotes and most valuable appendices added.

It was not enough, as the manuscript in question so plainly shows, that the altars were ordered to be utterly taken down and destroyed,—which was done to the dismay and amazement of a large majority of the people, who were awestruck by the punishment with which those were threatened who actively interfered in behalf of the ancient rites,—but the sacred cross-marked slabs, which had been duly blessed in God's name, with consecrated chrism, were to be purposely and deliberately profaned. To lay them down in the church porch or middle aisle, so that the people on entering were compelled to tread upon them, was not, in Archdeacon Aylmer's opinion, a use sufficiently "common" or profane; so certain of them were sometimes placed as steps leading to the nearest pig-stye, or even put to a more infamous and disgusting use—too disgusting to refer to more particularly: and this under the direct official authority of the Primate of

harness of their horses had been borne before the priest through many a crowd of kneeling villagers when the Blessed Sacrament was carried from its resting-place over the altar to the bedside of the sick and the dying. The banners, the hearse, the lights, and almost every article of the Church's furniture, were connected in their minds with the solemn funeral services, which, in their plaintive melody, show forth more fully than anything else that is left to us the wistful longing of the faithful here for the kingdom where sickness and death, marrying and giving in marriage, and all other sorrows and joys of this phenomenal existence, shall have passed away."—*English Church Furniture, etc.*, edited by E. Peacock, F.S.A., pp. 21, 22. London, 1866.

[1] *English Church Furniture, Ornaments, and Decoration at the Period of the Reformation, as exhibited in a List of Goods destroyed in certain Lincolnshire Churches*, A.D. 1566. Edited by Edward Peacock, F.S.A. London, 1866.

England[1] and Dr. Nicholas Bullingham, the intruded "Bishop of Lincoln."

A mere brief abstract, with a few startling examples of what was actually done in detail, must now be set forth with care. For after a study of this, the romance-writers of the Reformation may henceforth write in vain. Most of the recorded inventories are alike, both in form and phraseology; the destruction being systematic and complete. Every trace of the old religion, its mystic sacrifice and solemn rites, was carefully removed; while the language employed, relating to the ancient solemnities and their *ornamenta*, was violent, contemptuous, and coarse, as will be too clearly seen.

At Ashby, near Sleaford,[2] as may be read, the images of the rood were burnt, and the altar-stones used to pave the church. At Aslacbie "the Mass-books, the processioners, the manual, and all such peltrie of the Pope's sinfull service, was made away, torn, and defaced in the second or third year of Our Sovereign Lady that now is." The same was the case at Ashwardbie. Here "all the Mass-books and all books of papistrie were torn in pieces, and sold to pedlars to lap spice in." At Bardney, the old priest, Sir Robert Cambridge, had removed the service-books; but the candlesticks and other ornaments were broken and sold. The altar-stones of the church of Barkeston were put to profane uses, having been laid down in pavement at the town bridge, while the holy-water vat was turned into a vessel for milk. At Belton, in the Isle of Axholme, a representation in alabaster of All Saints, with "divers other idolls," were cut in pieces, burnt, and defaced. What the churchwardens profanely call "a sepulchre, with little Jack,"—*i.e.* the Blessed Sacrament,—had been smashed a year ago, "but little Jack was broken in peces this yeare by the said churchwardens." Here, too, the altar cloths were said to be "rotting in pieces in the bottom of a cheste." At Bichfield, the torn-down altar-stones had been placed on Broad Bridge to bear up the bank. At Billingborough, the churchwardens certified to Bishop Bullingham that "all the trumpery and popish ornaments were sold and defaced, so that there remaineth no superstitious monument within our parish church." The sacring-bell of Burton Coggles Church had been given to William Eland, who contemptuously hung it by his horse's ear. At Bomnbie, the pix had been used for a salt-cellar;

---

[1] "The churchwardens shall see that the altar-stones be broken, defaced, and *bestowed to some common use.*"—*Injunctions of Edmund Grindal*, 1571. London : William Serres.

[2] For details, see pp. 29–171 of Mr. Peacock's important volume.

while at Botheby, when Archdeacon Aylmer held his visitation, the rood-loft had been sold to one Richard Longland, church-warden, who made a bridge of it by which his cattle might reach their pasture. The altar-stone was disposed of to Mr. Francis Pennell, who made a fire-hearth of it. At Braughton two pixes which held the Sacrament had been given as playthings to a child; while at Braunceton the altar-bread box of bone or ivory became the money-box of John Watts. Here Robert Bellamy bought two corporas cases, "whereof his wife made of one a stomacher for her wench," and of the other, when ripped up, a purse. The pix cloth of this parish had been secured by John Storr, whose "wief occupieth yt in wiping her eies." These arrangements were sanctioned at Lincoln by the bishop and others on the 18th of March 1565. At Croxbie, when some plumber was mending the leads of the nave, and needed a fire for his work, the crucifix and the images of Our Lady and St. John were thrown into it and burnt. Of the rood-loft, a Mr. John Sheffield, ancestor of the present Earls of Mulgrave, made a ceiling in his house; and of one of the altar-stones a sink for his kitchen. At Croxton, the tabernacle for the Blessed Sacra-ment was converted by some earnest Reformer into a dresser upon which to set dishes. Of one of the chasubles at Denton, a certain William Green made a velvet doublet; the sepulchre from the chancel John Orson turned into "a presse" for his own clothes. At Dowsbie the churchwardens had secured two suits of vestments, of which they made cushions and bed quilts; while at Durrington it is thus recorded:—"Altar-stones ij—one is broken and paveth the church, and the other is put to keep cattall from the chappall wall; and yet standeth edgewaies on the ground." At Gonwarbie, two copes and two chasubles were sold to a tailor, and a holy-bread basket to a fishmonger "to carrie ffish in;" while at Grantham, St. Wulfran's shrine was sold to a goldsmith, and the proceeds devoted to the purchase of a "sylver Pott, parcell gilt, and an ewer of silver for the mynis-tracion of the holye and most sacred Supper of Oure Lorde Jhesus Crist called the Holye Communyon." Three altar-stones from Habrough Church were first broken, and one of them was then laid in the porch,[1] so that the people should be obliged

---

[1] These pages are being prepared for the press at the little village of Chearsley between Thame and Aylesbury, where the Buckingham family of Francklin were once lords of the manor, and founded a chantry; and I find that one of the altar-stones, with its top downwards, placed as a step at the south porch of the church in Queen Elizabeth's reign, still remains. It measures 4 feet 8 inches by 2 feet 1 inch, is nearly 4 inches thick, and is bevelled round its edge.

to tread upon it on entering; while stepping-stones for man and
dog at the churchyard stile were made of the other two.   The
Vicar of Haconbie must have been a person somewhat deficient
in piety and reverence; for the rood here with Mary and John
were burnt under his direction, as well as an elaborate reredos
of alabaster, "full of images."   The altar candlesticks were also
broken, two purple velvet vestments were cut up and made into
cushions; while the vicar himself was foremost in his energy for
such reform.   Of the tabernacle veil he made a hanging for his
own hall, of two banner cloths he made window-curtains for the
vicarage parlour, and of an altar canopy of velvet he made himself a tester for his bed; where, when awake, he and his lady, by
due contemplation, with their eyes turned upwards, could constantly realise the practical advantages of the "Reformation."
The holy-water stoup this religious and reverent divine deliberately turned into "a swine's troughe."   At Horblinge the MS.
service-books were sold to a mercer, who tore them up to wrap
spice in; the rood-loft to a certain John Craile, who made of it
a weaver's loom; three altar-stones were used for swine troughs
and bridges; while two old vestments were given to Richard
Colson, a scholar, who, it is on record, "haith made a player's
cote thereof."   The altar-stones at Kelbie are "defaced and laid
in high waies and serveth as bridges for sheepe and cattall to go
on; so that there now remaineth no trash nor tromperie."   At
Langtoft, one altar-stone was placed at the bottom of a cistern,
another was used in mending the church wall, and a third inserted
in a fire-hearth.   A bedstead was made out of the rood-loft of
Osbombie by John Audley—a member of an illegitimate branch
of the baronial family of that name.   At Market Raisen the
"rood with Mary and John—with the rest of the idolatrous
images belonging to the abominable mass," had been burnt three
years previously.   The cross cloth of Stallingbrook had been sold
to some strolling players; that at Tallington the churchwarden,
John Wright, took and hung up in his hall; an amice from
Thorpe was given to a poor woman, with which to make a shirt
for her child.   At Thurlby the altar-stones were set up edgeways
to make churchyard stiles.   At Waddingham the banner cloths
and cross cloths were made into coats for the children of
strolling players; while at Welby what is styled the "linen
baggage" was made into shirts and smocks.   The high-altar stone
at Witham had been placed at Mr. Harington's fire-back.   At
Wrought, in the Isle of Axholme, "the rest of such triflinge toyes
and tromperie apppertaininge to the popish masse and popish
prelate was made away and defacid in King Edwarde's time."

In certain of the cases here detailed, no doubt many of the *ornamenta* noted as "stolen" were removed by devout people in the hope of seeing better times and another change, when they would be brought out again for use.[1] Many such, carefully hidden away, have been from time to time discovered. A Lincoln antiquary[2] of taste and repute some years ago gathered a large collection of old vestments and fragments of hangings from different parts of the diocese.

Now, when it is remembered that Bishop Bullingham and Archdeacon Aylmer, under whose authority the frightful deeds thus put on record had been done, were not only perfectly in harmony with Queen Elizabeth, the chief ruler of the Church of England, but entirely at one with their episcopal and archidiaconal brethren of both provinces, it is clear that the work of destruction, carried out in the diocese of Lincoln, was in no manner peculiar; that it did not differ either in method or completeness with the same kind of work done in other dioceses; and that what took place in that of Lincoln, just referred to, was likewise carried out and completed in every other diocese throughout the kingdom. Bishops Pilkington,[3] Sandys, Grindal, Overton, Meyrick, Bale, Bullingham, and Parkhurst were each and all thoroughly agreed in their principles and course of action. In substituting the new religion, which had been set up for the old one which had been deliberately and

[1] Mr. Peacock thus wrote:—"I should not have published it had I not felt that the text illustrated in no ordinary manner the spirit of the Reformation. There is nothing in the annals of the French Revolution more sickening to a Christian man than some of the entries in these pages. I did not point out in my 'Preface,' as I wished to write entirely without partisanship, the fact that from many of the churches (*e.g. Scotton*, p. 135; *Market Raisen*, p. 124, para. 8) things are said to have been 'stolen.' Surely these repeated entries imply that Catholic-minded persons removed the things to keep them from profane hands. I think that in many cases where the vestments are said to have been ripped up for bed-hangings, 'quishinges,' etc., that the persons who did so only made believe to put them to household uses for the sake of saving them. The John Thimbleby (p. 108) 'wat haith defacid' a cope and a vestment was certainly a Roman Catholic. So, I think, were the Ffairfaxes mentioned under Langtoft (p. 111)."—Author's MSS. and Excerpts, "Letter from E. Peacock, Esq., dated 13th September 1866."

[2] The late E. J. Willson, Esq., F.S.A., whose son has inherited the collection.

[3] Whittingham, Dean of Durham, under Pilkington, in his frightful excesses quite equalled the dark deeds of Bullingham and Aylmer; for he made the stone coffins of the priors of Durham, whom he termed "servants of the synagogue of Satan," into swine troughs, and the holy water stoups of brass, which stood within each of the doors of the cathedral, into vessels for ignoble uses in the kitchen of his house.—See Machyn's *Diary*, p. 59, and Anthony à Wood's *Athenæ Oxon.* vol. i. p. 195. London, 1721.

duly abolished by Parliament (the adherents of which were being persecuted and exterminated), were only carrying out the obvious and avowed intentions of those State officials who had placed them in high ecclesiastical positions expressly to carry out the changes and so-called "reforms" resolved upon.

Of course to any English Churchman of the Oxford school, the proceedings in question will no doubt be read with some pain. It is no easy task to show that the revived doctrines and Catholic practices, now so largely current in every diocese of our beloved country, and, many of them, so generally popular, were utterly repudiated by the dismal prelates, whose violent and heretical language is so awful in itself and so disquieting to dwell upon; and whose destructive labours it is so distasteful to put on record. Men, who in a spirit of self-sacrifice now repair churches, cleanse the font, rebuild the broken-down altar of the Lord, beautify His sanctuary, adorn with pictured pane and Mosaic representation the chancel wall,—who open their restored churches for the daily office; who, in the face of secular courts and senseless "judgments," believe in baptismal regeneration, practise confession, pray for the departed, and have been led, step by step, to restore the Christian sacrifice and Eucharistic adoration; and who, furthermore, look upon themselves, now clothed in sacerdotal garments, and standing facing the crucifix at lighted altars, as sacrificing priests of the new law,—can surely have but very little in common with the vulgar anti-Catholic bishops of Queen Elizabeth's day, whose profane and awful words, when read at a distance of three centuries and more, make a reverent person shudder; and the dark record of whose blasphemies and active wickedness, when calmly faced, sends a thrilling shiver through the heart of a Christian, and makes every decent Englishman—unparalysed by indifference and not choked by false Science—blush for shame that such officials ever belonged to so moderate and respectable an institution as the Church of England by law established, now appears.

The change for the better which in several respects has taken place of late years in this communion, as those external to it allow, is, in truth, little short of miraculous. In Queen Elizabeth's reign, the bishops and ministers, having only little to give, of course gave but little. But "to him that hath shall be given." The grace of baptism used aright merits more grace—the gift of contrition and the admitted efficacy of prayer. An imperfect knowledge of the Most High, duly made use of, merits more knowledge. That which is used for God's honour and glory is never squandered, and cannot be altogether lost. Nor are men, after they have known the grace of baptism, what they were before.

In the present day, some Englishmen frequently complain of the policy, principles, and action of the bishops of the Established Church under difficult circumstances, and when dealing with delicate and complex cases ; and ofttimes they complain without just cause ; for, as a rule, those dignified officials are perfectly true to the duties imposed on them, and obedient and faithful to their present Master—the British public.[1]   Too much independence should not be looked for from them.   The water-spring can never rise above its source ; nor, to use another simile, are grapes gathered from thorns.   In the present day Her Most Gracious Majesty's bishops, notwithstanding their extraordinary but precedented Oath of Homage, are obviously far superior in character to those of Elizabeth, the first female Governor of the Church of England ; for they are decorous, moral, and moderate. It is true that they are sometimes more active in defending the temporalties and position of the Establishment than the Creeds which it still professes to maintain ; in other words, some seem to value more highly their temporal than their spiritual trusts— yet they are almost always active, well-informed, worldly-wise, and shrewd.   No bishop of the times in which we live would, for example, think of marrying, or rather of taking into his keeping as mistress, the attractive spouse of a butcher, as did John Poynet ; nor would any modern Archbishop of Canterbury, as did Cranmer,—after the woman in question had obtained a divorce, and the amorous prelate was waiting to welcome her to bed and board,—publicly officiate at the questionable nuptials, and so seal his suffragan's happiness.   Nor, in truth, would a modern Anglican prelate of the exalted rank of Archbishop Sandys put up at an inn during his visitation rounds, and so far forget himself as to allow the wife of the host to be discovered in his sleeping-chamber during the darkness and quiet of midnight. With all their drawbacks and difficulties, therefore, English Churchmen have much for which to be thankful.   What has been already accomplished may be reasonably regarded as an earnest of what it is still possible to labour for, with zeal and credit, and it may be, after all, with success.

---

[1] The reader who is curious to see how gradual, but certain, has been the change from the " Royal Supremacy," invented at the so-called " Reformation " to the " Supremacy of Public Opinion," may read with interest, and possibly with profit, an article on that subject in the *Reunion Magazine*, vol. i.   London, 1879.

CHAPTER V.

A copy of the Bull of Pope Pius V., already duly published and set forth, was affixed to the door of the English ambassador's house at Paris; and another was placed on the gate of the Bishop of London's Palace at St. Paul's, late at night on May the 24th, 1570, by John Felton, a gentleman of Southwark, and Cornelius Irishman, a priest. Of these the former was tried for high treason at Guildhall on the 4th of August, and found guilty. His attachment to the old religion was evidently deep, earnest, and enthusiastic, as the risk he had run showed. Under the severest and most cruel torture, borne without shrinking, he absolutely refused to name his accomplices; he declined, moreover, to acknowledge that he had received the copy made use of from the chaplain of the Spanish ambassador; he gloried in having thus promulgated the document, and asserted his perfect readiness to die a martyr to the faith of his fathers. To the "heretical system," as he termed it, which the queen and her advisers had set up, he professed his cordial repugnance; he declined, after the decision of the Pope, to acknowledge Elizabeth as his sovereign; but personally, as he asserted, bore her no malice whatsoever, hoping that she would one day renounce her heresy and accept the faith; while on the morning of his execution, August 8th, as a token and testimony of earnest sincerity, he drew a diamond ring of the value of four hundred pounds from off his finger, and sent it by the Earl of Sussex as an offering to the queen.

Though she professed to despise the sentence pronounced by the Pope, and though her advisers appeared to treat it with the utmost contempt, it is tolerably clear that neither the one nor the others at all liked it; and it is perfectly certain that it was a cause of much suspicion, uneasiness, and alarm to both. Making it a subject of conversation with her ambassadors, she is said to have declared it to be an insult to all the European sovereigns; and induced the Emperor Maximilian to endeavour to get it withdrawn. The Holy Father, on being solicited to do this, at once perceived, as all but Cecil and his allies saw, that the blow had been keenly felt. But before his Holiness could give any reasonable answer to the emperor's request, he must first know whether Elizabeth acknowledged his authority. This was a preliminary and crucial point which could not be overlooked. Having procured intervention regarding the Bull, it might be presumed that she did. But to the definite question, "Does the Queen of England regard the sentence as valid or invalid?" he must have an unambiguous and reasonable answer. If Her Majesty looked upon it as valid, why did she not at once seek reconciliation with the successor of St. Gregory and the Chief Bishop of Christendom? If invalid, there was, of course, nothing to revoke; for, from her own standing-point, the act was null and void. The pitiful revenge, which, with written oaths and strong language, she had threatened, was altogether beneath the Pope's notice. As the earthly father of the Christian family, and acting in his Master's name, he had, as he remarked, only done his duty. If, therefore, the queen did not repent and alter her policy, events must take their course.

Her Majesty's advisers, therefore, lost no time in taking fresh action consequent upon the publication of this Bull. Parker, Grindal, and Sandys, judging from their advice, held that it was a matter to be treated with contempt; but whether this was their true and secret opinion appears exceedingly doubtful. Cecil certainly did not agree with them, but thought otherwise. For a local insurrection in Norfolk, in which Esquire John Throckmorton took a leading part, appeared to give some grounds for disquiet. On the 2nd of April 1571, consequently several fresh laws, most carefully and artfully framed, were duly and finally passed;[1] and such was the practical response made by the queen to the Pope. Henceforth if any one called Elizabeth a heretic, or gave her the title of schismatic, or declared her to be an usurper or an infidel, he was liable to be charged with treason and punished. What the punishment for treason was no one was ever allowed to forget. Any one introducing a Papal Bull into England was likewise held to be a traitor; and, if the fact were proved, the usual punishment followed. All persons who should, by writing or printing, dare to affirm that any one particular person was the heir of the queen, "except the same were the natural issue of her body"[2]—a phrase of remark-

---

[1] Some propositions relating to persons who refused to communicate at the new service of the Supper were so extravagant, that, when certain peers complained of their tyrannical character, they were withdrawn.

[2] At one period most unpleasant rumours were afloat, amongst others a

able significance—were to be imprisoned for twelve months for
the first offence, and to suffer the penalties of *præmunire* for the
second.   Furthermore, if any English people were found sending
over relief to their expatriated relations, who, because of the fury
of the persecution and the impossibility of exercising the Catholic
religion at home, had gone abroad, very severe punishments at
once ensued.   Finally, those who went abroad without licence,
as well as those who had obtained written permission to go,
were to return at once after a warning by proclamation, at the
risk of forfeiting all their goods and chattels, and the profits of
their lands during lifetime, to the queen's use.   Tyranny is no
term with which to describe such proceedings.   The darkest age
of barbarism—when cruellest despots, without responsibility or
conscience, governed undraped savages—could scarcely produce
parallels to the policy of this fearful woman and her unprincipled
advisers.

Her government was in fact a pure and simple despotism—a
despotism of the darkest dye.[1]   The Court of High Commission
and the Star Chamber Court were the principal instruments
by which such alarming despotism was carried out ; and if
unpopularity met any man of rank or mark ; if, in the hearing of
a spy of Cecil's, or of some long-eared and contemptible informer,
he uttered a word or sentence which might be twisted and turned
against him ; or if the queen found him less pliant or obsequious
than she thought he ought to be, he stood henceforth in the
greatest danger of liberty or life.   Both those who adhered to
the old religion, and those who were for proceeding further along
the road of reform, alike suffered.

The queen, jealous of the prerogatives and powers with which
Parliament had endowed her, was resolved to make all her
subjects of one religion—that which, mainly for State purposes,
had been recently excogitated and set up.   This bore a certain
relation to the old, for some of the leading dogmas of Christianity
were embodied in it ; but other doctrines which served to
preserve a due balance, and which together made up a complete

report that the queen was likely to become a mother.   But Lord Leicester
thought it his duty to write to Sir Francis Walsingham to inform him that
the queen's indisposition was but slight, and that the rumour in question was
unfounded.

[1] Those who assisted in erecting this system, though continually condemning the proceedings of Bonner and others in Mary's reign, seem never to
have been struck by their own great inconsistency.   Bonner, so unjustly
maligned, was at least upholding and maintaining a system which was as
old as the time of St. Austin of Canterbury, whereas the new institution of
Cecil and Parker was of quite recent date.

circle of divine truth, were rejected. The ecclesiastical somersault which Her Majesty herself had made between the faith she
professed to hold on the morning of her coronation and that in
which she now appeared to believe, was a somersault which she
expected all her subjects to be capable of taking, and ready to
take.

The Court of High Commission enabled her effectually to
carry out her plans, and especially to answer the Pope. By this
she formally gave to certain prelates and State officers exceptional
powers : their authority extending over the whole realm, and
over all ranks and degrees from peer to peasant. These Commissioners were empowered to exercise a complete control over
both the faith and opinions of all ; and, according to their
discretion, to punish all men, in any way and by any method
short of death. It was open to them to proceed against delin-
quents by law, if they thought fit ; but, on the other hand, if
these Commissioners thought it desirable, they might employ
imprisonment (without trial or conviction), the rack, or any
customary torture, so as to obtain their desired ends. If any
man was even suspected—no matter regarding what, where, or
why—they were empowered, *ex officio*, to administer an oath to
him ; by which, as they maintained, he was bound, as a good
subject, to reveal his most inward thoughts, opinions, and convictions ; and not only thus to accuse himself, but his nearest
and dearest friend or relations, and this on pain of death. Such
ingenious and frightful tactics opened the door to dark acts
of injustice worthy of the heartiest reprobation. Moreover,
whenever they pleased, these High Commissioners could fine
and imprison men as and when they willed, without fear or
rebuke. They claimed alike an absolute control over the souls
and consciences, as well as over the bodies, lands, and monies
of Englishmen,—and all this on the hypocritical and false plea
that such a policy was essential for delivering their countrymen
from a "slavish subjection to a foreign prince and prelate." In
the action of these courts nobody's conscience was regarded,
whether Catholic or Puritan ; in fact, no one was expected to
possess a conscience, while no mercy was shown to any who
presumed to exhibit the least independence. Furthermore, no
practical remedy for the existing evils seems to have been as yet
devised, even by those called upon to suffer in patience and
endure.

The nation at this period was, in truth, sick at heart. The old
nobility could not act together, were sometimes jealous of each
other, and had lost much of their influence. The new men, ever

so avaricious and grasping, cared little for the poor; and in turn were themselves cared not for by any of those beneath them. The abbey and church lands were now theirs; but their first thought was to make the most of their new possessions, and so the poor were deliberately passed by. New notions were eagerly clutched at. Some of the nobility openly advocated change, and in certain cases did so with a lack of good breeding and a singular want of taste.[1] There was an almost universal restlessness of thought; disorder everywhere reigned, and poverty was wide-spread. Men by hundreds rose of a winter morning who knew not how to sustain their ordinary wants during the day; social misery increased, dissatisfaction was rampant. The successful thieves—for this is what they were—who had ennobled themselves, or induced the queen to make them peers, had ruder imitators in the lowest ranks of the people; who, if they could obtain success in no other manner, became cut-purses and highwaymen. For them, under the new order of things, might became right.

Take, for example, one well-known case of legal wickedness and murder. Dr. John Storey, a distinguished civilian who in King Edward VI.'s reign had done all that lay in his power to oppose the changes in religion, and who, under Queen Mary, had been commissioned to see that the rood and its attendant images, with a figure of the patron saint of every church, had been restored, was now to suffer death. He had done this good work of reparation and restoration so energetically and enthusiastically that the innovators, no bad judges of who were their friends and who their enemies, held him in particular abhorrence. The earlier Reformers had often singled him out for special abuse; for he had frequently exposed their heresy and self-seeking, had drawn a most powerful contrast[2] between the old religion and

---

[1] The Duchess of Suffolk, wife to Mr. Peregrine Bertie, a renowned Protestant, had had a small rochet and chimere (the domestic dress of a bishop) made for one of her poodle dogs, which, in contempt for the Bishop of Winchester, she put on the animal's back, with its fore-legs in lawn sleeves. The dog itself she was polite enough to name "Gardiner."—See *Memoir of Peregrine Bertie, Eleventh Lord Willoughby de Eresby, etc.* London, 1838.

[2] The contrast has been vigorously drawn in recent days by Mr. J. A. Froude, though his conception of the Catholic religion and Catholic practices is as inexact as it is queer. Some assertions he makes, if made in earnest, are exaggerated caricatures, altogether unworthy of a writer of history :— " The Catholic believed in the authority of the Church; the Reformers in the authority of Reason. Where the Church had spoken, the Catholic obeyed. His duty was to accept without question the laws which councils had decreed, which Popes and bishops administered, and, so far as in him lay, to enforce on others the same submission to an outward rule which he

the new, and was exceedingly plain spoken and zealous for the faith. On Queen Mary's death he had prudently withdrawn to the Netherlands, where he received an appointment in the local Custom-house. There he was often brought into contact with English merchants. On one occasion, evidently by previous arrangement with the authorities at home, he was seized bodily, when searching an English vessel, and brought by force to England. Though guilty of no transgression save that of self-expatriation, so that he might observe without let or hindrance the religion of his forefathers, he was at once put into confinement in the Tower;[1] and at the age of seventy years cruelly executed. The Oath of Supremacy [2] was at once tendered him; but he refused to take it, as contrary to his faith and conscience. Neither argument nor threat could move him. He had never had a doubt that such a she-supremacy, the acceptance of which it was endeavoured to impose upon him, was both ridiculous and profane; and no inducements held out of a few

regarded as divine. All shades of Protestants, on the other hand, agreed that Protestants might err; that Christ had left no visible representative, whom individually they were bound to obey; that religion was the operation of the Spirit on the mind and conscience; that the Bible was God's Word, which each Christian was to read, and which, with God's help and his own natural intelligence, he could not fail to understand. The Catholic left his Bible to the learned. The Protestant translated the Bible, and brought it to the door of every Christian family. The Catholic prayed in Latin; and whether he understood his words, or repeated them as a form, the effect was the same, for it was magical. The Protestant prayed with his mind, as an act of faith, in a language intelligible to him, or he could not pray at all. The Catholic bowed in awe before his wonder-working image, adored his relics, and gave his life into the guidance of his spiritual director. The Protestant tore open the machinery of the miracles, flung the bones and ragged garments into the fire, and treated priests as men like himself."— Froude's *History of England*, vol. vii. pp. 23, 24. London, 1863.

[1] On the walls of the Beauchamp Tower the inscription, no doubt cut with his own hand, still remains, thus :—

1570 : IHON . STORE . DOCTOR .

[2] "Bishop Burnet acquaints us, in his *History of the Reformation*, that Queen Elizabeth scrupled at first very much to accept the supremacy. And well she might. For she could not but know herself unqualified by her very sex, even for the lowest degree of any ecclesiastical dignity or function. Yet she accepted it, and discarded the Pope, as her father had done before her, though upon a different motive. For Henry did it to be revenged of the Pope; but Queen Elizabeth's motive was 'because she knew very well,' says Dr. Haylin, 'that her legitimacy and the Pope's supremacy could not stand together.' So that although her policy was not quite so bad as her father's, it was mere policy and interest of state that determined her to this capital article of her Reformation, and the considerations of religion had no part in it."—*England's Conversion and Reformation Compared*, p. 302. Antwerp, 1725.

K

more years of life (he had already reached the appointed three-score years and ten) could lead him for an instant to alter his noble determination. He was consequently condemned to be drawn, hung, dismembered, disembowelled, and quartered; and thus, his punishment deliberately prolonged, the poor old man suffered.   When cut down from the hanging-post alive—an important part of the sentence—he is said to have struggled with, and struck the executioner, who was drawing out the bowels from his ripped up and bleeding body; but, of course, Storey, wounded, maimed, and half-strangled was soon overcome, and groaning heavily, then died for his religion and his conscience in excruciating agonies.

Thus men of independence and vigour, the grey-haired as well as the hale and lusty, were put out of the way.   It needed a firm faith in the unseen world, and a full reliance on the Almighty's promised help in time of need, to enable them thus nobly and calmly to meet death.   God grant that, if the valley were shadowy and dark for such sufferers, the land beyond was fair and peaceful and bright to their disembodied souls!

But even this bloody method failed of its purpose. Uniformity was never attained; divisions, as will be seen, steadily increased.

Dr. Bonner, Bishop of London, whose dignity and revenues had been usurped, died a prisoner in the Marshalsea on the 5th of September 1569. He was unpopular because he had taken an active part, in Mary's reign, against the innovators; and various writers have united in his condemnation. But exceedingly little has ever been produced to show that the popular conception of this prelate's character and actions was either just or true. Moreover, those who live for the sake of popularity frequently get exceedingly little for their pains. In sowing over-abundantly they often reap but very sparingly. Bonner was more than once offered his liberty if he would change his religion; but he died as he had lived, a consistent man and a good Catholic, preferring to the smile of the present world the welcome of his Master and the eternal joys of the world to come. He was buried at nightfall in the churchyard of St. George's, Southwark.[1]

[1] Bishop Sandys thus wrote to Cecil:—"Dr. Bonner had stand excommunicate by a sentence in the Arches' eight or nine years and never desired absolution. Wherefore by the law Christian sepulture might have been denied him; but we thought not good to deal so vigorously, and therefore permitted him to be buried in St. George's Churchyard.   And the same to be done not in the day solemnly but in the night privily."—Bishop Sandys to Sir W. Cecil, 9th September 1569, *Remains of Archbishop Sandys*, p. 307. Parker Society.

Bishop Thirlby[1] died at Lambeth Palace, where he had been confined for eleven years, on the 26th of August 1570, and was buried, without Catholic rites, in the midst of the choir of the parish church of Our Lady of Lambeth.

It should here be noted that many principles which those who had formed the New Church had entirely put out of consideration in constructing it, were at once true and important; and some of these were very soon seized upon and adopted by the Puritan leaders—many of whom were laborious scholars, and, though sometimes pedants, men of rare ability. The inherent truth of such principles and their obvious reasonableness ensured them both respect from the populace and acceptance; while in some instances they were received with enthusiasm. An *Admonition to Parliament*, presumed to be from the pens of Wilcox and Field, two Puritan divines, who lectured at Wandsworth, contained the bitterest language against the New Church, and was greedily bought up and read. Whitgift on the side of the Establishment, and Cartwright on the Puritan side, both engaged in controversy concerning it. Long sermons and longer controversies were at that time all the fashion. This particular discussion lasted no less than six years. At its end neither batch of disputants seemed to be wiser than at the beginning. At Cambridge, one Charke, a preacher, was also anything but complimentary to the new hierarchy. It is true that as a body the members of it were a very commonplace lot, with no higher notion of their office than that they were State officers,—perhaps, after all, a not inaccurate estimate,—yet, when this university divine maintained that "Satan had introduced bishops, archbishops, metropolitans, patriarchs, and popes," neither Dr. Matthew Parker nor Dr. Edwin Sandys could have been exactly flattered. The polite and impressive language they had so often applied to the Holy See and its occupants was now in turn applied to themselves. Nemesis had arrived sooner than was anticipated. When, moreover, the Puritans[2] taught, for instance,

[1] The only predecessor of Cardinals Wiseman and Manning in the See of Westminster.

[2] They objected altogether to bishops and specially to the superiority of bishops over other ministers. With them all "preaching ministers" were alike. They also disliked the Ecclesiastical Courts (as in subsequent times they had the best reasons for doing), the "vain repetition" of the Lord's Prayer, and the existence in the Table of Lessons of any parts of the Apocrypha. They further objected to the use of the sign of the cross in baptism; to the ring and the words of betrothal in marriage; to the observance of festivals; to the chanting of Psalms; to the use of organs or other musical instruments; and, above all, to the habits—the surplice, silken hood, cope, rochet, and chimere of the ministry.

that the Church ought always to be independent of the State, they only recommended an obvious truism; for Cæsar has nothing to do with the things of God. When, again, they maintained that women should have no part in Church government, except to listen, learn, and obey, they knew themselves to be supported both by apostolic teaching and by universal precedent throughout Christendom.   Here they and the Pope were at-one.   This doctrine, therefore, they constantly declared in private, and often preached in public.   The Supreme Governess, of course, did not approve of such homilies, and swore when she heard of their delivery.   But whether Her Highness liked them or not, the Puritans continued to preach on.   As a consequence, divisions multiplied, and new sects were born.

As a maintainer and defender of these principles one remarkable man stood in the forefront, and for some time gave considerable trouble to the authorities.   Thomas Cartwright, born in Hertfordshire, about 1535, received his education at St. John's College, Cambridge.   In Queen Mary's reign he had withdrawn from making preparation for the ministry, and for a while made his living as a scribe.   On Elizabeth's accession, however, when the tide had turned, he went back to Cambridge, where he was elected a Fellow of Trinity College; but being disappointed of further promotion, as some have asserted, went off to Geneva, where he cordially accepted the Calvinistic theories in all their logical sharpness and terrible conclusions; and then returned in 1570, when he was made Margaret Professor of Theology.   The controversy concerning clerical vestures was then raging furiously and being conducted with vigour, in which he took a leading part against them.   But he carried his contention with the queen's New Church still further.   He was opposed to bishops themselves, their incomes, courts, and officers, as well as to their lawn rochets and satin chimeres; and in due course, because of his ability and plain speaking, was soon looked upon as the head and leader of the Puritan party—a party patronised by Lord Leicester.   Thus the new bishops were not only compelled to face and receive the controversial fire from Dr. Allen, Stapleton, and others, who for several years had so ably and consistently maintained the ancient faith, but were now likewise taken in the flank by the racy and raking arguments of Cartwright and his allies.   They were thus between two fires.

The policy and method of Cartwright in appealing to this or that text of Scripture, or in quibbling and arguing about antiquity, entirely took the wind out of the sails of the Establishmentarian prelates.   They knew not what to say.   If one controversialist could appeal to the Bible, so could two, or twenty, or two hundred, and why should they not? They each did so. No one could determine the controversy. No one could finally decide it. Private judgment untrammelled and unchecked had come in. Authority had been turned out. Thus confusion became worse confounded.[1] Babel was being painfully rebuilt.

Again, this honest and out-spoken Puritan was highly incensed at what he looked upon as the pompous state and extravagance and good living[2] of the bishops: "He is much offended with the train they keep," are Parker's own words of complaint to Lord Burghley, "and saith that three parts of their servants are unprofitable to the filling of the Church and Commonwealth; and he is very angry with their furniture of household."[3] All this annoyed and mortified the archbishop greatly, who, whatever he may have been, was very modest in his opinion both of his personal and official powers. For he thus implored Lord Burghley to induce the Supreme Head to step in and settle the dispute concerning the value of episcopacy:—"Sir, because you be a principal Councillor, I refer the whole matter to Her Majesty and to your order. For myself, I can as well be content to be a parish clerk as a parish priest. I refer the standing or falling altogether to your own considerations, whether Her Majesty and you will have any archbishops or bishops, or how you will have them ordered."

The abject and humiliating position of this great official,—this first Protestant archbishop,—thus set forth in his own words, could not possibly be more abject or degrading. He has evidently no principles to maintain, and therefore none to resign. But he is even ready to sacrifice his office, as well as himself,—to give up the whole question of episcopacy (which with him evidently could have been no question of principle),—if the Head of the Church, the new She-Pontiff, and her principal secretary should in their infallible judgment decree that His

---

[1] Eventually the ministers themselves admitted as much. "Because that is generally known throughout the whole Citie (of London) that no one parish or parson can agree together, & that the cause thereof is the privatt readinge in houses . . . we humbly require that these readers may be forbidden and some straight punishment for this great and horrible sin may be appointed, or else the preachers hereafter commanded to hold their peace."—Address of the London Clergy to Convocation, A.D. 1580.—MSS. of Anthony á Wood, No. 8494, fol. 30, Bodleian Library.

[2] "Tin cupps for the Supper suffice; but my Lord of Durham now hath them of gold for his lady and impes."—A True Protestacion, etc., p. 31. London, 1575.

[3] Lansdowne MSS., Brit. Museum, No. xvii. folio 93.

Grace ought to do it. In this Parker proved himself a worthy successor to Thomas Cranmer.

That prelate, who, twenty-six years previous to Elizabeth's accession, had first stood forward to make a breach with the Holy See, and who, to his earthly king and patron, had proclaimed himself ready at all risks and at any cost to act independently of his legitimate superior, bore a heavy responsibility upon his shoulders. Where he had passed, others, like Parker, were ready to follow. The acts of Cranmer at his consecration had been so bold and unprincipled, and at the same time so adroit and well-suited to the temporary purpose of the king his master, that all the complex and miserable evils which have afflicted this nation since—the final separation, with division subdivided by division—may, in truth, be traced upward to the frightful sacrifice of principle perpetrated when this wretched man became Archbishop of Canterbury.

In truth, no one acquainted with the facts of his true history has presumed to deny that he was a despicable character; and that the only noble act he did was at the close of his life, when he appropriately let his right hand first suffer at the stake, because it had been the instrument by which a degraded and corrupt mind had wrought out so many evil deeds. His notorious obsequiousness to his successive masters, Henry, Seymour, and Dudley, was only equalled by the barbarous cruelty exercised by him upon the various obstinate and wrong-headed sectaries who, from time to time, found themselves in his power. In one respect this archbishop is distinguished from all other persecutors, even from pagans, in that he not only actively promoted the capital punishment of those who disagreed with him in religion, but of those likewise who agreed with him in it. In Henry's reign, for example, he took a leading part in bringing to the stake Lambert, Anne Askew,[1] Frith, and Allen, besides condemning many others to the same awful punishment for denying a bodily presence of our Lord in the Sacrament of the Altar. Under King Edward,—the Calvinistic child who was the pliant and pietistic tool of others,—Cranmer had secured the conviction

[1] At the church of Snodland, in Kent, there is, or was when the author visited it several years ago, a highly coloured and most impressive stained-glass window, of all the tints of the rainbow, in which certain of the reforming bishops are represented, above the Communion Table, in the most gorgeous Eucharistic vestments—"the garments of Babylon," as they would have termed them. In one of the lights is a highly idealised representation of Cranmer; in another—with somewhat of inconsistency, not apparent doubtless to those who put it up—a representation of this very "Anne Askew" whom he had brought to the stake.

of Arians and Anabaptists—two of whom, Joan Knell and George Van Parr, he actually caused to be burnt, personally preventing the king from pardoning the poor wretches, by authoritatively and unctuously assuring him that "princes being God's deputies, ought to punish impieties against Him."[1]

But to return to the method by which the New Church was practically ruled—a point of great practical moment. For many persons nowadays hold that what they term "recent innovations"[2] had no place in the pure conception and perfect scheme of the "Reformers,"—a remarkable delusion, utterly contrary to historical facts ; totally opposed both to the policy of the queen and the unvarying practice of each of Her Majesty's prelates.

The Church of God, as we all admit, was ever governed by lawful authorities, the bishops ; the Church of England from its first creation by the Reformers was ruled by Royal Commissioners, who settled its constitution, arranged its Prayer-Book, sanctioned and legalised its Ordinal, and managed its temporal affairs. These, with a few exceptions, were laymen, some of them lawyers, others needy gentlepeople who had apostatised, or "new men" of base birth and low origin, who had already risen from the ranks by servility, want of good principles, and by intrigue ; and who reasonably desired to rise higher, and secure more of the good things of this world by fresh deeds which will not bear the light of day. Their scheme of setting up a local church which they could mould, alter, and dominate as they willed was a master-stroke of state-craft. But it was also mischievous, wicked, and wrong. "God's mill grinds slowly." At length, however, some—waking from a deep sleep, stretching out their hands, yawning with a will, and rubbing their eyes— begin to see the situation as it *is* (not as it *seemed* to them in their rosy dream), and are now too accurately realising what was done.

Elizabeth's Commissioners, of whom Archbishop Parker was chief, were to make strict inquiries concerning all erroneous, heretical, and dangerous opinions. They were to find out who were absent, Sunday by Sunday, from the Church services, as well as those who frequented the private prayer-meetings and preachings of the Puritans. They were to give their best

---

[1] Burnet's *History*, part ii. book 1.
[2] The existence of the Privy Council as the Final Court of Appeal in spiritual questions, for example ; the abolition of the Arches' Court and the Chancery Court of York ; the substitution of a new Parliamentary Court for the whole of the two provinces ; and the setting up, by statute, of a new and non-spiritual judge.

endeavour to suppress all heretical and seditious publications; all anonymous and other libels and squibs, then becoming numerous,[1] against the queen, and her officers both of Church and State, and if possible to get hold of both writer and printer, and nail their ears to the pillory, or cut them off; they were, moreover, to deal with all adulteries, bigamies, fornications, and other offences against the ecclesiastical law—which had enormously increased—and to punish the offenders with so-called "spiritual censures."

Catholics and Puritans alike both suffered.

In 1571, two Puritan members of Parliament, Strickland and Snagg, boldly proposed to amend the Prayer-Book in a Protestant direction; but they were soon put down. The queen, as Supreme Governess, maintained, accurately enough, that such proposals struck at the very root of her prerogative, as no doubt was the case; and that she, as Head of the Church, being alone charged with the care of it, distinctly forbade Strickland to go forward with the measure. At first he declined, and was pardonably sulky over the question; but, on being warned of the consequences of his resolution, and having been brought before the Privy Council, he was most arbitrarily and illegally forbidden to attend the House at all.[2] This strong measure, however, was more than the Commons chose to allow to pass unchallenged. They, therefore, protested, and Strickland soon took his seat again.

[1] It was made felony "to write, print, or set forth any manner of book, rhyme, ballad, letter, or writing, containing any false or seditious matter to the defamation of the Queen's Majesty or to the encouraging of insurrection or rebellion within the realms."—*Statutes of the Realm*, vol. iv. p. 659.

[2] Her Majesty's arbitrary action on this occasion was severely commented on. Some said that as Parliament had made her the Head of the Church, she was obviously inferior to Parliament, and must abide by its decisions. On the other hand, the prompt action she took in the case of Strickland, if justifiable with one member of Parliament, might subsequently have been applied to all. The Puritans were furious, and considerable sensation was created. Besides such action as that recorded above, the queen interfered personally in the election of members of Parliament. In Oxfordshire and Buckinghamshire she sent written orders to those known to favour the innovating section, to see that her allies, and those who would actively support them, should alone be elected. Amongst such were Sir Henry Lee of Quarrendon; the Cheynes, a knightly family of Drayton Beauchamp and Chesham-Bois; and the Packingtons of Aylesbury; all connections by marriage, and all more or less of a Gallio-like type. The long disfranchised borough of Galton was at that period notoriously under the influence of a certain Madam Copley. But this lady had not repudiated the ancient faith, and was consequently held to be "not well affected." So the queen gave directions that Madam Copley's nominees should be passed over, and only "loyal" men returned.—See Loseley MSS., and Author's MSS. Excerpts.

In the meantime, those who were directly affected by the issue of the Pope's Bull, found themselves in still greater straits. Foreign Catholic sovereigns with their hands full of troubles and responsibilities of their own, had apparently allowed its promulgation to pass unnoticed; while, amongst those of the old religion at home, there had at once arisen serious dissensions with regard both to its terms and its object, as well as to its immediate effects. Some maintained that it had been irregularly and unauthoritatively issued. Others argued that no one was bound to take action upon it, until the Christian nations of Europe had first determined upon accepting it in combination, and of actually putting it into practice. Argument, as experience teaches, is often easier than action.

While opinions thus differed, and nothing was done, it became tolerably evident that the innovators did not intend to be at all checked or circumscribed by any such inaction. Cranmer, by his laxity regarding oaths, had some years previously taught how an Archbishop of Canterbury might become entirely independent of the Pope; and the queen's advisers, having accurately and perfectly learnt their lesson, applied the principle involved in it with boldness and spirit. Having first repudiated the Pope, they then abolished the Christian sacrifice.[1] In so doing, they were independent of every existing authority, being amenable to no one, and superior to all. In action they were wholly unchecked by any considerations of what might be said in criticism—a position scarcely conceived of nowadays when public opinion owns such an extended, and, in some cases (where prejudice does not come in), beneficent and advantageous influence.

When, therefore, to say mass was to be guilty of high treason,[2]

[1] In the abolition of the Christian sacrifice, Protestantism and Mahometanism appear to stand on a level. In the recommendation of penance and self-denial, however, the latter apparently has the advantage of the former. Here it may be noted that one of the queen's leading bishops is profane rather than witty (as he evidently intended to be) in the following pedantic and laboured paragraph regarding the mass:—"How many toys, crossings, blessings, blowings, knockings, kneelings, bowings, liftings, sighings, houslings, turnings ' and half-turnings, mockings, mowings, sleepings and apish playings, soft whisperings and loud speakings, have we to consecrate our own devices withal, or [i.e. before] it can be gotten done!"—*Pilkington's Works*, p. 498, Parker Society. London, 1842.

[2] "Treason, by the law of England, and according to the common use of language, is the crime of rebellion or conspiracy against the Government. If a statute is made, by which the celebration of certain religious rites is subjected to the same penalties as rebellion or conspiracy, would any man, free from prejudice, and not designing to impose upon the misinformed, speak of persons convicted on such a statute as guilty of treason, without expressing in what sense he uses the words, or deny that they were as truly punished for

and to hear mass, of felony,—each offence punishable with an infamous death,—it certainly behoved all those who could take a broad and wide view of the position to be prepared for some kind of action, unless the faith were to be actually allowed to die out. Of course penal laws, like the enactments referred to, could never change the nature or essence of things. They could not make certain actions, for the punishment of which these laws had been specially passed, to become crimes in the sight of God and man, if they were not so before. Murders, treasons, and rebellions, great and acknowledged sins, have generally been punished with death; but can any reasonable being—can any person in his right mind, assert that to say mass was a sin at all, or a sin of a like dye, or had ever before been looked upon as such, or that it merited a similar punishment, or indeed any punishment at all? The most holy and sacred mass was simply the august sacrifice of the new law, instituted by Our Divine Lord Himself, and offered to Almighty God day by day, from east to west, in all preceding ages, and in every Christian kingdom, from the foundation of our holy religion to the period in question. Is it credible, then, that, as in other Christian countries, all the bishops and priests of Great Britain through a period of nine hundred years should have been guilty every morning of committing a crime, equivalent in its punishment to that for murder or rebellion?[1] The very notion thus stated, though absurd enough, suffices to prove that the enactment of these sanguinary statutes,—executed for generations, and some of them remaining as laws of the land within the memory of

their religion as if they had been convicted of heresy? A man is punished for religion, when he incurs a penalty for its profession or exercise, to which he was not liable on any other account. This is applicable to the great majority of capital convictions on this score under Elizabeth. The persons convicted could not be traitors in any fair sense of the word, because they were not charged with anything properly denominated treason."—Hallam's *Constitutional History of England*, 6th edition, vol. i. p. 164, note.

[1] Some of the more daring innovators persisted in maintaining that all "mass-mongers," as they termed the old clergy, because of their office, were "conjurors." The Protestant bishops in their sermons had deliberately encouraged this kind of language, with profane epigrams about "Hocus-pocus." For example, Grindal, when Bishop of London, wrote to Cecil on April 17, 1571, alluding to the examination of Cox *alias* Devon, an old priest who had been taken that day. The Council, the bishop hopes, will surely punish him for his magic and conjuration. Devon, it appears, had said mass at the house of Sir Thomas Wharton of Newhall, Essex; at Sir Edward Waldegrave's; and at Stubbe's, in Westminster. On the 19th, the Earl of Oxford encloses to Cecil "an Inventory of all such implements of superstition as were found in the chamber near Lady Wharton's bedchamber at Newhall, Essex," after the pursuivants had ransacked it.

those still living was one of the blackest stains on Elizabeth's character.

The direct consequences of such legislation have already been only indirectly hinted at, though some few have been plainly set forth. In the latter portions of this sketch of the Church under Queen Elizabeth, certain dark deeds which resulted from that legislation will be duly put on record. With several writers they have been deliberately kept in the background.

Before the result of the recent legislation against recusants is considered in detail, it is necessary to glance for awhile at another part of the picture, and to note certain obvious features in the new order of things, which, by way of contrast, may better enable the reader to take in exactly what had been done.

Many of the new clergy were zealous in their labours, and had little disposition to let their moderation be known unto all men. For, as it was mainly the over-zealous and fanatical who had been promoted to high places since the queen's accession, so fanaticism and over-zeal, held to be the highest virtues by those who expected promotion, were often rampant.

Just as the queen's first Parliament had been packed with "good and true men,"—that is, with persons known to Cecil as favourable to his own designs and a change in religion,—so likewise had the two Convocations of the English provinces. When those clergy who on principle had resisted the innovations, had either resigned, been imprisoned, or expatriated, there were no great difficulties in duly manipulating the elections for proctors. The deans and other officials were, of course, all of one way of thinking; and every care was taken that the representatives of the chapters and parochial ministers should be of a like stamp and in harmony with them, as far as harmony could be looked for.

As early as the year 1562, the Lower House of the Convocation of Canterbury, clearly indicating its "reformed" character, had formally made requisition to the bishops, firstly, that "no person abide within the church during the time of the Communion, unless he do communicate; that is, they shall depart immediately after the Exhortation be ended, and before the Confession of the communicants"; and, secondly, that it be added to this Confession that "the communicants do detest and renounce the idolatrous mass."[1]

Deacons—whether distinct from "readers" does not appear —on their being licensed were expected to promise as follows: "I shall not openly intermeddle with any artificer's occupation

[1] Strype's *Annals*, vol. i. p. 508. Oxford, 1824.

as covetously to seek a gain thereby, having in ecclesiastical living the sum of twenty nobles or above by year,"[1]—a position which, from some documents consulted, it is tolerably clear that no ordinary "reader" could have held.

The furniture now needed for the churches, but not always supplied, consisted of a font, a pulpit, a table (*i.e.* a board), some tressels, a large Bible, and a Prayer-Book each for the parson and clerk. John Foxe's *Book of Martyrs*, a volume of controversial misrepresentations and falsehoods, which still stands without a rival, was specially ordered to be procured and left open in some side aisle, in order that all might read its gross and wicked assertions, illustrated by rude but thrilling and effective woodcuts, and so swell the ranks of the innovators. The queen's "Injunctions" and the "Paraphrase" of Erasmus likewise had to be procured by the churchwardens, together with the two volumes of savoury *Homilies*, recently published, for the non-preaching ministers to read out to the people.

The parish clerk, who in out-of-the-way places[2] was no doubt conservative enough, and no great promoter of change (for change was not likely to benefit him much), went on the even tenor of his way, as of old, making as few practical alterations as possible. In many places, as at St. Just's, in Cornwall; Wincanton, in Somersetshire; Thame, in Oxfordshire; St. Margaret Pattens, in the city of London; and at Our Lady's, Bury St. Edmunds,[3] he still wore the accustomed linen rochet— sometimes without sleeves, as more convenient. No doubt he continued likewise to observe many of the ancient traditional rites and ceremonies, not specified by any printed or written direction, as a matter of course; to ring the bells as of yore, marking peal from chime,[4] the clang of the marriage-bells from the solemn toll of the great bell for funerals. It was more probably his pious custom to begin and end all services, regular or occasional, with the sign of the cross; to strike his breast at

---

[1] Strype's *Annals*, vol. i. p. 515. Oxford, 1824.

[2] Mass was said in several remote parishes, throughout the whole of the reign of Elizabeth, *e.g.* at Morwenstow and Lanherne, in Cornwall; at Stonor Park, Oxon.; at Thame Prebendal House Chapel, as well as at Thame Park; at the Manor House, North Weston; at Waterperry House; at Wing, in Buckinghamshire; Nash Court, in Kent; Raglan Castle; and in many parish churches in Lancashire and Carlisle, where the local nobility and gentry connived at such breach of "the law"; in some places even unto the period of the Great Rebellion.

[3] Author's MSS. and Excerpts.

[4] In hundreds of country parishes throughout England and Wales, the mass-bell is still rung on Sunday mornings at eight o'clock, though there be no service held of any sort or kind.

the Confession; reverently to cover his face with his hands at the *Miserere* as usual;[1] to respond as of old at baptisms and churchings; to have the cross borne at the head of a corpse at funerals; and, generally, to sever as few as possible of those traditional threads[2] which both in church and churchyard linked so firmly the living with those who had worshipped there in the past, and who now slept their last sleep beneath the green grass, under the shadow of some old church-tower.

Except amongst the upper classes and the more prosperous tradesmen and yeomen, the people seemed to have still buried their dead, when interred in the churchyard green, in a shroud and winding-sheet, without coffins. Most of the nobility and gentlepeople owned vaults in the churches or chantry chapels, and were interred with exceeding great heraldric pomp—strictly according to their true and recognised rank. Of this the heralds took especial care, for they duly marshalled the procession, formally sanctioned the coat-armour put up, and were not unrewarded as regards fees. The clergy likewise by custom were commonly interred in the choirs or chancels, and often, as of old, with their feet towards the west. In these cases leaden and oak coffins were always used. But the large majority of persons during Elizabeth's reign were evidently buried without coffins. The long winding-sheet was folded again and

---

[1] The fact that these traditional observances were forbidden in the later years of Queen Elizabeth, by her bishops in their "Visitation Articles" shows, by implication, that they were still practised in some places.

[2] As late as the first year of James I., one Howell Thomas was buried openly in the parish church of Caerleon, with all the ancient rites. Father Robert Jones said the funeral mass early in the morning, after which a large concourse of persons, hooded and bearing lighted tapers, preceded the corpse to the burial-place. The ancient offices seem to have been used, for no minister was present, while at the close of the funeral ceremonies, one Lander ventured to predict that mass would soon be said publicly again.— *State Papers, Domestic, James I.*, vol. xiii. 52a, A.D. 1603. Even later than this, public feeling was so strong on the subject of the burial of the dead, that an attempt at excommunication on the part of the minister of Allesmore, near Hereford, was completely defeated by force. It seems that a devout Catholic woman died; but, as the old rites had been used in her sickness, the minister maintained that she was excommunicated, and could not be interred in the churchyard. The clerk dug a grave, but the minister ordered it to be filled in again. The body remained unburied for more than eight days. At length her neighbours determined to inter the corpse. So they rose early on the appointed day, and with torches, tapers, and the ancient ringing of bells, they boldly went to the churchyard and peacefully effected their object. The minister had appealed to the bishop, who sent his officers to take the people into custody; but the number of Catholic sympathisers so increased, that this was out of the question, and serious riots were feared. —See *Treatise on Mitigation*, by Robert Parsons.

again round the stiff body, after which the latter was bound closely with swathings of clean and white linen, with a frill both at head and foot ; then placed on a bier, or sometimes in a parish coffin kept for the purpose, over which during the funeral service a wooden hearse stood, commonly covered with a silken pall.

In certain dioceses, as in that of St. David's, already referred to, some young and vigorous bishop—"a mightie proper enemy to the Pope and all his fond and pernicious tromperie"—had done his best to crush out all Catholic customs, and to destroy reverence and decency; but in others, and specially in that of York, where the wolds were wild, the parishes extensive, and the country population scattered ; and, perhaps, mainly because parsons were scarce, and ministers few in number,—the parish clerk, retaining his old duties, was duly authorised by the Primate of England[1] not only to read the first Lesson, but to monotone the Psalms at mattins and evensong, and to recite the Epistle in the monthly and quarterly service of the Lord's Supper.   In some cases, when no minister was to be had, the clerk appears to have churched the women, catechised the children, and buried the dead.[2]

Here and there, especially in certain large towns, well-meant attempts to preserve to the newly-arranged services some kind of order and decency were sometimes made.   So long as former traditions survived this was not so impracticable.   But such services were not popular; the churches had fallen into such decay—there were broken windows around, damaged roofs above, and damp pavements beneath—that the people failed to attend them, save under pressure from authority, and fear of punishment for being absent.   Thus week-day services ceased, and only Sundays came to be at all observed.   For then lists of all absentees were made out by churchwardens and sidesmen, who stood at the chief entrance with ink-horn, pen, and paper, while once a quarter lists were returned to the diocesan authorities. In newly-founded grammar schools, however, and in alms-houses, some kind of prayers, usually a modification of mattins and evensong, were almost always enjoined to be said daily—to the credit of their founders.

[1] The clerk, at least, in the diocese of York, was expected to be both able and ready to read distinctly the first Lesson, the Epistle, and the Psalms, with all the ordinary responses, and to keep the church clean, swept, and sweet.   Whether he was ordained at all, and if so by what form, is uncertain. The old clerks had almost always received the four minor orders.—Archbishop Grindal's *Articles to be Enquired of*, etc., A.D. 1571.   London : William Serres.

[2] Author's Excerpts and MSS.   Elleker Letters, No. 17.

Loose doctrines continued, at the same time, to be taught with regard to the need and nature of episcopacy. Whatsoever the Pope was believed to maintain as true and necessary, that (whatever it might be) was still openly opposed, caricatured, and condemned. Yet when the ultra-Puritans became potent, those in authority in the Established Church were obliged to shift their ground a little. Bishop Pikington of Durham, for example, remarked : " I agree that James, brother of our Lord, was bishop there at Jerusalem, as the ancient writers testify; but that he said or did anything like the popish clouted Latin mass, *that* I utterly deny." [1]

Elsewhere the same Protestant authority wrote :—

" In all these ages were some that both knew, taught privately, and followed the truth; though they were not horned and mitred bishops, nor oiled and sworn shavelings to the Pope. Such popish bishops, I am sure, no man is able to prove to have been in every See of this realm continually since the apostles' time, nor elsewhere. When he has proved it, I will say as he does." [2]

Confirmation, no longer a sacrament, but only a mere rite,[3] in which the subjects confirmed themselves, was then looked upon by the great majority as most probably a work of supererogation, and was in no way appreciated. Hence very few confirmations were held anywhere; for, in truth, nothing approaching a ceremony, unless the queen were the chief subject of it, was now tolerated, much less run after. When apostles could bestow a power of speech to the stammering or stupid, or when to those preaching to strange nations (as some remarked) a special "gift of tongues" was thus imparted, laying on of hands was all very well. But when nothing visible ensued, as was certainly then the case, it became merely an empty and idle ceremony. Long sermons or wearisome "prophesyings," as they were termed, were then all the rage. What were termed

---

[1] *Works of Bishop Pilkington*, p. 496, Parker Society. London, 1842.

[2] *Ibid.* p. 598.

[3] " The *rite* of Confirmation, as I desire to point out, is something altogether different to the *Sacrament* of Confirmation. The latter is as old as Christianity, administered both in the East and West ; whereas the former, the 'rite,' was first invented by the English Reformers. It is, as we all know, a service in which persons make a promise in the face of the congregation 'to ratify and confirm' the pledge made on their behalf by their sponsors—a very impressive service; a kind of 'renewal of vows.' But this is not a sacrament, as any bishop of the Established Church would frankly and passionately maintain."—Sermon by the Bishop of Dorchester, O.C.R., reported in the *Daily Chronicle*, September 1878.

"theatrical displays"[1] had quite gone out of fashion. When, therefore, Dr. John Underhill, in 1589, was sent to Oxford as bishop, this interesting rite had not been administered for more than a quarter of a century ;[2] and when an obscure person, named John Jegon, was appointed to the See of Norwich in the spring of 1603, there had been no confirmation in that part of the country for the space of twelve years.[3]

It was a long time before the people became accustomed to wedded bishops and parsons' wives. Several smitten and insinuating prelates who had made offers of marriage to the daughters of knights and esquires were cruelly repulsed, and this sometimes even when the watchful *paterfamilias* was himself an innovator, and "most godly and worshipful." Sir John Harington records some notable incidents relating to this subject ; and it is well known that for several generations after the changes under Elizabeth the inferior clergy had to be content with the pink-faced and fresh daughters of husbandmen, with "serving-maids," or, as a doubtful alternative, with "ancient widows."

When Dr. John Whitgift was Bishop of Worcester (A.D. 1577–1583), though the revenue of the See was not very great, he always came up to Parliament well attended,—his servants in purple liveries and staves of office, his ambling nag caparisoned with a richly embroidered saddle-cloth, his chimere of new and shining satin, and his lawn sleeves perfectly clean and undarned, —a fashion much gone out, because many of the prelates were so miserly, and consequently so personally shabby; but one which was greatly liked by the queen.[4] It happened one day that Bishop Aylmer of London, meeting His Lordship of Worcester with such an orderly troop of attendants, demanded of him how he could afford to keep so many men, upon which Whitgift answered, with a sharp twinkle of the eye and a smile, that it was because he kept so few women.

The distracted bishops, pulled hither and thither by controversial partisans, were now so troubled by the Puritans that

---

[1] "With respect to Confirmation, I do not suppose you approve of the theatrical display which the Papists have admitted among their sacraments. But if those who rightly instructed in the Catechism are admitted to the Lord's Supper with public testimony and imposition of hands (which we know that Christ also practised to young children), I do not see what occasion there is for any one to quarrel about it."—Rodolph Gualter to Bishop Cocks, Letter 94, 2nd series *Zurich Letters.*

[2] This melancholy fact is apparent from documents existing in the Diocesan Registry at Oxford.

[3] *A Replicacion to an Auncient Enemy, etc.,* p. 31.   London: Serres.

[4] *Brief View of the State of the Church of England,* by Sir J. Harington, p. 8.   London, 1653.

formal Injunctions were issued in the summer of 1571, forbidding reading, praying, preaching, or administering the Sacraments[1] in any place, public or private, without licence. This was certainly needed, if anything approaching to order was to be retained; and was not determined on a day too soon, for the disorder then existing was of so remarkable a kind that, to some, it seemed likely to be subversive of all peace, either in Church or State, and threatened to produce anarchy. A sermon in those days, instead of ending with a devout formula, often closed amidst controversial expostulations and noisy assertions, and sometimes ended with a free fight. A parsimonious Chelmsford church-warden,[2] who, on one occasion, had provided a certain amount of wine for use at some religious commemoration (let us hope it was a love-feast, and not "the Supper" of the Prayer-Book), had the empty flagon thrown at his head, because he had not supplied sufficient for the spiritual wants of the militant and excited "saints." Such disorders were by no means singular. The Act of Parliament[3] which had been passed in the spring of the year had already gone as far as it was possible to go in conciliating the wandering preachers and communistic prophets. Probably a full third of the beneficed clergy were either (1) only "readers" or old parish clerks; (2) persons who, when abroad, had received a "call" from some of the foreign sects, or who had been "ordered" by a minister;[4] (3) persons who had been appointed preachers by the Superintendents of Foreign Protestants in London, Sandwich, Canterbury, Dover, Norwich, and else-where; or (4) old men who, either in religious houses or as seculars, had, in previous reigns, received minor orders and the office of the sub-diaconate or diaconate; or (5) persons who, believing themselves "sent," and wholly repudiating forms and

---

[1] Unless a man could preach fluently without a manuscript, the Puritan leaders doubted if he were "called," though possibly "ordered." "As for those unlearned ones, whom you call, neither are they ministers, though you so term them; neither have authority to minister Sacraments, though you give them power, except they can minister the Word by preaching also."— *An Answer to Certain Pieces of a Sermon made at Paul's Cross*, by Dr. Cooper, Bishop of Lincoln. London, 1572.

[2] *The Brownists of Chelmsford, etc.*, by a Congregational Minister, p. 37. Chelmsford, 1821.

[3] Statutes, 13 Elizabeth, cap. xii.

[4] "One Badam, an old worn-out minister of Gloucestershire, deprived of all living by the Superintendent of Hereford [*i.e.* John Scory, bishop] for his lewd conversation, and among the rest *for making ministers for money*, with-out his lordship's knowledge, etc."—*An Ancient Editor's Note-Book*. Library, Stonyhurst College. From this it is clear that an old minister [neither bishop nor priest] simoniacally pretended to make "ministers."

L

ceremonies, had never been ordained at all.   Inquiries which
some of the bishops had carefully made, convinced them clearly
enough of the true state of affairs ; and, as it was quite impossible
by any existing legal machinery to turn out at least one-third of
the persons beneficed, amounting to no less than three thousand,
it was clear that what could not be cured must be endured.
Complaints had long been made that anybody and everybody
who believed himself to be under the guidance of the Spirit,[1]
insisted both on praying and preaching in parish churches as
well as by market-places and on village greens.   Persons of the
humblest class, and with no attainments,—some could only read
with difficulty, and often stumbled much in reading at all,—
came forward on their own authority to curse the religion of their
ancestors, with impressive oaths and terrible language ; to interpret
the mystical imagery of the Apocalypse in a sense "disadvan-
tageous to the foreign Bishop of Rome," and at the same time,
as some reason for their astounding dogmatism, to maintain the
certainty of their own predestination to eternal life, and their
sure guidance from on high.   As regards "reforms," those
already carried out by the Spiritual Governess, Parker, and
Cecil were not worthy of the name.   Instead of having had one
Pope of old, all the new prelates, as it was maintained, now
themselves wanted to be popes ; they wore the outlandish
garments of Babylon, fined and persecuted "the saints" (as the
Puritans modestly called themselves), cited them to their courts,
where legal sharks abounded, and steadily resisted that further
"godly reformation," which was still, as they argued, so sorely
needed.   When Archbishop Parker summoned Sampson and
other Puritan leaders to Lambeth, His Grace soon found out
how fanatical and disobedient they were, and how entirely
exhortations to conformity were contemptuously disregarded.

It was determined, therefore, to allow all those who were in
possession of benefices—whether ordained or not, and whatever
they were, laymen, ministers, or priests—to retain their respective
preferments by simple subscription to such of the "Articles of
Religion" of 1563 "as only concern the profession of the true
Christian faith and the doctrine of the Sacraments."   Conditional
ordination was never even contemplated.   With the same aim,
certain words of the twentieth Article, viz. "The Church hath

---

[1] The "farmers of benefices" were quite content to employ such persons,
because their services could be secured for a small payment ; and, consequently, seldom inquired about "ordination."   The Bishops' Courts, moreover, granted all kinds of dispensations, from which considerable fees were
received.

power to decree rites and ceremonies, and authority in controversies of faith," were somehow omitted in a new edition of these Articles which Jewell, Bishop of Salisbury, had prepared for publication; and this with the express intention of more effectually smoothing the path of the Puritans, and of avoiding further contests or agitation. Such, however, was never secured. For agitation was still carried on, and contests were more frequent than ever. The large concessions already made to the Puritans were, of course, accepted. And, be it noted, these were no sooner accepted, than fresh agitators began at once to demand further and still greater changes.

The chief point, however, which should never be forgotten by those who look back on the past, but of which few are really aware, is that, at the period referred to, the question of the necessity of episcopal ordination was settled, at the distinct suggestion of the bishops themselves, — with the pontifical authority of the Supreme Governess herself, and by and with the consent of Parliament,—in the plain sense of its *not* being necessary at all. Thus the loose and lawless opinions of Cranmer, Barlow, and Bale concerning ordination were not only commonly current throughout the New Church, but were actually approved and ratified by this new and special enactment; formally confirming those whose ordinations were avowedly questionable, doubtful, or invalid, in the full, free, and peaceable possession of their respective benefices.

Were the solemn warnings, let it be here asked, of Bishops Thirlby and Scott, of Abbot Feckenham, and Bishop Watson, uttered in all solemnity on Queen Elizabeth's accession, but utterly disregarded, the warnings of the lawful teachers of the Church of England,—not greatly needed when, in less than twenty years, such a fundamental and complete revolution could have been thus effected?

Alas, for the poor of our crowded cities! Alas, too, for the poor scattered over the wealds and wolds of our dear old England, robbed thus of their brightest heritage, the faith of their fathers: offered henceforth, in lieu of the promised Bread and a foretaste of the peace up above, only the discordant wranglings of dreary disputants, and—a stone!

What has already and hitherto been set forth will thus serve to show how thoroughly the work of destruction had been done. Not only had the people of England been cruelly cut off from communion with the rest of Christendom—against the will of a large majority, and obviously without the knowledge of what was being done, on the part of a still larger; but all religion was being deliberately corrupted and destroyed,[1] and all authority weakened.

Those who, for their own selfish purposes, had set to work to make a new Church for the English people, may possibly have done their best, in the process of its being first planned, then arranged, then manipulated anew, altered again, reformed afresh, and still made dependent, weak, and uninfluential; but the lesson they all so entirely forgot—a lesson which is more than ever needed at the present day—is that "all power" has been given to the Son of Man on earth as well as in heaven; that He has mercifully delegated that power to be exercised for the benefit of all races and nations to His One Universal Church, and that no local communion, isolated and apart, can in such sinful isolation convey the full benefit of God's royal gifts to any.

The authority of prince as well as prelate, indeed, comes from the same divine source—God Almighty; and this is true, though now rejected by those who think themselves wiser than their forefathers.   Furthermore, the destruction of one, as the experience of Christians teaches, ensures the certain weakening of the other, and *vice versâ*.   It can cause no surprise, consequently, that, when the old and legitimate Christian authority of the Holy See was rudely abolished in England, all authority became weakened; or that, in due course, it was discovered that the destruction of the altar under Elizabeth had directly led to the overthrow of the throne under Charles I.   Putting aside the question of a she-supremacy, the monstrous and impracticable doctrine that children should rule their parents, and subjects their kings; that a disjointed rabble, excited by godless self-seekers and political fanatics, may lawfully and properly set aside both patriarch and prince, as and when they will, and as often as they like, is a doctrine which, more than any other, has

---

[1] As Dr. Mossman has acutely observed:—"The position taken up by the English Church at the time of the Reformation was that a national, or local, or particular Church has a right to sit in judgment upon the Church Universal; that a part of the Church has a right to decide for herself whether or not the doctrines which she has hitherto held in common with the whole Church Universal are true or false, and accept them or reject them accordingly; a right to decide whether or not the canons of the Church Universal are in accordance with the laws of Christ and His Apostles, and abrogate them, or establish them accordingly; a right to decide for herself, as against the rest of Christendom, which Sacraments were ordained by Christ, and which were not; and a right to decide finally what ritual and ceremonies of the Church are lawful and edifying, and so to be retained; and what, on the other hand, are unlawful and unedifying, and so to be rejected, as tending to superstition and idolatry to be abhorred of all faithful Christians."—*The Keys of the Kingdom of Heaven: a Sermon.*   London, 1879.

tended to bring about that alternate disorder, confusion, mistrust, and revolution by which the once-Christian nations of Europe are now in these latter years of civilisation, culture, and progress, periodically cursed. The most influential modern Evangel is obviously the gospel of the Gatling-gun—the glad tidings of fire, sword, and force. The so-called "progress" of once Christian races turns out to be only the impressive progress of a crab—their culture, a mere knowledge of how to pamper the body, paganise the mind, corrupt the conscience, and starve the immortal soul.

CHAPTER VI.

THE action which had been taken at Rome produced one direct effect, viz. that the persecution of those who clung to the old religion became at once more merciless, bitter, and unrelenting. While some few persons endeavoured to escape the penalties imposed by occasionally going to the new services, the large majority resolutely and firmly declined to do so.

As regards the old clergy, " Queen Mary's priests," as they were still called, some notoriously conformed in the hope of another change, or possibly in order to have greater liberty and licence. Others, however, stood firm unto the very end, living and dying in the faith of their forefathers.

Of the former an acute writer thus remarks : " When punishments are inflicted on the one hand, and considerable advantages offered on the other; when non-compliance is attended with bitter sufferings, and temporising encouraged with rewards, a sudden change in matters of religion is justly ascribed either to the fear of the one or hope of the other. And this was the case from the very beginning of Queen Elizabeth's Reformation. Great numbers of the inferior clergy who came over to it were frightened into a compliance, and taught to conform by the sufferings of others. They saw their bishops imprisoned, and all those of their own rank who had refused the Oath of Supremacy turned out of their livings and reduced to beggary. So that they had no other choice left but either to conform or starve, having nothing but their benefices to depend upon for a livelihood. A terrible temptation to those who are not armed with virtue strong enough to undergo a lingering martyrdom! But the greatest part were prevailed upon by the powerful charms of liberty and ease. For, besides the liberty they were sure to enjoy of gratifying their incontinence, as the effect soon showed, the queen had by the plenitude of her ecclesiastical power contrived such a commodious Reformation for them that, if they would but conform, they should keep their benefices, and at the same time be eased of the most painful part of the duties annexed to them."[1]

Of the Catholic laity by far the greater number had deliberately declined to attend the new services. Enactment had been added to enactment, statute to statute, but all in vain. They could not conform. Their consciences were altogether against it. The new religion, made only a few years ago, was certainly not from God. The new ministers had no proper ordination, and many of them no ordination at all. One contradicted another, and all was confusion; while the new doctrines were heretical or erroneous. They, therefore, would not conform.[2] Hence they lay at the mercy of their enemies. At any moment they might be arrested and hurried off before the appointed courts to be interrogated on oath as to whether or not they had been to church, where, when, and how often they had received the Lord's Supper, and whether they held the parson's written certificate that this had been publicly done. If not, they were condemned as recusants to fines and imprisonment; and if, having previously communicated, they had repented of the act and been reconciled by some priest, they forfeited their lands and goods, and were liable to be confined in prison for life. Thus, to say mass, as well as to hear mass, was a crime. To receive a confession, as well as to make a confession, was the same. To teach the Catholic faith as brought hither by St. Augustine, or to be taught it, was the like. To know that a priest was at a certain place, and not to seize or betray him, was a crime. To give him food, shelter, or money was also a crime. To remain away from the services of the desolate and ruined churches was a crime; torture, imprisonment, and death were the punishments. So that the rack and gibbet and the gallows were in constant requisition; while the prisons and the dungeons were choked with innocent victims.[3]

Elizabeth's Inquisition, for such it was, was empowered to exercise an absolute control over men's opinions, and to punish

---

[1] *England's Conversion and Reformation Compared*, p. 260. Antwerp, 1725.

[2] The above is duly and exactly paraphrased from replies to the inquiries of the Commissioners, of whom Grindal was one.

[3] "Of our late persecution in general it is so extreme as the like was never. All prisons are full of all sorts, old and young men, wives, widows and maids. It is not enough to use all allegiance by way of protestation; unless they can get one to renounce the Pope and confer with the ministry; or else to be committed and indicted for £20 by the month, and all further misery to be inflicted that they can possibly devise."—*The Troubles of our Catholic Forefathers*, 3rd series, p. 50. London, 1877.

all according to the discretion of its members. Ordinary evidence might be received in the ordinary manner ; but torture and imprisonment (what these were will be soon seen in detail) were likewise to be used whensoever thought necessary. Thus this hypocritical woman, aided by men like Cecil and Walsingham, the bishops and the judges, as well as the ordinary justices of the peace,[1] punished in a most barbarous manner persons absolutely guiltless of any crime whatsoever, and this by punishments hitherto reserved for the most dark and deadly crimes.

But the tyranny of inflicting fines for recusancy, *i.e.* for declining to attend the new services, was the most tyrannical. If persons honestly and conscientiously believed that attendance thereat involved the sin of apostacy (and most of their religious teachers so taught them), surely their consciences were not to be forced by such odious laws. But bribery had then become a science ; the bribed were exceedingly numerous, and money with which to reward them was notoriously scarce. Hence this plan of fines was cleverly adopted. Old families paid them ; upstarts and time-servers received them. The actual punishment for refusing to attend the queen's new services was no less than twenty pounds a lunar month, or about two hundred and fifty pounds a year ; which, according to the value of money in the present day, would be equivalent to an annual fine of three thousand two hundred and fifty pounds per annum. Hoards and children's marriage-portions, put by year by year from the time of their birth, thus soon decreased, and subsequently vanished. Numbers of noblemen and gentlemen endured this tyranny, and anxiously endeavoured to pay these demands, so long as their property enabled them to do so, by selling their estates (and this, of course, by forced sales and at great disadvantage) ; but if at any time the fines were in arrears, a statute recently passed authorised the immediate seizure of all their personal property in addition, together with two-thirds of their real estates every six months, so long as the arrears were unpaid. Sometimes an annual composition was received instead ; but this was regarded by Elizabeth and her ministers as a great favour.

Thus, under this woman's disastrous rule, the Catholic gentle-

---

[1] A justice of the peace was defined as "an animal, who, for half-a-dozen chickens, would dispense with a dozen laws" (Sir Simon D'Ewes' *Journal*, p. 661, London, 1682) ; while as regards bribes offered to, and received by, some of the superior judges, Recorder Fleetwood (quoted in Wright's *Letters*, vol. ii. p. 247) asserts that it had grown to be a trade in the court to make means for reprieves. "Twenty pounds for a reprieve is nothing, though it be but for bare ten days."

man's manor-house or mansion afforded him neither security nor safety. The walls may have been thick, and the moat around them broad and deep. Within, memorials of the past, and of those who had crossed the dark river, told silently of the peace of the grave. In the courtyard the peacock may have sunned itself undisturbed, or the swans moved gracefully upon the still waters. But the pleasant quiet of the old home was a mockery; while its material stability maybe only reminded its thoughtful owner how insecure was now his own altered lot. Peace was denied him; he experienced no such protection as just and righteous laws in a Christian state should always provide. His house was no longer his castle, as the ancient phrase stood. For the indiscretion of friends, or the ill-will and malice of foes; the dishonesty of tenants, or the carelessness of servants; a word uttered by accident; the sight of a rosary or crucifix, might cause the immediate break-up and desolation of his ancient and pleasant home, and bring him face to face with ruin. In by-ways and retired nooks, under high patronage, the disguised spy constantly skulked or crawled, in order to betray and impoverish the descendants of English gentlemen who, both at home and abroad, had been valorous and valiant in the field, just and honest in their due positions at home, the stay and strength of England—hitherto a happy country, where truth had found a temple and freedom had been secured and loved.

As for the poorer recusants, who owned consciences, and whose only comfort was their faith, they were in a like sorry plight. They, too, were cited, charged, and condemned. But how could any of such miserable creatures, who with the greatest difficulty had kept body and soul together, pay the fines and compositions which had been imposed?[1] They could not. For no sheriff's official can draw blood out of a flint stone, nor can any man give what he does not possess. They were sent off to prison therefore; huddled together in rank and filthy dungeons, and fed on black bread and brackish water. On one occasion as many as eighty-two had stood in the dock at Oxford at once. At York two hundred and three were condemned and imprisoned either there, at Beverley, or at Hull, in the course of three days, until at length the various counties petitioned to be

---

[1] In the course of an inquiry into the existence of bondsmen in England at the time of and after the Reformation, Mr. Furnivall has been shown, by Mr. Selby and Mr. Bond of the Record Office, two grants by Queen Elizabeth in the seventeenth year of her reign (A.D. 1575) to Sir Henry Lee, as a reward for his services, of all the fines and compositions he could extract from three hundred bondsmen and women.

relieved of their care and cost.   Then, after having been stripped
to the waist (women as well as men), these prisoners were sometimes tied up to a post, first flogged until the blood streamed
down their backs; and then, having had their ears bored with a
red-hot iron, were sent off without either money or food, to do
as they could or starve.   If they were not possessed of twenty
marks, they were to quit their native land within three months,
and to suffer death, without any fresh trial or further process, if
they returned.

One fact at length became clear, viz. that unless some actual
and practical means were taken without delay by which to keep
alive an interest in the ancient faith, and unless authorised
officers were appointed to maintain and defend it, it must surely
cease to exist, and this in no long period.   The priests ordained
in Queen Mary's reign were, one after the other, dying out.[1]
Poverty, anxiety, and imprisonment had made their hair pre-
maturely grey, and weakened their bodily powers.   They had
lost their spirits, and their energies had faded and failed.   The
illegally-deprived bishops were kept in confinement, and consequently could not keep up the supply of clergy.   A true vocation
for the office and due preparation were at least needed.   How
could the latter be given when persecution was rampant?   Who,
then, would propose a remedy—who supply the want?   What
could be done?

Dr. William Allen, already referred to, of good and ancient
family,[2] was the patriotic and far-sighted person who so
charitably and boldly stood forward to give an answer and
provide a remedy.   From the outset he had clearly enough seen
the magnitude of the evil and the true nature of the remedy
required.   With an intimate knowledge of his contemporaries,
and a sincere devotion to the Church of his baptism, he set
himself in good earnest to accomplish the task which the
religious revolution then effected in his native land made it so

[1] One priest "for avoiding searches he hath been compelled five days and
nights to lie in the woods, and other times to walk on hills and forests, and
lie in hay-barns.   He hath reconciled one hundred and sixty.   He hath been
driven to sit up four whole nights together to do works of charity, sometimes
hearing an hundred several confessions at one time."—*An Ancient Editor's
Note-Book*, MS., Stonyhurst College.

[2] He was a son of Esquire John Allen of Rosshall, co. Lancaster.   His
sister, Mary Allen, married one of the Worthingtons of Worthington, an
ancient Catholic family of rank and lineage.—From some MS. notes by a
relation, the author discovers that in 1808 there was a striking portrait of the
cardinal at Kiddington House, Oxfordshire, in which he was represented in
rochet, scarlet mozetta, and biretta.   It belonged to the late Charles Browne
Mostyn, Esq.

essential for him to undertake. He was learned and eloquent, bold and discreet, a good tactician, and patient under difficulties. From the first he had let his fellow-Christians know that Catholic authority could never tolerate any attendance at the new Zwinglian services. On that point his trumpet had never given any uncertain sound. To him, therefore, many seemed to look up with confidence and trust as to a guide. And they did not look in vain.

He resolved without delay to open a college at Douay, in Flanders, for the education of English Catholics for the priesthood, on the model of those valued institutions at Oxford and Cambridge, which were now shut to them at home. Friends and allies who had been consulted on the subject, not only gave their sincere approbation to the scheme, but rendered substantial and efficient help. Men denied themselves sorely in order to aid; contributions came in profusely, more at first than were actually required. When at the inauguration of the college, the mass of the Holy Ghost was said by Dr. Allen in the private chapel of his new institution, only six companions, five of them being Oxford men, knelt behind him at the elevation, imploring the Almighty's blessing on their joint labours. So soon as the start had been first made, difficulties seemed to vanish marvellously. Men planted and watered, but God gave the increase. First came the blade, then the ear, then the full corn in the ear. In a short time more than a hundred and fifty exiled Englishmen, mourning over the desolation of their country, but full of resolution, zeal, and devotion, had been enrolled on the books of the college, in order to study theology, receive the sacerdotal character, and then return to their native shores at the risk of their liberties and lives to keep the lamp of Divine Truth burning in their once happy island-home.[1]

Theirs was a noble work. In less than five years, ninety-six priests, charitable, zealous, and fearless, anointed with the unction of the Holy One, had landed in England to perpetuate the ancient faith. Later on more came, in a like spirit of self-sacrifice ready to face death; and though, for many generations, and through more than three centuries, it appeared as though

[1] "This seminary or college counts amongst her *alumni*, or such as have been some time her members, one cardinal, one archbishop, twelve bishops, two other bishops-elect, three archpriests with episcopal faculties, eighty doctors of divinity, seventy writers, many of the most eminent men of divers religious orders, and what is most glorious of all, above one hundred and fifty martyrs, besides innumerable others who have either died in prison for their faith, or at least have suffered imprisonments, banishments, etc., for the same."--Richard, Bishop of Debra.

the chill of a permanent winter had as it were, throughout all seasons, settled upon a garden where the spiritual flowers and fruit had once been beautiful and rich; yet after much patient waiting, and many a prayer that the dew of heaven might fall, a second spring appeared when men least expected its balmy breath and bursting buds; and so the flowers of grace again adorned the earth, and the welcome time of the singing of birds came back once more.

But to revert to facts, and to continue the record. Archbishop Parker died of the stone, having suffered much, on the 17th May 1575. Below the middle height, his features were heavy and dull; his hands large, his form portly; and he is said to have been somewhat rough in his manners and wanting in refinement. From Queen Elizabeth's standing-point — save in the case of having secured for himself a wife, Mistress Margaret Harleston—he proved himself to have been politic, discreet, and duly subservient to the State authorities; sufficiently pliable to have caused them no inconvenience by the assumption of an independence which he did not possess, and never cared to hanker after; and was found to be at all times a useful and prudent adviser in ecclesiastical questions. More considerate than others of the new bishops for those of the old faith, he appears to have been a learned man, particularly in history and antiquities; and in this respect was unlike the majority of his brethren; moreover, he was not stained with those obvious vices which overtook so many of the "Reformation" prelates; and when he saw how the Supreme Governess disliked them, he gave no sanction whatsoever to the fanatical extravagances of the Puritans[1] and their various sects. He was a commonplace, but somewhat dull and insipid, Erastian. From the wreck which had overtaken the abbey libraries, however, he wisely gathered several literary and paleographic treasures, which still remain as a memorial of him at Lambeth Palace, while his *Antiquities of the Church, and Lives of the Archbishops,* is a learned antiquarian volume. He was buried with some heraldric pomp in the chapel of that prelatial mansion, and an altar-tomb was placed over his remains.[2]

[1] In Lodge's sketch of the life of Parker, he declares truly enough that at that time "all the exterior decencies of devotion were reviled as remnants of popery, and ecclesiastical propriety was viewed merely as the means of spiritual pride."—Lodge's *Portraits*, vol. iii.

[2] The remains of this prelate were buried in the midst of the chapel; but in the time of the Great Rebellion, that building was "converted into a dancing-room, they [the rebels] having first beat down Archbishop Parker's tomb in the middle of it, and thrown his bones upon the dunghill."—See

Edmund Grindal, first Bishop of London, afterwards translated to York in 1570, was appointed Parker's successor as Primate of all England, in the early part of the year 1576. He was a Cumberland man, who had been educated at Cambridge, patronised by Ridley, and had taken a moderate part in the disputes concerning the character and comprehensiveness of the Book of Common Prayer when the foreign Reformers wished it to be further "reformed." He, too, was an Erastian, though puritanically inclined, and a great persecutor of his opponents.

An amusing anecdote is on record of the high-handed manner in which the queen practically maintained her supremacy over the bishops whom she had made, and may be here recounted. Cocks of Ely, a noted Puritan, then dwelt at his official town house to the north of Holborn—a spacious and magnificent edifice with hall, chapel,[1] library, parlour, gate-house, and hostelrie, of rich second-pointed architecture, surrounded with a garden and well-wooded grounds of no less than twenty acres. Sir Christopher Hatton,[2] one of the queen's later favourites, a person of handsome figure and an accomplished dancer, often looked upon the stately palace and fair surroundings of the bishop,—the situation was pleasant, the air pure, the land productive,—and at last, like Ahab of old, coveted a portion. The queen on learning this, ordered Cocks to transfer by legal deed a certain part to the new Vice-Chamberlain, and with no delay. But the bishop looked at the proposal from another point of view, and pleaded that as he only held the property in trust for the See, and owned but a life interest in it, he was altogether unable conscientiously to alienate any portion.

Upon which the Supreme Governess, who notoriously disliked consciences, wrote to him as follows :—

"PROUD PRELATE,—You know well what you were afore I

Trials for High Treason, etc., part i. p. 411.   London, 1720. The empty tomb now stands at the south-west part of the building, in a corner to the right of the chief entrance.

[1] The chapel, dedicated in honour of St. Ethelreda of Ely, after having been in a state of humiliating degradation for centuries, was purchased by the Fathers of the Order of Charity, and solemnly opened for divine service in the presence of Henry Edward Manning, sometime Cardinal-Archbishop of Westminster (who preached with great unction and charity), in 1879. Mass is again said daily; and a relic of the patroness is placed under the altar.

[2] There is an excellent portrait of Sir Christopher Hatton, from the brush of Kettel, at Dytchley Park, Oxfordshire. It was a present from Hatton himself to Sir Henry Lee, K.G., and descended to the Lord Viscount Dillon, through his ancestress Lady Charlotte Lee.

made you what you now are.   If you do not immediately
comply with my request I will unfrock you, by God.

"ELIZABETH R."

His lordship, being no doubt impressed by the threat and the
oath conjoined, and seeing that the person who had made a
bishop could most probably unmake one, did as he was told.   The
gate-house of his palace on Holborn Hill, and a considerable
part of the adjacent property, were speedily and duly made over
to Sir Christopher, who still gives the name of " Hatton Garden "
to a modern street in that changed locality.

As early as the year 1575, a congregation of Dutch Anabaptists, numbering nearly thirty persons of either sex, was
seized in London on Easter Sunday and committed to prison.
This sect[1] was one of the most direct and offensive products of
the so-called " Reformation."   Its members rejected the doctrine
of the Trinity, repudiated baptism, and denied the lawfulness of
war, oaths, and magistrates.   All this, of course, made them
specially obnoxious.   Four of the persons seized and accused
recanted their errors at St. Paul's Cross.   Eleven were condemned to be burnt, but were banished instead.   Two men,
however, John Wielmacher and Hendrick Ter Vort, were actually
burnt at Smithfield, and died enduring great agonies.[2]   Foxe, the
author of what is called his *Martyrology*, wrote to the queen[3]
urging her to inflict some other death than burning, as burning
was only the Pope's method of punishment, as he falsely asserted
—conveniently forgetting the cruelties which Servetus received
at the hand of John Calvin, and those endured by Lambert,
Allen, and Frith from Archbishop Cranmer.   But the queen,
who hated the Puritans more than the Catholics, would not, and
did not, interfere.

In the meantime, persecution was steadily carried on in every
part of England.   Terror and misery everywhere ensued.   Many
persons were banished.   The treatment through a considerable

---

[1] Its lineal descendants at the present day are a great curse to the country.
For in many places they still do much to prevent the lower classes having
their children christened, so that many thousands year by year die unbaptized
and unregenerate.

[2] "Two Dutchmen, Anabaptists, were burnt in Smithfield, who died in
great horror, with roaring and crying."—Stowe's *Annals, in loco.*

[3] On another and similar occasion it is on record that the queen calling to
mind "that she was the Head of the Church ; that it was her duty to extirpate
error ; and that heretics ought to be cut off from the flock of Christ that they
may not corrupt others," signed the death-warrant of two Nonconformists,
who were burnt to death in Smithfield.—Rymer's *Fœdera*, xv. 740, 741.

period of Doleman and Jackson, two priests of Queen Mary's reign, and others of like standing, may be gathered from the confession of Robert Gray, a priest, taken by that cruel and infamous priest-taker, Richard Topcliffe.[1]   Every endeavour was made to find out what religious services were held at Lord Viscount Montagu's house at Cowdray, near Midhurst, and at Sir Robert Dormer's mansion at Wing, in Buckinghamshire. Watchers were stationed near and servants bribed.   These noble families were related to each other, and warmly upheld the ancient faith.   William Browne, grandson of the first Viscount Montagu, born in 1578, entered the Society of Jesus, and died a lay brother abroad, aged fifty-nine.   His sister Dorothy had married Edward Lee of Stantonbury.[2]   Their mother Mary was one of the Dormers of Eythrope and Thame.   All these, amid the greatest difficulties, practised the ancient religion, and always carefully protected the old clergy.   Many of these latter who had resigned their preferments for conscience' sake were provided for by the Montagus.   At Wing and Eythrope there were priests' hiding-places, and it is on record that Sir Robert Dormer every year laid by a considerable sum of money to distribute to those poor outcast clergy of the old faith[3] who patiently suffered poverty rather than conform to the new state of things, and who found a home at no great distance from the mansion of this Catholic nobleman.

Some writers, either misinformed or inexact in their statements, have boldly asserted that priests of Queen Mary's reign were never persecuted, and that no undue persecution was inflicted on any of the older clergy at all until the Bull of Pope Pius V. had been issued.   But this is quite inaccurate, as the following original document conclusively proves :—

[1] See *State Papers, Domestic, Elizabeth*, vol. ccxlv. folio 138.   Author's MS. Collections.

[2] Father Roger Lee, S.J. (son of Edward Lee, and Amicia his wife, dr. of Sir Edmund Ashfield of Ewelme, Oxon.), was of this family.—See *Records of the English Province*, vol. i. pp. 456 *et seq.*   London, 1877.

[3] The following examples of how the old clergy were sometimes treated is worthy of note :—" Sir Michael Bowton, priest [an old man *in marg.*], about thirteen years since being apprehended and committed to prison to Ouse-bridge, was called before the judges the next assizes after, and because he would not tell them his place of abode, they burned him through the ear for a rogue."—*Notes by a Prisoner in Ousebridge Kidcote*, p. 307.   Mr. William Bandersby, an old man and priest, was committed to the castle, where he died in 1587.—*Ibid.* 322.   Mr. Richard Bowes, an old priest, sometime Priest-Vicar of Ripon Minster, *i.e.* from 1554 to 1569, but who would never do any Protestant service, nor come to church, was committed to York Castle, where he died.—*Ibid.* 322.

"Sir John Bowlton, priest, committed the first year of Her Majesty's reign, first to York Castle, from thence to Ousebridge, where he remained ten or twelve years close prisoner, and from thence removed to Hull Blockhouse, there remained about eight years, and then banished beyond the seas. Sir Nicholas Grene, priest, being committed twenty-eight years since to Ousebridge, where he remained five years and then died. Sir Henry Comberforth [priest] committed prisoner to Ousebridge twenty-six years since, where he remained six years, from thence removed to Hull Blockhouse, remaining there close prisoner about ten years and there died. So likewise Sir Thomas Bedall and Thomas Bell. The last named was committed twenty-four years since to Ousebridge, where he lay all one cold [est] winter as hath been seen of frost and snow, in the stocks: divers preachers coming the same time to confer with him; then removed to the castle."[1]

The timid as well as the more bold and devout adherents of the ancient faith, when their means would permit, sought an asylum from such persecution in foreign countries. When this became known to the Court, proclamations for their return were speedily issued ; and if they did not at once come back, their lands and goods were seized and sold at mere nominal prices to the supporters and adherents of the authorities and those in power. In one year no less than sixty-eight fugitives were so treated.[2] Thus opposition was successfully borne down, for all opponents were legally robbed and ruthlessly ruined. If such a policy deserved the name of "statesmanship," Queen Elizabeth's advisers were statesmen indeed.

Many of the bishops were likewise active in taking proceedings against all recusants. If any of their lordships appeared to be indifferent on the subject, or apathetic, Cecil employed some mutual friend or agent to jog their memories, and remind them of their duties. Occasionally he did this himself. Purity of faith, in that conscientious and religious statesman's opinion, was the first and greatest need. The Pope's religion, he piously observed, was most impure. Therefore the official believers in a better, as he pointed out, should strive to make others believers also. To ferret out the obstinate or timorous, to worry again and again those who had been ferreted out, and were then very probably in prison, was one of the chief and most charitable duties of the Protestant prelates. Grindal, a person of consider-

---

[1] *Notes by a Prisoner in Ousebridge Kidcote.* Original MS. at Stonyhurst College.
[2] Strype's *Annals*, vol. ii. Appendix No. 102.

able energy, was both constant and earnest in what he called the "blessed work." He always did it with a good will; but, as he informed Cecil regarding a most devout person upon whom he had tried his hand, was not always very successful:—"I can do no good with Sir John Southworth for altering his opinion in religion . . . the man is altogether unlearned, carried with a blind zeal without knowledge. His principal grounds are 'He *will* follow the faith of his fathers; he *will* die in the faith wherein he was baptized.'"[1]

Surely if this persecuted gentleman was satisfied with the religion which Christendom for fifteen hundred years had universally acknowledged to be the only true religion, he might not unreasonably have been allowed the same liberty as that claimed by Grindal and Cecil themselves.

When this prelate, who was great at sharp sayings and epigrammatic retorts, became Archbishop of York, he wrote a letter to Cecil, then Lord Burghley, concerning Dr. Vavasor, a physician of that city, who declined to give up the ancient faith, and was such an experienced and adroit controversialist that the archbishop himself, having in a public disputation been put to shame before a public audience, acted (as his own words allow) thus:— "My Lord President and I, knowing his disposition to talk, thought it not good to commit the said Dr. Vavasor to the Castle of York, where some other like affected prisoners remain; but rather to a solitary prison in the Queen's Majesty's Castle at Hull, *where he shall only talk to walls.*"

In the city of York, A.D. 1576, at the suggestion of the Queen's Council, more specific and definite inquiries were made as to the number and status of the recusants. The same process was adopted in other places, and similar machinery put in motion.[2] At York the city authorities were peremptorily ordered to supply careful and detailed information to the Earl of Huntingdon, Lord President of the Northern Council. From the dates of the official letters despatched from London—the later communications becoming more demanding and exacting in their terms— it is clear that the action enjoined upon the authorities in question was very distasteful to them; for these evidently put off the disagreeable work of examining the poorer citizens as long as

---

[1] *Remains of Archbishop Grindal*, p. 305. Parker Society. Letter 56, to Cecil, 3rd August 1569.

[2] As early as 19th June 1573, one of the old clergy, Sir Thomas Woodhouse, had been executed at Tybourne for denying the queen's supremacy, and this was done with the customary cruelties. He was a Norfolk man, and of a knightly family.

possible.   Perhaps no more touching returns can be found amongst such legal documents as those subsequently furnished and still on record.   The poor all tell their plaintive story with wonderful simplicity.   Between the new and the old order of things there was a difference, apparent enough both to eye and ear, and so great that none could mistake the one for the other. The innovators and their innovations were utterly distasteful to all under examination.   The consciences of those who clung to the ancient faith would not allow these poor people to accept the "reforms" thrust upon them.   One remarked that "her conscience would not serve her to do so."   In another case an aged respondent who, though poor and feeble, had been evidently well taught and owned true instincts as to right and wrong, averred that compliance "would damn her soul."   But, to go into particulars.   From the existing minutes of the examinations it may be seen how close were the inquiries concerning even the trading class and those below it.   One, Elizabeth Wilkinson, the wife of a miller in the parish of All-Hallows-on-the-Pavement, in response to questions, "sayeth she cometh not to the church because there is neither priest, altar, nor sacrifice."   Isabel, wife of William Bowman, locksmith of the parish of St. Cross, "sayeth she cometh not to the church, for her conscience will not serve her, because there is not the Sacrament hung up, and other things as hath been aforetime.   And further she sayeth that she doth not believe that such words as the priest readeth are true."   "Margaret Taylor," wife of Thomas Taylor of the same parish, "sayeth that she cometh not to the church because there is not a priest as there ought to be, and also that there is not the Sacrament of the Altar."

Instead of a priest, vested in his sacrificial garments attended by his server, and offering day by day the mystical sacrifice at the sacred altar in the dim and distant sanctuary, as had been the case from the coming hither of St. Austin the Monk, the poor now beheld the altar-stone thrown down, and perhaps used as a doorstep, the priest imprisoned, the lamps stolen, the sacred vessels profaned ; and, in lieu thereof, some "weighty minister" in a black garment reading prayers once a week from a pulpit in the nave to a fanatical and small congregation, whom he faced,[1] but did not edify.

---

[1] "To the intent that the people may the better heare the Morning and Evening Prayer, when the same by the minister is saide, and be the more edified thereby, we do enjoine that the churchwardens of every parish in places as well exempt, as not exempte, at the charges of the Parish shall procure a decent low pulpit to be erected and made in the body of the church,

Isabel Portar, already in prison,—and thus punished before she was properly charged with any offence,—the wife of a tailor in the parish of St. Mary, Castlegate, "sayeth that she cometh not to the church because her conscience will not serve her; for things are not in the church as it hath been aforetime in her forefathers' days." Janet Stryckett, widow, of the parish of the Holy Trinity, in Micklegate, "sayeth she cometh not to church because her conscience will not serve her; for the bread and wine is not consecrated as it hath been in time past."[1] Alice Lobby, the wife of a tanner in the parish of All Hallows, likewise "cometh not to the church because her conscience will not serve her; for she sayeth she thinketh the baptism is not as it hath been; and sayeth she will not receive (at the 'Supper') so long as she liveth."[2]

The above are only a few specimens of the replies out of many. They all, more or less, tell the same tale—a heavy tale of individual suffering.

The process of further action was eminently simple and extremely effective. It had been carefully devised round the Council-board of the Supreme Governess in London, and worked admirably. The first weapon was a severe fine for being absent from church; and this, if not promptly paid, was secured by an immediate distraint. Pots and pans,[3] jewels, "pillow-beres," "coverlids," coffers, and hangings were at once ruthlessly swept off and sold. For silly and superstitious "Papists"—as they were termed—there was, of course, no pity. If such persons owned consciences, it was all the worse for them; for consciences were obviously unprofitable possessions, and only brought mis-

wherein the minister shall stande with his face towards the people when he readeth Morning and Evening Prayer."—Injunctions given by Edmund Grindal, A.D. 1571. London: William Serres.

[1] In the Book of Common Prayer then in use, there were no manual acts whatsoever, nor any consecration ordered to be done, in or at the saying of the appointed prayer.

[2] MS. Records of the Proceedings of the Court of the Lord Mayor of York.—MS. Collections at Stonyhurst College, Angl. A. "By William Hutton, an ancient Catholic prisoner upon Ousebridge."—The Troubles of our Catholic Forefathers, 3rd series, pp. 233 et seq. London, 1877.

[3] "Our miseries are daily multiplied; we expect every hour dissolution. Our friends abroad are spoiled to their skin; what by the pursuivants, and what robberies they suffer by the under-sheriff and his followers it is long to tell you—neither pot nor pan, nor bedding, nor ring, nor jewels, nor anything whatsoever escapeth their hands. The oath is offered by the justices even at their pleasure, yet some of them cannot but in their hearts detest the injury, Divers priests have been banished of late, and now more are apprehended and like to be banished."—From a Letter by G. Lumbton. MS. Archives, Old Clergy Chapter, Westminster.

fortune. In the battle of life, in that day, those who regarded their consciences lost; while those who boldly disregarded them won triumphantly. The cottage room, therefore, was left empty (its pantry and bread-aumbry rifled), and sometimes the bed-loft over it likewise. If the grave offence of not going to listen to the squabbling preachers and Zwinglian pastors were repeated, imprisonment followed the act of distraint. Tradesmen, yeomen, and husbandmen who themselves conformed were all pressed hard to ensure the conformity of their wives;[1] while every obstacle was put in the way of those who sought to bring up their children in the ancient religion. Schoolmasters of the old faith were equally persecuted with the priests. Subsequently all lodgers, servants, and wayfarers,[2] who were occasionally housed in charity were also brought under the supervision of these energetic officials who exercised local authority; for by this means, a wandering priest, who, at the risk of his liberty and life, went about to minister to the poor, the desolate, and to prisoners, was sometimes secured, imprisoned, and subsequently either banished or executed.

Now, therefore, that the ancient faith, which had made England so great and happy for ages, was thus cast out, there seemed some chance of the total extirpation of all who dared to remain its adherents.

Though it had been and was a religion of charity and hospitality, though the repulsive name of "pauper" was then unknown,—for all, whether rich or poor, were regarded as brethren in the One Fold, all owned one Master and possessed a common interest in securing the common good,—yet in great probability (as men then alive thought) Elizabeth and her tools would complete the change they had so resolutely undertaken and commenced.

---

[1] "21° Februarii, 20° Elizabeth. — And now John Widdon, William Wilkinson, William Plowman, Richard Durham, Thomas Langton have submitted themselves to bide the order of this court for arrearages (sic) due by every of them for their wives' offence for not coming to the church, contrary to the ordinance of this city therefore lately established by this court."—MS. Records of the Proceedings of the Court of the Lord Mayor of York, folio 83b.

[2] "The sheriffs of this city, taking occasion to view the prisoners in the Kidcotes upon Ousebridge, they found amongst those that are committed for not coming to church, certain mass-books, pictures, holy water with strencles [sic—strencle, aspersorium or holy-water sprinkler], beads, pairs of vestments, wax candles and girdle, and a great canvas bag belonging to some man, having in it some unlawful books: wherefore it is supposed that some seminary priest did resort and frequent the company of the said prisoners in the said gaols, and there did say mass, persuading the said prisoners to remain in their disobedience."—MS. Records, etc., 14th February 158¾.

But Dr. William Allen was doing what lay in his power to resist the work, and was doing it wisely and well.   Between him and the Supreme Governess there rolled the sea—happily for his liberty and life ; he, therefore, from his new residence, could defy her death-dealing power, while she, frantic with the sincerest vexation, and savage with feminine spite, was unable to defy his. He had been steadily training a series of zealous and fearless teachers of the old religion ; and now they had come, in twos and threes, to do their work.   They did it well, in the spirit of the martyrs of the Forum and Amphitheatre of old, and soon had their reward.

The protomartyr of Dr. Allen's College at Douay was Cuthbert Maine,[1] born at Yalston, near Barnstaple, in Devonshire.   He had an uncle who, having been ordained under Queen Mary, had conformed to the new order of affairs, and was comfortably beneficed in the West of England.   This uncle entered him at St. Alban's Hall, in the University of Oxford, where he graduated, and having been ordained, subsequently became Fellow of St. John's College.   There he lived for some years and secured the regard and respect of its members and authorities ; but, subsequently, not liking the new religion, he went over to Douay, where he formally renounced all heresy and schism, and was in due course ordained a priest.   Anxious to atone for his past errors by some marked exhibition of zeal, he volunteered for work in England, and in company with another priest, Mr. John Paine, reached his old home in 1576.

Here he became chaplain to a certain Esquire Thomas Tregean who lived on his ample estate near Truro ; and for nearly a year laboured incessantly amongst the Cornish people, who were all deeply attached to the ancient faith.

In the summer of 1577, William Bradbridge, Bishop of Exeter, was holding a visitation at Truro, when the sheriff, a certain Esquire Greenfield, was ordered to· search for one Bourne who had been convicted in London of a misdemeanour, and to do so in the house of Tregean, where Maine passed as the esquire's steward, and in which house report declared that the delinquent was hiding.

The sheriff and his officers, offering a great show of violence, searched the house by force, and finding Maine there, accused

---

[1] See Bishop Challoner's *Memoirs of Missionary Priests,* vol. i. pp. 37–45 ; *Apology and True Declaration of the Institution and Endeavour of the Two English Colleges, etc.,* by Dr. William Allen ; John Stowe's *Chronicles,* p. 677 ; *Athenæ Oxon.,* by Anthony à Wood ; and the old edition of the *State Trials.*

him of being the person sought for, but this he denied. However, on searching him carefully, they found an *Agnus Dei* hung upon a ribbon round his neck; and upon discovering this, at once took possession of all his books, letters, manuscripts, and other property, which they carried off in triumph to the bishop. Amongst these was a printed copy of a document from Rome, announcing a jubilee, which he had purchased at a bookseller's shop at Douay.   They likewise soon lodged Maine in prison at Launceston, "putting great gyves about his legs, and chaining him to a bed-post."

At Michaelmas he was indicted of five separate offences :—(1) That he had obtained a Bull from Rome absolving the queen's subjects from their allegiance, and had so absolved divers. (2) That he had published this Bull in Esquire Tregean's house. (3) That he had maintained the usurped power of the Bishop of Rome, and so denied Her Majesty's spiritual supremacy. (4) That he had unlawfully brought into the kingdom a popish *Agnus Dei*. And (5) that he had said mass in Mr. Tregean's house.   Maine's reputation stood high amongst his Cornish friends and neighbours.   He was of a sweet disposition, with no harsh word for his enemies, and he owned a large circle of friends.   Moreover, he was most self-denying, patient, and devout; and this was all well-known to the spectators, amongst whom he had great sympathy.

The jury had been "carefully selected so as to serve the Quene's Majestie well and truly," which obviously means that it had been duly packed.   The Earl of Bedford, one of the new mushroom noblemen, who took a great interest in all such proceedings, was present; but Judge Manwood presided.   With the exception of the *Agnus Dei*, which was found upon Maine, but of which there was no proof that he had brought it hither, there was literally no evidence against the accused of any sort or kind. Surmises without reason, there may have been in abundance. Reasonable surmises there were but few.   But as for proofs, there were none.   As regards the Bull, it merely proclaimed a jubilee.   It was not an official copy certified by a notary, but only a printed version issued by a foreign bookseller.

However, the judge informed the jury that, in a case like that before them, where plain and positive proofs were wanting, strong presumption should be allowed to take their place; adding that it was their bounden duty by their verdict to protect the queen and condemn the accused.

They did so, with Lord Bedford's avowed approbation, and brought in Maine guilty of high treason.   He was held to have offended against the law of 1571. Sentence was pronounced in the usual form.

But it appears that, as certain of the other judges were dissatisfied with the verdict, some delay was occasioned in carrying it out. The matter was brought before the Privy Council ; but such was the iniquity of the times, that, notwithstanding the opinion of several of the judges that the verdict went beyond the evidence, it was resolved to carry it out as a terror to the Pope's allies. The Sheriff of Cornwall, going up to London by command, was knighted for having done his part of the work so efficiently, and took back the death-warrant duly signed.

On the 26th of November a serving-man informed Maine that he was to suffer in three days.

Maine thanked God for this information, and told his informant that if he had anything worthy of his acceptance he would gladly give it, for he had done him greater service than any other. He spent the remaining hours of his life in devout exercises, meditation, mental prayer, and holy contemplation. The second night before he suffered, some prisoners confined in an adjoining apartment beheld a strange and unusual light gleaming over him, though he had neither fire, lamp, nor candle.

On the morning of his execution, in the presence of several ministers, his life was offered him if he would renounce the old faith, go to the new services, and acknowledge the spiritual supremacy of the queen. Only let him accept these terms, by an oath on the Geneva Bible offered to him, and all his assumed treasons should be forgiven and forgotten.

But with a firm resolution he laughed them to scorn. "What should it profit a man," he asked triumphantly, "if he should gain the whole world, and lose his own soul? Or what should he give in exchange for his soul?" And when they held out a copy of the Scriptures, he took it in his hands, drew the sign of the cross with deliberation over it, kissed it, and then declaring in a loud voice, said : "The queen never was, never can be, and never shall be, the Supreme Head of the true Church in England."

He was to be drawn a quarter of a mile to the place of execution. The sledge or hurdle was prepared, the horses were harnessed and attached to it, when some of the officials suggested that the head of Maine should be so hung over the side of the sledge, to which he submitted himself to be bound, that he might be killed before he reached the gallows. To this the sufferer readily consented, only it was disallowed by the sheriff's deputy.

In the market-place of Launceston, a gibbet of unusual height had been put up, around which a temporary barricade of stout posts and rails had been placed. On arriving there, and having been unbound, he knelt down and prayed with great devotion. During this act the crowd observed a remarkable silence. He was not permitted to address the people, though many had come to hear his words of defence, heartily sympathising with him.

Before he ascended the ladder, he kissed it, as he likewise did the rope.

Just before the executioner was about to remove the ladder, one of the justices cried out to Maine : "Now, villain and traitor, you know that you must die ; tell us, therefore, whether Sir John Arundell and Squire Tregean knew of these things for which thou art condemned."

"I know nothing of these," he meekly replied, "save that they be good and most godly gentlemen." And then, drawing the sacred sign on forehead, lips, and breast, he said : "O Lord, into Thy hands I commend my spirit, for Thou hast redeemed me, O Lord, Thou God of Truth."

Some of the more brutal officials would have had him cut down at once, but this was disallowed. When the rope was severed, however, life was by no means extinct ; but, falling with his head on the side of the platform, which caused a shudder and scream from the populace, he was stunned ; so that, as one account puts on record, "he was little sensible of the ensuing butchery."

His sentence otherwise was duly carried out. He was dismembered, ripped up, disembowelled, beheaded, and quartered. His head was set upon a pole at Wadebridge, a noted highway near Launceston, and his four quarters were exhibited at Bodmin, Tregony, Barnstaple, and Launceston.

One event followed, which left a deep impression on the Cornish people. The hangman, within a month of this act of legal butchery, lost his reason, and became a violent maniac, dying a frightful death in great agony.

With Cuthbert Maine no less than sixteen persons, some gentlepeople and some yeomen and servants, were condemned in a *præmunire*. They had been reconciled by this zealous priest to the old religion. At the next assizes, Tregean himself suffered by a similar judgment, and was thrown into the common gaol at Launceston, while his ample estate and beautiful home were seized by the Crown. Through the long period of twenty-eight years he remained a prisoner. Though he had been known personally at Court, and was much regarded by many, the queen refused to listen to any proposal for the alleviation of his long sufferings. Save for his religious ardour, and for the consolation from on high which he received, the years went wearily by. On the queen's death, the old man, so worn and changed that he was unrecognised by his few living friends, obtained his liberty from King James, but only on condition that he at once expatriated himself. His children were reduced to penury, and he himself died an exile at Lisbon in 1608.

From this time forward, persecution never ceased. The hurdle and the horses, the hanging-post and the rope, the knife of the blood-bespattered executioner, and the cauldron of boiling and bubbling pitch, were in constant and continued requisition. Almost every year, and in some years every recurring month, witnessed the cruel execution of those who followed in Maine's footsteps. Fresh heads of seminary priests were consequently stuck up on poles above the prison gates; more portions of their quartered bodies were exposed to the sun of summer and the winter snows. Perjury, priest-hunting, and gross acts of injustice were then popular amusements. The grimy rabble often enjoyed the sport, more especially those influenced by the Protestant ballad-singers; and grinned with anticipated satisfaction at the idea of being free spectators of a morning's butchery.

Two priests suffered in 1578, four more at Tybourne in 1581. No less than eleven were hung, drawn, and quartered with the usual barbarities in the succeeding year. Of these a considerable number, though first technically hung, but at once cut down, were ripped up alive, had their bowels taken out before their own eyes, as the official sentences expressly ordered, and the sufferers were then beheaded and quartered. In 1583 two priests thus suffered at York, and two others in Hampshire. Five priests died, after like cruelties, at Tybourne, and one layman, in 1584; a priest and a layman were thus put to death in Lancashire, and a schoolmaster at Wrexham, in the same year. In 1585, at Tybourne and York, four were likewise legally murdered—two priests and two laymen. In 1586 no less than seven priests suffered at Tybourne, two in the Isle of Wight, two at York, and one at Gloucester. At York, likewise, Esquire Richard Langley and Robert Bickerdike, a gentleman, were thus executed. Margaret Clitheroe, whose sufferings and death will be recounted and recorded in a later chapter, was in this year pressed to death. In 1587 seven priests suffered; in the following year no less than twenty, with nine laymen. Five priests and four laymen were drawn, hung, and quartered in 1589; nine priests and two lay-

men in 1590; seven priests and seven laymen in 1591; two
priests and one layman in the following year; four priests and
one layman in 1593; six priests and four laymen in 1594; four
priests in 1595; five laymen in 1596; one priest and two laymen
in 1597; four priests and three laymen in 1598; one priest and
two laymen in 1599; six priests and seven laymen in 1600; and
several more of both orders in the last three years of this terrible
woman's reign.   Of those who were imprisoned for years, some
throughout their lifetime, Dr. Bridgewater provides a list of
more than twelve hundred; but recent researches amongst the
State papers have shown that this number does not probably
embody one-sixth of those who, including the rank of yeoman,
then suffered by imprisonment or expatriation for conscience'
sake.

Even as late as this reign the greatest part of London was
contained within its actual walls, where gardens for fruit and
flowers, and pleasaunces for recreation, adjoining the picturesque
timber-houses with quaint dormer windows and high-pitched
roofs, abounded.   In the whole area now constituting the
parishes of St. Margaret, St. Martin, St. Paul in the Convent
Garden, St. Ann, St. Giles, St. George, Bloomsbury, and St.
Mary-at-the-Bourne there were not, at that time, two thousand
houses.   The little sanctuary of St. Pancras was the church of a
small suburban hamlet.   Clerkenwell and Shoreditch were then
but thinly populated; Stepney and Statford-Langton only large
villages.   Spitalfields, Goodman's Fields, and Limehouse Fields
were green open spaces with luxuriant blackthorn and privet
hedges; here and there a farmhouse stood shaded with clumps of
dark elms, or rows of stately poplars, or of lime-trees where the
bees were musical.   Spitalfields was first built upon in this reign,
a district where the Huguenot silk-weavers from France secured
a home.   Hitherto its hospital had stood in fields; so named
because of it.   With the exception of Bermondsey, where the
solid walls of its abbey still towered above the squat cottages
around; and Southwark, with its lofty church of Our Lady and
the house of the Bishops of Winchester; and Lambeth, with its
palace, parish church, and archiepiscopal ferry, the tract southwards of the Thames was flat, marshy, and thinly populated.
Willow trees, on both sides, bordered the two chief roads to
Kennington and to Kent.   The waters of the Thames often
overflowed, and made Lambeth a village flanked on either side
by broad marshes and spongy meadows, where the water-flag and
the oat-grass flourished luxuriantly, and where such flats stretched
to the south-west towards the manor-houses of Kennington and

Clapham, and to the solid walls of the water-girt mansion then called Vaux's Hall.

The churches, both of the city of London and its environs, were at this time more than half empty, and the people grew so irreligious and openly wicked that the contrast between the past and the present startled many. Chancels in their neglected state and desolation were boarded off from the naves. For they were unused and not wanted. There the spider spun its web unharmed, and the dust of many seasons lay thick and undisturbed upon the desolate stalls. Early on Sunday mornings, soon after sunrise, the bells of the city spires were sometimes chimed as of old; but there was no Christian sacrifice offered, and no worshippers gathered. Selfishness and self-seeking were rampant. Old religious duties and customs, one after the other, were abandoned and died out. Miserable disputes here and elsewhere[1] were carried on with bitterness and bad feeling by the new ministers. Butchers took part in "prophesyings," and disputed concerning St. Paul's teaching. Some men wrangled over the official dresses of the ministers—what they should wear, and what they should leave off wearing; others became fanatical, and even mad, by reason of their perplexing disquisitions concerning the free-will of man and the foreknowledge of the Eternal. Certain persons believed themselves to be already of the family of the saints and the company of the chosen, and declared that nothing they might think, say, or do, could alter, by one iota, their predestined and blessed position. Others again (these were "weaker vessels"), gnashing their teeth and tearing their hair, despairingly proclaimed themselves lost throughout eternity; while few or none of the onlookers who witnessed their phrenzy cared to argue with them to the contrary. Necromancy was practised largely. The queen and Walsingham frequently consulted Dr. Dee, as of old; while that person became quite a proficient in the occult sciences. Demoniacs increased in number, and superstition on all sides was welcomed. At the same time a steady wave of unbelief rolled forward, and few worked to stem its progress. Authority had been so purposely

---

[1] " Since your departure from Norwich the preachers of the city have taken in hand (both for their better exercise and also for the education of the people), prophesying, which is done once in three weeks; when [some] one first interprets a piece of the Scriptures, which at present is *Paul to the Romans*, for an hour, and then two others reply for half an hour, when we end with prayer.

" My Lord Bishop, at his last giving orders, admitted none that had no knowledge of the Latin tongue or that exercised any secular occupancy; by means whereof John Cayme was not admitted, for he lacked the Latin and was a butcher."—*State Papers, Domestic, Elizabeth*, vol xii. n. 27.

banished, and licence everywhere recommended, that many, knowing not what to believe, believed nothing; and, as a necessary
consequence, often became less decent and moral in their ordinary
habits than the inferior animals which they despised and ill-
treated.[1]

But terrible sights met the eyes of the citizens on every side;
bequeathed by the legal butchers of Tybourne. Over the gate-
ways of the various prisons, stuck upon poles, were placed the
heads, and sometimes the arms and legs, of those who had died
for their religion. No one could come up to the city of London
from Kent, or pass over old London Bridge to return to that
pleasant county, without seeing from twenty to thirty heads,
which had been first boiled and tarred, and then dried and
become withered under summer heat and winter winds, exposed
on poles over the gateway battlements at either end of the bridge.
Children looked up with horror; men shuddered involuntarily as
they gazed on these dark, eyeless heads, with their matted hair,
drawn features, and white, protruding teeth; and tears often fell
down the cheeks of women, when such ghastly sights suddenly
met their glance; for they knew that those advisers of the queen
then in power had the will to rack and to fine, to imprison, flog,
and kill all and any who should oppose the changes which had
been so generally effected, or resist the policy sanctioned by the
Council. However, in 1582, the people began to murmur that
the Court authorities were now making London "but as one
shambles for human flesh,"[2] so numerous were the heads exposed
upon the towers of the bridges, and the limbs hung here and
there in public places.

The prisons of London were still full of "recusants." About
this time there were no less than thirty-two priests in the Marshalsea,[3] nearly the same number in the Tower, eighteen in the Gate
House at Westminster, eleven in the Compter in Wood Street,
nine at St. Bridget's Fountain or Bridewell, five in the prison-
house known as the "White Lion," twenty-two in the Compter
in the Poultry, fourteen in the Clinke or "Hall of Winchester" in

---

[1] The whole of the above account is faithfully paraphrased from the actual
records and written lamentations of eye-witnesses.

[2] On the strength of this complaint, four or five of the condemned
"recusants" were sent up to York to be executed. The gallows stood near
Knavesmoor, a common near to the city, and opposite to a place called
Hobbmoor Lane. During the reign of Elizabeth, no less than forty-nine
persons suffered here for adherence to the Catholic faith.

[3] See *State Papers, Domestic, Elizabeth* (A.D. 1580), vol. cxlviii. n. 33, 35,
61; vol. cxlix. n. 184; vol. cxc. n. 25, 42, 44, 74; and vol. cxcv. n. 74.
(These last named refer to later years, *i.e.* to the year 1586.)

the Bankside, Southwark, seven in Newgate, and three in the King's Bench Prison.   Some of these had been closely confined more than twenty years, and had been racked, otherwise tortured, half starved, and most cruelly used on many occasions. More than two hundred laymen[1] were likewise imprisoned in one or the other because of their religion.

In 1580 numbers of persons fled from England to France and Belgium.   Dr. William Allen, still President of the College which had been removed from Douay to Rheims, entertained no less than fifty expatriated Englishmen within a single month.   Sometimes whole families came, weary and utterly sick at heart; having been unable to endure the fines, persecution, imprisonment, and contumely which they had so long experienced in the land of their birth.   The President has left on record his conviction that the devotion thus exhibited to the cause of God and His Church was a standing miracle of grace.   Many of these, noblemen's and gentlemen's sons in the flower of their age, resigning the comforts of home and the hopes of future position and usefulness, gave themselves up to a course of preparation for the priesthood; so that they might again return to their native land, anointed with unction from on high, to strengthen and sustain the weak, and help to rebuild its waste and desolate places.

One of the chief argumentative weapons of the new leaders had continually been that all priests were impostors, and that under the gospel dispensation the very idea of a priest had no real existence, the office being entirely superfluous; for that the Saviour of the world was the alone and only true Priest, and all others were but impiously and profanely usurping His office without authority, Scripture warrant, or reason.   They asserted likewise that the sacrifice of the mass was a blasphemous fable and a dangerous deceit; that the blessed Sacrament of the Altar was "a god made in co-operation by the bakers" and "Queen Mary's shaven conjurors," with other blasphemies too awful to repeat.   For themselves they were, as they maintained, but plain ministers of the Word, not priests; preachers, not offerers of any kind of sacrifice except that of prayer and praise.   A sacrifice of bread and wine had not then been conceived or invented.

---

[1] One Richard Fulwood, a layman, thus details his own miserable lot in Bridewell:—" He had, he said, hardly enough black bread to keep him from starving.   His abode was a narrow strongly-built cell, in which there was no bed, so that he had to sleep sitting on the window-sill, and was months without taking off his clothes.   There was a little straw in the place, but it was so trodden down and swarming with vermin that he could not lie on it.   Besides all this, he was daily awaiting an examination by torture."—*Records of the English Province*, vol. i. p. 494.   London, 1877.

The " elect," when worshipping, of course offered themselves, their souls, and their bodies as a sacrifice, but nothing more. This they fearlessly asserted the Prayer-Book and " Articles of Religion " taught, and nothing further. Possibly they were not wrong.

In answer to this and such like, which abounds in the ponderous and unread literature of the period, and the points of which are reproduced again and again, Dr. Allen thus quaintly but forcibly replied. His words are given exactly as they were first printed :—

"Because one special reproch given us pertaineth not to our persons, but to the whole order of priesthood, we may be bold to adde a worde or two for our defense specially concerning that terme, ' Massing Priests,' whereby the new pulpits (the very chairs of the skorneful) merily or mockingly call us and our brethren. Which name yet given us also in public wriling of authorities, is not doubtles of skornefulnes, which must needes be far from the editers of such : but as we take it, for distinction and difference betwixt us Catholike and in deede onely, and the other of the new creation, whom the people, for some resemblance of their actions in the ministerie to the wonted celebration of divine things, often call priests, though they list not to be so called, as in deede the ministers cannot of right have any such calling, having no more power, right or authoritie to minister any Sacrament (other than Baptisme, which in some cases women may also do) then they have to make a new moone or another sunne. The Church of God knoweth no other priests, neither hath Christ instituted any other order of priests, but of these whom contemptuously they call ' Masse Priests.' It is that sort, and none other, to which our Saviour gave power to consecrate His body and blood and offer the same, which is to say Masse." [1]

But to return to the innovators. In and about the year 1580, many ministers, some of them evidently not ordained at all, [2] took livings and would only *preach* to their congregations, refusing altogether to baptize or to celebrate the Sacrament of the Lord's Supper, and these were termed "no-sacrament ministers " ; [3] upon which Archbishop Grindal wrote to his diocesan officers, and asked for the names of such offenders. The Privy Council

[1] *An Apologie and True Declaration of the Two English Colleges, the one in Rome, the other in Rhemes*, pp. 88, 89, A.D. 1581.

[2] Two modern authors of ability, perfectly able to give a faithful judgment, write as follows :—(1) "If the rectors and vicars of the parishes, *whether priests or laymen*, were the very scum of the earth, and contrast so very unfavourably with their successors of the present day, the comparison of our bishops with those promoted in the reign of Edward VI. will exhibit this contrast in a still more striking light."—*The Reformation and the Prayer-Book*, by Nicholas Pocock, M.A. London, 1879. (2) "*Some of the best of them* [*the ministers*] *were ignorant ranters*, utterly unfit to cope with the trained dialecticians who were being reared so carefully beyond the seas."—*One Generation of a Norfolk House*, by Augustus Jessopp, D.D., second edition, p. 74. London, 1879.

[3] Strype's *Life of Grindal*, p. 363, and Grindal's *Remains*, p. 413. See also " Letter from the Lords of the Council," in Grindal's Register, folio 191.

likewise interfered, ordering them to be sent up as recusants. But there were too many of such to make it easy to put them down.

Persecution, however, went on apace.   More seminary priests arrived, while Puritanism developed in several directions and increased.   In 1581 Chaderton, Bishop of Chester, wrote to the Council, urging them, on the one hand, to bring in a Bill making traitors and felons, without benefit of clergy, of "all vagrant priests as walk about in disguised apparel seducing Her Majesty's subjects." He also, on the other hand, complained that conventicles were not put down, and urged that the preachers should be compelled to reside upon their benefices. As regards the state of his own cathedral, he gives a most deplorable account. Religion in Chester, apparently, had been reformed off the face of the earth. For all the good which that interesting fabric did, it might as well have been clean pulled down. "In this cathedral church of Chester neither the dean nor any prebendary hath been resident or kept hospitality of many years. Neither is any parson or vicar of any parish within the city a preacher."[1]   Overton, of Lichfield and Coventry, in April of the same year, complains, in a melancholy strain, of the state of the county of Salop, though it be "one of the best and conformablest parts of my diocese." There, "of one hundred all most presented for recusancy, they could get one only to be bound, the rest refusing most obstinately to come before them."[2]

In other parts they were more successful. Cheshire and Lancashire clung closely to the old religion ; in certain counties, however, where the ancient nobility had been ruined, and their places supplied by Court nominees, "new men," and ready tools, the "Reformers" apparently had their own way.

In 1580 Dr. William Allen[3] induced Pope Gregory XIII. to send some of the Jesuits into England to aid in preserving the ancient faith. Two Oxford men, Robert Parsons, Fellow and Dean of Balliol College, and Edmund Campion, Fellow of St. John's,[4] were chosen for that purpose. They arrived in the

[1] *State Papers, Domestic, Elizabeth*, letter dated December 1, 1581.
[2] Lansdowne MSS. Brit. Museum, No. 33, folio 14.
[3] Of this divine, Anthony à Wood gives the following character :—"Certain it is that he was an active man, and of great parts and high prudence ; that he was religious and zealous in his profession ; restless till he had performed what he had undertaken ; that he was very affable, genteel, and winning ; and that his person was handsome and proper ; which, with an innate gravity, commanded respect from those that came near, and had to do with him."
[4] See *The Life of Edmund Campion*, by Richard Simpson. London, 1867 A model biography and a mine of information regarding Elizabeth's reign.

summer, and losing no time in beginning their work, before the Christmas feast came round, had reconciled to the Church of their fathers many who had lapsed. They acted in the spirit and purport of the Bull of Pope Pius V. For, as some might have asked themselves, if, in such a matter, the Father of Christendom could not speak with authority, who could? If he was not to be obeyed, to whom was obedience due? If His Holiness was unable to devise a remedy for the sorrows of England, to whom should the afflicted turn?

In the work of Parsons and Campion, friends aided them with zeal and devotion. So that they preached by pre-arrangement at different places, and exhorted with all diligence and earnestness various gatherings of sincere adherents and followers. Men of great gifts and of the highest culture, their influence began to be widely experienced at once; they always found an attentive audience, and seldom passed on to some other place without obvious results from their labours. In August of this year Parsons wrote his celebrated *Challenge*, which, having been made public by an esquire of Hampshire named Thomas Pounde, soon secured a circulation throughout the whole kingdom.

At Stonor Park, about five miles to the north of Henley, in Oxfordshire, a family of antiquity and repute had long resided— the Stonors. They were earnestly attached to the ancient faith. In the attractive and interesting picture gallery, which runs from east to west on the north side of their pleasantly-placed mansion, are various representations of those of many generations who have always been leal and loyal to the faith of their forefathers. In the adjoining church, standing towards the east of the house, mass has been constantly said without break or discontinuance down to the present day. In that sacred edifice no abomination of desolation has ever been set up. There, under the protection of an influential family, in a house placed towards the lower slope of a hill, away from main roads, and amid the shelter of beechen woods, Parsons was allowed to set up a private printing-press. One volume after another was put forth, being sold at Oxford as well as in London; each book full of wholesome truths for the innovators, and telling arguments for the deluded and misled in general. The authorities were beside themselves with anger and annoyance at being unable to unearth the offenders or discover the press. Spies and agents were despatched to secure them.

Parsons, who had been appointed one of the members of the Spanish ambassador's household, had his headquarters in London. But Campion, after moving about discreetly for some months, betrayed by one, George Elliot,[1] was taken in the house of Esquire Yates, at Lyford, in Berkshire, on Sunday, July 16th, 1581, just after he had preached to a congregation of nearly sixty listeners, a considerable proportion of whom were young students of the University of Oxford. Lyford House was then a turreted and moated building of some antiquity, — a county family's pleasant home, — in which several carefully-arranged hiding-places existed. Elliot had himself been a servant at Ingatestone Hall in Essex, and at Orpington in Kent, but was then a government spy, on active duty; and, knowing one of the servants at Lyford, entered into conversation with him at the gate of the drawbridge. Elliot's recent apostacy and infamous character were quite unknown to the servant, who admitted him to mass, and informed him in confidence that Campion would preach. The latter was taken in due course, at once given over to the care of the Sheriff of Berks, and carried through Abingdon, Reading, and Colnbrooke to London. There he was committed to the Tower. Both the Lord Chancellor and the Lieutenant of the Tower tried to induce him to betray his allies and friends. But he declined. So within a week he was placed upon the rack, and endured its tortures.

To quote from a contemporary authority: — "At his first racking they went no farther with him; but afterwards, when they saw that he could not be won to condescend somewhat at least in religion, which was the thing they most desired, they thought good to frame matter of treason against him, and framed their demands accordingly; about which he was so cruelly torn and rent upon the torture, the two last times, that he told a friend of his that found means to speak to him, that he thought they meant to make him away in that manner. Before he went to the rack he used to fall down at the rack-house door, upon both knees, to commend himself to God's mercy; and upon the rack he called continually upon God, repeating often the holy name of Jesus. He most charitably forgave his tormentors and the causers thereof. His keeper, asking him the next day how he felt his hands and feet, he answered *not ill, because not at all.*"[2]

Some controversies were held with him in the chapel of the Tower by certain ministers. "That he might want no good

[1] See a document in the handwriting of this man, amongst the Lansdowne MSS., British Museum, *Burghley Papers*, vol. xxxiii. Pluto, folio 16 *et seq.*, endorsed "10 Aug. 1581. A declaracon of certain Papists, etc., writ by G[eorge] E[lliot] is by one that was servant to the old Ladye Peter."

[2] From an old Latin MS. sometime at Douay, written by an eye-witness of Campion's death, and quoted in *Memoirs of Missionary Priests*, by Bishop Challoner.

pretence to yield to their desires," it is written, "they often brought to him such divines as they had to confer with him, and to persuade him privately to relent somewhat to their sect." But this was of no avail. Though worn with agony and weak with racking—so weak that his numbed arms hung by his side, and he could not stand—he was quite able to give an answer to the worrying and wearying divines. He would not succumb, and did not give in. Having been deliberately allowed to recover a little, the authorities proceeded to rack him a third time; so that when, three weeks later, he was put on his trial for high treason, he was positively unable, according to custom when charged, even to lift up his hand.

Seven persons were arraigned with Campion, and like him were condemned to die. He thus spake:—"I protest before God and the holy angels, before heaven and earth, before this world and the bar whereat I stand, that I am not guilty of any part of the treason contained in the indictment, or of any other treason whatsoever."

But the jury, having been informed by Popham, the Attorney-General, that "it was the queen's will that the prisoners should be found guilty," did as they were told.

On December 1st, 1581, he, in company with Alexander Briant and Ralph Sherwin, were executed at Tybourne, with all the ordinary horrors.

A relation of Campion's was informed by the Lieutenant of the Tower that if Campion could be induced to go over to the queen's religion, he should not only receive a pardon, but obtain "an office worth £100 by the year"; and when Campion was preparing to suffer, a like offer is said to have been made by Sir Francis Knollys.

A minister who wished Campion to join in prayer received this answer :—

"You and I are not of one religion. I pray you, therefore, content yourself, and leave me alone. I bar no one of prayer; but, for myself, I desire only them of the household of faith to pray with me, and, in my agony, I wish to know only one Creed."

The end was of the usual kind. The details of this tragedy were like those which had been done before and should so frequently be done after. The three sufferers were drawn on a hurdle to Tybourne; they were then hung and cut down alive. They were at once dismembered and disembowelled; their heads were taken off and their bodies quartered, and these were first thrown into a caldron of boiling water, and afterwards smeared over with pitch, before being exposed on poles in different parts of London.

The following four verses, in modern spelling, are given of a rare and beautiful " Epitaph " by Henry Walpole :—

> " His prison now the City of the King,
>   His rack and torture joys and heavenly bliss,
> For men's reproach with angels he doth sing
>   A sacred song, which everlasting is.
> For shame but short, and loss of small renown,
> He purchased hath an ever-during crown.

> " His quartered limbs shall join with joy again,
>   And rise a body brighter than the sun,
> Your malice keen tormented him in vain,
>   For every wrench such glory hath him won.
> And every drop of blood, which he did spend,
> Hath reap'd a joy which never shall have end.

> .   .   .   .

> " His hurdle draws us with him to the Cross,
>   His speeches there provoke us for to die,
> His death doth say this life is but a loss,
>   His martyred blood from heaven to us doth cry :
> His first and last, and all conspire in this—
> To show the way that leadeth us to bliss.

> " Blessèd be God, Which lent him so much grace,
>   Thankèd be Christ, Which blest this martyr so ;
> Happy is he, which seeth his Master's Face ;
>   Cursèd all they that thought to work him woe :
> Bounden be we to give eternal praise
> To Jesu's Name, which such a man did raise." [1]

A melancholy incident relating to the Thimbleby family of Lincolnshire must now be recorded.   Their ancestors had been seated at Pelham since the reign of Edward III., and were a knightly family of honour and good repute.   One of them, in prison at Lincoln, A.D. 1581, for refusing to attend the new services, and for declining to receive at the Supper, desired greatly to see his young wife, likely soon to become a mother. His request was allowed by Thomas Cowper, the bishop of the diocese.   But, as her name was amongst a list of those un-favourable to the "reformed" faction, when she was admitted to her husband's cell, she herself, under some order from authority, was actually detained by force.   Either the shock of this act of perfidious inhumanity, or the frightful stench of the place, brought on sickness and premature labour ; and, in her

---

[1] The original is reprinted *verbatim* in Dr. Jessopp's most interesting Memoir of Henry Walpole, entitled *One Generation of a Norfolk House*, pp. 106–110. London, 1879.

hour of weakness, in the presence of her helpless and distracted husband, she was cruelly denied by the gaoler the assistance of any matron. It seems probable that her husband, Gabriel Thimbleby, died in prison. Probably a speedy death mercifully ended her own sufferings.

But to return to the north-west. In the early part of 1583, at the Sessions held before Chaderton, Bishop of Chester, in conjunction with John Byron, three old priests, Williamson, Hatton, and Bell, were indicted for high treason; and no less than twenty-six persons were each fined two hundred and forty pounds because they had not attended the new services for at least twelve months. Of these one was a knight,—Sir John Southworth, a most determined and noble confessor of the faith, of whom another prelate, Grindal, could make nothing satisfactory to him,—four were esquires, three were gentlemen, ten were priests, three were schoolmasters, and the rest yeomen, husbandmen, and labourers. Four women, though indicted, were not arraigned, and seven other women appear to have escaped.[1] Thirty-eight, however (including six women), were speedily lodged in Salford Gaol. The offence of each was that he or she conscientiously refused to have anything to do with the new religion, its obligations, its authors, or its authorities.

In the meantime the new prelates and the newly-made ministers, so soon as they were consecrated or ordained, appear to have sought out wives for themselves as a consolation in their loneliness. It must, of course, have been very depressing to have lived alone, year after year, in out-of-the-way villages, with little to study but the *Martyrology* of Foxe, Jewell's *Apology*, and the two books of published *Homilies*. Such reading was, no doubt, rather "painful" than profitable. Wives, therefore, when they could secure them, served to take up their attention, while the prattle of children amused them. It is astonishing, consequently, how successful they became in this very practical part of their duty. Dr. Cotton's lady of Salisbury presented him from time to time with no less than nineteen. The bishop's chapel was often turned into a nursery; the parson's wife was fruitful as the vine on the vicarage wall, and often more blessed with olive-branches than the neighbouring squire's or the parish constable's; bishops left their daughters handsome portions, often secured knighthood for their sons,[2] and the children of the clergy were in due course looked upon as respectable members of society.

[1] *State Papers, Domestic, Elizabeth*, vol. clxvii. No. 40. Dated *in dorso*, January 22, 23, 1583.
[2] Two of the sons of Sandys, Archbishop of York, were knighted, viz.

In those days even the oldest prelates, though wanting in certain gifts, were bold and not bashful. For example, Thomas Godwin,[1] already a widower, Bishop of Bath and Wells, and "aged and diseased, and lame of the gout," as Sir John Harington puts on record, married as his second spouse a widow from London, not one of the "ancient widows" already noticed, but one "livelier and right merrie." It reached the queen's ears that this wrinkled and dilapidated old man, with one foot in the grave, had indeed wedded a girl of twenty; and Her Highness, invariably meditating on matrimony in some form or another, called him a "bigamist," and expressed the greatest indignation. Upon which the Earl of Bedford, who happened to be near and knew the lady, said merrily, and with much dry humour: "Madam, I know not how much the woman is above twenty; but I know that a son of hers is a little under forty."

But this rather marred than mended matters.

One other bystander remarked : "*Majus peccatum habet.*"

Another, to the queen's amusement, for it was the single topic always welcome, told methodically of three sorts of marriage. First, that of God's making, when Adam and Eve, two young folks, were coupled ; secondly, of man's making, when one is old and another young, as St. Joseph's marriage; and thirdly, of the devil's making, when two old folks marry,[2] not for comfort, but for covetousness, and such they said was Bishop Godwin's.

In the autumn of 1584, Thomas Watson, Bishop of Lincoln, the last survivor in England of the ancient episcopate, and a marked contrast to the amorous old gentleman just referred to, after a close imprisonment of nearly a quarter of a century, four years of which were passed in Wisbeach Castle, passed to his rest and reward. He had seen sixty-eight summers, and had long suffered from the ague. No passing-bell was rung from the adjoining tower of St. Peter's Church, then in the hands of the new preachers. His life had been one continued series of trials ever since Elizabeth's accession.[3] At Wisbeach his lordship was

---

Sir Edwin by Elizabeth, and Sir Miles. Each of these, though laymen, had been respectively made Prebendaries of York Minster for the sake of the endowments. The latter received the honour of knighthood in the first year of King James I.

[1] Consecrated Bishop of Bath, etc., at Lambeth, September 13, 1584.

[2] *Brief View of the Church of England*, by Sir J. Harington, pp. 114, 115. London, 1653.

[3] The bishop was placed there, at Lord Burghley's suggestion, in 1580.— *State Papers, Elizabeth*, Addenda, vol. xxvii. No. 21. In Father Parsons' *Account of the Persecution* (p. 60, A.D. 1582), he describes the scandalous

insulted by the Protestants in the grossest and most infamous manner.[1] Trusty friends were sometimes enabled to let him know, wherever confined, of the downward course of events throughout the country, and of the miserable religious desolation existing—a desolation which he was so powerless to alter. The seasons came and went during his last imprisonment; but for him there had been little change. Seed-time and harvest were alike. During the winter the sea-mists, drifting landwards, almost always hung over and hid the castle walls. Broad pools and patches of stagnant water, green with rank weeds, and wide marshes and sterile flats lay outspread all around for miles. The muddy river Nene was constantly overflowing its broken-down banks, so that the moat of the castle frequently flooded the adjacent garden and orchard. Of foliage, save a few stunted willow trees, there was little or none in sight; for when summer came round, the sun's heat soon parched up the rank grass in the courtyard, and withered the dandelion and snapdragon which grew upon its massive but dilapidated walls.[2] It was a dreary spot,[3] rife with the saddest memories; where, during half a life-

treatment which the imprisoned were then receiving; being deprived of all their books, and kept in separate rooms; not being allowed any intercourse whatsoever, except at table. The Bishop of Ely, as may be seen from a letter to the Privy Council from Carleton and Michel, the keepers of the castle, "hath appointed a preacher unto the recusants, a man of holy life, learned, and able to give an account of his doctrine strongly."—*State Papers, Domestic, Queen Elizabeth*, vol. cxliii. No. 17. To have pestered them with the modern heresies, over and above their imprisonments, was adding insult to injury.

[1] It may be gathered from an original letter still remaining in the Record Office, written by a Catholic prisoner in the Tower in 1581, that the bishop was subject to an insult almost incredible. "Not many days since," the account runs, "an infamous woman, the tool of some ruffians, was introduced into the chamber of the Bishop of Lincoln (who remains still in prison at Wisbeach), and dared in the most shameless way to solicit to sin that most holy man, worn out as he is with cruel treatment. When the old man, with all his might, endeavoured to drive the impure beast from his cell, her evil instigators, who awaited the result, even threatened him with blows."—*State Papers, Domestic, Elizabeth*, vol. cxlix. n. 61.

[2] "The building, which covered two acres of land, stood in the midst of four other acres, at the boundary of which was a strong high wall, and on the outside next the town was a ditch or moat, forty feet wide; and there was no way to the castle but by a drawbridge in the west front. . . . The great tower was the residence of the constable or governor. Underneath were dismal dark vaults for the confinement of prisoners, which made this tower sometimes be called the keep or dungeon. In this building was the great hall."—*Historical Account of the Ancient Town and Port of Wisbeach*, by William Watson, Esq., F.S.A., pp. 123-129. Wisbeach, 1827.

[3] Father Weston thus writes concerning this prison :—" When we reached it [*i.e.* Wisbeach Castle] we were divided and sent into separate rooms,

time, several martyrs and confessors of the faith continued to suffer in humility and patience, waiting for the breaking of a better day, doing God's will, and longing for their promised crown.[1]

wherein we lived day and night under bolts and locks, excepting at the hours of dinner and supper, and half an hour before and after our meal, when we could breathe the air and walk about a little. This was a public prison, common to all the thieves and criminals, and situated within the enclosure of the bishop's palace. It stood upon a high terrace, and water filled a moat all around it. Everything, however, at that time was ruinous and dilapidated, particularly through the rapacity and avarice of the heretical prelates; who, not caring for posterity, and only mindful of their own convenience, had despoiled the building of its best material, selling the lead off the roof, the beams, the iron, and the glass, and thus abandoning the other parts to ruin and decay."—*Life of William Weston*, p. 239. London, 1875.

[1] The Burials' Register contains only four words—"John Watson, doctor, sepultus"; and in this entry "John" is a mistake for "Thomas." There is no stone to mark his grave, nor any memorial whatsoever. As early as the year 1748, the Rev. W. Cole carefully searched for one, but in vain.—See Cole's MSS., Brit. Mus., vol. xviii. folio 90. Dr. Christopher Wordsworth, sometime Bishop of Lincoln, courteously informed me that there is no portrait of his illustrious predecessor, either at Riseholme or Lincoln.

CHAPTER VII

THE first prisoner sent to Wisbeach Castle for refusing to adopt the reforming policy was John Feckenham, O.S.B., the last Abbot of Westminster. He was a prelate of great learning, of most virtuous life, and of much kindness of heart. During Queen Mary's reign he is reported[1] to have frequently befriended the Lady Elizabeth; but when the latter came to the throne, and he found that she contemplated setting up a new religion, and becoming its Supreme Governess, he spoke out with the greatest plainness of language. Notwithstanding this, it is said that at her accession she felt disposed to offer him the vacant Archbishopric of Canterbury, if he would only take the Oath of Supremacy, and co-operate with her and her advisers in making a new national religion; but this he firmly refused to do. Soon after this he had been sent to the Tower; then he was placed in the custody of Horne, Bishop of Winchester; subsequently he was sent back to the Tower by Elizabeth, then to the Marshalsea, and at last to Wisbeach, where he died in the twenty-seventh year of that queen's reign, having thus been a prisoner for conscience' sake during the long period of more than a quarter of a century.[2]

Allusion has already been made to the cruelties practised on such prisoners. One of the most daring and impudent acts of the innovators was to provide a minister of the new religion to preach at, and argue with, those in confinement at Wisbeach; and then make these poor sufferers pay his stipend and find him in food. Bishop Richard Cocks, apparently, was the ingenious gentleman who devised and carried out this brilliant idea; but though one man may take a horse to the trough, twenty cannot

[1] See Anthony à Wood's *Athenæ Oxonienis*, vol. i. p. 222; and *State Papers, Domestic, Elizabeth*, vol. cxxxi. n. 48, and vol. cxliii. n. 17.
[2] The sin of which, in the eyes of Queen Elizabeth's Council, this noble confessor, in conjunction with Heath, Watson, and Tunstall, had been guilty, was maintaining the independence of the spirituality: nothing else. He refused to give to Cæsar the things of God.

make it imbibe the water, and so in practical effect this beneficial scheme fell flat, and failed of its purpose, as the following letter so graphically sets forth :—

"The Lord Bishop hath appointed a preacher unto the recusants — a man of holy life, learned, and able to give an account of his doctrine strongly. The men restrained, before us both and others, have been called divers times and as often required to hear the preacher, and abide the prayer; but they all with one voice generally, and after that every man particularly answering for himself, denied to allow either, saying that as they are not of our Church, so they will neither hear, pray, nor yet confer with any of us of any matters concerning religion."[1]

Even children at this period were not exempt from persecution. Four Lancashire youths of birth and rank, Worthingtons of Worthington, were seized and sorely tried, with a view of getting them to betray their relatives and friends.[2]   A pursuivant, accompanied by the under-sheriff of the county and twenty javelin men, seized them at the house of their friend, Esquire Sankey of Great Sankey, near Warrington, on February 12th, 1584. They were at once examined as to the whereabouts of their uncle, Father Thomas Worthington, a priest whose life had been marked by devotion and self-denial.   They were asked when they had last seen him, when they had attended mass, and where; but little information was obtained from them.   The two eldest, therefore (neither then sixteen years of age), were taken before the Bishop of Chester and the Earl of Derby, but without any result.   On their second examination the two younger were likewise brought up with their brothers.   One of the former was not yet twelve years of age.   The unusual nature of the proceedings attracted a crowd interested and attentive.   It appears that on the appointed examination day the guards had intentionally kept the children without any food at all until the evening, when they were plied with wine, so as to half stupefy them, and render them possibly more talkative and probably easier to be dealt with and entrapped.

One of them at once complained to the Commissioners of this treatment.

"They had evidently intended to deprive me of my mind by

[1] George Carleton and Humphrey Michel to the Privy Council. — *State Papers, Domestic, Elizabeth*, vol. cxliii. n. 17.
[2] The account in the text, much abbreviated, is taken from the second part of the Addenda to Bridgewater's edition of John Gibbons' *Concertatio Ecclesiæ Cath. in Anglia, etc.* Trèves, 1594. See also *State Papers, Domestic, Elizabeth*, vol. cxc. n. 25, dated "June 12, 1586"; *Prisoners in the Gate House;* and Strype's *Annals*, vol. iii. p. 420.

giving me strong drink!" he exclaimed; "but by God's goodness
they have altogether failed, for my mind is quite clear, though
my body be in sore pain.   I am, therefore, unable to appear
before your honours as I should do."

They were all examined, however, on subjects of their religion,
and every endeavour made to find out their uncle's whereabouts,
and to make them betray their friends and criminate themselves.

Lord Derby, partly by threats and partly by promises, having
offered to make the eldest youth his page of honour, if he would
only consent to attend the new services, was unable to obtain the
information wanted, or to effect his desired object.

Nor was the bishop more successful.   Consequently these four
children were at once imprisoned in Manchester, and told that
as they were guilty of high treason they would be duly punished
for it.   An officer of the bishop, Bull by name, was commissioned
by his lordship to take them in hand at once.   They were then
confined in the House of Correction.   So, dragging the eldest
out of bed one morning, he administered to him, in his brothers'
presence, a severe and cruel flogging with several ash rods.   But
this was of no avail; neither he nor the others, as they declared,
would go to the "services of the Calvinists."   They were consequently taken thither and to sermons by force; but this policy
only sickened them more.   Neither threats nor bribes in the
long run sufficed; and though the bishop attempted to bribe
them to conform, he utterly failed.   They were true to their
fathers' faith; and two of them, it appears, went abroad and
were subsequently ordained.

Prior to that event, however, they seem to have been again
secured by the authorities in London, on the plea that they were
about to be sent abroad by their relations to be educated and
made priests.   Their uncle was taken by Topcliffe at Islington,[1]
who reported him to Burghley and the Privy Council to have
been eminently "wilful, perverse, and arrogant."   This, of
course, was the character given to all who were resolute in
declining to co-operate with the innovators,—as regards the
upper classes at that period only a considerable minority.

At the visitation of Corringham, in Lincolnshire, on the 8th
of April 1566, three altar-stones had been taken down, two of
which were used as pavement for the church, and the other was
sold to Mr. Topcliffe.   This person, it appears, is the "Richard
Topcliffe" just referred to, who so frightfully persecuted the
"recusants" and "seminary priests."   He belonged, apparently,

---

[1] Thomas Worthington was taken at the house of Mr. Richard à Wood of
Islington, an ancestor of the celebrated historian of the University of Oxford.

to an old family of the country,[1] and had himself married a daughter of Sir Edward Willoughby. In the female line he was descended from the ancient Yorkshire families of Waterton and Fairfax. He had been brought up a Catholic, and had not only apostatised, but become one of the cruellest and most shameful persecutors, and a rack master. It is melancholy enough to see the "new men," ready tools of the authorities, taking an active part in overthrowing the old religion; but ignorance and fanaticism often go hand in hand, and when self-seeking is a man's sole aim, little good ensues; but here was a case in which a Lincolnshire gentleman of blood and family, having renounced the faith of his fathers, became, step by step, the supple tool of his inferiors, and at last a merciless, degraded, and disgraced ruffian.

Bishop Cocks of Ely, Berkeley of Bath, and Davies of St. David's, had died in 1581; Grindal, Archbishop of Canterbury, two years afterwards; Watson of Winchester in 1584; Barnes, Bishop of Durham,[2] in 1587; and Sandys, Archbishop of York, in 1588. Thus the leading and more active innovators, one after another, were called away to their last account. The persons who succeeded them were, as a rule, singularly commonplace in their characters. The single theologian of the Reformation-era, John Jewell, had not made any great impression at Salisbury, where the ordinary religious desolation, so current generally, was likewise experienced.

All this time the poor complained constantly of the unjust manner in which they were oppressed, and of the difficulty in

---

[1] *English Church Furniture*, etc., edited by E. Peacock, F.S.A., p. 62. London, 1866.

[2] The following account of this man, who was consecrated Suffragan Bishop of Nottingham by Thomas Young, Archbishop of York, on March 9, 1567, translated to Carlisle in 1570, and to Durham in 1577, and died August 24th, 1587, is given by a contemporary :—"Richard Barnes, an *apostata* priest, twice married, a common drunkard, Bishop of Durham, accustomed to drink seven times every meal, and as many between meals, every draught containing a pint ; and in his Public Consistory to offenders, accustomed to use most obscene and filthy words, fell at length with intemperance into a fever, and so into a frenzy. One night as he was about to rise out of his bed, he fell out of his bed, and was like to have broken his neck ; but for that time and with great difficulty recovered. Soon after, his disease brought him to his last exigent, when, as past speech, Toby Matthew, willing him in sign of his faith to hold up his hands, he always held his fingers to his mouth, which one, Ralph Hilton, his base [born] son, marking [it] swore, and said Mr. Dean did mistake his father, for that his finger to his mouth did desire nothing but drink. And so desperately he died, and was buried the next night at midnight."—*An Ancient Editor's Note-Book*, MS., Stonyhurst College.

keeping body and soul together. Petty tyranny amongst inferior officials was rampant, for which, too frequently, there was
neither remedy nor redress.   Anciently the great nobles had
stood between the Crown and the people; so that while the
former could not oppress those under them, the latter were in
no great danger of being oppressed, for their local lord was their
patron, friend, and protector.   The natural and proper rights
of all classes were thus safe from the power of any single
passionate or wayward ruler.   For generations the influence
and independence of the greater noblemen, supported by their
considerable wealth arising from broad lands; and the personal
devotion of their faithful retainers, had always been a valuable
check upon regal tyranny.   Dukes and earls in their own
localities had long been as little kings.   Standing alone, they
were strong; when in combination with others, they were
stronger.   When, however, it was seen how under Henry VIII.
such exalted and powerful noblemen had been so easily ruined
and brought to the block by this tyrant, the nobility in general,
as a class or "estate," began to lose their ancient legitimate
prestige; the local poor their natural protectors; and thus
regal tyranny,[1] fostered by a few needy adventurers without
either conscience or principle, became practically unchecked
and rampant in their revolutionary changes, arbitrary deeds, and
cruel punishments.

Two boys of the town of Wisbeach, born of poor parents,
likewise suffered, Thomas and George Fisher by name.   They
had been admitted to the castle to attend upon the prisoners as
servitors.   Naturally clever and observant, by degrees they each
became greatly influenced by what they heard and saw.   The
old religion, as so many persons quietly and privately maintained, was a strong and remarkable contrast to the new, and
though these youths had been brought up under the latter, in
no long time they became sincerely attached to the former; and,
at their own request, were carefully instructed in its tenets and

---

[1] As Canon Barry remarked in his recent *Lectures on the Reformation* :—
"From 1485 onwards the Royal power in England gradually became despotic
under form of law.   The Tudor despotism was a despotism exercised as it
were with the consent of the people.   They began to look at the king as
having a sacred character; they accepted him as a centre of national unity,
and came to reverence him as 'the Lord's anointed.'   The Royal power
became a very formidable thing.   The same thing occurred in other parts
of Europe, especially in France, Germany, and Spain.   Monarchial power
was on the increase, and rallied round it a strong national spirit everywhere.
As yet it was England in alliance with the papal power, or observing an
armed neutrality.   But a conflict was at any moment likely."   (A.D. 1879.)

duties. This being reported to the governor, offended him greatly, who, on a certain day when a sermon was to be preached in the parish church "by a painful and weighty minister," commanded them both, as a test, to be present at its delivery. But, in respectful language, they asked to be excused. They would rather not go. They had recently learned what the religion of their fathers was, and, if they might be allowed to make choice, they preferred it to that now set up. The governor became furious. Was ever such insolence and heresy known, and from two boyish knaves? As a punishment they were stripped to the waist, and publicly flogged in the market-place, in the presence of a large concourse of people, and then put into irons. Being subsequently set free, the eldest escaped abroad, and became a student at the college at Douay. But the younger, on a certain occasion, was found serving one of the old priests at mass, and was imprisoned in company with some of the worst and most depraved criminals. At length he was brought to trial, accused of being an ignorant recusant, and upbraided by the magistrates for being so foolish and for bringing so much misery upon himself and his parents.

"It is true that I am very ignorant about many things," he replied; "but of this one thing I am quite certain, notwithstanding my ignorance, that the Catholic faith is the only faith for salvation, and that it is a deal older, by many centuries, than your new religion."

"How can you, an ignorant boy, know which is the oldest religion, or anything about it?" asked the magistrate.

"Why, in this way, sir," the youth replied; "your own chroniclers, your own ministers, admit as much. Holinshed, who must have known, says so."

The magistrate denied that the writer in question had admitted anything of the sort, replying: "You lie, sirrah!"

Upon this the youth triumphantly drew out from his breast-pocket a single leaf of the "Chronicles" of Holinshed, and presented it to the official.

It contained a description of the coming hither of St. Augustine, with litanies, Catholic prayers, silver cross, and pictured banner, and had been given to him by one of the prisoners at Wisbeach, as evidence of the antiquity of the old religion—a leaf which might be judiciously produced when it was required. The youth himself, being poor and unable to pay fines, appears to have been dismissed with a warning.

In the year 1576 the Commons had petitioned the queen "to amend the discipline of the Church,' which had fallen into a state of great uncertainty and laxness. In fact, nothing could well have been worse than it was. The disorganisation in every diocese was complete and perfect. Everybody wished to govern, and declined to obey. Presbyters looked upon themselves as rulers, called synods, appointed fast-days, and ordained other presbyters.[1] In fact, every one did as he liked. The ecclesiastical courts were sinks of jobbery and iniquity, farmed by persons who paid for their offices,—handing over a yearly sum to the authorities who had let them out to the highest bidder,—and then worked them to their own profit and advantage.

The queen, in reply to the petition, informed those who had signed it that the bishops had been directed to examine the matter, and that if they failed to do their duty in a reasonable period she would speedily supply the want and rectify the evil by her own spiritual supremacy. But nothing had been done.

On one occasion, in 1577,—to pass from the ailments of the ministers to those of the Supreme Governess,—the queen suffered so acutely from toothache that she believed herself to have been bewitched. This conviction grew in force from the fact that some representations or images of Her Majesty, Cecil, and Walsingham had been recently found (or were said to have been found) concealed in the house of an ancient priest who sojourned at Islington; while Dr. Dee's personal tuition had made her singularly superstitious. This poor innocent priest was believed to have been practising "malign magic"; for the ordinary royal physicians, instead of relieving their patient, entered into a violent controversy as to what potions ought to be given, and practically did nothing. Perhaps these physicians were also bewitched. Her Majesty's pains and aches by consequence continued, and even grew in violence, so that the Lords of the Council thought it their duty to interfere and take the matter in hand. A foreign doctor, Fenatus by name, had been highly recommended to them by some of the Protestant exiles; but the queen mistrusted all foreigners, and Walsingham feared the man might turn out to be "possibly a Jew or even a Papist." So they bade him write a prescription without even seeing the royal patient. This, of course, was a difficult undertaking.

---

[1] Independent synods had been set up to which only the "elect" were summoned; in various counties, classes and gatherings for the exposition of Scripture and prayer had been formed; "ordination," so-called, by presbyters had been given to persons who were supposed to own special gifts of speech; and unauthorised fast-days were appointed, wholly independent of the queen's bishops.—See Strype's *Life of Whitgift*, vol. iii. pp. 244-256, and the "Articles" exhibited against Thomas Cartwright.

Howsoever, after having penned a long Latin letter, very devout, but rather wordy, explaining his own entire unworthiness to treat so mighty a queen for the toothache, he "drew a bow at a venture," and reasonably enough recommended a fomentation of narcotic herbs, which, however, did no good at all. The alternative which he had wisely suggested, and which certainly went to the root of the matter, was to have the tooth drawn. But to this the queen would not submit. She could not abide the pain. Though in her name the rack and the little-ease were in constant use on "seminaries," yet she herself quaked and sickened at the very sight of a steel forceps. Her heart, as it seemed, came up into her mouth. However, in order to brace up her nerves, Aylmer, Bishop of London, at the Council-board, told her that "although he was an old man and had not many teeth to spare, she could see a practical experiment upon himself, if she thought well," and forthwith he bade the surgeon take out one of his own teeth in the queen's presence. This having been done "without much blooding and no cries," the queen, in turn, timorously submitted to a like operation, and so was relieved. The "witch-craft" was thus defeated.

 Year by year throughout her reign, the queen, as a matter of pleasure and recreation, visited different parts of the country, and was received with great state and often with extravagant pomp by the nobility and gentry. Many of them seriously crippled themselves by the outlay necessary for such entertainments, and greatly impoverished their estates in so receiving her. She came with her Court and servants, whom her chief allies and gracious people of rank were likewise expected to entertain; and she always looked for special amusements,—masques, bear-baiting, tiresome speeches full of flattery, morris-dancing, hunting, and hawking. Sometimes no less than two hundred servants accompanied her. Lord Leicester entertained her at Kenilworth; Sir Henry Lee at Quarrendon, near Aylesbury; and from time to time the chief nobility and gentlepeople of every county. When she left their houses, she expected to receive presents of money, jewellery, and other valuable and acceptable gifts. The queen on one occasion took Berkeley Castle in her progress. During her stay no less than twenty-seven stags of a rare race of red deer were killed, while many others were "stolen and havocked," which so annoyed Lord Berkeley that he actually there and then disparked the place. The queen, on hearing of this, counselled his lordship to be more prudent in what he said and did in the future; informing him that Lord Leicester liked the situation of his family castle very much, and hinted that, if he was not more careful, he might lose it. The morality of such a contemplated robbery was quite in accordance with this autocratic woman's morality in general.

At Euston, in Norfolk, the queen was most hospitably entertained by a young esquire named Edward Rookwood (who had lately been married), at his pleasant mansion near Thetford, in August of the year 1578. His residence was of no great size, and, in selecting it as a resting-place, the queen passed over several large mansions near. This may have been for a purpose. When Her Majesty was about to leave, she, of course, thanked Rookwood for his reception of her—she could have done nothing less—and gave him her hand to kiss. But the 'Earl of Sussex, Her Majesty's Chamberlain, having learnt that he had been excommunicated for "papistrie," called him forward and rated him with bitterness and violence.[1] His lordship asked Rookwood how he who, because of his religion, was wholly unfit to accompany any Christian person, and was fitter to be put into a pair of stocks, had dared to come into the queen's "reall presence." Rookwood was then ordered out of the room, and at Norwich was committed to prison. An oaken image of the Blessed Virgin, which had been taken down from the lady-altar of a neighbouring church, and had been carefully secreted in a hay-loft, was accidentally discovered by some of the Court servants. The queen expressed her horror at the "sight of such a wicked idol"; which

---

[1] Richard Topcliffe, the rack master and official torturer, has left a record of these events, the spelling of which I have ventured to put into modern shape :—"This Rookwood is a Papist of kind newly crept out of his late wardship. Her Majesty, by some means I know not, was lodged at his house, Euston, far unmeet for Her Highness, but fitter for the blackguard ; nevertheless (the gentleman brought into Her Majesty's presence by like device), Her Excellent Majesty gave to Rookwood ordinary thanks for his bad house, and her fair hand to kiss ; after which it was braved at. But my Lord Chamberlain nobly and gravely understanding that Rookwood was excommunicated for papistry called him before him ; demanded of him how he durst to attempt her real presence, he unfit to accompany any Christian person : forthwith said he was fitter for a pair of stocks, commanded him out of the Court, and yet to attend her Council's pleasure ; and at Norwich he was committed. And to decypher the gentleman to the full (a piece of plate being missed in the Court, and searched for in his hay-house), in the hay-rick such an image of Our Lady was there found as for greatness, for gayness, and workmanship I did never see a match ; and after a sort of country dance ended in Her Majesty's sight, the idol was set behind the people who avoided. She rather seemed a beast raised upon a sudden from hell by conjuring, than the picture for whom it had been so often and long abused. Her Majesty commanded it to the fire, which in her sight by the country folks was quickly done, to her content, and unspeakable joy of every one, but some one or two who had sucked of the idol's poisoned milk."—*Lodge*, vol. ii. p. 186.

was burnt on the village green in her presence and with her marked approbation.

As she journeyed from place to place, every endeavour was made to keep the poor, the poverty-stricken, and the diseased out of her sight. If they came too near her moving retinue, they were summarily punished with great and sharp severity. It was often her custom, however, to speak condescendingly and freely with her people, from whom by close questioning and most pertinent inquiries—having beckoned them to her presence —she frequently found out the true state of the locality. The old religious houses were in ruins, their lands ill cultivated. Beggars abounded, and so infested some parts of the country— Bernewode Forest in Buckinghamshire, and that of Charnwode in Leicestershire, for example—that travelling was dangerous. Moreover, the churches[1] everywhere, not only all but empty or ill-attended and utterly uncared for, were going steadily to ruin.

Anciently, as no one can deny, the parish church was looked upon with affection as the common home of all. By right of the new birth at the font, every one was equal in the sight of God when kneeling at mass, or worshipping at evensong, whether knight or knave, earl or husbandman. Low and squat were the oak-bound cottages of wattle[2] and thatch which clustered together picturesquely in remote spots round spire or tower ; and, sheltered by ancient trees, were the humble but well-loved homes of a people blessed in the natural order, and marvellously sanctified by gifts of grace. But there was one building in every such village, of which, howsoever simple in itself, the form and outline were the seemliest for its sacred purpose that mind could plan or local hand design. Of it, the stones had been reverently hewn and chiselled, the window tracery artfully drawn out and carved, the roof of oak, the font and altar made of the best that could be gotten, and duly blessed in God's Holy Name. The church was the chief building both of town and village. In such humble temples the glowing prophecies of an elder dispensation had their literal fulfilment ; for while the pine-tree and the box-tree

---

[1] "The parish churches themselves—those amazing monuments of early piety, built by men who themselves lived in clay hovels, while they lavished their taste, their labour, and their wealth on 'the House of God'—were still dissolving in ruin."—*History of England*, by J. A. Froude, Reign of Elizabeth, vol. ii. p. 93.

[2] "Wattle," a composition of mortar, mud, and straw, of which cottage walls in Elizabeth's time were commonly built. In numbers of villages at the present day a similar material is largely used, and in some parts still bears the same name. In other parts, it is termed "watchyt."

beautified the place of God's sanctuary, there, too, the realities of the gospel perfectly fulfilled the ancient types of the law. The daily sacrifice was ever offered, both for quick and dead. The Lamb of God took away the sins of the world.

Day by day and week by week the people thus so abundantly blessed came to worship. They were all of one faith and one mind. Year by year children were born and new born, young men and maidens were united in marriage, the sick were anointed, the suffering cared for; and in due course the graveyard, across which the shadow of tower or spire crept slowly, received the bodies of those who had done their work and run their race, and, sleeping in Christ, were there laid up for the resurrection morning.

When these poor and humble folks died, they seldom forgot the church or its needs, but by testamentary disposition directly evidenced their faith and charity.[1] Even the husbandman often bequeathed something towards maintaining the lamp before the rood, over and above the sum apportioned for his own mortuary mass and month's-mind. Kneeling, from time to time, before the outstretched arms of his dying Redeemer, he had learnt, more exactly than sermon could ever inform him, of the deep meaning of those simple words of the belief—"Jesus Christ was crucified"—and of his merciful Lord's undying love. Those in the ranks of yeomen or merchants often gave, in addition, six shillings and eightpence, or thirteen shillings and fourpence, for the church, a suit of vestments or silver *pax* for some special altar, twelve or twenty pounds of wax for the choir lights or Paschal taper, and always a settled sum for funeral doles to their poorer neighbours. No one went to an open grave without saying a prayer for the dead person's soul. The rich from moated mansion or crenelated castle gave in proportion to their abundance; so that the treasures of the Lord's House, even in the poorest villages steadily increasing, were both worthy of the respective givers and of the object.

But at the time at which Queen Elizabeth made her progresses throughout the land all this had been changed, and so changed that men marvelled how such a radical and startling change could have been accomplished in little more than a single generation.

Sometimes unjust persecution works its own cure. Here,

---

[1] Having been recently permitted to examine at leisure the original MS. wills of certain parts of Oxfordshire and Buckinghamshire, the author, who read portions of several hundreds, from the year 1530 downwards, is confident of the accuracy of his statements in the text.

however, it had been so systematic, relentless,[1] and determined that most of those who had stood forward to resist innovation—homeless, ruined, and outlawed — were swept away by the unchecked tide of change, which, so to speak, had flooded and overwhelmed the land.

In the year 1585, no less than seventy-two priests were banished ; while from a calculation made from various returns to the Privy Council of certain dioceses, there could not have been less than four hundred and fifty about that period still in prison.[2] What to do with them greatly puzzled the authorities. Some one, evidently a person of wisdom and foresight, had prepared a written suggestion which was no doubt read, and which, still preserved amongst the State papers, is headed " The Means to Stay the Declining in Religion." It stands thus :—

"*Remedies for the Restrained.*—The execution of them, as experience hath showed, in respect of their constancy (or rather obstinacy) moveth many to compassion, and draweth some to

---

[1] " Many Catholics have fled the realm ; others live in obscure, unknown places by contrary names. Some commend themselves prisoners to noblemen, whereof one so prisoner, his patience, demeanour, and purity of life were such that the lady of the said house said to some secret friends of hers, ' If all Papists lived so well as my lord's prisoner did, Protestants must needs be in an ill state towards God.' "—*An Ancient Editor's Note-Book*, MS., Stony-hurst College.

[2] See, amongst other documents, *State Papers, Domestic, Elizabeth*, vol. clxxviii. n. 72 ; vol. cxc. n. 44 ; vol. cxciii. n. 67 ; vol. cxcix. n. 15 ; and vol. ccii. n. 61, etc. etc. What these prisons were has been most forcibly stated by Canon Raine of York :—" It is impossible to speak in terms of too strong reprobation of the state of the northern prisons in the seventeenth century, and of the conduct of their keepers. They were dens of iniquity and horror, in which men and women herded together indiscriminately.. . . Some of them had no light and no ventilation ; several were partly under water whenever there was a flood. The number of prisoners who died in gaol during this century is positively startling. And how could they live in such places where they were treated worse than savages themselves? The ordinary conveniences and necessaries of life were denied to them. They were at the mercy of the gaolers for their food and for everything they possessed. They had the meanest fare at the most exorbitant price. If they resisted, there were irons and screws that compelled them to be silent. There were also the greatest inequality and injustice in the treatment of the prisoners. Those that had money had many indulgences. They were allowed to go to places of amusement without the walls of the gaol, and some were even permitted to lodge beyond the precincts, subjected only to some trifling surveillance. Peter Prison in York and the hold in Ousebridge were a disgrace to any civilised country. The cells in the latter place would almost have rivalled the notorious Black Hole. Air, light, and ventilation were absent, and the waters of the river rushed in when they were above their usual level."—*Depositions from the Castle of York relating to Offences committed in the Northern Counties, etc.*, Surtees' Society Publications, A.D. 1861.

affect their religion, upon conceit that such an extraordinary contempt of death cannot but proceed from above; whereby many have fallen away.

"And, therefore, it is a convenient thing to be considered whether it were not convenient that some other remedy were put in execution. And in case the execution of them shall not be thought the best course, then it is to be considered what other way were fit to be held with them.

"There are of these seminaries two sorts, some learned and politic withal, and of great persuasion; others simple, having neither zeal, wit, nor learning.

"For the first, they are to be sent to Wisbech, or some such-like place, where they may be under honest keeping, and be restrained from access and intelligence; for that being banished, they might do a great deal of harm.

"For the second, they may be banished, as others before, upon penalty to be executed if they return.

"Such as were banished and are returned are to be presently executed."[1]

This document, by whomsoever written, was thought to be of so much importance, and of such practical value that, as Sir Francis Walsingham wrote to his ally and friend Phillipps, its suggestions were exactly adopted by the Council. Here is the letter[2] :—

"My lords do mean to take order with the seminary priests by banishment of some, executing of others, and by committing the rest to Wisbech, or some such-like place, under some honest keeper. I have thought good to send you a register of their names; to the end you may confer with the party you wot of, and to desire him to set down their intentions to do harm in their several kinds.

"I take it there will be found very few of them fit to do good. And so I commit you to God. At Barnes, the 25th December 1586.—Your loving Friend,   FRA. WALSINGHAM."

In what way "order was taken" may be learnt with exactness

---

[1] *State Papers, Domestic, Elizabeth*, vol. cxcv. n. 114. The number of poor recusants was so great that at one sessions in Hampshire no less than four hundred were presented as offenders against the law; while in the north-west county of Lancaster six hundred were presented (see Strype's *Annals*, vol. iii. p. 478, Appendix 98). Thomas Cowper, Bishop of Winchester (A.D. 1584), suggested to the Council that one or two hundred "lustie men well able to labour" might be sent to Flanders as pioneers and workmen for the army (*Ibid.* 169).

[2] Cotton MSS., Brit. Museum, Caligula, C. ix. f. 566.

from the following letter,[1] preserved amongst the State papers, evidently from the pen of one who was extremely well informed :—

"'They lately threatened Mr. Sherwin, a priest, with renewed tortures, and then to execute him and his companions; but he, preferring a present death to longer life, was not at all dismayed by their threats.

"We shall, I hope, very shortly learn what will become of us. We all indeed greatly desire to pay the debt of Nature at once, rather than to languish on by a daily death. However, there is no one here who does not earnestly pray our Lord Jesus Christ to grant His aid, whereby to render us worthy to suffer for His glory all torments and tortures, nay, even death itself, otherwise so bitter to Nature, rather than to offend the Divine Majesty in the least degree contrary to each one's conscience.

"It is, I think, patent and a known fact to many, that some of our afflicted ones have endured the most terrible tortures, than which, on account of their excessive torments, death itself is far preferable, constantly and willingly ere they would consent to the most abominable crime (i.e. apostacy). Of which things there are certain living witnesses, especially Luke Kirby and Thomas Cottam, two venerable priests, who were subjected to a certain iron instrument of torture called in English the 'Scavenger's Daughter,' enduring this most bitter torture for an entire hour or more. Others—namely, the Reverend Mr. Skinner and Mr. Briant, twice; Mr. Johnson, indeed, but once—were cruelly tortured on the rack, attended with the most exquisite sufferings. Mr. Alart lay stretched upon it for three hours in torture; but beyond this, or at least more severely for that time, he was not tortured. And after the same manner they dealt with a portion of the rest of his companions, not without some great attempts to bring them to a compliance being made.

. "Some were thrust down into a certain underground dungeon, very deep, and being shut in on every side, involved in the densest darkness. Amongst these were Johnson, Bristow, and Brian, all of them priests, some of whom spent two entire months in this chamber of horrors. As for the others, all of them, together with your Superior, were thrust into certain obscure and dark corners, deprived of hope and assistance, without beds or other necessaries of any kind. Thus they dealt with Stanislaus Bristow and the others. The greater portion of them from this time are confined separately in squalid and dismal cells, where

[1] This is believed to be from the pen of the Rev. Edward Rishton. The original is in Latin.—*State Papers, Domestic, Elizabeth,* 1581, vol. cxlix. n. 61.

they are not allowed at any time to see any one, much less to speak with a friend.

"Mr. Brian, of whom I spoke before, was for some days worn out, and well-nigh killed with hunger.   At length, for the greater increase of his pain, he was most atrociously tortured by needles being violently thrust under his nails.   (Ah, miser!)

"By these things which are written, most dear brothers in Christ, it is well known what, and what kind of tortures the sons of God, and the true servants of Christ, patiently endure for their firm defence of the orthodox faith; and should it be required of them, are ready willingly to undergo still greater.

"This only thing we implore of His mercy, that He will of His goodness grant us patience and perseverance even to the end.   Which that we may the more speedily obtain, we earnestly implore your prayers for us, and the more so as we are not without some apprehension, seeing that the Prefect of the Tower yesterday, and again to-day, was summoned to the Court, in order that, as we believe, he might be informed with certainty what is decided upon about us."

The cases here referred to by Mr. Rishton were only ordinary examples of what was being continually carried out by the authorities.   Amongst the State papers, document after document has come to light showing the artful malignity, the cruelty, as well as the perseverance of the persecuting and triumphant faction.   Although in ordinary histories of this period little or no reference is made to such acts; yet no adequate conception of the true state of affairs can be had without some study of the various records of these odious barbarities.

Throughout this queen's reign there were not wanting occasional tokens, mysterious, supernatural, and, as some would say, in a measure miraculous,[1] of the grave displeasure of the Almighty

---

[1] On the other hand, to some of those who suffered, singular tokens of the Almighty's favour were graciously given.   For example, the Rev. Stephen Rousham, who was executed at Gloucester in 1587, was thus singularly favoured.   He had been banished, but had returned, and of him *An Ancient Editor's Note-Book* gives the following particulars:—"A man of singular perfection, he had in his lifetime many heavenly visions, as great lights in windows and places where he was alone, and sometimes with others.   His crown of martyrdom [was] showed him most gloriously, being yet a minister, and in schism.   Afterwards a priest and in prison, God the Father, Christ our Saviour, our Blessed Lady, glorious souls of Saints, full often appeared unto him, leaving behind them such odoriferous smells, and sometimes lasting many hours with him, that for the space of one day and a half he thought himself in heaven, his joys were so great and strange.   This heavenly company had divers speeches with him in their several appearances to him, which he would not utter, neither did he reveal this but a little before his martyrdom to a dear worshipful friend, after a long visit to him."—*Records of the English Province*, vol. iv. p. 340.   London, 1878.

with the once Christian people of this country. A strange sign, which none could explain nor account for, here; a gloomy and mysterious prediction there; a sharp punishment by some unknown and fatal disease in another quarter, by which, with no preparation, numbers were hurried away to the particular judgment-seat of their Maker; a solemn warning, of which few could mistake the purport, was from time to time faced and noticed. But these supernatural interventions were too often passed by and disregarded. When, as was the case, misbelief had eaten into the very heart of the nation, such signs and tokens were either despised or laughed at. The old and authorised teachers had been set in a corner; while the whole multitude, ever seeking after what they called "the Truth," and never finding it, drearily brayed and fondly babbled over things sacred, hearing nothing but the discordant voices of angry controversialists in perpetual din and dismal contest. No one learnt; few obeyed. Every one taught; all sought to be guides. Those who then made up the common herd—each one for himself—thus rode to the devil on his own hobby and by his own road.

Of such supernatural warnings, a few examples shall now be provided. To the fools who say in their heart, There is no God, such will be as foolishness; to the Catholic, perhaps, not unworthy of note.

Within two years of the queen's accession an occurrence had taken place which caused an unusual stir in Wales. The record of it is simple enough, and may easily be recounted. An ash-tree, it appears, had been blown down during a severe and destructive storm which passed over the park of Sir Thomas Stradling at St. Donat's, in Glamorganshire. When certain people came to examine that portion of the trunk which was thoroughly split up, they found within it, much to their consternation and awe, a strange representation of a distinct and plainly-defined cross.[1] Some persons who first examined it confidently declared that its appearance was a token of the Almighty's wrath, and that it plainly indicated that many storms would be experienced by the nation if those doctrines which the cross symbolised were cast out and abolished. The few who first witnessed the portent, for such it was regarded, spread the above opinion throughout their respective villages, which led hundreds of persons from all the adjacent places to come in crowds to look upon it. When

---

[1] In some editions of Archdeacon Harpsfield's *Dialogi Sex, etc.*, may be found a rare plate of this miraculous cross. The volume in quarto was first published at Antwerp in 1573; other issues of it were made later; some, however, without the engraving.

it was seen, the people were overcome with terror.   God Almighty,
they said, would punish them all if they took to the new religion.
On this point controversies arose; while the excitement and
interest so increased that the Queen's Privy Council, at Cecil's
suggestion, felt called upon to consider what should be done.
The people were in a ferment.   Sir Roger Vaughan and Esquire
Edward Lewis, of the county of Glamorgan, were consequently
formally commissioned to make special inquiries with regard to
this "Cross of St. Donat's."   They did so at once; but without
any particular result, though they sent up to the Council at
Richmond several curious depositions of eye-witnesses and others
on the subject, which leave little doubt as to the fact.[1]   The
general impression amongst the populace was that the shameful
destruction of the crosses in churches and churchyards, which
had again taken place, was thus solemnly condemned by this
impressive portent.

A prophecy, long ago fulfilled, is one of the points of the
following notice.   The restoration of Glastonbury Abbey is by
no means so improbable as our forefathers may have supposed.

An old monk of Glastonbury, Austin Ringwode,[2] who, having
the fear of God before his eyes, though turned out from his sacred
home, dwelt in a cottage no great distance from it,[3] and through
many long years, observing without relaxation his old rule,
constantly interceded with God for his miserable and afflicted
countrymen.   He lived under the spiritual direction of Father
Bridgewater, in the greatest retirement and on the sparest diet;
gave himself up constantly to prayer, self-denial, and fasting;
and, in his later years, was favoured with celestial visions of a
most consoling nature.   To some friends who went to render
him assistance when he was smitten down with a sore plague, he
predicted that "many woeful troubles" would "fall upon the
people because of their sins"; that "the lands would be untilled
for divers years; and that a bloody war" would overtake the
country as a punishment.   He, furthermore, averred that some
of those then living would not die until they had beheld these

---

[1] *State Papers, Domestic, Elizabeth*, vol. xvii., A.D. 1561.
[2] He is alluded to, as is also his prediction, in a tract, *A True Relation of
Master Austin Ringwode, etc.*, published in the year 1652, in London, in
which the prophecy is assumed to have been fulfilled by the Civil War.   The
Rev. William Cole, on visiting Glastonbury in the eighteenth century, read
the inscription upon his gravestone.—See also Harleian MSS., Brit. Museum,
No. 6998, fol. 53.
[3] Certain other of the old monks continued to live within sight of the abbey
walls, and to observe their rule as far as possible.   One monk, who had
secured certain relics of the abbey, died at a great age.

portents. He said, moreover, that "the abbey would be one day
. repaired and rebuilt for the like worship which had ceased, and
that then peace and plenty would for long time abound."
Ringwode died in the winter of 1587, and was buried at
Glastonbury.

A mysterious kind of plague that swept off many persons of
rank and birth at Oxford is allowed by certain writers on both
sides to have been a judgment from heaven, and a warning to
the innovators and persecutors to desist from their unhallowed
work.

This warning was made in the case of the memorable trial or
Roland Jenks, a Catholic bookseller in Oxford,[1] who, for speaking
some words against the queen's religion, was condemned, in the
Assizes held at Oxford in July 1577, to have his ears nailed to
the pillory, and to deliver himself by cutting them off with his
own hands, which sentence was no sooner passed when immediately upon the spot a strange, mortal distemper, the like of which,
as to its symptoms, has never been heard of before or since, fell
upon the judges, justices on the bench, sheriffs, jurymen, and
hundreds of others that were present at the trial, and carried
them off in a very short time. Let us hear Mr. Anthony à
Wood, the well-known and accurate historian of the University
of Oxford, whose account of this history is on record.[2] His
words, translated from the Latin, are as follows :—

"It was ordered, therefore, in the Convocation held on the 1st
of May 1577 that the criminal, Roland Jenks, should immediately be apprehended ; and being put into irons, should be sent
up in order to be examined before the Chancellor of the University and the Queen's Council. In the meantime, all his goods
are seized, and in his house are found Bulls of Popes, and libels
reflecting upon Her Majesty. He was examined at London, in
presence of the persons aforesaid, and then was sent back to
Oxford, there to be kept in prison till the next assizes, which
began on the 4th of July, in the old hall in the castle-yard, and
lasted for two days.

"He was brought to the bar, and was arraigned for high
crimes and misdemeanors ; and, being found guilty, was condemned by a sentence in some manner capital, for he was to lose
his ears. At which time (although my soul dreads almost to
relate it) so sudden a plague invaded the men that were present
(the great crowd of people, the violent heat of the summer, and

---

[1] The above account, with the authorities for its statements in detail, is
given from the narrative of the pious and accomplished Bishop of Debra.

[2] *Historia et Antiquitates Universitatis Oxoniensis*, i. p. 294.

the stench of the prisoners, all conspiring together, and perhaps also a poisonous exhalation breaking suddenly at the same time out of the earth) that you might say Death itself sat on the bench, and by her definite sentence put an end to all the causes. For great numbers immediately dying upon the spot, others struck with death hastened out of the court as fast as they could, to die within a very few hours. A mournful ditty was shortly after published on this subject by a young university man, which, for brevity sake, I shall omit. But it may not be amiss to set down the names of the persons of greatest note who were seized by that plague, and breathed out their souls. These were Sir Robert Bell, Chief Baron of the Exchequer, and Nicholas Barham, sergeant-at-law, both great enemies of the popish religion. . . . To the above named must be added Sir Robert Doyley, the High Sheriff of Oxford; Mr. Hart, his deputy; Sir William Babington; Messieurs Doyley, Wenman, Danvers, Fettyplace, and Harcourt, justices of the peace; Kirby, Greenwood, Nash, and Foster, gentlemen; to whom are to be joined, to say nothing of others, almost all the jurymen, who died within two days."

Anthony à Wood adds, out of the Register of Merton College, the following account of the symptoms of this strange disease:—

"Some getting out of bed (agitated with I know not what fury from their distemper and pain), beat and drive from them their keepers with sticks; others run about the yards and streets like madmen; others jump head foremost into deep waters. The sick labour with a most violent pain, both of the head and stomach; they are taken with a frenzy; are deprived of their understanding, memory, sight, hearing, and other senses. As the disease increases, they take nothing; they get no sleep; they suffer none to tend or keep them; they are always wonderfully strong and robust, even in death itself; no complexion or constitution is spared; but the choleric are more particularly attacked by this evil, of which the physicians can neither find the cause nor cure. The stronger the person is, the sooner he dies. Women are not seized by it, nor the poor, neither does any one catch it that takes care of the sick, or visits them. But as this disease was strangely violent, so it was but of a short continuance; for within a month it was over." So far the Merton Register.[1]

---

[1] "The substance of this history," as the same writer remarks, "may be found also in Sir Richard Baker's *Chronicle*, and in Fuller's *Church History*, book ix. p. 139. To say nothing of the Catholic writers, in whom I have found it, who are F. Parsons, *Epist. de Persecutione Angl.*, published in 1581; Mr. Rishton, *De Schismati Angl.* i. 3; Ribadaneira, in his Appendix

A remarkable occurrence—betokening the frequent use of the executioner's knife—took place on the occasion when Father Campion the Jesuit was sentenced to death, and seems to have been a warning to the judge. It is given from an authentic record :—

"When Judge Ayloffe was sitting to keep the place when the other judges retired, while the jury consulted about the condemnation of Father Campion and his company, and pulling off his glove, found all the hand and his seal of arms bloody, without any token of wrong, pricking, or hurt; and, being dismayed therewith, wiping, it went not away, but still returned. He showed it to the gentlemen that sat before him, who can be witnesses of it till this day, and have some of them upon their faiths and credits avouched it to be true.[1]

As a rule, such warnings and portents remained all unnoticed by those in power. Other persons occasionally were not unimpressed.

One of the most serious and practical losses to the country in general, a loss more especially felt by the upper and middle classes,[2] was that which had ensued because of the utter destruction of the monastic system, viz. the universal lack of any machinery for education. In previous generations, the sons and daughters of the nobility and gentry had commonly received their education at the abbeys and convents of old; and there is no reason to believe that this education was not both solid and

to Dr. Saunders' *History*, cap. 13; Yepez, Bishop of Tarraçona, in his Spanish *History of the Persecution*, i. ii. cap. 9, who relates also, cap. 11, some other examples of the like judgments upon the persecutors, etc. I find also the same history had reached Douay by the following month, where it is recorded in the Register or Diary of the College, August 1577. Mr. Jenks survived his punishment many years, for by the same Diary he was at Rheims in 1587."

[1] "Life of Father Thomas Cottam," p. 168, *Records of the English Province.* Manresa Press, 1875.

[2] Many of the lower classes in agricultural districts could neither read nor write, though there were, of course, considerable exceptions. They learned their *Pater noster, Ave Maria*, and *Credo* by heart, instructed by the parson of the parish, and said their rosary on a knotted ring or a string of beads. They heard the Bidding-Prayer in their native tongue; many parts of the baptismal and marriage services were said in English; while the sermons were plain and homely, and wanting in that everlasting criticism and controversy which so distinguishes those of the present day. The poor gained much of the accurate religious knowledge they possessed from the expressive and telling pictures in the churches; and perhaps were after all quite as happy and contented as their Board School trained descendants, who are illuminated by penny newspapers, and instructed to despise the Catholic religion; and know neither in theory nor practice their duty to God and to their neighbour.

sound, as well as pious and sufficient, notwithstanding the false
assertions of the Commissioners and the sneers of the over-cynical
Erasmus.   Then, however, all such places of education had been
utterly destroyed.   At Glastonbury several hundred youths, year
by year for generations, had been Christianly and virtuously
brought up; and so it was elsewhere in every English shire.
The practical change which such a revolution had made can now
scarcely be realised.   The inconvenience and loss must have
been excessive, and added largely to the existing ill-feeling.   In
fact, so serious did some of the reforming party think it, that the
Council urged upon their trustiest allies—those who had secured
so much of the monastic property—to do what was possible and
practicable in their own particular localities towards remedying
the evil.   The queen's personal friends [1] were likewise exhorted
to aid.

For the new country clergy could do nothing in this crisis of
want of education.   Taken from "the lowest of the people,"
they were often so ignorant that they could scarcely read the
Scriptures in English without special preparation, and knew no
more of Latin or English Composition than the general class of
mechanics from whose ranks so many of them had been taken.
In the dioceses of London, Canterbury, Norwich, York, and
Lichfield, judging by the registers and books of institution,
batches of persons were ordained either readers or ministers,
thoroughly unworthy of the offices—gauging them from the new
standing-point.   The very low state of public education in
general towards the middle of Elizabeth's reign may further be
collected from a provision in Archbishop Parker's foundation of
three scholarships at Cambridge in 1567.   These are to be
supplied by the most considerable schools in Kent and Norfolk,
and are to be "the best and aptest schollers, well instructed in
the grammar, and (if it may be) such as can make a verse."

It was essential, therefore, that something were done, and done
promptly, to remedy the evil.   So the authorities stirred up
persons of influence in various parts of England, especially those
who had favoured the innovating policy, to provide means and
machinery for educating the young.   Sir Nicholas Bacon, in
consequence, secured two specific charters founding a grammar
school at St. Alban's.   At Aylesbury, Sir Henry Lee, K.G.,

---

[1] Author's MSS. and Excerpts. Letter of Robert Beale, Clerk of the
Council, to Sir Henry Lee of Dytchley and Quarrendon, Knt.   It was, no
doubt, because of this that Sir Henry founded the grammar school at Aylesbury, near which part of his property lay, and in which his lady, Lord Paget's
second daughter, was buried.

founded a similar institution, to which a subsequent benefactor, more than a century afterwards, added a munificent donation. At Thame,[1] in Oxfordshire, in 1559, Lord Williams of Thame established an admirable school, where for generations the sons of the nobility and gentry living near received a good education. At Bromeyard, in Herefordshire, another efficient and welcomed school was set up. In the county of Kent, Sir Roger Manwood, by the queen's special authority, instituted a grammar school at Sandwich.[2] Others at Maidstone, at Cranbrook in 1574, and at Faversham in 1576, were likewise established. At Reading the Corporation resuscitated an old school connected with the abbey, at the queen's special request; and having undertaken to pay the master's salary, received in return from Her Highness a charter, bearing date 23rd of September 1560, and a grant of certain lands which then produced about forty-one pounds per annum. At Wycombe, in the year 1561, the queen granted the buildings and site of the Hospital of St. John the Baptist in that town for "the maintenance of one pedagogue or master for the good instruction of children or youth," and gave to it certain lands in Penn, Hughenden, and Great Marlow. Archbishop Grindal founded a school at St. Bees, about the year 1583, but died before the work was completed. At Ashborne, in Derbyshire, another was set up, two years later, on the petition of Sir Thomas Cockayne to the queen; and a third at Dronfield, near Chesterfield,[3] by Henry Fanshaw, Esq. James Pilkington, Bishop of Durham, had obtained a charter for the foundation of a school at Darlington on June 15th, 1567, the common seal of which bears a representation of the queen crowned and with a sceptre. At Chepping Barnet, Lord Leicester founded a school by Letters

---

[1] See *Some Account of Lord Williams of Thame, Founder of the Grammar School and Alms-Houses at Thame, together with a Copy of His Will, etc.* Thame, 1873.

[2] "That the scholemaster be firste allowed by the Ordynarie, and hy examynacion fownd meete bothe for his learnynge and discreacion of teachinge; as also for his honest conversacion and righte understandinge of Godes trewe religeon nowe sette fourthe by publique awcthoritie."—*Statutes of Sandwiche Grammar School.*

[3] "*Item,* I ordain that the scholars do upon every Sunday and Holy-day in the morning resort orderly unto the school, and that they go from thence with their master and usher before them into the church, two and two in rank; that they carry their service-book with them, and answer the versicles and the psalms as the clerk of the parish doth; that they kneel at such times of the celebration of Divine Service accordingly as it is in that behalf prescribed in the 'Book of Common Prayer,' and that they stand up at the reading of the Creed, and bow at the sacred name of Jesus," etc.—*Statutes of Dronfield School.*

Patent dated 24th March 1573 ; and at Hawkshead, in Lancashire, Sandys, Archbishop of York, did the same in 1588. At Market Bosworth, Sir Wolstan Dixie, Lord Mayor of London, founded a school in 1592. At Halifax in Yorkshire and at Woodstock in Oxfordshire, grammar schools were founded in 1585. In the north similar schools were erected, under the queen's direct sanction, at Appleby and Kirkby-Stephen ;[1] while in the extreme West of England, Bodmin, Launceston, Saltash near Plymouth, and Penrhyn were benefited by the setting up of similar institutions. Of most of these the statutes were drawn up with wisdom and discretion; and the Christian, apart from the Catholic, principle was everywhere and thoroughly recognised.[2]

Notwithstanding the several important educational foundations of this reign, however, there were not two hundred grammar schools existing throughout the whole country. These, of course, were under the direction of the new bishops, who licensed both the chief or head master and his ushers—often forbidden, in their deed of licence, to marry, or to have any woman or children at the school-house[3]—and who were enabled to exercise the same jurisdiction over them as over the ordinary ministers of their dioceses. As a rule, the "grammarians" seem to have been learned men of mark and ability, and often presented a strong contrast in these particulars to the recently-ordained

---

[1] From the statutes of the School of Kirkby-Stephen (1566) it appears that Lord Wharton, its founder, desired that the scholars, with the master, should daily sing together certain psalms in the chapel where his tomb stood, after they had recited their prayers in the choir. "Knaveshness, malpertness, or stubbornness" in the boys were to merit "reasonable correction."

[2] In the mischievous educational changes of later years, made ostensibly because of "our miserable divisions," the Christian principle is now given up under Queen Victoria, just as the Catholic principle had been abrogated under Queen Elizabeth. All religious tests are now abolished ; boys who attend need not be baptized ; "women may be gonors" [Query? governesses] of the schools ; head masters need not be in Holy Orders ; and a perfect revolution has been once more effected.

[3] "Imprimis, I do ordain and will that the schoolmaster to be learned, sober, discreet, and unmarried ; such a one as hath taken a degree or degrees in the Universities of Oxford or Cambridge, undeformed, and of the age of thirty years at the least."—*Statutes of Witton School*, co. Chester. "We desire that the master and undermaster shall both be forbidden to keep their wives (if they have married any, or hereafter shall marry) or any part of their family within the walls, rooms, attics, or apartments of the masters ; for they have been built for the purposes of teaching and learning, and ought to be kept in a state of complete quiet and silence, so that no improper disturbance may arise in any way to interfere with the studies of the school."—*Statutes of Thame Grammar School*, chap. x. Bishop Robert Pursglove, in founding the school at Guisborough, in Cleveland (19th June 1561), ordered that "no Scot nor a stranger born be master, nor no married priest or layman."

clergy.   Many of the former did a good work, and were held in
high repute.[1]   As for the general body of schoolmasters, they
came to be looked upon as a special and favoured class, being
exempt from the payment of certain taxes and other burdens
which pressed so severely upon other classes at this period.   It
should be remembered that, in the beginning of Elizabeth's reign,
all benefices had been taxed to the amount of a thirtieth part of
their value to provide education for poor students.

About this time William Carter was executed for having reprinted and sold a "Treatise on Schism," which gave great
offence to the authorities.   Full of pointed arguments and
pertinent reflections, it is said to have been from the pen of a
most brilliant writer and powerful controversialist, Dr. Gregory
Martin, an exile, and had been first printed at Douay in 1578.
One passage in it, relating to Holofernes, was thought to have
recommended the murder of the queen ; but this interpretation
appears far-fetched and more than doubtful,[2] although the judges
assumed it to be evident.   Eventually the jury, thus misdirected
on a matter of fact, convicted the accused, and on January
10th, 1584, he was executed as a traitor, with the customary
barbarities.

The halter and knife, in fact, were still in constant requisition.
Sometimes, too, the stake, the faggots, and the lighted torch.
For example : Matthew Hammond, a plough-wright, of Hether-
sett, near Norwich, and a Nonconformist, pronounced an obstinate
heretic by the Bishop of Norwich, was burnt at the stake on
May 20th, 1579, in the ditch of that city ; as was also Francis
Kett, about ten years afterwards, i.e. in 1588, who appears to
have been an Arian.   On each of these occasions the queen
justified herself in signing the death-warrant on the plea that as
Supreme Governess it became her personal duty to punish
heretics at the stake.   On February 12th of the year 1584, five
seminary priests were put to death at Tybourne ; blood had been

[1] At Thame the trustees of Lord Williams' Will had so high an opinion of
the first "Informator," Edward Harris of New College, that they procured
for him Letters Patent granting him the office for life.   Some of his relations
had been monks at Notley Abbey and the Abbey at Thame Park ; and he
was a man of good ability and considerable learning.

[2] "The whole object of the author was to warn his brethren against the sin
of schism.   For this purpose he advised the Catholic gentlewomen to imitate
Judith ; as she abstained from profane meats, so ought they to abstain from
all communication with others in a worship which they believed to be
schismatical.   By doing this they would destroy Holofernes . . . After an
attentive perusal of the whole tract," continues Dr. Lingard, "I cannot find
in it the smallest foundation for the charge."—Appendix, Note QQ. to vol.
vi. of *The History of England.*

flowing in fact, and legal butchering going on so steadily, that foreign nations criticised the queen and her advisers sharply.[1] These criticisms had their due weight. Two treatises, in reply and explanation, accordingly appeared, one a "Declaration of the Favourable Dealings of Her Majesty's Commissioners," etc., and "A Declaration of the Traitorous Affection borne against Her Majesty by Edmund Campion, Jesuit, and other condemned Priests." To these Dr. Allen retorted in a very powerful volume *On the English Persecution*, which created so great a sensation both at home and abroad, that Lord Burghley[2] entered the arena, and published *The Execution of Justice in England, for Maintenance of Public and Christian Peace, against certain Stirrers of Sedition, etc.* This fell somewhat flat; and Dr. Allen thought it deserving of notice, and so wrote "A True, Sincere, and Modest Defence of the English Catholics, that suffer for their Faith both at Home and Abroad, against a Slanderous Libel."

On the part of the queen and her advisers, fresh Acts of Parliament and further enactments were far more efficient than *ex parte* tracts and treatises. These latter, however, as penned by their opponents, had caused the Council great consternation. They saw, or professed to see, dangers gathering on all sides, and plots thickening. Some one had been captured at sea, a Scotch priest named Creighton, and had tried to destroy a manuscript containing, as it was asserted, notes of a plan for the country's invasion by the Spaniards, but in vain, for the MS., or something which did duty for it, was secured. The friends of Queen Mary of Scotland were reported to be exceedingly active in trying to aid her; and Francis Throckmorton and others were severely racked and then executed for treasonable correspondence with the Spanish ambassador.

Consequently, in the latter part of the year, two new and important Acts of Parliament were passed. (1) The first was made "for the surety of the queen's most royal person, and the continuance of the realm in peace."[3] This enactment legalised an association which had been formed to protect Her Majesty from assassination, and to revenge her death if assassinated. Its

---

[1] A comparison between the deeds of the pagan emperors of Rome and those then being done in the queen's name gave great offence. The sting of the remark lay in the justice and accuracy of the parallel. The queen smarted under it.

[2] Some assert that he himself was the author of the first defence of the Commissioners.

[3] 27 Elizabeth, cap. i.

members,[1] at the head of whom was Lord Leicester, pledged themselves to punish with death any one who attempted her life; and also excluded from the throne—this was directed against Mary Queen of Scots—any one who should either authorise such an attempt, or profit by it. (2) The second Act was directed against Jesuits, seminary priests, and other "such-like disobedient persons."[2] These were to leave the kingdom within forty days, under the penalty of treason. If anyone received them or aided them, it was treason. All students in the seminaries abroad were to return within six months and take the Oath of Supremacy, or else were regarded as traitors; and when they returned they were not to come within twenty miles of the Court for ten years. Persons sending a son to these seminaries were, for every such offence, to forfeit one hundred pounds, and to incur the penalties of *præmunire;* if they forwarded money to any son already there, he was henceforth precluded from inheriting any estate or other possession from the sender.

Whittingham, a noted lay-divine of that period, was a strong Calvinist; and the only ordination he had received was a call from a fanatical assembly of this self-satisfied sect at Geneva.[3] Yet, without either question or protest, he had been made Dean of Durham by Letters Patent; and, if the Supreme Governess had willed it, she might have made him High Admiral, a state-bishop, or a peer. If the chief officer at Durham Cathedral were unordained, can it be doubted that in inferior positions the unordained were numerous? After having been dean for some years, however, a complaint was laid against him that "he was neither deacon nor minister according to the laws of the realm, but a mere layman." In this prolonged contest Sandys, Archbishop of York, a decided personal opponent of the dean, eventually proceeded to excommunication. Of this the Lord Treasurer strongly disapproved; nor were the proceedings looked upon with favour by Dr. Hutton, then Dean of York, who resisted Sandys' high-handed policy with much vigour. A long, excited, and involved discussion took place on this point. In itself it is wearisome, tedious, and of slender interest.[4] It was eventually

[1] Mary Queen of Scots proposed to join, and offered to sign the declaration agreed upon, but was not permitted to do so.

[2] 27 Elizabeth, cap. ii.

[3] Any one who cares to wade through a wordy account of it may do so in the various letters from foreign Protestants in the Parker Society's publications.

[4] What had taken place under King Henry VIII., as regards episcopacy and ordination, may be set forth in the late Lord Macaulay's own words:—

settled in a manner which clearly and conclusively proved that at the period in question the imposition of the hands of the Genevan ministers was considered by all in authority quite as efficacious and sufficient as the imposition of the hands of the new English prelates. Whittingham retained his deanery until his death. The so-called "ordination" of the foreign sectaries, Scotch as well as continental, was thus held to be just as good as any other ordination. At that time such was the teaching of the queen's new communion. Parker, Grindal,[1] and Sandys fully recognised ministers of this kind, gave them licences to officiate in London, Canterbury, and elsewhere, superintended them, and looked upon them as part and parcel of "the true and blessed congregation of the elect."

"The founders of the Anglican Church took a middle course. They retained episcopacy; but they did not declare it to be an institution essential to the welfare of a Christian society, or to the efficacy of the Sacraments. Cranmer, indeed, plainly avowed his conviction that in the primitive times there was no distinction between bishops and priests, and that the laying-on of hands was altogether unnecessary."—*The History of England, etc.*, p. 53. London, 1848. And again :—"He (the king) appointed divines of various ranks to preach the Gospel, and to administer the Sacraments. It was unnecessary that there should be any imposition of hands. The king—such was the opinion of Cranmer given in the plainest words—might, in virtue of authority derived from God, make a priest, and the priest so made needed no ordination whatever. These opinions Cranmer followed out to their legitimate consequences. He held that his own spiritual functions, like the secular functions of the Chancellor and the Treasurer, were at once determined by a demise of the Crown. When Henry died, therefore, the archbishop and his suffragans took out fresh commissions empowering them to ordain and to perform other spiritual functions, till the new Sovereign should think fit to order otherwise. When it was objected that a power to bind and to loose, altogether distinct from temporal power, had been given by our Lord to His Apostles, the theologians of this [the Erastian] school replied that the power to bind and to loose had descended not to the clergy, but to the whole body of Christian men, and ought to be exercised by the chief magistrate as the representative of the society."—*Ibid.* p. 56.

[1] In 1582 Archbishop Grindal's Vicar-General gave a formal written licence to John Morrison, a Scotch Presbyterian preacher, both to preach and to minister the Sacraments throughout the province of Canterbury. This document distinctly exhibits the true position of the question of Orders, for it states that Morrison had received imposition of the hands of the General Synod, *i.e.* the presbyters and elders of the county of Lothian; and that the faith of the new communion of John Knox was conformable with that newly set up and established by the authority of Parliament in England.—On the other hand, it seems that a certain Serjeant Manwood, subsequently a judge, wrote to Archbishop Parker, asking that the vacant living of Old Romney, might be given to Nicholas Jones, his brother's son-in-law, who, however, had already been refused it once, for two good reasons: first, that he was not a member of any university; and, secondly, *because he had never been ordained.*" Here it may be noted that some of the new prelates were more lax than others.—Parker MSS., C. C. Coll., Camb. No. cxiv. folio 935.

The case of Travers, the earnest and outspoken lecturer of the Temple Church in London, is equally to the point. He had been originally educated at Cambridge, was a good Oriental scholar; and, having gone to Geneva several years previously, there made the acquaintance of Theodore Beza. Thus he became settled in his misbelief as a Calvinist; and going to Flanders, was made a minister at Antwerp,[1] where, with Cartwright, another notable Calvinistic Puritan, he preached to the workmen at the English factory. In 1584 he returned to England, and on the strength of his foreign ordination, was at once made chaplain to Lord Burghley; who subsequently secured for him the appointment of lecturer at the Temple. His abilities as a preacher were considerable, his oratory powerful; his learning, though one-sided and narrow, was solid; his method systematic, and his rhetoric remarkably telling and effective.[2] He consequently gained a great influence over the councillors of the Temple, and secured an enthusiastic following. When the celebrated minister, Richard Hooker, who inclined to ancient principles, was made master of that corporation on March 17, 158$\frac{4}{5}$, he himself commonly preached in the morning, and Travers in the afternoon. What the former "grave and painful divine" (as his contemporaries termed him) asserted in his thoughtful sermon after mattins, that the lecturer was accustomed flatly to contradict in his eloquent discourse which followed evensong in the afternoon.

This state of things, though then common enough in many country places, was not unlikely to breed grave dissensions and inconvenience in the city of London. The lecturer at the Temple, however, was then neither peculiar nor alone in his policy. Hundreds of ministers had no other orders, and an innumerable number plainly contradicted the neighbouring preachers to their right hand and to their left. But in London these offences became very notorious. So Travers was brought before the Court of High Commission, and after no great consideration an order was signed to silence him. Policy, not law, influenced the decision. He appealed for redress to the Lords of the Council, asserting somewhat loosely and vaguely that "by virtue of the communion of saints all ordinations, whether by

---

[1] For the testimonial of his ordination at Antwerp by the Presbytery, dated 14 May 1578, see Fuller's *Church History*, book ix. p. 214.

[2] Fuller writes flatteringly of Travers, that his "utterance was graceful, gesture plausible, matter justifiable, method plain, and his style carried with it *indolem pietatis*, a genius of grace flowing from his sanctified heart."— *Church History*.

presbyter or bishop, were of equal value in the Church of Christ."
But this did not serve him. Archbishop Whitgift disallowed
the proposition.[1] Such loose principles, it was seen, might
seriously inconvenience the bishops, now that the Puritans were
so rapidly gaining in strength, numbers, and influence; so that,
under Archbishop Whitgift's advice, Travers was condemned
both for want of Orders and for lack of jurisdiction, in very plain
terms.[2] Afterwards he went to Ireland, at the invitation of
Adam Loftus, Archbishop of Dublin, where orders were held to
be of very slender importance, and became provost of Trinity
College; but Calvinism was not over-popular there—as Bale had
long ago discovered—and he made several enemies, so resigning
this appointment, he eventually returned to England, where he
ended his days.

In 1586, the state of morals in London had become so
frightful, while among the preachers or ministers the peace-
makers were few and the sowers of discord and brawlers so
many, that John Aylmer, the bishop, who at once states and
deplores the evils, ordered the Commination Service to be said
at least three times a year, to avert the looked-for wrath of God.
In so doing, we may reasonably wonder if he ever called to
mind the atrocious acts of sacrilege which he himself, when
Archdeacon of Lincoln, had perpetrated or directly sanctioned
twenty years before.   In the utter moral corruption then existing,
the nation was only reaping what had been so recently sown by
these "Reforming" prelates and their party.

Several of the clergy, to judge by the actual words of this
Bishop's Visitation Articles,[3] were believed to keep suspected
women in their houses, to be grossly incontinent, given to

---

[1] Archbishop Whitgift, in 1589, was the first prelate of the "reformed"
Church who claimed for episcopacy the joint character of "apostolic" and
"divine." Hatton, Bancroft, Bilson, and Andrewes followed him subsequently in maintaining the truth and importance of the same principle.
But, like Hooker, they were uncertain, ambiguous, and feeble in setting it
forth; while, in almost every case, they hesitated to condemn the Puritans,
except on the policy of expediency.

[2] The actual terms of the order condemning Travers were as follows:—
"That he was no lawfully-ordained minister according to the Church of
England; that he preached without being licensed; that he had openly presumed to confute such doctrine as had been publicly delivered by another
preacher, without giving warning of these controversial sallies to the lawful
ordinary; and that this liberty was contrary to a provision made in the
seventh year of this reign, for avoiding disturbances in the Church." The
authority of Parliament, not that of the old canon law, was thus brought to
bear upon him.

[3] Imprinted at London by Richard Johnes, dwelling at the Rose and
the Crowne, neere unto Holborne Bridge, 1586.

drunkenness, indecency,[1] idleness, hunting, hawking, and dicing, to be table-swearers, dancers, liars, and false dissemblers; while many in all parts, as well in the Province of York as in that of Canterbury, notoriously ministered, or pretended to minister,[2] without having received any ordination of any sort or kind. Illiterate, ignorant, and uninstructed, the more violent and vulgar they were in frantically denouncing the religion of their grandparents—women as well as shopkeepers joined in the work[3] —the better they found themselves suited to the depraved taste or religious excitement and Calvinistic blasphemy of the multitude, and the greater was the favour shown them by those ministers of the queen who superintended the ancient dioceses, and were officially pledged to root out the old faith. Infants at this time were no longer baptized, as many old parish registers abundantly show; while the Lord's Supper was now celebrated at night, and Evening Communion introduced by these "Reformation" worthies.[4] The most rampant revolutionary utterances, often ridiculous in themselves when not painfully blasphemous,

---

[1] In January 1581, Davye Wood, a drunken preacher, scandalously ill-treated his wife, and when two women interfered, exposed himself to them.— *Vide State Papers, Elizabeth*, vol. cxlvii. n. 4.

[2] Archbishop Parker, had some years previously, *i.e.* in 1575, inquired "whether any have intruded themselves and presumed to exercise any kind of ministry *without imposition of hands and lawful calling by ordinary authority*, and whether any admitted but to deaconrie *usurpe the office of the minister. Item*, whether any lay persons take upon them to read openly in the congregation Divine Service in any church, chapple, or oratorie, without there be thereunto upon some urgent cause or great necessity *for a time licensed by the ordinary*. Whether such have been allowed, and how long they have served, and whether any of them have taken upon them to solemnise matrimony, *or to minister any Sacrament.*"—*Parker's Articles of Enquiry*, 1575. London, John Daye. It is evident, therefore, from the early years of Queen Elizabeth's reign, that the greatest laxity had prevailed; and that, in fact, ordination by a bishop was not thought at all necessary to enable a person to hold an ecclesiastical benefice.

[3] The common people of England were wiser than the wisest of the nation; for here the very women and shopkeepers were able to judge of predestination and determine what laws were to be made concerning Church government; and then what were fit to be made or abolisht: that they were more able (or, at least, thought so) to raise and determine perplext cases of conscience than the wisest of the most learned colleges in Italy: that men of the slightest learning, and the most ignorant of the common people, were mad for a new, or super, or re-reformation of religion."—Quoted in Isaac Walton's *Life of Richard Hooker*.

[4] "Baptizing of infants, although confessed by themselves to have been continued ever sithence the very Apostles' own times, yet they *altogether condemned*. . . . The Eucharist they *received* (pretending our Lord and Saviour's example) *after supper*."—Hooker's *Preface*, p. 186, vol. i., Hooker's *Works*, Ed. Keble. Oxford, 1845.

were sometimes mistaken by the open-mouthed and deeply impressed listeners for special revelations from the Divine Spirit of Truth.   Frantic prophets, with staff and scroll and lying lips, jabbered of things sacred without any regard for sense and decency, or thundered forth curses and anathemas for the Chief Bishop of Christendom ; while the true glad tidings of salvation, which had cheered the hearts of thousands in life, and comforted the way-worn and weary in death for well-nigh ten centuries, were rejected with contumely and scorn.

CHAPTER VIII.

In the summer of 1583, as already briefly recorded, Edmund Grindal, who, by the queen's favour, had been Primate of all England for nine years, had gone to his last account in the palace of Croydon. A Cumberland man, educated at Cambridge and patronised by Ridley, he was always puritanically inclined, differing in but few particulars from the ordinary herd of commonplace Elizabethan prelates. The so-called "prophesyings" already referred to, found in him a sincere and bold admirer. These "religious exercises" had largely aided in making confusion worse confounded all over the country; having directly tended to degrade religion, to extend frivolous and profitless controversies, to foster self-delusions, and even to endanger social order, by bringing all authority into contempt and disrepute. The excitement they sometimes produced was in itself inherently mischievous, as the queen and some of her advisers had good cause for believing. But Grindal, having in a bold and outspoken letter declined to put down the pestilent discussions in question, though expressly ordered to do so by the Supreme Governess herself, was promptly and duly suspended from his archiepiscopal office without further ado. The royal lady who had conferred that dignity upon him, thus temporarily took it away again, without direct charge or any trial, to his great annoyance and chagrin. He was furthermore peremptorily commanded to remain a prisoner in his own palace in Surrey—an order at once dutifully obeyed; and, had it not been for his death, there is good reason to believe that he would have been shortly evicted absolutely. The poor perplexed man, who had then grown blind, physically as well as morally, fretted sorely over the disorders of the time and because of his punishment; some affirming that, exhausted with worry and worn-out with disappointment, he died of a broken heart. Certainly the existing state of public affairs, when contrasted with the harmony and unity of the days when he was a Cumberland youth, happy amid the hills and lakes of a beautiful country, could not fail to have struck him keenly. No one remembered him after death. He who in the spirit of a pagan had distinctly forbidden prayers for departed Christian souls,[1] was himself soon and altogether forgotten when dead and buried.

The following, relating to this period, from an old and authentic record of persecution, tells its own tale :—

"Mrs. Anne Landers, in one of the cruel searches which the Lord President did continually cause to be made in and about York, was apprehended for her religion, together with many other gentlewomen, and committed prisoner to Ousebridge. Her husband, an attorney, was apprehended for going about to defend his wife by law, and sent prisoner to London, and condemned to the pillory; from whence, fearing the infamy of that punishment, he wrote to his wife to yield somewhat to the times in matter of religion, which was a cause to her of unspeakable grief and abundant tears for many days. At length she wrote back to her husband her resolute mind to suffer all manner of crosses rather than to offend Him Who had died upon the Cross for her, and desiring him to do the like; and so he did, suffering patiently the punishment of the pillory for the cause above mentioned. After this she had liberty for a while; but, being taken the second time, she was committed to York Castle about the year 1579, where she did much good by example of her godly life and charitable works. From thence she was removed to the castle of Hull. The terror and fearful report of the hard and cruel usage there of Catholics did not dismay her, being suddenly separated from her husband and children, and committed to a cruel and unmerciful keeper. There she lived five or six years, suffering with great constancy, patience, and Christian fortitude, and comforting all other afflicted Catholics, her fellow-prisoners, and relieving them with great alms. At length she was called for by warrant to London to the same prison where her husband was, where she lived as godly as she had done before; and lastly they both departed this life in the Counter [or the Clink]."[2]

During all these years nothing could have exceeded the disorder and confusion which existed. Everything was out of gear.

---

[1] Grindal, in 1571, had specially enjoined in his *Injunctions* "that neither on All Saints' Day, after evening prayer, nor the next day after (of late called All Souls' Day), there be any ringing at all other than to common prayer, when the same shall happen to fall upon the Sunday. And that no months' minds or yearly commemorations of the dead, nor any other superstitious ceremonies be observed or used, which tend to the maintenance either of prayer for the dead or of the popish purgatory."—London : W. Serres, 1571.

[2] *The Troubles of Our Catholic Forefathers*, 3rd Series, p. 323. London, 1877.

Restlessness was universal. Men both unordained and un-licensed still continued to officiate.[1] The old order of things had been duly and deliberately destroyed by brute force; though whether this could have been done unless much wicked-ness and corruption, much self-seeking, worldliness, and in-difference had existed,[2] seems more than doubtful.

The state of the fabrics of the churches, and the nature of the services in them had rapidly gone from bad to worse. Many more of the former were then becoming ruinous. In some dioceses, notoriously those of Oxford and Norwich, numerous churches and chapels were deliberately allowed to become utterly desolate. Men could not be secured to serve them, for the new owners of the great tithes were often only eminent for their super-fine rapacity. In certain of the churches, no service of any sort or kind had been held for nearly twelve years. There was often no one either to look after the fabric, to keep up the straggling hedges or impaired fences of the churchyards (in which swine[3] often grubbed up the graves); no one to let fresh air into the building, or to preserve the remaining fittings from the alternate evils of mustiness and damp on the one hand, or of dry-rot and pilferers on the other. Doors at last lost their rusted hinges and imperfect fastenings; dust accumulated; storied windows were broken; starlings found a shelter under the roofs; spiders undis-turbed spun their webs in convenient angles; bell-towers were turned into dove-cotes and places for breeding pigeons, by some local yeoman. The bells, no longer needed, were sold—for they brought in something; the lead was stripped of the aisle roofs; sometimes the chancel was altogether destroyed, so as to avoid

---

[1] "Whether any doe presume to saie service in your church or chappell openly *who is not a lawfull minister* and sufficiently licensed by the ordinarie or this archdeaconrie under the seal of his office?"—*Visitation Articles of John King, Archdeacon of Nottingham.* Oxford, Joseph Barnes.

[2] As the Rev. T. E. Bridgett so frankly admits:—"I cannot forget that Our Lady's Dowry in England was not destroyed by an incursion of un-baptized heathen nor by Protestants brought up from infancy in anti-Catholic prejudice, and taught to connect the honour of the Son in some strange fashion with the dishonour or neglect of the Mother. No, alas! the enemies of Our Lady had been children of the Catholic Church."—*Our Lady's Dowry.* London, 1875.

[3] There is a peculiar inscription on the outer wall of Chiswick churchyard, thus:—"This wall was made at ye charges of ye right honorable and truelle pious Lord Francis Russell, Earle of Bedford, out of true zeale and care for ye keeping of this churchyard and ye wardrobe of Godd's saints, whose bodies lay herein buryed, from violating by swine and other prophanation. Wit-nesseth, W. Walker, 1623." This was Francis, fourth Earl of Bedford, who married Katherine, daughter of Giles Brydges, third Lord Chandos, and was the father of the first Duke of Bedford.

the cost and difficulty of repairing it ; while in certain cases these combined evils eventually led to the absolute destruction of whole fabrics.   So that even now in many parishes it is impossible for any but the duly-initiated to trace even the foundation stones on some secluded slope of what until Queen Elizabeth's day had been a fair and stately house of God.   Many such at the hands of the "godly" were wholly "reformed" off the face of the earth.[1]

It is now necessary to deal at some length with one of the darkest events of Elizabeth's reign, — bearing as it does so directly on the ecclesiastical policy of her advisers.   How the judicial murder of a royal guest and kinswoman was compassed by the English queen shall now be told.

The well-meant advice which Catharine de' Medici had given to Queen Mary to return to Scotland turned out to be most unfortunate.   Her long minority enabled rival factions to have brought the country into a state bordering upon civil war, while deeds of infamy and ferocity were done there, with scarcely a parallel in history.   John Knox, the notorious apostate monk, was then carrying out what some imaginative persons still term a " Reformation "—the chief consequent effects of which have been schism, heresy, disorder, misbelief, and eventually infidelity.[2] Subsequently after many trials, personal as well as political, Queen Mary became a prisoner in the hands of her own subjects. When she succeeded in escaping from their prison walls, and at Elizabeth's invitation came to England, she found herself only too secure in the keeping of her wily and deadly enemy.[3]

---

[1] In the diocese of Oxford (though portions were then in that of Lincoln) may be mentioned the churches of North Weston, Easington, Quarrendon, Creslow, Mursley, Littlecote near Stewkley, Medmenham, Saunderton, Deyncourt near Woburn, and Rowsham in Wingrave, as ruined or razed. The late Rev. W. Hastings Kelke, in a paper on the *Desecrated Churches in Bucks* (*Records of Bucks*, vol. iii. p. 127), asserts that the whole number in Buckinghamshire alone may be estimated at no less than sixty.   The Oxford diocese now also comprises Berkshire as well as Oxfordshire.   Supposing that each of such churches would have accommodated a hundred worshippers (a low calculation), this destruction thus robbed the people of six thousand sittings.

[2] In almost all town parishes in Scotland there are in the present day at least three buildings used for preaching and prayer according to the rules and rights of the Established religion, the Free Church religion, and that of the United Presbyterians ; but these all differ.   Independent of these leading sects, there are many others of inferior importance and influence, more or less Christian in certain of their tenets.

[3] " *Her imprisonment can only be justified as an act of State necessity.* There is no other plea.   To have opened her prison doors and bade her go forth free would have made her the active chief and rallying-point of Catholic

It was the peculiar and almost unique position of Queen Elizabeth which from the outset of her reign gave her advisers such an obvious advantage, in pressing their reforms and revolutions upon the English people. Edward VI. was dead; Mary Tudor was dead; and, as Elizabeth was notoriously illegitimate both in fact and law, Mary Queen of Scots was, without any doubt, the direct and immediate heiress to the throne of England, and was also wife of Francis, heir to the king of France. The English people, who knew all this well and accurately enough, saw at once that their island-home seemed thus more than likely to become a mere province of France—a humiliation too great to be borne. Thus many practical questions, as they arose in turn during Elizabeth's reign, were considered by politicians with this grave alternative directly staring them in the face. No other method of treating these questions than that adopted could have so successfully won the confidence of the great cities and centres of renewed life. On the subject of national independence, moreover, the husbandman and hind were as much united in sentiment with the merchant and the townsman as Lord Burghley could have desired. The formal frivolities which were tolerated regarding the queen's matrimonial arrangements; the numerous reasonable and unreasonable proposals for her royal hand; the anxious debates round the council-board concerning the different candidates—juvenile, antique, or adventurous—who came forward for the honour of becoming her husband, all arose from an exact knowledge of the situation's gravity. Therefore it came to pass, not unreasonably, that so many leading men alike stood forward as active opponents of Mary Stuart and warm supporters of Queen Elizabeth. It was not at the outset (when men began to take sides) a choice of two religions, the old and the new, the Catholic and the Protestant, for nine-tenths of the people were at heart Catholics; but it was a great national and political question, in which every Englishman was naturally and deeply interested, viz. whether the kingdom should become subject to foreigners, the Scotch and the French, or retain its ancient independence at any cost under Elizabeth. This position of affairs gave notorious advantages to Burghley in carrying out his anti-Catholic policy, and he was certainly not slow to use them.

For more than eighteen long and wearisome years the Queen of Scotland, who came as a guest, had been kept in captivity.

disaffection, and of the power of Rome against England. *The same cause compelled her execution."—Introduction,* p. 26, to *Documents from Simancas relating to the Reign of Queen Elizabeth,* edited by Spencer Hall, F.S.A. London, 1865.

The treatment Her Majesty received, judged of, not by historical romances of anti-Christian or Protestant historians, called upon to bolster up a bad cause, but by the actual MS. letters of those more immediately engaged in harassing her, is such that, after the lapse of three centuries and more, the queen's trials stand out from the thick darkness around, and she becomes deserving of the truest and most profound sympathy. She was often treated most insolently and cruelly by her keepers. Beset with spies, and surrounded with enemies anxious to please Elizabeth, Queen Mary's life must have been a burden. On one occasion, Amias Poulet, her gaoler, because she refused to open her private cabinet for his inspection, threatened to break it open with bars.[1] Upon this the queen produced the keys. Poulet then rifled it, and took possession of its contents for his mistress.

At the age of forty-three Queen Mary's hair had become perfectly white. Yet her noble Christian virtues of constancy and fortitude were always remarkable; and, by the grace of the Most Highest, her spirit never gave way. Many influential foreigners were horrified at the treatment she received, and so expressed themselves, to the intense annoyance of Elizabeth. Queen Mary's allies and partisans, both in Scotland and England (as they were bound to do), made several attempts to aid her,— they would have been unworthy of the honour of her friendship had they done less,—but their plans were either ill-laid, or, by the instrumentality of government spies and false friends, were cleverly defeated.

Eventually Sir Francis Walsingham succeeded in entangling a number of young Catholic gentlemen—Salisbury, Tichbourne, Travers, Barnewall, Tilney, Windsor, and others[2]—in a scheme which was known as "Babington's Plot," and which apparently involved a plan for dethroning Elizabeth.[3]   Pooley and Gilbert

---

[1] "After many denials, many exclamations, and many bitter words against you (I say nothing of her railing against myself), with flat affirmation that Her Majesty might have her body, but her heart she should never have ; refusing to deliver the key of her cabinet, I called my servants and sent for bars to break open the door, whereupon she yielded ; and causing the door to be opened, I found there in the coffers mentioned in Mr. Ward's remembrance five rolls of canvas containing five thousand French crowns, and two leather bags, whereof the one had in gold one hundred and four pounds, two shillings," etc.—*The Letter-book of Sir Amias Poulet.—Poulet to Walsingham*, p. 289. London, 1874.

[2] For an account of their trial, see *State Trials*, vol. i. pp. 64-71. London, 1720.

[3] Babington had been in France recently, and had brought letters for Mary, and, in return, she is stated in his indictment to have written letters to him, 'in which she not only signified that she allowed and approved of such

Giffard, though with other professed sentiments and trusted by Mary's friends, were the secret agents of the Secretary of State, and, as the plot developed, deliberately betrayed the trust reposed in them. Letters which passed amongst the Scottish queen's allies were opened by Thomas Phillips, a noted reader of cypher-writing, engaged by Walsingham, and an agent thoroughly adroit in the art of counterfeiting seals; they were read, copied, and then sent on to the person for whom they were intended, so that evidence of the plot in writing might be duly obtained. By such tactics Walsingham secured such information as enabled him in some way to connect Queen Mary with Babington, and eventually to bring about her death on the scaffold. Babington and his thirteen allies were accused of concocting a plot to murder the queen, and of a conspiracy to raise a rebellion in favour of Mary. Seven of the prisoners acknowledged their guilt; of the other seven, five were convicted. Two successive days, September 20th and 21st, were appointed for their execution. Their punishment was to be drawn, hung, and quartered, and this, it is to be feared, was done with the deliberate intention of inflicting as much pain as possible.[1] The queen degraded herself by expressing a particular wish that they might suffer some kind of death more barbarous and excruciating than the ordinary horrors referred to. To this it was objected, by the law officers, that such an alteration or addition would be illegal. She then consented that the existing law should have its course, on the express condition that the executions were "protracted to the extremitie of payne" in the sufferers, and in the face of the populace. On the first day the hanging of each was by deliberate intention a mere pretence, for they were only half-choked or strangled a little, and then promptly cut down alive. The detailed cruelties of the executioners which ensued, with their savage slowness, and bloody knives, were endured by these generous youths with noble patience; but the populace, horribly disgusted, became so excited at such deliberate barbarity, that, on the morrow, the others were hung till they were quite dead, and then dismembered, disembowelled, and quartered as usual.

To return to Queen Mary. Some of the letters made use of,

intended treasons, but therein also urged and solicited Babington and his confederates, by promises of great reward, to fulfil the same." The truth of this assertion, as regards any design on the life of Elizabeth, is very doubtful; but it answered the purpose of the framers of the Association, and it was forthwith resolved to proceed to the judicial murder of the unhappy prisoner. Her secretaries (Nau and Curle) and her papers were seized, and both subjected to rigid examination.

[1] See Howell's *State Trials*, vol. i. pp. 1126-1158.

and from which the English Council acted, were no doubt forgeries; for the gospellers and leaders of the so-called "Reformation" were adepts at the art of forgery. And it seems quite reasonable that, if Babington and his allies had determined on accomplishing that of which they were suspected, they would at least have exercised ordinary prudence in their plans and arrangements.

The Earl of Leicester, who was not without experience on the subject, had recommended that the Queen of the Scots should be secretly poisoned, and had even sent a Protestant minister to Sir Francis Walsingham to prove logically that, in accordance with the teaching of Scripture, a queen who is an idolatress deserves nothing short of death.[1] Elizabeth, fearing the effect of a public trial and execution of the Queen of Scotland, complained that Sir Amias Poulet and Sir Drue Drury, did not somehow or another manage adroitly and secretly to shorten the life of Mary; but, as these two knightly gaolers (as will be shown further on) appeared horrified at the suggested idea of assassination, there was nothing left but a trial and an execution.

On the 11th of October 1586, preparations for the form of a trial were commenced and gone through at Fotheringhay Castle in Northamptonshire. Including the Lord Chancellor and Burghley the Lord Treasurer, Henry Grey, Earl of Kent, and George Talbot, Earl of Shrewsbury, no less than twenty-five peers arrived as actors in the tragedy. A letter from Queen Elizabeth was delivered to Mary, announcing the purport of these formal proceedings, who, on seeing it, composedly remarked that she was sorry to be charged with that of which she was innocent; and reminded those present that she too was a queen, and in no way amenable to foreign jurisdiction. Her Majesty requested the Chancellor to explain what was meant by his mistress's extraordinary and inaccurate expression, that she was "living in England under Elizabeth's protection," but he evaded giving any answer to so pertinent and difficult a question. For some time she refused to plead; but, after Sir Christopher Hatton had suggested that with some persons such action might imply guilt, she reluctantly consented to defend herself. This last resolution was surely a mistake.

The formal charge was two-fold: first, that she had conspired

---

[1] The Protestant literature of the period (too profane and offensive to quote) is all based on the gross assumption that "Eucharistic Adoration," as it is now termed by certain English Churchmen, is flagrant idolatry; and that idolaters ought not to be suffered to live.

with traitors[1] and foreigners to procure the invasion of the realm ;
and secondly, that she had likewise conspired to bring about the
death of the queen. The first charge Mary declined to allow,
for it was obviously inadmissible. English statutes could not in
any way bind one who was not an English subject, but the
sovereign of another realm. She, as the Queen of Scots, was the
equal of Elizabeth ; and between such there was no other law
than the law of nature. That law fully justified her in seeking
to secure her liberty. And who, after all these late years of
trial and sufferings,—what man could blame her, if she received
such aid as had been tendered her, in the hope of securing
her deliverance from an unjust and shameful captivity? With
regard to the second charge, she firmly and emphatically denied
it with tears ; calling God the Trinity to witness of its utter
falseness and of her own innocency. Here, be it noted, that
only copies of the intercepted letters in the Babington case were
produced ; the originals were not forthcoming, nor was the
accuracy of the copies used either asserted or proved. Friendless, and almost alone, this poor lady, worn with sufferings and
sorrow, had been in confinement for no less than nineteen years.
With no knowledge of law, and unaccustomed to judicial pro-
cesses, she was no match for the low-minded upstarts and
unscrupulous lawyers who pretended to sit in judgment upon
her. All that trickery could accomplish, forgery compass,[2] and
contrivance devise, was devised and accomplished to secure her
death. Intense hatred of the Christian religion, and a fear of
its being restored again in its integrity, had much to do in giving
point and purpose to the aims of the commissioners.[3] Moreover,
this desolate lady was not only refused the aid of all counsel or
witnesses in her defence, but even of her own papers, which,
after her caskets and coffers had been secretly broken open and
rifled, were stolen and denied her. As regards certain copies of
letters produced, "she protested," as Lord Burghley himself
admits, "that the points of the letters which concerned the

[1] "That Babington's conspiracy was with with the privity (*cum scientiâ*) of
Mary."—Sentence of the Commissioners.
[2] "Forgery (I blush for the honour of Protestantism while I write it) seems
to have been peculiar to the Reformed. . . . I look in vain for one of those
accursed outrages of imposition amongst the disciples of Popery."—Dr.
Whitaker's *Vindication of Queen Mary*, vol. iii. p. 2. And again, the same
writer, on pp. 45, 46, and 54, writes : "Forgery seems to have been the
peculiar disease of Protestantism," etc., to the same effect.
[3] As Camden put on record : when Lord Buckhurst pronounced judgment
upon the queen, he clearly admitted as much, for he bade Her Majesty
"look for no mercy, seeing that her life was incompatible with the safety of
the Protestant religion."

practice against the Queen's Majesty's person, were never by her [Mary] written, nor of her knowledge."[1]   Babington alone could have told the truth, and him they had already put to death.   The attempts made by Walsingham and others to inculpate Mary's own servants and attendants failed.   Some of these on oath denied the perverted interpretation put upon their words.   The Court was then adjourned to Westminster, where, on the 29th of October, after much legal chicanery and contemptible shuffling, they found the Queen of Scots guilty.

On the following day, Sir Amias Poulet informed her that as she was now dead to the law, she had no right to any of the insignia of royalty.   He, therefore, made her servants remove the cloth of estate, dais, and canopy; and then with ill-bred and unmannerly insolence, not looked for from a Somersetshire gentleman, he covered himself and sat down in the queen's presence. In place of the royal arms of Scotland, the queen's servants, at her command, put up some engravings of Our Saviour's Passion and death, which Poulet wrote of as "stuff."   He further told the queen, that "as a woman in her situation could not need further recreation," he should at once remove her billiard-table, which was done.   As she informed the Archbishop of Glasgow, she felt keenly these premeditated and unworthy insults; and wrote to Elizabeth, calling such action useless cruelty.

No notice seems to have been taken of the Scottish queen's reasonable complaint.   A wise cunning secured its being ignored.

Elizabeth, however, on learning what the commissioners had done, appeared to be extremely reluctant to go a step further and to sign the death-warrant, as well she might be; for the whole proceedings had been conducted on the principle that as Mary, who had been the English queen's guest, was thus her prisoner, she was justified, now that Mary was in her power, in taking away her life.   Both Burghley and Walsingham saw, and put their opinions on record,[2] that without such a step they themselves stood in grave danger—as no doubt would have been the case—if the old Catholic party could by any means have once again secured the upper hand.   Throughout Europe a thrill of horror ran, when the proceedings at Fotheringhay—for a short time kept secret and for a much longer misrepresented—were first made known; and it required all the arts of dissimulation and

[1] Lord Burghley to Secretary Davison, October 15.—*Ellis' Letters*, pp. 111–112.
[2] *State Papers.*   Sir F. Walsingham to Lord Shrewsbury, October 6th, and Lord Burghley to Lord Leicester, dated October 26th, 1586.

double-dealing of Elizabeth's confidential advisers to remove the
bad impression which these illegal and unprecedented proceedings[1] had produced.   In truth, it may be gravely and certainly
doubted whether such *was* removed.

But for Elizabeth's hesitation there were no doubt some
grounds.   True, the Spanish king was well enough engaged in
Flanders ; the·French monarch, greatly perplexed and engaged
with religious wars at home, was practically powerless ; but
there was the danger of driving the Catholics and Mary's allies
to desperation, as well as some dread of the well-deserved
infamy which, accurately enough, she knew would cover (as it
most righteously has covered) her name, because of this iniquity.
Elizabeth herself had suggested assassination, but it had been of
no avail ; her friend Leicester, with equal futility, had hinted at
poison ; but neither assassin nor poisoner had been forthcoming.
Anyhow, therefore, if the execution must take place, it should
be done either privately without the queen's cognisance, or else
in response to a specific request for the same from Parliament.

This was planned for, and soon cleverly arranged.   The Lords
and Commons, duly manipulated and sufficiently sanctified by
the sacred presence of six grave ministers in lawn sleeves and
satin,[2] joined in a solemn petition that the sentence of the
commissioners might speedily be carried into effect, for the
honour of God and the safety and glory of the realm.   When,
as some pointed out, idol-worshippers and mass-mongers combined to plot against the Lord's anointed, it was certainly

---

[1] On this point a high-principled author of the last century thus writes :—
" The judges in Queen Mary's case were not to act by reasons of State, but
by rules of law and justice ; and the whole course of the proceedings, in
taking the confessions of men who were executed, and might have been kept
alive ; of persons who were then alive, and might have been brought to the
trial ; in proving letters by copies, and producing no originals ; in condemning a sovereign princess, who had been so long imprisoned for using every
means (but those of assassination, which were not proved) to recover her
liberty ; these things were not easily reconcilable to the laws of England, or
laws of nations ; and therefore I am glad not to find Lord Willoughby's name
in the Commission."—*Memoir of Peregrine Bertie, eleventh Lord Willoughby
de Eresby, etc.*, p. 61.   London, 1838.

[2] Lord Burghley wrote to Davison, as follows, on the 9th of November
1586 :—" Yesterday, in the Parliament, grew a question whether it was
convenient for the two Archbishops (Whitgift and Sandys) and four other
bishops to accompany the other Lords Temporal in their petition to Her
Majesty for execution of the Scottish Queen.   Some scruple I had whether
Her Majesty would like it, because in former times the bishops in Parliament were wont to absent themselves.   Yet I do not think [it] unlawful for
them to be present and persuaders in such causes, as the execution tend to
the state of the Church, as this doth."—*State Papers, Domestic, Elizabeth*,
vol. cxcv. n. 11.

Q

time to act. The bishops were unctuous in their phrases and portentously solemn in their long - winded warnings. Their lordships, as they asserted, had nothing at heart, but the pure and unadulterated Gospel. This alone was their comfort, their hope, and their reward. As the speaker, with such profound biblical knowledge impressively pointed out, Her Majesty should beware of foolishly and wickedly imitating Saul, who had spared Agag, or King Ahab, who had failed to put Benhadad to death. One, Sir James Croft, whose nauseous cant and hypocrisy were super-eminent, moved that some earnest and devout prayer. to God the Holy Spirit might be made, to incline Her Majesty's too tender heart to grant this their reasonable petition ; and asked that this devout prayer might be speedily printed, as well for daily use in Parliament—so anxious for direct enlightenment from Heaven—as for all the members thereof in their private devotions at home.[1]

The queen in a similar spirit — disgusting because of its obvious insincerity and hypocrisy—on receiving the petition and hearing of the devotional exercises of the Commons, took up the idea thus suggested, and replied, with corresponding cant, that she likewise must take time to deliberate and also betake herself to prayer at the throne of grace. She, too, "commended herself to be directed by God's Spirit ;" while the Lord Chancellor, in answer to an assertion from Elizabeth, that it was desirable that some expedient should be devised for the safety of the kingdom, short of the judicial murder of the sovereign of an adjoining kingdom, which she dreaded,—informed her that any such unwise and disastrous expedient was to be avoided, and could not possibly be adopted. It was the block and the axe and the Queen of Scots' decapitation and death which were needed. Nothing less.

Lord Buckhurst was consequently enjoined to inform Queen Mary of the unanimous judgment of the commissioners, now ratified by Parliament, and of the joint petition of both houses to Elizabeth. Sir Amias Poulet, her gaoler, and Robert Beale, Clerk of the Council, accompanied him.

His lordship told her that it was quite vain and useless to look for mercy, for her notorious attachment to Popery, mass-mongering, and idol worship rendered her life wholly incompatible with the safety and security of the new religion ; and insultingly offered the services of the Bishop or Dean of Peterborough to enable her to prepare for death.

[1] See D'Ewes' *Journal of the Votes, Speeches, and Debates during the Reign of Elizabeth*, pp. 491-404. London, 1682.

She replied with dignity that the judgment was wholly lacking in justice; that she had never sought the least injury to, much less the murder of, the English queen; that her true crime was evidently her religion, for which she was perfectly ready to die; and that she must altogether decline the aid of the ministers in question. She asked and secured the services of her own almoner, and then wrote three letters, entrusting them to her servant, one to the Holy Father, another to the Archbishop of Glasgow, and a third to the Duke of Guise.

In London—where public opinion, so far as it then existed, had been for several months corrupted by false news, and by groundless alarms deliberately circulated—the proclamation was with due formalities made public. The bells of the churches rang merry peals; in some instances the parish ministers "gave God the thanks"; bonfires blazed at Westminster, Clerkenwell Green, and Tower Hill; the more depraved creatures of the Court appeared in a state of frenzied ecstasy. Walsingham told Lord Shrewsbury that it was to be hoped that the queen might be moved by these "earnest instances, to proceed thoroughly in this cause." This man's hope, alas! was all too soon realised.

In a letter to Elizabeth, the Queen of Scots made four dying requests: first, that her dead body might be taken to France, and placed beside her mother's tomb; secondly, that she might send a jewel, with her maternal blessing, to her son James,[1]; thirdly, that her servants might have a free passage home and retain the legacies she intended to leave them; and fourthly, that she might not be put to death in private, lest her enemies should assert that she had ended her days in despair, or had not died in the Catholic faith. In this dignified letter, there is throughout no expression whatsoever which can be twisted into anything like a plea or petition for mercy. She regrets the suppression of her own letters before the Commission, a most shameful act of injustice; and ventures to remind Elizabeth that the day would come when she herself would have to give an account of her actions before a just and unerring Judge. It was a touching and true letter, in every respect worthy of the high character and noble antecedents of this royal sufferer; and its

[1] "From her own son she might have hoped [for] some sense of duty, some desire to save. But when this so-called Scottish Solomon—as being the son of *David*—heard of the trial, he simply remarked, 'Mary must drink the ale she has brewed.' When he consulted his Council, the Earl of Bothwell told him roundly he deserved to be hanged the day after, if he allowed the execution to take place."—*Documents from Simancas*, Introduction, p. 28. London, 1865.

perusal brought tears to the colourless face of Elizabeth, as Lord Leicester informed Walsingham. But, with unroyal discourtesy and unwomanly harshness, no notice whatsoever was taken of it. No answer was returned.

The King of France, on hearing what had taken place, at once sent M. de Bellievre to expostulate with Elizabeth, but for some time she carefully avoided seeing him. Fraud and cunning met the king's agent at every step he took in endeavouring to accomplish his mission. At last he was enabled to inform her, face to face, that his royal master would most strongly and earnestly resent the execution of Queen Mary.

"Sir, have you the authority of your sovereign to employ such language to us?"

"Yes, madam," he replied, "I have. For the king, my master, expressly commanded me to use it."

"Is your authority signed with his own hand?"

"It is, madam."

"Then I require you," responded the queen, "to testify as much in your writing."

This he did; upon which Elizabeth resolved to reply by letter, which she promised to send in due course. In that she assumed a lofty spirit, and rebuked the king with Tudor vigour for what she asserted was his uncalled-for interference.

The resident French Ambassador, as well as Queen Mary's son James—the latter by the intervention of Sir Robert Keith, Sir Robert Melville, and the Master of Gray (some at heart enemies of Mary,) endeavoured to avert the coming deed of iniquity, but all in vain. Their expostulations and suggestions were treated with marked contempt.

On the 1st of February 1581, a letter was sent to Sir Amias Poulet at Fotheringhay, jointly signed by Sir Francis Walsingham and William Davison,[1] which charged them, at Elizabeth's suggestion, with lack of care for her service; for had it been otherwise, they would have long ago, in some way or another, killed and got rid of the royal captive. Of her guilt, after the trial, they ought to have no doubt; while the oath of association, which they had already taken, should have perfectly cleared their consciences before God, and their good repute in the eyes of their fellows.

Sir Amias Poulet, though a sour and bigoted anti-Catholic, and accurately enough perceiving that Queen Mary was no friend

[1] See "Note" to this chapter, in which the letter in question, and some other subsequent communications throwing much light upon its meaning, are given at length.

to the new religion, was too honest and intelligent to sacrifice his conscience to Elizabeth's will. He could never make so foul a shipwreck of his conscience, he replied, nor leave so great a blot on his posterity, as to shed blood without law or warrant. Drury, his co-gaoler, he added, was of a like mind.

The queen, as Davison her secretary soon discovered, was intensely annoyed at the reply of Poulet and Drury, and burst out into loud expressions of anger and vexation, well garnished with her favourite oaths, at their scrupulousness. The commission for Queen Mary's execution, however, had been duly signed on the 1st of February, and despatched by Beale to Fotheringhay.

Immediately prior to this period, the Scotch ambassador had been urgently asking a brief delay of eight days before the sealing and signing of the death-warrant. But Elizabeth, tortured in conscience, worried with expostulations, and fearing further discussion, once again swearing a profane oath, savagely replied, "No, not for one hour."

The death-warrant reached Fotheringhay Castle on a cold and bleak day in the early part of February. The Earls of Kent and Shrewsbury, who brought it, were introduced into Queen Mary's presence at once, and read the illegal sentence.

"My lords," she answered, "the day long looked for and long desired has come at last. And what better end can I have than to render up my life for my faith? For thus, and because of this it is that I am to suffer. Nevertheless, as to having compassed the death of the queen, your sovereign," she continued, placing her right palm on a New Testament which lay open upon her table, "note my latest words : I call the living God to witness that I neither sought it nor even imagined it."

"Madam," interposed the Earl of Kent, "that book there is a Popish testament, not Christ's free and blessed Gospel. An oath on such a book is of no value."

"It is a Catholic book," she exclaimed, "and for this reason I value it all the more, and you ought the more to regard my oath taken upon it."

"Madam," continued the earl, "your life must have been the death of our new religion, while your death—God grant it !—will be the life of it."

"Heard you that?" asked the queen of her attendants. "My Lord of Kent has now betrayed the secret. It is my religion, then. It is my religion," she repeated, with intense emphasis on the word "religion," "which is the cause of my death."

She then requested the assistance of a priest and the aid of her confessor ; but this, she was informed, was not only contrary to the law of the land, but repugnant to the principles of the Queen's Highness's religion and the restored Gospel, and dangerous to the souls and bodies of the commissioners. They could not possibly tolerate confession, idolatry, massing, nor superstition. Her reasonable request, therefore, was thus cruelly and shamefully denied. Its denial abundantly serves to show to what practical infamy Elizabeth's despicable tools had descended.

The last night of Queen Mary's earthly life, when necessary business was despatched, waa spent in self-recollection, meditation on Our Blessed Redeemer's Passion, and in mental prayer. If the Sacraments of the Church were denied her,[1] — those divinely-appointed aids for gaining strength to pass the valley of the shadow of death securely—yet, when these were intentionally refused or could not be had, her holy religion abundantly sustained her soul in these latest trials. She slept but little, she ate sparingly ; and, when not engaged in her religious duties, bade farewell, with kind words and some suitable memorials for all, to her devoted and sorrow-smitten servants. On their knees they asked forgiveness for all their defects and shortcomings. She, on her part, forgave them cheerfully ; and in turn asked their forgiveness likewise. She then gave them her hand to kiss. This parting touched all even to tears. The remembrance of it would remain green and fresh as long as life lasted.

The doors of the great hall of Fotheringhay Castle were thrown open about seven. It was lit up within by a few pendant lamps. Outside, from a very early hour, Thomas Andrews, Sheriff of the shire, and several gentlemen of the county, with their retainers, on whose countenances the impress of ·sorrow was stamped, had long waited for admittance in the chilling cold of a February morning. The fog lay heavily all around ; the mists were thick, the ground white with frost. Many seemed terribly depressed ; the silence amongst those gathered was solemn and trying. Soon, however, the augmented guard of the castle passed in, and then nearly two hundred spectators, pressing forwards, filled the hall, save in its centre, on every side.

At eight in the morning Queen Mary entered the hall dressed in robes of state, bearing a book of devotions and an ivory crucifix in her hands, and attended by two of her ladies. These latter, however, were thrust back by force, and the doors of the hall closed.

---

[1] Conn, in his *Life of the Queen*, asserts that, by virtue of an indult from Pope Pius V., she administered the Holy Eucharist to herself on the morning of her execution ; but this, judging by her own letter to that Pontiff, is evidently a misconception.

When her attendants had been forced out, and their wailing was heard throughout the hall, Mary quietly remarked—"Certainly the queen your mistress, being a maiden, will vouchsafe in regard to womanhood that I have some of my own women about me when I die." A silence that might have been felt pervaded the whole assembly. As the queen spoke anew no one stirred. But from the commissioners there was no response.

"You might, I think, grant me a far greater courtesy were I a woman of lesser calling than the Queen of Scots." The Earl of Kent winced.

Observing that the authorities were looking at each other askance, and seeing some of them much cowed, she continued with greater vigour—"Am not I your queen's own cousin, a descendant of the blood-royal of Henry VII., a married Queen of France, and the anointed Queen of Scotland?"

At this the Earl of Kent relented; the two ladies were hastily readmitted, together with four of the officers of her household.

Melville, her old steward, overcome with grief on his admission, fell upon his knees in a paroxysm of sorrow, unable to speak.

"Good Master Melville," she said, giving him her hand to kiss, and raising him up, "cease to lament for me, for this day thou shalt see the certain end of Mary Stuart's troubles." She then graciously kissed him on the cheek.

Her two ladies-in-waiting, Jane Kennedy and Elspeth Curle, were permitted to remain with her, but her Majesty's reiterated request to see her clerical almoner, Le Préau, was again cruelly refused;[1] the lords "not thinking it proper to waste so much time about a priest." At the same time one of them heartlessly remarked that her beads, her *Agnus Dei*, and the crucifix she carried were, in their judgment, "superstition enough already."[2]

The preparations for her death, the raised and railed platform in the middle of the dark-draped hall, the covered block, the axe, and the masked executioner in black velvet, never caused her to tremble, even when, in all their startling solemnity, they first met her gaze. With no quailing she advanced with her accustomed stately grace and majesty to the centre of the hall. Poulet assisted her to mount the scaffold, on which she said, "I thank you, sir. It is the last trouble I shall give you, and the

[1] In her letter to her confessor she complains bitterly of the cruelty of her enemies in refusing her his spiritual aid, and earnestly solicits his prayers.

[2] The Earl of Kent and Robert Beale, in their official account sent to the Lords of the Council, thus put on record this fact:—"Shee demaunded to speake with her prieste, which was denyed unto her, the rather for that she came with a superstityous paire of beades and a crucifix."—See Sir Henry Ellis' *Original Letters*, 2nd series, pp. 111-113.

most acceptable service you have ever done me."[1] She then
seated herself on a stool prepared for her, during the reading of
the warrant.

Here the queen addressed those assembled, in her clear and
beautiful voice, which throughout, even to her latest and last
most pious aspirations, had never failed nor faltered. In brief
and pregnant sentences of no ambiguity, for the last time she
solemnly protested her innocence of all plots against Queen
Elizabeth's life,[2] and maintained her unshaken fidelity to the
one ancient faith, which she thanked God she was thus enabled
publicly to confess. She reminded all present that she herself
was a sovereign princess, in no way subject to the English
Parliament, but brought there to suffer by injustice and violence.
"After my death," she declared, "many things at present hidden
in darkness will come to life. Rejoicing to shed my blood for
my religion,"—for she knew well enough why she was about to
suffer death,—"I place all my hope and confidence in Him, my
gracious Lord, Whose image I hold in my hand. I pardon all
mine enemies, whom my latest words shall not prejudice, from
the bottom of my heart; and from all to whom I have done
amiss or given offence, I humbly ask pardon, likewise."

Upon this Dr. Fletcher, Dean of Peterborough, pushing himself
forward, began a preachment, in which he contrived to be at once
coarse, canting, and insulting. This was the burden of his
words:—His royal mistress, the supreme and beneficent Governess of them all, was bound to execute justice on the body of
the condemned one, but, like a mother to all, was most anxiously
watchful for the good of her soul. Elizabeth, as he asserted,
had therefore commissioned him to bring her into that fold, in
which the true sheep were fed on Gospel-truth; and to induce

[1] On the very same day this man thus wrote to Mr. William Davison:—
"Sir Drue Drury, with his hearty due commendations unto you, prayeth
your favourable mean for his revocation, which he would not desire (notwithstanding his great and urgent occasions) *if the cause of his abode were not
through the mercy and favour of our good God clearly removed, to the great
comfort of himself and all other faithful Christian subjects.* I will say nothing
of his careful service in this place, because his zeal to religion, duty to his
sovereign, and love to his country are very well known unto you. The
children of God have daily experience of His mercy and favour towards such
as can be content to depend on His merciful providence, Who doth not see
as man seeth, but His times and seasons are always just and perfectly good.
The same God make us all thankful for his late singular favours [*i.e.* the
murder of the queen !!], and thus I leave to trouble you, wishing you all
felicity in Our Lord Jesus. From Fotheringhay, the 8th of February 1586."—
Letter-book of Sir Amias Poulet, pp. 364-365. London, 1874.
[2] In her written letter to the King of France—penned just before her death
—she declares that she dies quite innocent of any crime against Elizabeth.

her to renounce the communion of that idolatrous and apostate Church, which by law had been abolished, and in which if she remained and died, she would be most certainly damned.

Queen Mary, thus persecuted by this repulsive and extravagant fanatic, entreated him on such an occasion to hold his tongue and let her be at peace. But he was not to be put down. Though she quietly turned away from him and his disquieting noise, which was all she could do; yet he went round to another part of the platform, stared at her, thumbed his Bible, selected his text, and began his disturbing utterances once again.

At last Lord Shrewsbury, who saw that the onlookers were much wanting in sympathy with the preacher, suggested that he should give over preaching and proceed to prayer. He did so at once. His prayer, however, was only the same sermon put into other words. He exclaimed, he lifted up his voice, and he cursed. But Mary heard him not.

Engrossed in devotion, she was repeating the beautiful Psalms, *Beati quorum, Miserere*, and that of Compline, *Qui habitat*, during the Dean's "exercise" as it was termed; when one of the peers, touched by the creature's heartless cruelty, suggested that he should stop and stand aside. He did so.

The queen then arose, and uttering a most touching intercession for the afflicted Catholics of the country, for her son James, and for Queen Elizabeth, heard by all in painful silence, held up her crucifix and exclaimed—"As Thine arms, O Blessed Saviour of the World, were stretched out upon the Cross, so now, O Lord, receive me into the arms of Thy mercy and forgive me all my sins."

"Madam," retorted the Earl of Kent,[1] "leave alone such Popish trumpery; and bear Christ rather in your heart than in your hand."

"I cannot hold in my hand the representation of His Passion," she meekly but firmly replied, "without at the same time bearing Him in my heart."

Upon this her two maids, bathed in tears, began to disrobe

---

[1] This man (Henry Grey, sixth Earl of Kent) was of an ancient family; but evidently a person in great want of good breeding. His grandfather, one of Henry VIII.'s favourites, became so inveterate a gamester, that he impoverished his estate, and died ignobly at the George Inn in Lombard Street in 1523. The sixth earl, his grandson, was a sour Puritan of a bad type. He married an old woman and died without lawful issue. Sir William Dugdale wrote of him in very mild terms that "he evinced much more zeal" for Queen Mary's "destruction than befitted a person of honour." Like many other of the base peers of that period he was in truth a disgrace to his race, rank, and dignity.

her.   But the executioners interfered, as it was said to be their
duty, and they looked for certain perquisites.   The sight of the
queen thus being prepared for death touched to the heart a large
number of the spectators.   Her servants were greatly overcome.
One was in paroxysms of grief.   But her Majesty bade them
bear up with fortitude, gave them her parting blessing, and asked
their prayers.

One of them placed a handkerchief over her eyes, upon which
the headsman and his assistant guided her towards the block.

Kneeling down, she exclaimed repeatedly, "Into thy hands,
O Lord, I commend my spirit."   Save these beautiful words,
nothing was heard but the sobs and groans of the onlookers.

And now the executioner raised the axe.   But the sounds of
weeping evidently disconcerted him.   It fell with a flash, and
inflicted a deep wound on the skull.   The poor sufferer never
moved.   At his third stroke the head of the saintly queen rolled
on to the scaffold.   The deed of shame and infamy was now
complete.

Holding it up, as usual, he cried out—as a shudder ran through
the crowd at the sickening sight, and a wail of agony arose—
"God save Queen Elizabeth !"

"Amen !" responded the dignified minister who had been cut
short in his preaching, "and so may all her enemies perish !"

"So perish all the enemies of the Gospel !" exclaimed the
Earl of Kent, throwing up his velvet cap as a token of satisfaction.

But there was no single response, no one said "Amen.",

Pity, admiration, and sympathy now filled the hearts of many,
as the sobs which were heard indicated ; for truth and justice
had been grossly outraged by the murder then committed by
Elizabeth ;[1] while the repulsive cant which had been there
exhibited sickened to the heart's core several of the red-eyed
onlookers, whose secret sympathies were against the innovators
and their cruel policy of tyranny and blood ; and who deplored
all the evil consequences which were seen to exist, by reason
thereof,—and which, though years have intervened, still live
on.

The queen's body, after embalmment, was buried some months

---

[1] To use the words of Whitaker, the accomplished historian, Elizabeth was
one "who had no sensibilities of tenderness and no sentiments of generosity ;
who looked not forward to the awful verdict of History ; and who shuddered
not at the infinitely more awful doom of God.   I blush, as an Englishman,
to think that this was done by an English queen, and one whose name I
was taught to lisp in my infancy as the honour of her sex and the glory of
our isle."

afterwards at Peterborough,[1] but subsequently removed by her
son James[2] to Henry VII.'s chapel at Westminster.

William Davison, one of the Secretaries of State, — who
throughout these proceedings had been the tool of Queen Mary's
enemies, and had thus seen the bloody deed, which they had so
artfully planned, completed, — was sacrificed,[3] in order that,
when the opinion of Catholic Europe was expressed—as the
Court agents abroad informed them it soon might be—a scape-
goat should be at hand to bear their dark and weighty sins.
The queen had been specially angry with Lord Burghley, and
he was in sore disgrace. But, as he declared to Her Majesty,
he submitted wholly to her blessed will; she was as light and
life to him; and thus endeavoured to soothe her by quoting
texts of Scripture or by nauseous flattery.[4] His mock humility
was so ably assumed and so artfully exhibited, that he was soon
restored to favour. Davison alone suffered. He was tried in
the Star Chamber, condemned to pay a fine of ten thousand
pounds, and imprisoned for years. But these tactics did not
shield the queen from the strong condemnation she so richly
and righteously deserved.

In the year of Grindal's resignation—to turn awhile to the
other side of the picture—Father Cornelius,[5] a Cornishman of
Irish extraction, came back to England—one amongst the

---

[1] The Puritans were extremely angry that Bishop William Wickham of
Lincoln, who preached her Majesty's funeral sermon, did not openly declare
his conviction of "her certain damnation."—See Fuller's *Church History*,
book ix. p. 181.

[2] The most scandalous case of dissimulation, falsehood, and hypocrisy
which is on record is that in which the queen, writing to James the son of
Mary Queen of Scots, makes a solemn appeal to Heaven that she was
entirely innocent of his mother's death; and, furthermore, that she held in
abhorrence the sins of hypocrisy and dissimulation.

[3] Of Davison's policy, under the charge against him, Dr. Lingard thus
wrote: "In court he acted with more reserve than prudence. To the
invectives of the Crown lawyers he replied, that to acknowledge the offence
would be to tarnish his own reputation; to contend with his Sovereign would
be to transgress the duty of a subject; that they did him injustice by reading
garbled passages from his answer, let them read the whole, or rather let
them read none: for it contained secrets not fit for the public ear; he would
only say that he had acted under the persuasion that he was obeying the
Queen's commands, and for the rest would throw himself on her mercy."—
History of England, by John Lingard, D.D., vol. vi. p. 232. Dublin, 1874.

[4] See Strype's *Annals*, vol. iii. p. 371, and Appendices Nos. 144–146.

[5] Father John Cornelius, *alias* Mohun, was born at Bodmin, in Cornwall,
of poor parents. Sir John Arundell of Traherne, an "occasional conformist,"
gave him an education at Oxford, but he subsequently went to Rheims under
Dr. Allen, and afterwards to the English college at Rome. Having been
ordained priest, he came back to England in 1583, and gained his rest and

numerous adherents to the old religious system. He laboured
assiduously and zealously for eleven years, during which he won
for himself great admiration from men and many remarkable
divine graces from Heaven. A sacred and solemn revelation,
full of expressive teaching, was made to him, six years before his
death, with regard to a deceased nobleman, thus :—

"John, Lord Stourton,[1] who was a Catholic, had through fear
in those terrible times conformed to the State religion, having
greater regard for his temporal than for his spiritual and eternal
interests. Lest, however, death should surprise him in this sad
neglect of his duty he entertained two priests in his house ; and
had taken all imaginable precautions that both should never be
absent at the same time, being fully resolved to die within the
pale of the true Church. But God's inscrutable providence and
just judgment did not allow this ; for when he met with the
accident which carried him off, both priests were absent at the
same time, nor could the most anxious search discover where
they were. Still, God in His great mercy infused into the
baron's heart so lively a sense of the horror of his sin, and so
deep a contrition, that, not satisfied with begging pardon of God
and promising within his own mind amendment and satisfaction,
he called together his wife and steward and all the family, and
with floods of tears acknowledged before them his crime and the
scandal he had given, declaring that he was willing to make
amends were it even by shedding his blood.

"He expressed his grief at being deprived of the rites of the
Catholic Church when he most wished to receive them ; and
protested that he died a Catholic, out of which religion there was
no salvation. Then, imploring God's mercy, he expired. He
not only besought them all to bear witness of this his act before
both men and the dreadful tribunal of God, but even, it is said,
made a confession of his sins to a servant man in sign of his
sincere repentance, desiring thereby to testify his full determination to have confessed to a priest, had time and opportunity
permitted.

"Father Cornelius, when asked his opinion if in this case it was
lawful to pray for the deceased lord, replied that it was both
lawful and obligatory."

reward by suffering a cruel death at Dorchester on July 4th, 1594. He had
previously been admitted to the Society of Jesus.—See *State Papers, Domestic,
Elizabeth*, vol. ccxlviii. n. 75, A.D. 1594. There is an original portrait of
Father Cornelius at the Gesù, Rome.

[1] John, eighth Baron Stourton (whose wife was Frances, daughter of
William, Lord Cobham), died 13th October 1588.

The following incident is related by Dame Dorothy Arundell, the half-sister of the deceased lord, in her " MS. Acts of the Blessed Martyr Cornelius " :—

" One day my mother, Lady Arundell, begged Father Cornelius to offer up mass for the soul of her son John, Lord Stourton, which he consented to do.   When at the altar he remained a considerable time in prayer between the consecration and the memento for the dead.   After mass was finished, he made an exhortation on the words, *Beati mortui qui in Domino moriuntur* —'Blessed are the dead who die in the Lord,'—and then told us that he had just seen a vision.   Before him was presented a forest of immense size, in which all was fire and flame, and in the midst he perceived the soul of the deceased lord, who, with tears and lamentable cries, accused himself of the evil life he had led for several years, especially whilst at the Court; and his dis-simulation in frequenting the Protestant Church, though still a Catholic, to the scandal and grievous hurt of the souls of his relations.   But above all, in the most bitter terms, he accused himself of having been one of the forty-seven chosen by Queen Elizabeth to condemn the innocent Mary, Queen of Scots, a crime for which he had experienced so deep a contrition that it had hastened his death.   After these avowals of the deceased lord to Father Cornelius, he exclaimed in the words of Holy Scripture, *Miseremini mei, miseremini mei, saltem vos, amici mei, quia manus Domini tetigit me*—' Have pity on me, have pity on me, O ! ye my friends, for the hand of the Lord hath touched me.'   Having implored the Father to assist him with prayers, the appearance, by which he had been recognised, vanished.

" Father Cornelius wept much in relating his vision to us, and all the household, who to the number of about eighty per-sons were listening to him, united their tears with his.   The server of the mass, John Carey, afterwards a sufferer for the Faith with Father Cornelius, saw and heard all that passed in the vision ; but as for myself and the rest of those present, we only perceived, while it was manifested, a glimmering reflection like that of live coals on the wall against which the altar stood." [1]

The sufferings and death of Margaret Clitheroe, already referred to, must now be narrated at some length.[2]   She was the

[1] See *Records of the English Province*, vol. iii. pp. 444, 445 ; and Life of Father Weston, in *The Troubles of Our Catholic Forefathers*, 2nd series, pp. 128, 129.   London, 1875.   An account is also given by Bishop Challoner in his *Memoirs of Missionary Priests.*

[2] The author is largely indebted for most of the facts related, to Father John Mush's *Life of Margaret Clitheroe*, as well as to Bishop Challoner's *Memoirs of Missionary Priests.*

daughter of Thomas Middleton, citizen and wax-chandler of York, and sometime sheriff. He, there is good reason for believing, was the third son of Esquire Middleton, of Stockeld,[1] and his wife Margaret, daughter of Sir Thomas Gascoigne of Gawthorpe. She married John Clitheroe,[2] a well-to-do tradesman of York, who became subsequently one of the city chamberlains.

"As touching her worldly state and condition," as her biographer declares, "she was about thirty years of age, and to her beautiful and gracious soul God gave her a body with comely face and beauty correspondent. She was of sharp and ready wit, with rare discretion in all her actions, a plentiful mother in children, and her husband of competent wealth and ability."

She appears to have been brought up without any very definite religious belief; but, having heard of the sufferings endured by so many for the old religion, she attached herself thereto with great sincerity and devotion. Declining to attend the services of the Calvinists, she was several times imprisoned; separated on two occasions for more than two years from husband and children. But, to quote her biographer again, "she turned all things to her good, and sucked honey out of the cruelty of her enemies. They persecuted, and she thereby learned patience; they shut her up into close prison, and she learned thereby to forget and despise the world; they separated her from home, children, and husband, and she thereby became familiar with God; they sought to terrify her, and she thereby increased in most glorious constancy and fortitude."

Her supposed offence was that she had harboured priests, and allowed mass to be said in her husband's house, and had sent her son Francis abroad to be educated in a foreign seminary. On March 10th, 1586, the vice-president of the. Northern Council and others, therefore, authorised her house to be searched. The sheriff's officers coming suddenly and finding a youth, whom they stripped and threatened with rods, induced him to show them the priests' chamber, where they found a portable altar, a missal, some altar-breads, and "church-stuff," *i.e.* priestly vestments; upon which discovery both she and her husband at once were committed to prison.

---

[1] Sir William Middleton of Stockeld, Knt., had by Margaret, his third wife, a son, Thomas. These Middletons were allied with the Vavasours, Wentworths, Calverleys, and Gascoignes. His grandson, William, signed the Pedigree in the Visitation of 1612 by Richard St. George.—See *Foster's Yorkshire Pedigrees*, p. 286. London, 1875.

[2] He had a brother, William Clitheroe, who had been ordained subdeacon at Rheims, on March 19, 1580, deacon at Chalons, and priest at Soissons on June 9th, 1582.

She was arraigned four days afterwards, and brought from the castle to the common hall. She was there formally accused of having, contrary to the laws, harboured and maintained Jesuit and seminary priests, traitors to the Queen's Majesty, and that she had divers times idolatrously, wickedly, and unlawfully heard mass, etc.

Mr. Justice Clinch, standing up, asked her thus,—"Margaret Clitheroe, how say you, are you guilty of the indictment, or no?"

To which, with a smiling face, she mildly replied, "I know of no offence whatsoever, of which I should confess myself guilty."

"You have certainly harboured Jesuits and massing-priests, sure enemies to the Queen's Majesty and the Gospel," retorted the judge.

"I never maintained any enemies of the queen," she replied, "and God defend that I should."

She thus declined, in a beautiful spirit of self-sacrifice, either to betray her friends, implicate members of her family, or injure those of the old clergy who had rendered her any spiritual aid.

"How will you be tried?" his lordship again asked.

"Having given no offence whatsoever, my lord, I need no trial," was her calm reply.

"But you *have* offended against the statutes, as these monuments of superstition and idolatry plainly show," continued the judge, pointing to some sacred vessels and vestments which lay on the table; "and, therefore, you must be tried, and at once."

"If you say I have offended, and that I must be tried, I will be by none save but by God and your own consciences."

Some officers of the court, taking up the albs and chasubles, here put them upon two common men; who, being vested in mockery, seized two chalices and a handful of wafer-breads, made the sign of the cross in mockery, bowed down in derision, and then holding them up with wanton winks and coarse grimaces, exclaimed, "Behold your gods in whom you believe!"

"How like you these vestments, Mistress Clitheroe?" asked one of the bystanders who had thus witnessed the antics of these irreverent buffoons.

"Well enough," she answered, "were they upon the backs of those who know how to use them to God's honour, as they were made."

She still refused to be tried, or to give any other answer to that she had already made. The judges adjourned the court until the morrow, when she was again brought up, to whom the judge spoke thus—

"Margaret Clitheroe, yesternight we passed you over without

judgment, hoping that you would be more conformable, and put yourself to the country; otherwise you must needs have the law. We see no reason for this your refusal.   There be but one witness, a youth, against you, and the country must consider your case."

"In deed and in truth!" replied the prisoner, "you have no witnesses against me but a child; and such, with a rod or an apple or a bag of figs, you can make to say what you will."

"It is plain," remarked the judge, "that you had priests in your house; for here be their pestilent garb and goods."

"As for good Catholic priests, why should I not have them, if they come but to do me and others good?"

"They be all rascally traitors, idolaters, and rank deceivers of the queen's subjects," remarked Mr. Hurleston, one of the councillors.

"God forgive you!" replied the prisoner, with feeling; "you could not say so did you know them.   I know them to be virtuous men sent by God to aid us who need them, and to save our souls."

She was again asked to plead; but, with a combination of boldness and modesty, still refused to do so.

Just as the judge was about to pass sentence, one of the new preachers, Wiggington by name, a noted Puritan, stood up and addressed his lordship with great earnestness.

"Take heed what you do, my lord," said he.   "You sit here to do true justice.   This woman's case is touching life and death. You may not, either by God's law or by man's, condemn her to die on the slender witness of a mere boy.   You should not judge her save on the credit of two or three sufficient men.   Therefore, look to it, my lord, look to it.   On your own head rests this cause."

"I may do it by law," retorted the judge.

"By what law?" at once asked the preacher.

"By the Queen's Majesty's law," replied the judge, "the only law we know of."

"That may be," Wiggington answered; "but not by God's law.   And God's law none of us may pass over, neither the Queen's Majesty nor any beside."

Margaret Clitheroe was once more requested to plead; but again answered as before.

On this, one Rhodes, a justice, is reported to have interfered, asking, "Why stand we here all the day over this naughty woman?   Let us with no more ado despatch her."   This was determined on.   Those in court, behind the barriers, and in distant corners, the interested onlookers, stretched themselves forward with anxiety to hear the formal sentence.

The judge solemnly rose, cleared his throat with an unctuous noise and upturned eyes, and thus delivered it :—

"Margaret Clitheroe! Having refused to put yourself to the country, this must be your sentence : You must return from whence you came, and there, in the lowest part of the prison, be stripped naked, laid down with your 'back upon the floor, and as much weight laid upon you as you are able to bear, and so to continue three days without meat or drink, except a little barley bread and puddle water ; and the third day, your hands and feet being tied to posts and a sharp stone being put under your back, you are to be pressed to death."

She heard the awful words without fear or shrinking, merely remarking, with humility and modesty, in reply, "If this judgment be according to your conscience, I pray God, when your own time comes, to give you a better judgment before Him. For this right heartily do I thank the Most High ! "

She was then pinioned by the sheriff's men, and led back to prison. There Sir Thomas Fairfax and others earnestly implored her to save herself and family by going even to one sermon at church. Some of the York ministers repeated this request, but in vain. One, Pease, asked, "Why refuse you to come to ' Our Church,' we having so plain and sure testimonies to show on our side for the truth ? "

" I believe in that One Church, not made by man, which hath Seven Sacraments and One unalterable Faith. In that I will to live and die."

Wiggington, the already mentioned minister, informed her that he had had a vision of the Person of Our Lord, who had assured him of his own election and salvation; and therefore he trusted she would regard him as a faithful minister.

Mr. Toby Matthew, Dean of Durham, and the Lord Mayor of York (who had married her mother), likewise tried to make an impression upon her ; but it was of no avail. She declined to give up the faith.

It was decreed that she should suffer on Ladyday, and at the York Tolbooth. She looked forward to her end without fear, and in full confidence of God's sustaining power to enable her to endure. She passed the last night of her life in prayer; and had fasted all the previous day. The prison-keeper's wife, though no Catholic, in charity promised to induce the executioners to hasten her death as soon as possible ; but the sufferer replied, "No, good Mrs. Yoward ; not so. God defend that I should procure any to be guilty of my death and blood."

Ladyday dawned brightly. The golden sunshine had early

R

lit the fretted towers of the Minster, and gilded the many spires of the parish churches; all around the city it fell on the bright green meadows watered by the Ouse. The clouds above were light, the air was clear, the sky blue. Nature seemed to speak eloquently of man's resurrection from temporal death; while the blessed feast-day itself told of God's grace and mercy, and of Mary's co-operation and obedience.

The two sheriffs of the city, one of whom, Gibson, was horrified at this legal atrocity, brought the condemned one to the place of execution before eight o'clock. She went cheerfully, walking bare-footed, and distributing her alms. Coming to the appointed place, quite calmly, she knelt down and prayed. Some ministers near, tormenting her for the last time with exhortations and vain words, asked her to join with them in prayer.

"I will not pray with you, nor shall you pray with me," she replied. "I will neither say 'Amen' to your prayers, nor shall you to mine."

She then interceded openly for the Holy Father, for the cardinals, for all true bishops and priests, and for all Christian princes, more especially for Queen Elizabeth, that God would turn her to the Catholic faith, and that so, after this mortal life, she might enjoy the peace of Heaven.

Fawcett, the other sheriff, said, "Mistress Clitheroe, remember that you die for treason."

"No, no, Mr. Sheriff," she answered; "deceive not yourself, I pray you. I die for the love of my Lord and Saviour and for the Ancient Faith."

"Put off your apparel, then, now," he continued; for you must die naked, as judgment was pronounced."

On her knees, and in piteous accents, with tears, she and other women earnestly asked that she might retain her linen undergarment. But this was rudely denied her. Then she further implored that, for the honour of womanhood, only women might undress her; and that the spectators would then avert their gaze. Eight beggars, four men and four women, had been hired to do the murder, and stood by ready for the work. Her clothes were removed, and thereupon the women drew over her body a habit of linen. She was then laid at length on the ground, with a kerchief over her face. A large, sharp flint stone, of many angular points, was placed under her back. Her ankles were tied together, and her wrists affixed by cords to two posts. A stout oak door, supported at the edges by these and other posts, was then placed upon her body. Heavy stones were then placed thereon. She continued to pray audibly, "O Jesu, good Jesu, good Jesu, have mercy upon me," as the hired and heartless ruffians rudely heaped stone after stone upon the door. The rough fall and increased weight of every addition produced unknown agony. But she is said to have struggled not, and only prayed more earnestly. The few spectators sickened at the sight, as during a full quarter of an hour the stones were being piled on to the amount of nine hundredweight; while the poor sufferer's agonising prayers to her Master grew fainter and feebler, for her frame quivered and her swollen tongue was dry. To some the minutes seemed hours. At length, after the crash of a weightier stone than any, no more prayers were heard; the suppressed sob of suffering and the awful and prolonged sigh of extremest agony, found relief and rest in death.

Thus of one more obstinate adherent of the old religion England was rid.

Should any reader conceive this to be an exceptional case of punishment even unto death, inflicted on a woman during Queen Elizabeth's reign, it becomes a duty to point out that such an idea is a complete misconception. Women as well as men were constantly treated with the severest cruelty. Record after record occurs of their imprisonment and torture. Hundreds died in the northern gaols, after years of suffering, worn out with punishment and misery. Mistress Margaret Ward, a lady of Cheshire, and Mistress Ann Line, a widowed gentlewoman, both suffered death at Tybourne; the first in 1588, for aiding a poor persecuted priest, Father Richard Watson,[1] to escape from Bridewell; the second, on February 27th, 1601, for having harboured a priest, as was supposed; for the "offence" was not proved. The first-named was often whipped most infamously, and tortured acutely. For eight succeeding days she was hung up by the hands to a beam, her feet scarce touching the ground; a sharp punishment, which sometimes caused her to swoon. She was then taken down, carefully tended until she revived and recovered. then scourged anew, and hung up in the same way once again. She was offered her liberty if she would go to church, but declined. When her aid to the poor priest was thrown in her teeth as an act of disrespect to the queen, she replied that if Her Majesty had the ordinary feelings of a woman, and had known how

[1] Of Father Watson, it is on record, "the authorities" thrust him into a dungeon so low and so strait, that he could neither stand up in it, nor lay himself down at his full length to sleep. Here they loaded him with irons, and kept him for a whole month on bread and water; of which they allowed him so small a pittance that it was scarce enough to keep him alive; not suffering anyone to come near him to comfort him or speak to him.—*Memoirs of Missionary Priests*, vol. i. p. 234. Derby edition.

Father Watson was suffering, she herself would surely have aided him to have escaped. When Mrs. Line was ready to die she embraced the rope as well as she was able, being old, weak, and ill, exclaiming, "I am about to suffer for having harboured a priest. So far from repenting for having done so, I rejoice ; and would, with all my heart, that instead of having harboured one I had entertained a thousand." Two priests, Mark Barkworth and Roger Filcock, suffered death at the same time.

About the period that Campion and Parsons arrived in England, it is said by some that Philip II. of Spain, who was also Sovereign of the Low Countries, in concert with the Guises of France, had begun to make military and naval preparations for the conquest of England. At all events they were commenced soon afterwards. It must be frankly admitted that Elizabeth had given him great provocation for going to war. She had artfully fomented rebellion against him, and by the aid of spies, secret agents, and traitors, had done him all the mischief in her power. She had notoriously intercepted and seized his treasure, had provokingly engaged foreign mercenaries to fight against his troops, had allowed her mariners to plunder and massacre his defenceless subjects, as well as those of his American colonies. When he quietly and privately complained, shuffling and sophistry were the only replies vouchsafed. When, again, he expostulated with dignity through his ambassador, she and her ministers descended to the use of obvious and acknowledged falsehoods. Yet for her liberty and life she had been indebted to Philip in byegone days. Throughout all the preparations, however, Walsingham had been indefatigable in watching them step by step, and in checking King Philip indirectly on all occasions and at every point. When he sought pecuniary aid from the Venetians and Genoese, the great money-lenders of the age, Elizabeth's ministers, perfectly aware of the negotiations, succeeded both in damaging King Philip's credit, and in causing him some inconvenience. But, having secured new vessels, naval stores, and efficient seamen from Denmark and the Hanse towns, and by great general efforts both in Spain and the Low Countries obtained co-operation, he began to make his final plans.

In 1587 it became evident from reliable information received, that the expedition would certainly sail in the spring of the following year. Accordingly every endeavour to meet the enemy was made by the queen's advisers, and a fleet was assembled of some size, consisting of about one hundred and forty vessels. These were furnished by the cities of London, Bristol, Harwich,

Sandwich, and other seaports; by the merchant adventurers and by private individuals. To Charles, Lord Howard of Effingham, who was of the old religion, was given the chief command. Under him were Raleigh, Hawkins, Drake, and Frobisher. Lord Henry Seymour, with a portion of the fleet, watched the coast of Flanders.

Three armies were gathered together, each consisting of about twenty-five thousand men. One was discreetly distributed along the southern coast, specially near probable landing-places; a second was placed near Tilbury Fort on the Thames, to protect the city of London, while it was arranged that a third should be in attendance on the person of the Sovereign. The queen, who stayed at Havering-at-Bower, St. Edward's ancient palace, absurdly arrayed in a breastplate, paid a short visit to this camp, where Lord Leicester,[1] though a most incompetent general, commanded, and Her Majesty made an artificial and somewhat bombastic speech to the troops:—"I am come amongst you," she remarked, "not for my sport and recreation" (an indirect reply to those who said that, as usual, she had only followed her favourite), "but, as being resolved in the heat of the fight, to live and die amongst you all. I am ready, for my blood and my people, to lay mine honour in the dust. I know I have but the body of a feeble woman, but I possess the heart of a king, and of a King of England too."

The people were enthusiastic in coming forward to defend their country. Those who adhered to the ancient faith were not less earnest and zealous than their neighbours. On this occasion, and indeed on all others, where patriotism was brought to the test, the Catholics proved that no degree of oppression and persecution could make them forget their duties as citizens or as subjects. Even Hume admits that Catholic gentlemen, though excluded from all offices of trust and authority, entered

---

[1] "As for your person," wrote Leicester to her, "being the most dainty and sacred thing we have in this world to care for, I cannot, most dear queen, consent that you should expose it to danger. For upon your well-doing consists all the safety of your whole kingdom; and, therefore, preserve that above all."—*Hardwicke Papers*, vol. i. p. 577. She was allowed to come for a few days to see the forts and troops, and spend a short time with her favourite, who, however, distinctly forbad her remaining with the army or in the camp. When Lord Leicester visited Lord and Lady Shrewsbury at Chatsworth, the queen had the execrable taste to write thus of him, acknowledging his hosts' attentions:—We should do him great wrong (holding him in that place of favour We do) in case We should not let you understand in how thankful sort *We accept the same at both your hands, not as done unto him, but to Our Own self, reputing him as another Ourself,*" etc.—*Lodge,* vol. ii. p. 155.

as volunteers in the queen's fleet and army. Some equipped ships at their own charge, and gave the command of them to Protestants; others were active in animating their tenants, vassals, and neighbours, to the defence of their hearths and homes. Thus, at a sore crisis, when internal dissensions might have produced national ruin, and when an excellent opportunity had arisen to disorganise the plans of the Council and to make their cruel enemies and persecutors then lick the dust, the afflicted and sorely-tried Catholics were nobly patriotic and marvellously self-denying. Facts like this are of far greater moment and value than words. These facts cannot be gainsayed.

On the side of the Spaniards there then lay near Lisbon a mighty fleet of nearly a hundred and forty vessels of war, with a corresponding number of transports—a grand and imposing sight. They had no less than twelve thousand seamen and galley-slaves, three thousand pieces of ordnance, and twenty-two thousand troops, officered by the noblest, the most refined, and the most gallant of Spain. In May, Philip visited the fleet, having received a blessed banner from Pope Sixtus V.[1] and His Holiness's good wishes for success. Perex, Duke of Medina Sidonia was in command, aided by Don Martinez de Ricaldi, a mariner of great experience. The king had an account of what he termed "the most happy Armada," set forth and printed in Latin and other languages, while Cardinal Allen addressed "An Admonition to the nobility and people of England and Ireland," in Latin, urging them to aid the Spaniards. and denouncing the queen in language as plain and forcible as that used of their opponents by her own new bishops. His Eminence, or Robert Parsons (for some say it was first drafted by him), seems to have caught something of the spirit of Bale, Pilkington, and Sandys. The "Admonition," however, did not involve a question of style or spirit, but of fact. It is to be feared that the facts stated therein are but too true, and cannot be denied nor disproved. As paragraph after paragraph is faithfully and impartially considered, melancholy though the strong and plain-spoken expressions and charges in it appear, yet it is impossible with any honesty to deny that they are in the main, and unhappily, correct and only too true. These are their exact terms in its old English form :—

[1] Felix Peretti—(A.D. 1585-1590)—a Pontiff of humble birth, but of great governing powers and high principles. He encouraged the Holy League in France, formed to defend the faith against the Huguenots; and was active both in maintaining the rights of the Chief Bishop of Christendom, and in putting down innovation and error.

"She [Queen Elizabeth] is a bastard, and daughter of Henry VIII., by his incestuous commerce with Anne Boleyn.

"She was intruded by force, unjustly deposing the lords of the clergy, without whom no lawful Parliament could be held, nor statute made ; and without any approbation of the See of Rome, contrary to the accord by King John, at the special request and procurement of the Lords and Commons, as a thing necessary to preserve the realm from the unjust usurpation of tyrants.

"As to her behaviour, she has professed herself a heretic. She usurpeth by Luciferian pride the title of Supreme Ecclesiastical Government, a thing in a woman unheard of; not tolerable to the masters of her own sect [this is an allusion to Calvin's and Knox's opinion on the subject]; and to all Catholics in the world most ridiculous, absurd, monstrous, detestable, and a very fable to the posterity.

"She is taken and known for an incestuous bastard, begotten and born in sin, of an infamous courtesan, Anne Boleyn, afterwards executed for adultery, treason, heresy, and incest, among others with her own natural brother, which Anne Boleyn her father kept by pretended marriage in the life of his lawful wife, as he did before unnaturally know and kepe both the said Anne's mother and sister.

"She is guilty of perjury, in violating her coronation oath.

"She hath abolished the Catholic religion, profaned the Sacraments, forbidding preaching, impiously spoiled the churches, deposed and imprisoned the bishops, and suppressed the monasteries.

"She hath destroyed most of the ancient nobility, putting into their houses and chambers traitors, spies, delators, and promoters, that take watch for her of all their ways, words, and writings.

"She hath raised a new nobility of men, base and impure, inflamed with infinite avarice and ambition.

"She hath intruded a new clergy of the very refuse of the worst sort of mortal men.

"She hath made the country a place of refuge for Atheists, Anabaptists, heretics, and rebels of all nations.

"She hath polled the people, not only by more frequent and large subsidies than any other princes, but by sundry shameful guiles of lotteries, laws, decrets, falls of money, and such like deceits.

"She sells laws, licences, dispensations, pardons, etc., for money and bribes, with which she enriches her poor cousins and favourites. Among the latter is Leicester[1] whom she took up

[1] "We are told that among the females, married or unmarried, who

first to serve her filthy lust; whereof to have more freedom and interest, he caused his own wife to be murdered, as afterwards, for the accomplishment of his like brutish pleasures with another noble dame, it is openly known he made away with her husband. This man over-ruleth the Chamber, Court, Council, Parliament, ports, forts, seas, ships, tenders, men, munition, and all the country.

"With the aforesaid person, and with divers others, she hath abused her bodie against God's lawes, to the disgrace of princely majestie and the whole nation's reproache, by unspeakable and incredible variety of lust, which modesty suffereth not to be remembered; neyther were it to chaste eares to be uttered how shamefully she hath defiled and infamed her person and country, and made her court as a trappe, by this damnable and detestable art to entangle in sinne, and overthrowe the younger sorte of the nobilitye and gentlemen of the lande; whereby she is become notorious to the Worlde, and in other countryes a common fable for this her turpitude, which in so highe degre, namely in a woman and a queene, deserveth not onlie deposition, but all vengeance, both of God and man; and cannot be tollerated without eternal infamie of our whole countrie, the whole worlde diriding our effeminate dastardie, that have suffered such a creature almost thirty years together to raigne both over our bodies and soules, and to have the chief regiment of all our affaires, as well spirituall as temporal, to the extinguishinge not onley of religion but of all chaste livinge and honesty.

"She does not marry, because she cannot confine herself to one man; and to the condemnation of chaste and lawful marriage, she forced the very Parliament to give consent to a law that none should be named for her successor, savinge the natural, that is to saie bastard-borne, child of her own bodie."

(Here is an allusion "to her unlawfull, longe concealed, or fained issue.")

"She confederates with rebels of all nations, and is known to be the first and principal fountain of all those furious rebellions in Scotland, France, and Flanders; sending abroad by her

---

formed the Court of Elizabeth, two only escaped his solicitations; that his first wife was murdered by his order; that he disowned his marriage with the second, for the sake of a more favoured mistress; and that to obtain that mistress he first triumphed over her virtue, and then administered poison to her husband. To these instances has been added a long catalogue of crimes, of treachery to his friends, of assassination of his enemies, and of acts of injustice and extortion towards those who had offended his pride or refused to bend to his pleasure."—*History of England*, by J. Lingard, D.D., vol. vi. p. 253. Dublin, 1874.

ministers, as is proved by intercepted letters and confessions, numbers of intelligencers, spies, and practisers, in most princes' courts, not only to give notice of news, but to deal with the discontented; and hath sought to destroy the persons of the Pope's Holiness and the King of Spain.

"She is excessively proud, obstinate, and impenitent, though she has been excommunicated eighteen years.

"She hath murdered bishops and priests, and the Queen of Scots."

The point and pith of this terrible series of charges is then set forth. Having noticed several examples of the depositions of kings under the elder dispensation, and of emperors by the Patriarch of Christendom, it proceeds to point out that the sentence of Pope Pius V. has not been pursued, for two reasons : firstly, because of His Holiness's death, and, secondly, because of Elizabeth's great power and influence. But her determined perseverance in wickedness, her frightful persecution of those of the old religion, and her constant incitation to continental rebels to revolt, have induced Pope Sixtus to urge upon Philip of Spain the work now undertaken.

How all this failed of its purpose; how the Armada, thought to be invincible, was speedily scattered; how the elements fought against the Spaniards; and how their admiral frankly admitted the loss of thirty ships of the largest class, and no less than ten thousand men, is perfectly well known. Philip was thus defeated, the foreign Catholics were sorely disappointed. Many English people were frantic with joy. The queen triumphed.

To revert once again to the innovators, their doings, and the consequences thereof.

In certain places where the gospellers had secured popularity for their new doctrines—popular, of course, with the fanatical and gloomy of a certain type, as well as with the speculative and logical, who followed Calvin,[1]—many of the old rules, and most of the existing directions concerning divine service, put forth in rubrics, injunctions, and visitation articles, were utterly ignored. Some of the ministers, like Dee and Cardan (in a later reign), practised witchcraft and invoked demons.[2] The amount of

---

[1] Dean R. W. Church, of St. Paul's Cathedral, with an evident dash of quiet irony, writes of "the *imposing greatness* of Calvin's theological position."—Introduction to *Hooker*. Oxford, 1868.

[2] "Whether there be any man or woman in your parish that useth witchcraft, sorcery, charms, or unlawful prayer, or invocations in Latin or English, or upon any Christian body, or beast, or any that resorteth to the same for counsell or help, and what be their names."—Sandys' Visitation Articles, 1578.

liberty in fact taken on all sides was considerable, but with some licence had no bounds; for the restless spirit of reform seemed to have taken possession of so many. They simply did as, and what, they willed. Thus change followed change, because the followers of these daring innovators were ever seeking after some new thing.

In many dioceses the "non-sacrament ministers" seemed likely to become a majority. Increasing in boldness, some of them, passing over the bishops, set up Presbyteries,[1] and held so-called "courts" or assemblies of their own, for judging their adherents. In these, all signs and sacraments were condemned. And, as legal presentments for schism or neglect were calmly ignored by such innovators, while some of the bishops confessed themselves altogether unable to suggest any remedy,[2] disorder continued to increase.

Only on Sundays in certain parishes were any services ordinarily held. From Monday mornings until Saturday nights, more especially in villages, the churches were too often locked up and left desolate. In certain towns, however, where the "prophesyings" were popular, such devotional exhibitions or exercises afforded considerable interest to many. They steadily developed in a Puritan direction, and became more extravagant year by year.

These "prophesyings" commonly began with a long prayer from the presiding minister, who occupied the pulpit; during which the men, standing, bent forward and covered their faces with the sleeves of their gowns. The women-folk squatted and sighed.[3] A mystical text selected from the Apocalypse always ensured an exciting sitting, for those who thought themselves

---

[1] 'Whether any new presbiteries or eldershippe be lately among you erected, and by them any ministers appointed *without orders taken of the bishops*, do baptize, minister the Communion, or deale in any function ecclesiasticall?" &c.—Articles of Enquiry of John Aylmer, Bishop of London, 1586.

[2] "My Lorde of Llandaffe [Gervaise Babington, consecrated in 1591, and who died in 1610] would faine end these terrible [Qy. ?] disputacions ; but sithense the coming of Morgan the minister, all hath bin perversitie and sore disputaciousnesse."—Author's MSS. and Excerpts. Original Letter from Robert Johnes, dated 1594. "Since the liberty of prophesying was taken up, which came but lately into the northern parts (unless it were in the towns of Newcastle and Berwick, where Knox, Macbray, and Udall had sown their tares), *all things have gone so cross and backward in our Church, that I cannot call the history of these forty years or more to mind, or express my obligations upon it, but with a bleeding heart.*"—*Works of Dr. T. Jackson,* vol. iii. p. 273.

[3] *Apologie for the Trewthe, as sette fforthe, etc.* by H. H., p. 19. London : At the Sign of the Swan in Paul's Churchyard, 1594. See also *History of the Martin Marprelate Controversy, etc.* London, 1845.

specially endowed from on high, seated and covered, and with their Bibles open and ready, gave free rein both to imagination and assertion. If the minister who began the proceedings had plenty of confidence in his own judgment, a stentorian voice, a fluent delivery, and what has been styled "the grace of obstinacy," he could not only talk down his contradictory opponents, but both command silence and ensure it, when the subject, in his judgment, had been well thrashed out, or when wind and words failed him. If he were both physically and morally weak, no one could safely predict the result of the "prophesying,"—it might end in an unsanctified noise, a shower of Bibles across the nave, and a free fight amongst the elect. No one under such circumstances could say that the new system was dead, where such obvious and tangible signs of active life were so plainly apparent.

Towards the latter half of the queen's reign, when developments more startling than ever were current, the suggestion, long previously put forth,[1] that, as a further reform, "the Lord's Supper" should be made a substantial meal, and be partaken of in the evening, the only suitable time of day for a supper, was very commonly followed. To wind up the proceedings of the "Sabbath," as the Lord's Day began to be called, in this manner was felt by some to be at once solemnising, appropriate, and elevating. On such occasions the "ordinance," as it was termed, partook largely of the nature of a solemn social assembly for singing sacred songs, making vague admissions of spiritual weakness, eating, drinking, and praying.[2] How far "the Order for the Administration of the Supper" in the Book of Common Prayer was used or followed, is open to question and consideration. The Communion tressels were spread with a table-cloth, loaves and wine were supplied in abundance, and in some cases profusely; platters or trenchers were placed round the table; a sop of bread and wine made in a porringer,[3] was partaken of with

---

[1] See page 68 of this book for the authority, given in the foot-note.

[2] At Thame, Oxon., at Easter 1560, two gallons of wine were provided; at Easter 1563, three gallons, a large amount, and no less than twenty-six loaves. It is thus also recorded:—" 1591. May 2nd. Item, delivered unto William Typpinge Two Cupps for the Communion-table, ij dozen and an halfe of Platters, one pann, six spones, and half a dozen of trenchers, ij table-clothes." The tressels there were not abolished until the year 1625, when thirty shillings were expended in providing a Communion-table.—Author's MSS. and Excerpts from the Parish Accounts of Thame, Oxon.

[3] There is a two-handled silver cup at Charing in Kent. It is said to hold a gallon of wine. The Tudor notion of making the Lord's Supper a full and substantial meal was perpetuated for several generations.—See *Archæologia Cantiana*, vol. xvi. p. 354. At Bonnington in Kent, there is no chalice,

spoons; and so, with a certain grave demeanour, the sitting saints[1] probably contrasted that, their homely and simple rite,—in which the body was refreshed, the mind deluded, and the conscience drugged,—with the now absolutely-abolished and truly-hated mass. It *was* a contrast indeed.

In other particulars, some reaction took place. The first person amongst the English ministers, who, by the general soundness of his principles, the clearness of his thoughts, and the ability with which he set them forth, began to stem the tide of this kind of confusion, innovation, and novelty (in his day so great, that all order and law seemed likely to be overturned, and distinct Atheism first became rampant in a once Catholic country[2]) was Richard Hooker, born of a respectable family near the city of Exeter, on Our Lady's Day 1554. When about twenty years of age, by the aid of an uncle who was chamberlain of that city, he was admitted a clerk of Corpus Christi College, Oxford, of which in 1577 he became a Fellow, and subsequently Rector of Drayton Beauchamp in Buckinghamshire; but was in 1584 appointed Master of the Temple in London, a position of prominence and importance. Here he was brought into controversy with the two notorious Puritans, Travers and Cartwright (of whom mention has already been made), who were deliberately aiming to effect still further and still greater fundamental changes both in the doctrine and discipline of the Church of England.

but a porringer (that is, a domestic cup), with two handles for porridge, is in use at the Holy Communion. The same is the case likewise at Frinsted and Postling in that county.—*Ibid.* vol. xvii. pp. 291-2. London, 1887.

[1] 'The state of the churches was deplorable; they had been left to fanatical neglect and ruin. The Sacrament was administered in the most irreverent manner; *the service for the altar* [Qy. the cup and platter] *was borrowed from the nearest house, and the communicants took their seats at tables which the Catholics termed "oyster-boards."* The estates of the Church were alienated by the bishops. The highest dignitaries had availed themselves of the spoliation of the churches, and shared the plate and costly carvings with the nobility and gentry. Many parishes were left without a clergyman; in almost all, the service was neglected."—*Documents from Simancas*, Introduction, pp. 17, 18. London, 1865.

[2] "To heighten all these discontents and dangers, there was also sprung up a generation of godless men; men that had so long given way to their own lusts and delusions, and so highly opposed the blessed motions of His Spirit, and the inward light of their own consciences, that they became the very slaves of vice, and had thereby sinned themselves into a belief of that which they would, but could not, believe: into a belief which is repugnant even to human nature (for the heathens believe that there are many gods), but *these had sinned themselves into a belief that there was no God.*"—*Life of Mr. Richard Hooker*, by Isaac Walton, ed. Keble, p. 37. Oxford, 1845.

Though Hooker had been brought up in the narrow school of Calvin, yet, when the new religion became duly developed in its various and contradictory forms, when moreover he saw to what lengths Travers and his adherents proposed to go,—what blank infidelity had ensued from such conflicts and controversies,—he himself stopped short; surveyed the actual situation with the power and grasp of a clear-sighted and vigorous mind, and gave to the Christian nations a treatise so deep, so exact, and so masterly, that his name remains as one of the greatest and deepest writers of his day. One of the Chief Bishops of Christendom highly commended his labours.[1] *The Laws of Ecclesiastical Polity* was commenced in the Temple about 1587, continued at Boscombe in the diocese of Sarum four years afterwards, and completed about 1594 at Bishopsbourne near Canterbury. The eminent writer, who was as modest and humble as he was thoughtful and learned, was of short stature, bent with literary labours and bodily mortifications, much tried by home troubles, and in no way externally remarkable. But the services he rendered to the institution of which he was so great a light and defender, the masterly method by which he led his readers back from the new to the old, will only be adequately realised when the miserable disunion of the sixteenth century, which he so deplored, is atoned for by the corporate reunion of a later age.

Hooker laid the foundation of a theological party in the National Church, whose principles were rather akin to those of Christian divines before the so-called "Reformation," than to those of Barlow, Cranmer, Sandys, Parkhurst, and Bale. From Hooker's day to the present, his principles have been always more or less acknowledged as good and true ; so that a considerable section of English Churchmen has been benefited and blessed through his labours.

Nevertheless, as regards the crucial question of ordination,—a question of life or death to the professing Catholic, though one of little or no moment to the newly-bred sectarian or Donatistic Nationalist,[2]—Hooker's trumpet gave a most uncertain and

---

[1] Pope Clement VIII. [Hippolytus Aldobrandini] said of Hooker, "There is no learning that this man hath not searcht into ; nothing too hard for his understanding ; this man indeed deserves the name of an author ; his books will get reverence by age, for there is in them such seeds of eternity, that, if the rest be like this, they shall last till the last fire shall consume all learning."—*Life of Hooker*, Keble's ed. of his *Works*, p. 71. Oxford, 1845.

[2] In quoting the following account of Hooker's position, the author must regretfully and frankly confess his inability to reconcile such distressing facts as many of those which are recorded in these volumes, with the late respected

unsatisfactory sound.   As regards current events, he saw around
him bishops who one and all did not believe that episcopal
ordination was essential, and who possibly had never themselves
received it; deans and prebendaries, like Whittingham and
Kinge, Alwood and De Saravia, who had received only so-called
"ordination" at the hands of presbyters ; and numerous churches,
as existing evidence proves, served by ministers not ordained at
all.[1]   In making his able defence of true principles, therefore, he

Mr. Keble's confident assertions regarding the then state of affairs.   That
thoughtful and eminent Tractarian in 1845 thus wrote :—"Now, since the
episcopal succession had been so carefully retained in the Church of England,
and so much anxiety evinced to render both her Liturgy and Ordination
Services strictly conformable to the rules and doctrines of antiquity, it might
have been expected that the defenders of the English hierarchy against the
first Puritans should take the highest ground, and challenge for the bishops
the same unreserved submission, on the same plea of exclusive apostolical
prerogative, which their adversaries feared not to insist on for their elders and
deacons.   It is notorious, however, that such was not in general the line preferred by Jewell, Whitgift, Bishop Cooper, and others, to whom the manage-
ment of that controversy was intrusted during the early part of Elizabeth's
reign.   They do not expressly disavow, but they carefully shun, that unreserved appeal to Christian antiquity, in which one would have thought they
must have discerned the very strength of their cause to lie.   It is enough with
them to show that the government by archbishops and bishops is ancient and
allowable ; they never venture to urge its *exclusive* claim, or to connect the
succession with the validity of the holy Sacraments ; and yet it is obvious that
such a course of argument alone (supposing it borne out by facts) could fully
meet all the exigencies of the case.   It must have occurred to the learned
writers above mentioned, since it was the received doctrine of the Church
down to their days ; and if they had disapproved it, as some theologians of no
small renown have since done, it seems unlikely that they should have passed
it over without some express avowal of dissent ; considering that they always
wrote with an eye to the pretensions of Rome also, which popular opinion
had in a great degree mixed up with this doctrine of apostolical succession.
One obvious reason, and probably the chief one, of their silence, was the
relation in which they stood to the foreign Protestant congregations.   The
question had been mixed up with considerations of personal friendship, first
by Cranmer's connection with the Lutherans, and after King Edward's death,
by the residence of Jewell, Grindal, and others at Zurich, Strasburg, and
elsewhere, in congregations which had given up the apostolical succession.
Thus feelings arose which came, insensibly, no doubt, but really and strongly,
in aid of the prevailing notion that everything was to be sacrificed to the
paramount object of union among Protestants."—Rev. J. Keble's Preface to
the *Works of Richard Hooker*, pp. lix. lx.   Oxford, 1845.
   [1] "Nearly up to the time when he [Richard Hooker] wrote, *numbers had
been admitted to the ministry of the Church of England, with no better than
Presbyterian ordination*, and it appears by Travers's *Supplication to the
Council*, that such was the construction put upon the statute of the 13th of
Elizabeth, permitting those who had received orders in any other form than
that of the English service-book, on giving certain securities, to exercise their
calling in England.   If it were really the intention of [the framers and makers
of] that act to authorise other than episcopal ordination, it is but one proof

was bound to consider such grave facts, which he, a mere country pastor, had neither power nor opportunity to alter. Nothing that he could think, write, or say, could undo the mischief already deliberately done. Hooker, consequently, adapted himself to circumstances, there was obviously no other alternative ; and though, if his admitted principles were faithfully applied, the fact that episcopal ordination was essential might be reasonably deduced from their acceptance, he not only nowhere so applied them, but actually regarded Dr. Adrian De Saravia [1]—ordained abroad by presbyters, if at all—as one perfectly capable of receiving his death-bed confession, of giving him absolution, and of administering the Lord's Supper. Here is the record :—

"About one day before his death, Dr. Saravia, who knew the very secrets of his soul (for they were supposed to be confessors to each other), came to him, and after a conference of the benefit, the necessity, and safety of the Church's absolution, it was resolved the doctor should give him both that and the Sacrament the day following. To which end the doctor came, and after a short retirement and privacy, they two returned to the company, and then the doctor gave him, and some of those friends which were with him, the blessed Sacrament of the body and blood of our Jesus. Which being performed, the doctor thought he saw a reverend gaiety in his face." [2]

Subsequently, the "Reformed" National Church — which, however, had happily retained a belief in the fundamental doctrines of Christianity, and in two of the Sacraments—began to throw off the heresies and errors of its first founders, and in due course abandoned some of them. For the influence of Hooker has never been lost. The rise of the Caroline school of theologians, often thoroughly Christian, if not quite Catholic ; the improvement deliberately made in the Ordinal in 1662, together with the expulsion of the fanatical and unordained ; the beneficial influence of Archbishop Sancroft and the later Non-

---

more of the low accommodating notions concerning the Church which then prevailed ; and may serve to heighten our sense of the imminent risk which we were in of losing the succession."—P. lxxvi. of the Preface by the Rev. John Keble to his edition of Hooker's *Works*.

[1] Adrian de Saravia came from Ghent. His father was a Spaniard ; his mother from Artois. As is generally allowed, he was never ordained, though he wrote in defence of episcopacy, held a controversy with Beza, and was made a Prebendary of Canterbury. He wrote three remarkable tracts : (1) "De diversis ministrorum evangelii gradibus ;" (2) "De Honore praesulibus et presbyteris debito ;" and (3) "De sacrilegis et sacrilegorum poenis."

[2] *Life of Mr. Richard Hooker*, p. 85. Keble's edition of his *Works*. Oxford, 1845.

jurors; and, more especially, the great work of reparation and restoration effected because of the Oxford movement of 1833, are all tokens that the Almighty has not forsaken us, but has yet some important work for the Church of England to do,—whether in a day of sunshine and grace, or after a period of storm and losses, none can know,—when the time for effecting corporate reunion, on the solid basis of authority and truth, shall in His merciful providence have at length arrived.

CORRESPONDENCE CONCERNING THE PROPOSED PRIVATE ASSASSINATION OF MARY, QUEEN OF SCOTS.

From the " Letter-Books of Sir Amias Poulet," Keeper of the Queen.

"To Sir Amias Poulet.[1]

"'After our hearty commendations, we find by speech lately uttered by Her Majesty that she doth note in you a lack of that care and zeal of her service that she looketh for at your hands, in that you have not in all this time of yourselves (without other provocation) found out some way to shorten the life of that queen, considering the great peril she is subject unto hourly, so long as the said queen shall live. Wherein, besides a kind of lack of love towards her, she noteth greatly that you have not that care of your own particular safeties, or rather of the preservation of religion and the public good and prosperity of your country, that reason and policy commandeth, especially having so good a warrant and ground for the satisfaction of your consciences towards God and the discharge of your credit and reputation towards the world, as the oath of association which you both have so solemnly taken and vowed, and especially the matter wherewith she standeth charged being so clearly and manifestly proved against her. And therefore she taketh it most unkindly towards her, that men professing that love towards her that you do, should in any kind of sort, for lack of the discharge of your duties, cast the burthen upon her, knowing as you do her indisposition to shed blood, especially of one of that sex and quality, and so near to her in blood as the said queen is. These respects we find do greatly trouble Her Majesty, who, we assure you, has sundry times protested that if

[1] Hearne's MS. Diary, vol. lxxxv. p. 89. From *Gwyn's Transcript.*

the regard of the danger of her good subjects and faithful servants did not more move her than her own peril, she would never be drawn to assent to the shedding of her blood. We thought it very meet to acquaint (you) with these speeches lately passed from Her Majesty, referring the same to your good judgments. And so we commit you to the protection of the Almighty.

"'At.London, February 1, 1586.

"'Your most assured friends,

"'FRANCIS WALSINGHAM,

"'WM. DAVISON.'

"This letter was received at Fotheringhay, the 2nd of February at five in the afternoon."

"An abstract of a letter from Mr. Secretary Davison, of the said 1st of February 1586, as followeth :—

"'I pray let this and the inclosed be committed to the fire, which measure shall be likewise mete to your answer, after it hath been communicated to Her Majesty for her satisfaction.'"

"'A postscript in a letter from Mr. Secretary Davison, of the 3rd of February 1586 :—

"'I entreated you in my last to burn my letters sent unto you for the argument' sake, which by your answer to Mr. Secretary (which I have seen) appeareth not to have been done. I pray you, let me entreat you to make heretics of the one and the other, as I mean to use yours, after Her Majesty hath seen it.'"

"'In the end of the postscript—

"'I pray you let me hear what you have done with my letters, because they are not fit to be kept, that I may satisfy Her Majesty therein, who might otherwise take offence thereat, and if you entreat this postscript in the same manner, you shall not err a whit.'"

"A. Poulet—D. Drury.

"A copy of a letter to Sir Francis Walsingham, of the 2nd of February 1586, at six in the afternoon, being the answer to a letter from him, the said Sir Francis, of the 1st of February 1586, received at Fotheringhay, the 2nd day of February, at five in the afternoon :—

"'Your. letters of yesterday coming to my hands this present

S

day at five in the afternoon, I would not fail according to your directions to return my answers with all possible speed, which (*sic*) shall deliver unto you with great grief and bitterness of mind, in that I am so unhappy to have liven to see this unhappy day in the which I am required by direction from my most gracious sovereign to do an act which God and the law forbiddeth.   My good livings and life are at Her Majesty's disposition, and am ready to so lose them this next morrow if it shall so please her, acknowledging that I hold them as of her mere and most gracious favour, and do not desire them to enjoy them, but with Her Highness's good liking.   But God forbid that I should make so foul a shipwreck of my conscience, or leave so great a blot to my poor posterity, to shed blood without law or warrant. Trusting that Her Majesty, of her accustomed clemency, will take this my dutiful answer in good part (and the rather by your good mediation), as proceeding from one who will never be inferior to any Christian subject living in duty, honour, love, and obedience towards his sovereign.   And thus I commit you to the mercy of the Almighty.

" ' From Fotheringhay, the 2nd of February 1586.

" ' Your most assured poor friends,

" ' A. POULET,

" ' D. DRURY.

" ' Your letters coming in the plural number seem to be meant as to Sir Drue Drury as to myself, and yet because he is not named in them, neither the letter directed unto him, he forbeareth to make any particular answer, but subscribeth in heart to my opinion.' "

"I copied these letters in December 1717, from a MS. folio book of letters to and from Sir Amias Poulet, when the Queen of Scots' Governor at Fotheringhay.   This book is in the hands of John, Earl of Poulett, his immediate descendant, and in that book is likewise contained a particular account of the trial of the Queen of Scots, which seems to be done by Sir Amias himself.[1]

[Poulet was too cautious to destroy the disgraceful letters he had been dishonoured by receiving from the secretaries of his sovereign.   He carried the originals with him to London, and there doubtless they were "made heretics of," as Davison had

[1] With this note by Mr. Gwyn, Hearne's copy ends.

urged. But mindful of his own reputation, he left copies with his family, that, if necessary, it might be known in what terms he had repelled the base proposal.]

"Poulet to Davison.

"'Sir,—The rule of charity commandeth to bear with the impatience of the afflicted, which Christian lesson you have learned, as I find by experience to my great contentment, in that you have been content to bear with my malapertness, wherein you bind me more and more to love you and to honour you, which I will do with all human faithfulness.

"'If I should say that I have burned the papers you wot ot I cannot tell if everybody would believe me; and therefore I reserve them to be delivered to your hands at my coming to London. God bless you and prosper all your actions to His glory.

"'From Fotheringhay, the 8th of February 1586.
"'Your most assuredly to my small power,
"'A. POULET.'"

The Letter-Books of Sir Amias Poulet, Keeper of Mary, Queen of Scots. Edited by Rev. John Morris. London, 1874. A volume which, I may be permitted to add, is full of historical interest and importance.

CHAPTER IX.

THROUGHOUT all these stirring times, times of excitement, confusion, and change, the peculiar disorder which everywhere existed in the National Church can scarcely now be realised. Unless records actually remained in black and white, of the exact state of the then existing degradation, which plainly set it forth in detail, few would be found to credit its existence. Writers interested in making out a case, by suppressing facts, passing over damaging records, and by artful special pleading, have for a long time succeeded in obscuring the truth. The bishops of that day are constantly complaining to the Council of their miseries, and are found metaphorically wringing their hands in despair of ever being able to bring order out of such disorder. Obedience, they assert, does not exist. Every one persists in doing exactly what he likes, and moral suasion is of little or no avail.

Dr. Bickley, Bishop of Chichester, believes that the times are sad because "so many preaching ministers will abide no correction."[1] He himself had been openly set at defiance, to his great humiliation, by some "proper insolent" preachers who, going from place to place, would not minister any sacrament "but only stir up the ignorant and mean with vain and vicious words," despising his lordship, his office and authority, and "the powers that be." They were "verie sore skornfull" when the queen was referred to as owning any spiritual authority.

Dr. Chaderton of Lichfield was very downhearted at the state of affairs, as he piteously wrote to the Lord Treasurer in the following terms?—

"Certes, my honorable lord, I am here in a very perilous country; and, if I may speak it without offence, the very sink of the whole realm, both for corrupt religion and life.[2]

---

[1] In 1583 it is on record that Thomas Underdowne preached in St. Michael's, Lewes, that anyone who had an inward persuasion and allowance that he was called by God might lawfully preach.—*State Papers, Domestic, Elizabeth*, vol. clix. Nos. 15, 16.

[2] Strype's *Annals*, vol iii. Part I. p. 35. Oxford, 1824.

Many of the persons ministering thereabouts were not even in deacons' orders, and others had declined to undergo any matrimonial inquisition of any sort or kind.[1] On one occasion at Lichfield, a "proper stout and comely wench" assaulted an "ancient justice," who had proposed to examine her according to law, by tearing his beard, and she threatened him with further punishment if he made any like attempt.

Complaints had been made, but without effect, for no remedy was forthcoming, that in one parish of this diocese, "the minister refused to wear the surplice, and that he would not keep the accustomed place of prayer, where service was wont to be said, but stood lower to the people, and turned not his face upward toward the east, but downward to the west, and used not the Order of Common Prayer."[2]

By the year 1583 a wave of change had completely passed over the diocese of St. David's. Externally the ancient faith had been on all sides efficiently put down. As regards externals, the sign of the cross, chrism, holy water, lights at the altar and at the reading of the Gospel, special vestments for the clergy, had all been swept away.[3] Here and there a tattered cope, which no one cared to possess, was sometimes hung over the edge of the pulpit; otherwise all sacerdotal vestments were totally abolished. The nature of Dr. Middleton's Visitation Articles was thoroughly innovating. Though those favouring the old religion were com-

[1] William Chaderton, Bishop of Lichfield, to the Lord Treasurer, A.D. 1582.—Strype's *Annals*, vol. iii. Part I. p. 141. Oxford, 1824. "Whether was your parson made *deacon* before his admission to the said benefice? . . . . Whether hath your parson married in such sort, as he ought to do, having two justices of peace's hands for the allowing of such?"—*Articles of Enquiry, Diocese of Lichfield*, A.D. 1582. Strype's *Annals*, vol. iii. Part I. pp. 164, 165. Oxford, 1824. *A Replicacion to an Auncient Enemy*, etc., p. 39. London, Serres.

[2] The Archdeacon of Canterbury bears similar testimony, thus :—"What shall I now speak of the notable decay of prayer, fasting, and alms, and univer sally of all virtuous living, of the disobedience of children to their parents, of servants to their masters, of fraud, deceit, circumvention, more practised than ever before in all contracts and bargains, of rarity of trusty true friends, and of decay of obedience to public laws and magistrates, and finally of all good order and public discipline."—*The Pretended Divorce between Henry VIII. and Queen Catherine*, by Nicholas Harpsfield, Archdeacon of Canterbury, edited by N. Pocock, p. 298. London, 1878.

[3] As Dr. Harding, in his *Confutation*, had so triumphantly asked of Jewell, "If ye show us not the use of chrism in your churches; if the sign of the cross be not borne before you in processions, and otherwheres used ; if holy water be abolished ; if lights at the Gospel and Communion be not had ; if peculiar vestments for deacons, priests, bishops, be taken away, and many such other the like, judge ye whether ye have duly kept the old ceremonies of the Church?"

pelled to worship in secret, the bishop of that See was obliged to report that in his diocese "there is now little Popery, but the people are greatly infected with atheism and wonderfully given over to vicious life."[1]   A certain official informs him that in no less than thirty-two churches there are neither services nor congregations. Some persons, he is distressed to find, "would welcome the idolatrous mass anew, but are sore disdainful to the preachers." At Breachfa two ministers had held "a godlie disputation," lasting several hours; and their hearers, having split themselves into two camps towards eventide, concluded the "exercise" by an appeal to blows and cuffs.   It seems to have been the pious wives of the two ministers[2] who first proposed an appeal to physical force, in which they and others of their sex heartily joined.   The local constables, feeling themselves incompetent to settle the knotty points of controversy with authority, left the opposing theologians and their respective adherents to fight out their battle.   Darkness failed to settle the controversy, but it happily sufficed to close the militant disputation.   For the "saints" left off squaring up to each other, mollified their respective bruises, and fought no longer.   A few years later, in 1586, it was reported—and no one need have been astonished at the report—that "in Brecknock, the livings are nearly all impropriate, with no preachers but ignorant and unlearned ministers.   Seldom or never is there evening prayer.[3]

One special difficulty of the bishops was that every ordinary minister now looked upon himself as an "overseer," a "preaching and presiding elder," or "a bishop,"[4] and denied altogether the value of the new "Parliament-approved ordering."   Authority, many asserted, came from the people, not from above; from the flock, *i.e.* the "godly," not from "great Eliza, the maiden

---

[1] *State Papers, Domestic, Elizabeth,* vol. clxii. No 29, dated "Brecon, September 16, 1583.

[2] On another occasion, as is on record, the zeal of the women was not hidden under a bushel.   "Lo! and behold, two of the wives of ministers also challenged him to dispute upon points of religion.   The female theologians, however, spent the labour of their preparation in vain; for the martyr remanded them to their spindles and needles, and especially recommended to them modesty and silence; for the more they observed these so much the wiser would they show themselves to be."—*Records of the English Province,* vol. iii. p. 462.   London, 1878.

[3] *State Papers, Domestic, Elizabeth,* vol. cxci. No. 17.

[4] A certain minister, Wright, who had received orders of Villers and other ministers at Antwerp, confesses that in his judgment "*every minister is a bishop.*"   He further affirmed that the preachers who followed the Prayer Book were dumb dogs, and that the ministers were thieves and murderers, and, moreover, that there were no lawful ministers in England.—Strype's *Annals,* vol. iii. Part I. p. 179.   Oxford, 1824.

Shepherdess."[1] One, John Daye of Norwich, in an epistle to the bishop, was both out-spoken and plain-spoken :—

"He said also that we urged orders so long as orders maintained superstition; but all other orders were no orders. He concluded by the first [chapter] of the Acts of the Apostles, that no man might appoint ministers, but the disciples in every parish. He would needs urge also that none might be suffered in the church but preachers."[2]

As to Bishop Middleton's assertion that atheism and immorality were on the increase, while parishes were destitute,[3] the existing evidence is conclusive on the point. Nothing, of course, could have been more conducive to the extension of such principles as the controversies by puffed-up Calvinists and self-elected teachers of irreligion.

In 1582, a minister of Stamford was accused of "wickedness and heresy, two gross crimes, namely, for lying with another woman, his wife being alive, and for likewise affirming the lawfulness of having two wives"[4] at the same time,—a somewhat more progressive reform than had as yet been sanctioned by his superiors. If an old Carmelite or a Cistercian, he reasoned, could lead some "one wench" to the altar, why could not a Stamford preacher "lead two?"

In 1584, the cases at the Quarter Sessions in London give an awful account of the state of religion. A minister's wife was accused of systematically transgressing the law in an infamous manner; while Heaton, the parson of St. Andrew's, Holborn, was also charged with most frightful crimes. This man's father, it is recorded, was in prison for incest.

On May 28th, 1582, Bishop Nicholas Robinson of Bangor had written to Sir Francis Walsingham[5] to justify himself against the reports that he had fallen away from true religion. In this letter he makes a free and full confession to the Secretary of State,—a delegate of the Supreme Governess,—and makes it in detail with much care and precision. He unfolds the whole course of his

---

[1] Author's MSS. and Excerpts. Robert Beale, Clerk of the Council, to Sir Henry Lee.

[2] John Daye to the Bishop of Norwich.—Strype's *Annals*, vol. iii. Part I. p. 26. Oxford, 1824.

[3] "There are whole thousands of us left untaught : yea, by trial it will be found that there are in England whole thousands of parishes destitute of this necessary help to salvation, that is, of diligent preaching and teaching."— Sampson's *Supplicatory to the Queen*, Strype's *Annals*, vol. iii. Part I. p. 327. Oxford, 1824.

[4] Strype's *Annals*, vol. iii. Part I. p. 169. Oxford, 1824.

[5] *State Papers, Domestic, Elizabeth*, vol. cliii. No. 56.

life since he became a preacher,[1] both before and since he was
Bishop of Bangor.

Notwithstanding what had been done in the work of "Reformation,"[2] as it was termed, notwithstanding that the old
churches, now stripped and desolate, looked more like Jewish
synagogues than temples for the worship of God the Trinity, and
for the celebration of Christian rites, numbers of the ministers
and others, more especially the advanced Puritans, thought that
much more ought to be swept away. It has been shown how
great had been their demands in the way of further change, and
how indisposed those in authority had shown themselves to be
as regards acceding to them. A little later, some of the bishops
began to see that Puritanism could only be opposed by reverting
to rejected principles; and began to teach that bishops governed
by divine right.[3] The queen's personal love of pomp and
display, when, as Supreme Governess, she herself was the object
of it, is well known. In churches and cathedrals visited by her,
she was still regularly honoured by external rites and signs. She
was received with genuflections, she walked under a canopy
borne over her, occupied the chief seat of honour near the
Communion-board, and was herself often the subject of praise

---

[1] It had been asserted in print that "the Superintendent of Bangor, one
Robinson, is no priest nor minister, but only a preacher.—*Modest Cure, with
a Cry from the Wilderness*. London, 1556. But he seems to have been
certainly consecrated a bishop at Lambeth on the 20th of October in that
year, by Dr. Matthew Parker, assisted by Bullingham and Ghest.

[2] Archdeacon Harpsfield of Canterbury thus wrote of the evil deeds of
King Edward VI. : "He averted, extinguished, and abolished not only the
rites and ceremonies of the Catholic Church, but divers articles of our faith,
and the chief Sacraments withal. *Then our churches were more like to Jews'
synagogues* (the image and cross of Christ, with the image of His blessed
mother and all His holy saints, being defaced and broken, the altars overthrown, and the precious body of Christ villanously profaned) than to
Christian churches : the walls all be-painted, like the Jews' temples, with
places of Holy Scripture ; and yet worse than the Jews' temples, for that the
meaning of these authorities was to make the world believe that to pray to
the saints, to pray for the dead, to worship Christ's body in the blessed
sacrament, was nothing but plain superstition and idolatry. Then should
you have seen in the place where Christ's precious body was reposed over the
altar, and instead of Christ His crucifix, the arms of a mortal king set up on
high with a dog and a lion, which a man might well call the abomination of
desolation standing in the temple, that Daniel speaketh of."—*The Pretended
Divorce between Henry VIII. and Queen Katherine*, by Nicholas Harpsfield,
LL.D., edited by N. Pocock, pp. 281-282. London, 1878.

[3] Sir Francis Knowlys tells Lord Burghley that he is of opinion that the
superiority and authority of bishops is derived immediately and independently
from Her Majesty. Mr. Martin and Dr. Whitgift the bishop have, in his
judgment, incurred the penalty of *præmunire* by claiming a divine right for
the bishops. *Domestic State Papers, Elizabeth*, vol. cccxxxiii. 62.

and glory in the anthems and hymns sung. In ordinary parish churches, instead of bowing to the altar or the cross, or to the crucifix on the rood-screen, many of the people now bent the knee either to actual representations of Her Majesty on canvas, or to her gorgeously-emblazoned coat of arms—everywhere then substituted for the representation of our blessed Saviour on the cross—the sole patch of strong and vulgar colouring amid the surrounding whitewash. In one Oxfordshire church,—that of Cuxham,—instead of the text "The fear of the Lord is the beginning of wisdom," some local scribe in a paroxysm of loyalty had written up in black letters, " The Fear of the Quene is the iniciacion of wisdome,"[1]—possibly incited to do it by some witty but daring recusant, who lived near, or it may have been some unsanctified Erastian.

On the other hand, under the not inappropriate name of Jezebel, Her Majesty was satirised for being too conservative and lukewarm. For example, at St. Edmund's Bury, under her elaborate and magnificent armorial bearings, the following text had been illuminated in red and black letters—"Because thou art lukewarm, and neither cold nor hot, it shall come to pass that I will spue thee out of my mouth ; " and another for the special consideration of the Bishop of Norwich, viz. :—"I have a few things against thee that thou sufferest the woman Jezebel, which maketh herself a prophetess, to teach and to deceive my servants ; to make them commit fornication, and to eat meat sacrificed unto idols."[2]

One minister, evidently a "vessel of charity," as he modestly termed himself, in preference to abusing or satirising Her Majesty, had, with much personal superiority and great condescension, previously prayed for her thus :—"Lord, we humbly beseech Thee to strengthen the Queen's Highness with thy Holy Spirit, that in the twenty-third year of her reign, she may cast down all the high places of idolatry within her land, with the Popish Canon Law, and all superstition and commandments of men, and to pluck up all filthy ceremonies pertaining to the same."[3]

Judging by what has been here set forth,—the state of profanity, contradiction, and self-pleasing which existed—it might have been conceived that the queen and her ministers had already done this tolerably[4] if not perfectly well. The further

---

[1] *Notes upon Stadham, Easington, and Cuxham Churches*, by John D'Oyley, p. 144. Oxford, 1773.
[2] Strype's *Annals*, vol. iii. Part I. p. 176. Oxford, 1824.
[3] *Ibid.* vol. iii. Part I. p. 66.
[4] From Heylin's *Affairs of Church and State in England under Queen Elizabeth*, pp. 174–175, ed. London, 1661, it is stated that "every man is

"Reformation" which these fanatical people desired was only duly and completely accomplished in a later age, by the fury, fire, and sword of Oliver Cromwell; for whose advent, however, they were then so efficiently paving the way.   The murder of the King, the further pollution of the dismal and altarless churches and the miseries of civil war later on, were the natural and reasonable sequences of an overthrow of all Christian authority, the casting away of five out of the seven sacraments of the New Law, and the atrocious cruelties to Catholics under Elizabeth. As in the sixteenth century our nation sowed, so, in due course, it deservedly reaped.   A portion of the harvest even now remains to be gathered in.

Some persons—such always exist, the pitiful skulks of society, or artful Gallios of the day—avoided taking sides.   They were content to follow those whom they judged to be their betters, and to hold their tongues.   Certain persons highly approved of the new liberty which had been secured, and liked it still better when, as in so many cases, it degenerated into the wildest licence.   They punctually went through mere external legal formalities, such as attending church, listening to sermons, or participating in "the Supper," as a matter of course; quieting their dulled consciences with the hope that if public affairs were so much out of joint these might soon become not so disturbed and less anomalous.   Others, like Cecil of old, whom they followed humbly and at a distance, allowed their predilections in religion to become entirely subservient to their temporal advancement.   Instead of renouncing the world, they worshipped it with devotion.   They were always careful not to express any strong convictions on ecclesiastical questions; and perhaps doggedly carried out the expressive maxim, that "if eloquence be silvern, silence is golden," with an approach to perfection. Or, with some art and forethought, they took both sides[1] at

left unto his private rule or canon, whether he will take the Bread into his hands, or let it stand at the end of the table, the Bread and Wine being laid upon the table, where it pleases the parish clerk or sexton to put them": that the new church "is constrained to suffer cobblers, weavers, tinkers, tanners, cardmakers, tapsters, fiddlers, gaolers, and others of like profession not only to enter into disputing with her, but also to climb up into pulpits, and to keep the place of priests and ministers": that "the residue of the Sacrament [in loaf bread] unreceived was taken of the priest or of the parish clerk, to spread their young children's butter thereupon, or to serve their own tooth with it at their homely table."

[1] See "Jack-of-Both-Sides, a godly and a necessary Catholic Admonition touching those that be Neutres, holding upon a certain religion, and such as those that hold with both parties, or rather no parties."   Richard Harrison, 1562

different times, and in accordance with the respective company in which they might find themselves ;—a position of some difficulty, conducive neither to honesty nor honour.

In the meantime the hangman was not allowed to slumber long, nor the gibbet to stand unused, nor the queen's goose-quill for signing death-warrants to remain for any time undipped in ink. The man-butcher likewise was frequently called upon to sharpen his blade and turn up the cuffs of his blue and blood-stained smock.

Constant rumours were artfully put about that various people were continually on the look-out to poison or get rid of the queen. This, however, — save in one or two questionable instances,—is more than doubtful ; for the gift of lying was so common, and the arts of forgery and fabrication were so frequently resorted to by the bevy of hired spies and bribed ruffians in the pay of the Court,[1] that small reliance can be placed even on the documentary evidence they produced in such cases. Their sworn words were often but as idle tales, their secret letters forgeries. Many of these rumours were deliberately and of malice invented, in order to justify further cruelty or as a plea for more confiscations and robberies. From the proceeds of such confiscations, the forgers and falsehood-mongers were richly rewarded. At all events, if there were so many persons anxious to get rid of so cruel and heartless a woman (and no one can wonder at it, if such were the case ; though the poisoner or assassin be contemptible), they appear to have been altogether

---

[1] "The Secretary Walsingham had for years had a little army of spies in his pay—wretches of blasted character and broken fortunes, fellows who were adepts at inventing plots or worming-out secrets, their trade eavesdropping, their daily bread gained by scenting out 'murders, stratagems, and crimes' ; where true intelligence was not to be gained, *false rumours and slanders of the blackest hue* served their turn as well. Sometimes they were dogging the steps of decrepit old 'Queen Mary's priests' ; sometimes *they were busy forging letters from people in high station ;* but always sleepless, suspicious, unscrupulous — men of infinite resources in the base expedients of the in-former's trade."—*One Generation of a Norfolk House,* by Augustus Jessopp, D.D., p. 248. London, 1879. On one occasion Lord Burghley sent twenty pounds as a present to one Stephen Powle, of Maiden Lane, a notorious spy, who had professed to have discovered a plot on the part of persons employed by the Pope to take away the queen's life by poisoned perfumes—a lying invention, which might probably be turned to some account. Later on he was sent to the Court of some German Protestant prince, to keep both his eyes open and ever to prick up his ears ; and in 1589 having, as he admitted, "received much comfort" from Lord Burghley's "fatherly speeches," and a promise of some office, never fulfilled, went off to one of the Swiss Cantons "to spend the remainder of his wretched days."—*State Papers, Domestic, Elizabeth,* vol. ccxxii. 77, 92, A.D. 1589, and vol. ccxxiii. I.

unable to effect their purpose.   And well is it, perhaps, that such was their failure, for the pangs of a sin-sick soul and tortured conscience throughout weary years were far keener than the internal pains of poison or the sharpness of polished steel.   For such sins against God Almighty, truth and justice, as the queen had committed during her long reign, she righteously deserved to suffer.   What mental sufferings she endured in her later miserable years and latest hours none can either know or tell.

In the autumn of 1588, no less than nine priests and ten laymen were executed, either for denying the queen's spiritual supremacy, or under one of the recent Acts against the Old Religion already alluded to.   The same sanguinary cruelties so shocking to contemplate and so revolting to describe, were undergone by all.[1]   And this, so soon after those who supported the Old Religion had shown their loyalty when the *Armada* was expected.

On the other side persecution went on apace.[2]   A certain ignorant Protestant, of low birth, William Hackett, created a considerable stir in the spring of the year 1591 by his extreme developments.   He had long been "an acceptable preacher" to many, and had acted in alliance with two eloquent but fanatical Puritans in the ranks of gentlepeople, named Coppinger and Arthington, who together wandered about the country, delivering very excitable and stirring addresses.   Hackett, who had previously maintained that the spirit of St. John the Baptist

---

[1] I borrow the following from a learned and independent writer :— "Scarcely a year passed by without these dreadful massacres, the details of which are more revolting and shameful than those who have not given their attention to the subject, or read the accounts written down at the time, could be readily brought to believe.   For ten years the butchery had been kept up remorselessly.   The victims, as a rule, were not hung by the neck till they were dead, but cut down while they were alive and conscious, then thrown upon their backs, the executioner's knife was plunged into their bowels, and the entrails and heart tossed into a cauldron of water which stood hard by.   In more than one instance the victim in his agony and despair struggled with the hangman, but it was only for a moment.   In some cases the crowd shouted out to the sheriff to 'let him hang.'   Sometimes a condemned man begged as a special grace that he 'might not be bowelled ere he was dead.'   The rabble looked on terror-struck ; but such scenes could not but brutalise them.   The appetite for blood is a strange passion, and once yielded to is prone to exercise a horrible fascination on some minds."—*One Generation of a Norfolk House*," by A. Jessopp, D.D., 2nd edition, p. 228. London, 1879.

[2] "Jan. ultimo—Six fond persons, Colman, Bolton, Evans, Hallegam, Benson, and Gates, mislyking of the service of the Church, committed to the Flete."—*Burghley State Papers*, W. Murdin, p. 764. London, 1759.

was guiding him, now styled himself "the Messiah," Coppinger assumed the office of "Prophet of Mercy," as he termed himself, Arthington that of "Prophet of Judgment." Their varied assertions and incoherent ravings were even more violent than the language of the official and authoritative *Homilies*. They boldly proposed to overturn the new religious system of the queen once for all ; and in the strongest and strangest language dealt out condemnation to all Her Majesty's bishops. Crowds followed them, and hung upon their words. On one occasion at Charing Cross, the excitement they caused threatened to produce a serious riot. At Lincoln a cruel and ignominious flogging at the cart's tail had only deepened Hackett's reforming zeal. Of Queen Elizabeth's loose morals, these Protestant prophets spoke with the greatest plainness ; while, on one occasion, Hackett, who followed Knox in his dislike of a woman having been made the Governess of a Church, deliberately defaced with a steel bodkin a portrait of Her Majesty and her Royal arms. Upon this he was at once arrested, charged with treason, tried, and hung in Cheapside.[1] Coppinger, poor wretch! was imprisoned, and there starved to death. Arthington recanted his errors and obtained a pardon.

Soon afterwards fresh enactments were passed against these Puritans.[2] In the thirty-fifth year of the queen's reign,—though axe and halter, torture-men,[3] and human butchers had been so constantly in requisition for Catholics, more work of the same kind must be done, and further legal powers secured. Grim and

---

[1] "1591, July 28th, one Hackett, a fanaticall sectary, hanged in Cheapsyde."—*Burghley State Papers*, p. 797. London, 1759.

[2] "They appealed to the public with all the bitterness of disappointed zeal ; and the friends of the Establishment were surprised and alarmed by a succession of hostile and popular pamphlets. The titles of these writings were quaint, their language declamatory and scurrilous, their object being to bring the hierarchy into discredit and contempt. But the queen threw over the clergy the shield of her protection. She issued a severe proclamation against the authors, publishers, and possessors of seditious libels, and the Court of the Star Chamber restrained the exercise of the art of printing to the metropolis and the two universities, to a single press in each of these, and to a certain number in London, with a prohibit to print, sell, bind, or stitch any work which had not previously obtained the approbation of the bishop or archbishop. Yet in defiance of these regulations, copies of the more obnoxious publications were multiplied and circulated through every part of the kingdom. They issued from an ambulatory press, which was secretly conveyed from house to house, and from county to county."—*History of England*, by John Lingard, D.D., vol. vi. p. 260. Dublin, Duffy and Sons, 1874.

[3] Topcliffe and Young were authorised to use "such torture as is usual for the better understanding of the truth."—*Domestic State Papers, Elizabeth*, vol. ccxxx. 57.

gaunt hanging-posts were too few and far between.   Representations of religious facts by way-side slope and on village-green,—
of the Incarnation, by figures of Our Lady and her Divine Child ;
of the Passion and Death of Our Blessed Saviour, by the Crucifix,
—had long ago been smashed, mutilated, or burnt.   In their
place, as tokens of the increased happiness and contentment of
the people, let more gibbets be erected, and new ropes woven.
An Act was, therefore, passed to "restrain the queen's subjects
in obedience," as it was termed.   She who herself was disobedient to the Patriarch of Christendom, found in turn that
others were disobedient to her.   Her only method by which to
influence the reason, conscience, and will of those under her, was
an Act of Parliament, with the glorious gibbet and efficient
strangling-rope set forth in its latest clause.   All persons, therefore, who dared to dispute the queen's ecclesiastical and
spiritual authority ; all who abstained from going to church ; all
who attended "any assemblies, conventicles, or meetings, under
colour or pretence of any exercise of religion," were to be put
into prison and kept there until they conformed.   If in the
course of three months they could not, or would not, make up
their minds to do this, they were at once to abjure the realm.
If, furthermore, they refused to depart, or dared to return and
show their faces after their abjuration, they were to be at once
"strung up."[1]   All these enactments were for the Puritans.

More suffering, however, was also in store and legalised for
those of the old faith.   Another Act[2] was at the same passed
against "Popish recusants."   Such were to repair to their own
homes and not to travel five miles therefrom.   If they did not
possess sufficient goods to satisfy the monthly fine of twenty
pounds for non-attendance at their parish church, they too were
to abjure the realm ; and if they refused or hesitated to do this,
they were to suffer as felons.   A previous statute had compelled
those abroad to return home, or else to endure the loss of their
goods.[3]

[1] Act 35 Eliz. c. i.
[2] *Ibid.* c. ii.
[3] Grant to Dr. Gyfford, one of Her Majesty's physicians, of the goods of
Germane Poole, *forfeited by reason of his continuance beyond the seas contrary
to statute."—State Papers, Domestic, Elizabeth*, vol. ccxxxiv. 70.
From the Council the following orders were despatched to the authorities
at York :—"To have a vigilant eye and regard to such as be harbourers and
maintainers of any priests, schoolmasters, or other persons, not yet confirmed
or reformed ; or such as have been of late beyond the seas and are returned,
and be no favorers of the godly and Christian religion now established and
professed ; and that you do certify their names, qualities, and dwelling-
places, or to whose houses and places they do resort or have access."—

The only method of avoiding these fines, penalties, and punishments,[1] was to make a formal confession, in which each person, whether Catholic or Protestant, was to acknowledge (the appointed words are substantially given) that he had grievously offended God in contemning Her Majesty's godly and lawful government and spiritual authority by absenting himself from church, and from hearing divine service and sermons, contrary to the godly laws and statutes of this realm ; that he acknowledged and *testified in his conscience* that neither the Bishop of Rome nor any other person hath or ought to have any power or authority over Her Majesty or within any of Her Majesty's realms and dominions. In the Protestant form of recantation, the sentence concerning the Bishop of Rome was omitted.

Before some of the effects of these new enactments are given in detail, a brief reference must be made to the case of one, distinguished above all the rest of the sufferers for his noble birth and high rank. The treatment of Philip seventeenth Earl of Arundel, godson of King Philip of Spain, was simply unqueenly and inhuman. Early in his career he had declined to carry the sword of state before the queen to chapel, which offended Her Majesty deeply. Soon afterwards, with unregal meanness, she sent Lord Hunsdon and Walsingham to "draw him out" as regards religion, artfully concealing herself with Lord Leicester in order to overhear the conversation. For this, in which he laughed at the she-supremacy existing, he in due course suffered persecution. He had long been condemned to pay a heavy fine as a recusant, and had been imprisoned for some years,[2] later with some relaxation. When the *Armada* was expected, however, he was watched carefully. Two fellow-prisoners, Esquire William Shelley and Sir Thomas Gerard, examined separately, were terrified into asserting that Lord Arundel had on a certain occasion induced an old priest to say mass for the success of the Spanish invasion ; but this assertion had only

"Articles sent to the Justices of the Peace within the City of York," 18° Junii, 20° Eliz.

[1] That these were sternly inflicted is clear from the following :—"On Friday last Sir Richard Knightley, Hooles of Coventry, Wigsome and his wife, of Warwick, were condemned in the Star Chamber, as furtherers of the book called *Martin Mar Prelate*, to pay, the first two thousand pounds, the second one thousand marks, the third five hundred, the fourth one hundred, and to be imprisoned during the Queen's pleasure."—Letter of Sir H. Lee to Lord Shrewsbury, dated Feb. 17, 1590.

[2] See *State Papers, Domestic, Elizabeth*, vol. ccxxv. 41, ccxxxi. 48. In a letter to Lord Burghley from the Tower, Lord Arundel declares that he "is full of all misery and void almost of any comfort." 30th of March, 1590.

been secured by a threat of torture and death, and the witnesses who had made it refused to face the Earl when put upon his trial before his peers.   Burghley on this occasion cross-examined Lord Arundel with art and skill; but it is clear, from a consideration of the evidence, that the latter had simply lifted up his prayers to Heaven for himself and his companions, all threatened with assassination, and that the charges were certainly not proven. At this trial, with remarkable dignity and power, he recounted the fatal ends of his ancestors.   His great-grandfather had been condemned without being heard, his grandfather had been beheaded for light and trivial matters, and his father — having been circumvented by his enemies—never bare any hostile mind against either queen or country.   After an hour's debate, however, the peers found Arundel guilty, and sentence of death was pronounced.   His condemnation was an act of policy, and an outrage both on justice and truth.   It should be noted that the charge on which alone he was unanimously convicted was that of having been reconciled to the faith of his forefathers.   In this alone his offence consisted.   No charge of treason was proved.

He made a request of the queen by letter to be allowed to see his wife, and the little boy, then five years old, who had been born during his captivity, and whom he had consequently never even seen.   But to this letter no answer was returned.

He was thus persecuted, as his father, the eighteenth earl of that name, had been before him, firstly because he was feared. For many of the old religion turned towards his family, hoping that some member of it might head a party against the detestable and cruel policy of those who for so long a time had secured the upper hand.   He was also persecuted because he had evidently declined to be the means of satisfying the unbridled lusts of the queen, who greatly admired his handsome person.   Her repulsive advances and nasty proposals were disgusting and revolting to a Christian nobleman of honour.   "He seems to have given some deep but secret offence, which, though it was never divulged, could never be forgotten," is the quiet but forcible remark of a great historian.   The queen, therefore, did not order his execution; for Sir Christopher Hatton[1] had strongly urged

[1] "There cannot be a doubt that he [Sir Christopher Hatton] was a party with his colleagues Burghley, Leicester, and Walsingham, to many questionable and unjustifiable proceedings, yet to his honour it must be recorded that we find him at times employing his authority to shield the poor and friendless from oppression, and to mitigate the severity of the law in favour of recusants under prosecution for their religion before the Ecclesiastical Commission."— *History of England*, by J. Lingard, D.D., vol. vi. p. 242. Dublin, 1874.

her not to do so. But she never let the poor prisoner know of her resolve, and, with a delicate refinement of cruelty, kept the axe, as it were, suspended over his head for nearly seven weary years. He daily looked for the reading of the death-warrant, and the end of his time of probation. She had already taken the life of his noble father by a legal murder. She, of course, had the power to repeat the sin in his case. He lay, therefore, absolutely and abjectly at her mercy, very ill-treated by the Lieutenant of the Tower.[1] Of this he feelingly complained in a letter to that functionary, which still exists,—a touching appeal from one who was sorely cast down. At length, in the year 1595, he was artfully poisoned. After eating some teal, he became frightfully contorted in face, and was in an agony of pain. His physician,[2] Dr. Martin, endeavoured to afford relief; but, after great suffering, he died within two months, in the eleventh year of his imprisonment. His name, as drawn by himself, may still be traced over the fire-place in the Beauchamp Tower. He was a most devout and saintly nobleman, enduring his severities with patience; worthy of his religion, lineage, and rank; and so merited the repose and bliss of a better world.

The Chaplain of the Tower was present at the Earl's funeral, whose elm coffin was certainly cheap and inexpensive. But the service read was not that of the Prayer Book, but one of the chaplain's own composing. It began with an exhortation. Exhortations in those days were invariably both popular and lengthy, affording scope for uncharitable rhetoric on the part of the author; and the chaplain's was no exception to the rule. As God had lain this peer's honour in the dust, as was asserted; so, as the Scriptures had recorded that it was right to bury even Jezebel, it could not be wrong to inter the Earl. For his lordship's death, God was praised in the words of the Song of Deborah, and thanked because in His mercy He had taken the Earl out of the world. Self-righteousness, scurrility of language, and bad taste, as we see, made up for the loss of the Christian graces of faith and charity.

---

[1] The Earl, shortly before his death, thus addressed the Lieutenant of the Tower:—"You must think that when a prisoner comes hither, that he bringeth enough sorrow with him. Do not, therefore, add affliction to affliction. There is no man, whosoever he may be, who thinkest that he standeth surely, but may very soon fall. It is inhuman to tread on one whom Misfortune hath cast down. God hath that man who is void of mercy in great detestation. Your commission is only to keep with safety, not to kill by severity."—*Life of Philip Howard in loco.*

[2] "Dr. Marten, Lord Arundel's doctor, has escaped to Dunkirk."—*State Papers, Domestic, Elizabeth,* vol. ccxxxiv. 48.

T

The queen with all her heart hated the Countess,[1] who became a constant victim of Her Majesty's venomous rancour. Throughout the last part of the Earl's imprisonment, when he daily expected death, he was never once allowed to see his wife, his children, or any of his relations. After his death, the pitiful spite of this wrinkled and feeble specimen of a Tudor woman who ruled, was as keen as ever. The Countess was confined to her residence, never even allowed to go to London for her physician's advice without first securing a formal warrant; and, whenever the queen came to London, the Countess was first ordered to quit it. Could tyranny any further go? Could royal malice be more intensified? Could feminine spite be more malignant or despicable?

The case of Esquire Edward Sulyard of Weatherdon, in Suffolk, is also specially noteworthy. He was a Roman Catholic, and wholly unable to pay the heavy fines of twenty pounds every lunar month which had been imposed. This was certified to the authorities, as also his readiness to offer forty pounds a year instead—all that his estate could afford. It seems uncertain whether his offer was accepted. Anyhow Sir Francis Walsingham forbade his being further molested. Out of one thousand three hundred and eighty pounds then, by accumulation, due, the poor gentleman had paid no less than five hundred and forty pounds, leaving eight hundred and forty pounds unpaid. For the payment of these arrears within three years, he was, however, required to obtain two sureties, whom he found in his cousin Esquire Edward Sulyard of Fenning, and in his friend and ally Esquire Thomas Tyrrell. On the approach of the *Armada*, notwithstanding that he had publicly signed a declaration that Elizabeth was his lawful Sovereign, and that he would defend her against all foreign foes, he was at once imprisoned. Soon afterwards he obtained leave to visit his wrecked and impoverished estate for a short time; on condition that he was afterwards confined, at his own cost, in a private house. He was further bound in a bond of two thousand pounds not to depart from it. In 1591 he obtained some liberty. Under the same penalty he pledged himself, firstly, not to go beyond six miles from his place of confinement; and, secondly, to present himself before the Council at ten days' notice, whenever he

---

[1] This lady, Anne, an admirable woman and no mean poetess, was the sister and co-heiress of Thomas, Lord Dacre of Gillisland. She survived her unfortunate husband until the year 1630. Her son Thomas, the twentieth Earl of Arundel, was one of the most distinguished noblemen that England ever owned. His collection of antiquities is possibly unique.

should receive it.   From that period to the death of the queen,
twelve years afterwards, he was in a constant state of imprisonment, sometimes in the Castle of Ely and sometimes in his own
house ; during which time he was often compelled to " lend "
money—as it was termed—to the queen, which, of course, was
never repaid ; and often to equip a trooper at his own sole cost,
for the Queen's Majesty's service. [1]

The Towneleys of Lancashire, some of the Hampdens in
Bucks, [2] the Bellamys of Harrow-on-the-Hill, the Lords Paget of
West Drayton, and others, were sorely harried and punished.
Guiltless of any offence but that of declining to attend a worship
contrary to their conscience, they were constantly fined and
imprisoned, and their property stolen.   Of one of the Towneley
family there is a picture still remaining in their ancient and
interesting mansion at Towneley, — a certain John of that
honoured name,—under which the following record of his long
and patient sufferings may still be read :—

> "THIS JOHN, ABOUT THE SIXTH OR SEVENTH YEAR OF
> HER MAJESTY'S REIGN THAT NOW IS, FOR PROFESSING THE
> APOSTOLICK ROMAN CATHOLIC FFAITH WAS IMPRISONED
> FIRST AT CHESTER CASTLE ; THEN SENT TO THE MAR-
> SHALSEA ; THEN TO YORK CASTLE ; THEN TO THE
> BLOCKHOUSES IN HULL ; THEN TO THE GATEHOUSE IN
> WESTMINSTER ; THEN TO MANCHESTER ; THEN TO
> BROUGHTON IN OXFORDSHIRE : THEN TWICE TO ELY IN
> CAMBRIDGESHIRE ; AND SO NOW, SEVENTY-THREE YEARS
> OLD, AND BLIND, IS BOUND TO APPEAR AND KEEP WITHIN
> FIVE MILES OF TOWNELEY HIS HOUSE.   WHO HATH
> SINCE THE STATUTE OF THE TWENTY-THIRD PAID INTO
> THE EXCHEQUER TWENTY POUNDS A MONTH, AND DOTH

[1] Even a poor lady of Buckinghamshire, Mistress Avicia Lee, a "recusant,"
was ordered through Robert Dormer, Sheriff of the county, to furnish a
light horseman for the queen's service at her own sole cost ; having already
for several years paid twenty pounds a month as a fine for not giving up her
religion ; and so had been brought almost to ruin.   The delivery of this order
was notified to the Council from Marlow, in 1585.   Within a few months she
outwardly conformed and went to her parish church, of which a testimonial
of conformity from the minister was then transmitted to London from Great
Missenden, dated March 19, 1586.   But like many others, though an
occasional conformist, she secretly practised the old religion, and died in the
faith and fear of God.—*State Papers, Domestic, Elizabeth*, vol. clxxxiii. 32, vol.
clxxxiii. 32 ; Author's MSS. and Excerpts ; Buckinghamshire Wills.

[2] An inventory was taken of the books and other Popish relics found in
the house of Mistress Hampden, of Stoke, in the county of Buckingham, and
carried away from thence by Mr. Paul Wentworth.—*State Papers, Domestic,
Elizabeth*, vol. clxviii. No. 47, Jan. 26, 1584.

STILL; SO THAT THERE IS PAID ALREADY ABOVE FFIVE
THOUSAND POUNDS, AN. DNI. ONE THOUSAND SIX HUN-
DRED AND ONE. JOHN TOWNLEY OF TOWNLEY IN LAN-
CASHIRE."

When such records of persecution meet the gaze, they cannot
but cause a blush on the cheek of all who have any regard for
their country's fair fame; and a feeling of the heartiest respect
for those who so bravely endured and patiently suffered.

But the case of Esquire Thomas Pounde of Belmont[1] is
even more noteworthy, and, because of the facts it lays bare
and the lessons it teaches, deserves to be recounted at some
length. Born on May 29th, 1539, he was the son of William
Pounde, Esquire, a wealthy country gentleman of Hampshire,
by Anne Wriothesley, sister of Thomas, Earl of Southampton.
His early years had been spent at the College of Our Blessed
Lady of Winchester, where he patiently studied, preparing
himself for forensic labours and legal responsibilities. When of
age, in form and figure he was tall, handsome, and graceful.
His features were regular and well-formed. His strength was
great, and he excelled in all gymnastic exercises, and such
sports as the country gentlemen of that period indulged in.
His mental capacities were considerable. Brave, courteous, of
remarkably polished manners, eloquent in speech (his voice
being sweet and musical), and of ready wit, he was always
perfectly self-possessed and quite at ease in the company of his
equals and superiors. As a scholar his abilities were considerable. He was a poet of no mean order, as existing specimens
prove. He wrote Latin prose with singular grace and purity,
and artfully penned many verses in that language of much
vigour and sweetness. On one occasion, when the queen was
received at Winchester College, Pounde recited, amid great
applause, a complimentary ode, which he himself had composed
in honour of Her Majesty.

He had always theoretically accepted the faith of his fathers,
and looked upon the new religion with something like contempt; but he had grown indifferent when, as a youth, he
became attached to the Court—one of the most lax, dissolute,
and irreligious of any in Europe—and was ready and willing to

[1] The authorities for the above narrative are Father Bartoli's *Istoria S. J.
d'Inghilterra*, ed. 1825; *The Rambler*, vol. ii. for 1857; *State Papers,
Domestic, Elizabeth*, vol. clix. 36, vol. cc. 59, vol. cci. 53, vol. clxxviii. 74,
vol. cxc. 44, vol. cxcv. 32 and 34, vol. cciii. 20, vol. cxcv. 115, and also
State Papers, Domestic, Elizabeth, A.D. 1582, No. 58, containing some of
Pounde's MSS.—a long poem, in two parts, no doubt intercepted by some
spy.

swim with the tide; so that subsequently he conformed outwardly to that form of misbelief and worship then popular. When he ceased to practise the old faith, he soon became indifferent and ungodly — tinctured by the indifference or wickedness of those around.

During the octave of Christmas 1569, the Court held high festival. The three masses for the Feast of the Nativity had been then abolished for more than ten years. Morning service, consisting of prayers, psalms, canticles, and collects, took their place. But few cared to attend these. A paganism in taste had long permeated all the Christmas festivities. Interludes, plays, masques, concerts, and dances took place day by day. The religious element, now thoroughly unpopular, had been cast out in the observance of Christmas; and few there were who did not far prefer the secular games, so exciting, to the dreary dissertations of the more fanatical sermon - mongers. Pounde had not only helped to compose masques, but, at at Kenilworth Castle, five years previously, had taken part in acting them. On this occasion, Lord Leicester being the host, they were arranged and carried out with unusual magnificence.

The flower of the nobility were there. Its youth and its beauty were gathered to do honour to the queen. Money had been spent in profusion by all those who arranged the entertainments; much of which of right belonged to the ancient Church, its abbeys and bishoprics [1]—for the more money they thus squandered, the better was the queen pleased.

An occurrence then took place, which changed the course of Pounde's life. It occurred thus:—

He was a remarkable dancer, and combining good looks, skill, and a most graceful figure, greatly attracted the queen. In one dance he so outstripped himself in grace and agility, that at its close Her Majesty seized him by the hand, which, with smiles and leers, she most approvingly squeezed; and then snatching Lord Leicester's velvet cap, placed it on Pounde's head, whom she thought, after his violent exertions, might otherwise catch cold. The queen was so delighted at his performance, that she commanded its immediate repetition. No greater compliment could have been paid him.

He repeated it in part, when, all of a sudden, becoming giddy and losing his balance, he stumbled, staggered, and fell close

[1] "1588, July. A grant to the Earl of Leicester of seven hundred pounds lands, whereof five hundred pounds to be resumed from bishopricks and two hundred pounds of attaynted lands."—*Burghley State Papers*, p. 788. Edited by W. Murdin. London, 1759.

to the queen's feet. The recent applause was soon followed by peals of laughter from all sides, and by shouts of derision.

Upon this the queen contemptuously kicked him with her foot, and with marked sarcasm — parodying the formula of making a knight—exclaimed, " Rise, Sir Ox," and then, turning away, joined the Court in laughing at what was mistakenly deemed his awkwardness.

He rose promptly, bent his knee to Her Majesty, and was heard to exclaim, with downcast eyes, " *Sic transit gloria mundi.*" He had been touched to the quick. Hurrying from the royal presence, he left the Court for ever, retiring to his paternal mansion at Belmont, and burying himself for days in solitude. There he blamed himself for the thirty years of past life, and made the firmest resolutions of future amendment. He was soon reconciled to the ancient faith, making restitution and doing severe penances for his lapse. He then left his paternal home, and gave himself up to solitude,—to prayer, self-denial, and mortification. He likewise bound himself by a vow to practise perpetual chastity, and resolved, after seven years of probation, to offer himself for the priesthood. He was likewise most earnest in making converts, and desired to become a member of the Society of Jesus. Betrayed by one of these converts, however, an insincere and false friend, he was taken before Sandys, Bishop of London, who interrogated him as to his religion, and then, in the year 1574, put him into prison. He was charged with no crime whatsoever, with no violation of the laws, and no accusation was made against him. He was nevertheless imprisoned on the strength of recent Parliamentary enactments, and frequently tortured with the utmost cruelty.

He thus suffered, firstly, because he had enjoined upon his co-religionists at Winchester and elsewhere, that they should steadily refuse "the Supper" of the ministers, and decline even to enter the desecrated churches ; and, secondly, because he was known to have been about to leave England without a licence.

Sandys came to him in prison and distinctly offered him his liberty, if he would but once attend the new services and hear a sermon. But he civilly and calmly answered—" If I cannot recover my liberty otherwise than by offending God, I am firmly resolved that my soul shall rather be torn from my body, than that this flesh shall go forth out of prison on such terms." [1]

[1] He is the only son and heir of his father, a Catholic, but his mother, being still alive, as yet enjoys the paternal mansion and estates which fell to him at his father's death. He is thirty-eight years of age, of a tall and

For this bold and unambiguous reply, evidencing his true nobility of character, he was retained in confinement for six months longer; but subsequently liberated on bail at the intervention of his relation, Lord Southampton. Thus for awhile Pounde was at liberty.

Hereupon he retired to his paternal house in Hampshire, where his widowed mother resided; but Robert Horne, Bishop of Winchester, irritated at his religious zeal and controversial acuteness, by which he secured many adherents; and terribly annoyed at his skill in public dispute and his brave bearing, handed him over with some others to the secular arm, as an obstinate and dangerous recusant. He was soon committed to the local prison, but subsequently sent to London and lodged in the Marshalsea.[1]

handsome figure, a flowing beard, and a pleasing countenance. In the prison he dresses most handsomely, thinking thus to inspire Catholics with greater courage, and also to conciliate the authorities. He has not yet made his philosophy, but is well up in his humanities, and wonderfully devoted to the study of the holy Fathers. He is eloquent in his native tongue, and equally fluent in speaking and writing, and much practised in the art of exhortation and persuasion. . . . . . For the greater part of the time I lived with him, I mention only what I have myself witnessed, he used to impose severe austerities upon himself, the ground being his miserable bed; he spent one hour at midnight in prayer, with great spiritual gust, and followed this by spiritual reading at daybreak. He would then resume his meditation for two, three, or four hours, and spend the rest of the day in reading the holy Fathers, giving two or three hours to prayer again in the evening. The heretics reported him as a superstitious fool or a madman: his domestics, and even some of his friends, thought the same of him, saying that he was imprudently severe against himself. But all this he courageously disregarded, and persevered in his manner of life, till they were forced to change their reproaches into admiration."—*Letter from Thomas Stephens*, dated 4th Nov. 1578, Public Record Office, Brussels.

[1] *State Papers, Domestic, Elizabeth*, vol. cxl. 40.—"He remanded Pounde offhand from the Marshalsea, London, to be immured in a distant prison. This was Stortford, or Bishops' Stortford, Castle, Herts, thirty miles from London, on the confines of Essex, a lonely place well chosen for his purpose. Pounde was thrust into a cell, a few feet under the ground, in which was perpetual night, no ray of the sun nor any gleam of light ever entering there whereby to distinguish between day and night. No one was allowed to visit him, for wherever this had been permitted, he had gained many to the Catholic faith. The bare and dirty ground was his bed, a pair of heavy fetters was put on his legs, and handcuffs on his wrists, with chains attached, besides many other sufferings added by his brutal gaoler. As the blacksmith was about to rivet the shackles upon his legs, Thomas endeavoured to kiss them, whereupon the smith inhumanly struck him with them on the head, and drew blood; when, with an undisturbed countenance, he exclaimed, 'Would that blood might here flow from the inmost veins of my heart for the cause for which I suffer!' The blacksmith was astonished at his fervour and patience under so great and so unprovoked an injury. And it pleased God, in reward for the merit of his patience, to give Mr. Pounde that soul, moving

The following paragraph from a contemporary letter exactly describes how this came to pass :—

"When before the bishop and a great assembly of spectators, he rendered so brilliant an account of his faith in the presence of them all, and so severely rebuked the bishop himself, that the latter was unable for very rage and confusion to say a word in reply. . . . After this they were all given into separate custody, and Mr. Pounde was thrust into the prison of the common thieves. But when the bishop saw that many were impressed by his example, and specially by his fastings and prayers, being things deemed simply impossibilities amongst them, he removed him from his diocese, as if he were a pest, and remanded him to London, where to this day he perseveres in prison to the great consolation and edification of many."[1]

Later on, upon a certain occasion, the renowned Father Campion had given to Pounde a MS. copy of his celebrated "Challenge,"[2] which, on reading again and again, he became so greatly impressed by the force of its arguments and its general power and point, that he communicated it to a Catholic neighbour, Benjamin Tichbourne; and a copy having been found by the Sheriff of Wiltshire, and sent up to the Privy Council, Watson, Bishop of Winchester, and others feared its effect so greatly, that no stone was left unturned to punish all who had aided in its distribution or publication.

This poor gentleman's life, in truth, was a continual martyrdom. For more than thirty years he was securely kept in prison, and for long periods in complete solitary confinement, enduring continuous tortures. After being for one year in Newgate, he had been removed to the Marshalsea;[3] then to Bishop's Stortford;[4] then to the Tower; then to the Compter on the south

the smith to demand of him whence he possessed so great confidence that he was of the true religion, seeing that in England 'Papist' and 'reprobate' were synonymous terms. The prisoner gave the man such strong reasons and convincing proofs, that he was vanquished and afterwards became a Catholic, in punishment for which act he was cast into prison, where he died piously in chains."—*Life of Thomas Pounde, of Belmont*, by Henry Foley, in *Records of the English Province*, vol. iii. pp. 592-593, to which the author is greatly indebted for several facts and much information.

[1] Letter from Thomas Stephens, dated 4th November 1578. Original, in Latin, in the Public Record Office, Brussels.

[2] *State Papers, Domestic, Elizabeth*, vol. cxlii. 20.

[3] "He is buried in a prison under-ground, totally dark and gloomy; having no other light than that of an oil lamp. . . . . He sleeps for the most part of the night on the damp ground ; bound sometimes with one, two, and often with three iron fetters."—*Letter from Father Parsons to the Father General*, given in Bartoli's *Inghilterra*, lib. i. cap. xvii. 134.

[4] When Pounde was at Bishop's Stortford, Norton, the rack-master visited

side of the Thames; thence to Wisbeach Castle, where for ten years he dwelt with many priests and laymen. In 1597 he was again sent to the Tower,—where altogether he had been confined for ten years,—subsequently to the City Compter; after that to the White Lion, then to the Gate House at Westminster; subsequently to the Fleet Prison, and lastly to Framlingham.

Having thus suffered imprisonment for the long period of years already mentioned; having, moreover, paid the value of more than two-thirds of the whole of his property into the Royal Exchequer in fines for recusancy;[1] being consequently harassed by debt, and driven by sheer necessity to do so, upon Elizabeth's death, he appealed to King James I., stating at length, in writing, some of the horrible cruelties which had been practised on so many of his Catholic friends and neighbours[2] because of their religion. He was thoroughly out-spoken and plain-spoken, and his words impressed the king greatly. His Majesty speedily referred the petition to the judges, who tried the case in the Star Chamber. There he defended himself most earnestly and adroitly, with consummate ability and remarkable boldness. From his own truly Christian standing-point, setting forth the legal cruelties constantly practised, he proved the full truth of the facts in his petition. The Attorney-General, however, informed the Court that any man who disparaged and disobeyed

him, and going back to Sir F. Walsingham, reported that he was a religious lunatic, and that Bedlam would be his most suitable place of residence. It may not be uninteresting to notice that this Norton's own wife, being possessed of an evil spirit, died in a state of violent madness.—*Document, State Paper Office*, dated March 27, 1582. Pounde himself thus described his state to a former friend and ally at Court :—"O God, Sir Christopher! I wolde you saw the spectacle of it, what a place I am brought into here. It is nothing but a large vast room, cold water, bare walls, nor windows, but loupholes too high too look out at ; nor bed, nor bedsteade, nor place very fit for any."—*Letter from Pounde to Sir Christopher Hatton*, dated 18th of September 1580.

[1] The late Mr. Richard Simpson, in *The Rambler*, for 1857, pointed out that Esquire Pounde once asserted to the Bishop of Winchester that he had paid upwards of four thousand pounds in fines alone rather than go to church for the new service and abandon his religion. "Multiply that sum by twelve," remarks Mr. Simpson, so as to calculate this amount by the value of money in this day, "and we shall have the present equivalent of the cost of Catholicity to an English gentleman of the sixteenth century."

[2] Bishop Cowper of Winchester wrote to Sir F. Walsingham, on Dec. 10th, 1585, against any favour being shown to the wife of one Mr. Pitts, of Alton, in Hampshire, committed to the Clink, who was a very obstinate person and natural sister to Nicholas Sander the traitor. *Her return to Winchester*, as the Bishop maintains, *would do more harm than ten sermons would do good.* "No man," he remarks, "whose wife is a recusant is sound himself."—*State Papers, Domestic, Elizabeth*, vol. clxxxv. 17.

the laws recently passed against the Patriarch of the West and
the Primate of Christendom, was plainly guilty of high treason.
Whosoever, he maintained, acknowledges the Primacy and Jurisdiction of the See Apostolic—obviously the case with Pounde—
makes the English sovereign a sovereign only by a very uncertain
tenure and himself an enemy and traitor to his king and country.
Priests who do so are rather apostates than apostles, adding
that a Gracchus should not complain of sedition, nor people of
the old but discarded religion, like this disobedient and self-
willed ecclesiastical layman, of severity.   Pounde was consequently condemned, for the Court had been duly and carefully
packed.   He was fined five thousand pounds and ordered to be
exposed in the pillory in three different places.

Subsequently, when the king had resolved to banish all priests,
His Majesty determined on releasing the laity in prison.   Pounde
was then permitted to go out, and received in addition a special
licence to go abroad.   But, because of old age and infirmity, he
retired to his old home, by that time desolate, disorganised, and
miserably dilapidated.

Since his retirement from Court, he had always lived a life of
singular devotion, recollectedness, and self-denial.   He took
food only once a day, until old age obliged him to modify this
rule.   From day to day he saw clearly that the next might be
his last.   He was therefore always most vigilant.   No fear of
death, however, ever prevented him from expressing openly his
religious belief, or from doing all that lay in his power to warn
people against the innovators and their dangerous principles.
For this he became ever liable to the gross, cruel, and disgusting
punishment for high treason.   But he was in no state of fear.
The hanging-post, the butcher's knife, and the caldron of boiling
pitch had no terrors for him.   The enemies of God might do
their worst.   They could but torture and mangle his body.   His
faith was keen and firm.   His feet were planted on a Rock.   He
constantly prayed, studied the Catholic Fathers with care and
attention, and wrote some useful and pertinent treatises against
existing errors.   In prison or out of prison he was always devot-
ing himself to building up the weak and wavering in the faith.
His calm demeanour under great trials, and his courageous but
mildly-spoken and musical words in the presence of heretics and
schismatics, greatly strengthened those who stood in fear of consequences.   For as to himself, he was ever prepared to do what
was right and true, rather than that which was politic and expedient; while he confidently left all consequences and results, of
what kind soever, in the hands of God.   The new religion—for

such in truth it was—not only had no charms for him, but was positively repulsive. Both in ordinary conversation and in careful writing he plainly and fearlessly maintained that Queen Elizabeth was not only not the head and ruler of the true old Church in England, but that she had not the shadow or a shred of spiritual jurisdiction, above any other woman, or over anyone,—which was of course the case. Over the new community, which had been made by Parliament, confined within the natural boundary of Her Majesty's dominions, she was of course wholly and truly supreme; and, as far as Parliament could make her so, she was, and was always recognised as, the Supreme Governess or Head of this newly-organised Church of England. The contrast between it, however, and the old Church was almost as great as contrast could be. The two institutions were remarkably dissimilar, as all could see, and as both sides admitted. Where authority had been intentionally cast out from a Christian state, disorder, discord, and chaos, must ere long come in like a flood. This, as we know, was too soon abundantly the case.

Pounde lived to die in the very same room of his old Hampshire home in which, seventy-six years before, he had first seen the light of day, "My dear and most-loved country," he exclaimed on his death-bed, "may God soon convert thee out of this wretched and pitiful captivity of schism, confusion, and heresy!" Its awful and Babel-like state was constantly before him, even to the end. His soul passed to the particular judgment-seat when the March winds were wild and keen, and when the crocus shot up its saffron leaves, and the snow-drop told of the resurrection of the dead. But the spring sunshine, falling through the pictured panes of Belmont, lit up the oaken room where, with a crucifix on his breast, he lay shrouded and coffined, waiting for a final resting-place in the neighbouring churchyard; and where a few devoted relatives, weeping over their loss, commended his righteous soul to the keeping of a merciful Creator, God the Trinity; and asked the blessed aid and intercession of the angels and saints in white near and about the throne, that the departed might soon enjoy eternal peace, and live in the light which never grows dim.

Of another somewhat similar case of persecution, which ended even more painfully and most sadly, Father Grene[1] has left on record the following brief account :—

"I remember about fifteen or sixteen years ago there was one Mr. Horsley, a gentleman of the North, as I have heard. . . . He was taken, brought to York, before the Council, who sent

[1] Father Grene's MSS. in the English College at Rome, vol. F.

him about nine of the clock in the night to the castle, where he had double irons laid on him, and took them merrily.   The next morning the Council sent for him and committed him to the Bishop's Prison, or Peter Prison, and laid irons on him ; and there straitly and cruelly he was used, for almost none could learn where he was committed till he was sent back again to Hull, and there monstrously abused ; for he was there arraigned and condemned to have his ears cut off, and cruelly they did [so]. Then the tyrants put him in a filthy place and prison called the Hall, and kept him straitly, for he was thought to be a Catholic ; and, therefore, they fined him, for he was glad to eat the crusts which some threw in at the window.   Thus starving him he died, and lay dead so long (how long none knoweth) that the rats had eaten his face and other places."

That the old religion should in due course have gradually lost its adherents in England is not to be wondered at, when such records of cruelty and torture as those just related are duly had in consideration.   In some parts the villages had become depopulated,[1] more especially those adjacent to the old religious houses.   Cottage after cottage had been removed, grange and manor and yeoman's mansion went to decay and ruin.   The only wonder is that any ancient families remained at all, to lift up their testimony by deed as well as by word through later times of misery, rebellion, and revolution ; and to bear witness to the Catholicity and continuity of the religion of St. Edward the Confessor and William Wainflete, in which, by divine grace, and greatly to the benefit of their native land, they continued to believe.

There were some tortures which were extremely agonising to those who endured them, and one might have imagined distressing to witness by those who were officially enjoined to make use of them.   One such form of punishment consisted in hanging people up to a beam with cords by the joints of their fingers or wrists, until, because of sheer agony, they swooned and lost all

---

[1] " Whereby is it come to pass that where before there dwelt many a good yeoman able to do the king and the realm good service, there is nobody now dwelling but a shepherd with his dog, but by the suppression of the abbeys ? Whereby is it that whereas men where wont to eat sheep, now sheep eat up houses, whole towns, yea men and all, but by the suppression of the abbeys ? What is the decay of tillage but the suppression of the abbeys ? What is the decay of woods and the cause of the excessive price of wood, but the suppression of the said abbeys, which did carefully nourish, supply, and husband the same ?"—*The Pretended Divorce between Henry VIII. and Queen Katherine,* by Nicholas Harpsfield, edited by N. Pocock, p. 299. London, 1878.

consciousness. On one occasion, as Sir John Harington states, Topcliffe was called upon to explain to the queen the method of this torture, and to give a detailed account of its results. The queen listened with attention, and Topcliffe was afterwards rewarded substantially for his efficiency and resolution. Here is a single example taken out of many :—

In the year 1594, " Father John Ingram, priest, being apprehended in the north country, brought to York to the Lord President, where he was kept in his porter['s] lodge about two months close prisoner, having secret conference with Dr. Favor and others, and dealt withal both with lenity and extremity. When they had used all the means they could, and could not prevail against him, they sent him to London to the torturers where he was hung [up] by the joints of his fingers and arms in extreme pain so long that the feeling of his senses was clean taken from him. After that they sent him again to York, where he was committed to Ousebridge, kept there close prisoner in a low, stinking vault, locked in a jakeshouse the space of four days, without either bed to lie on or stool to sit on ; from thence carried into the North, pinioned with a cord, where he was apprehended, committed to Durham gaol, brought at the Assizes there before the judges, condemned, and executed."[1]

Here follows the record of a form of persecution and torture which cannot be more distinctly referred to :—

" John Pearson, a venerable old priest, was imprisoned for many years at Durham for refusing to attend the heretical services. After enduring with great patience the close confinement of an underground dungeon, he was removed to another far worse, and thrust amongst a set of thieves. This was done at a time when he was suffering from a burning fever. Here, as if the very filthiness of the place, with its accompaniments, were not torture enough to a refined man of advanced age, the thieves out of mere malice became his tormentors. For while he was taking his meals, they . . . caused him such nausea that he could not retain the poor nourishment he had taken. By this more than savage treatment received at the hands of these pitiless wretches, he was, before many days were passed, worn out, and so passed to a better life."[2]

As it was in the North so it was in the South of England. For example :— In 1591, Roger Dickenson, who had been

[1] " Notes by a Prisoner in Ousebridge Kidcote," in *Troubles of our Catholic Forefathers*, 3rd Series, p. 314. London, 1877.
[2] " Notes by Father Grene," in *Troubles of our Catholic Forefathers*, 3rd Series, p. 315. London, 1877.

ordained at Rheims, and who ministered to those of the old religion near Winchester, was caught, arraigned for this "offence," as it was deemed, condemned, and sent up to London to be similarly tortured, in the hope of his betraying his friends and co-religionists, which he firmly and faithfully declined to do. With him suffered Ralph Milner, a poor married man, with a large family, having been convicted of aiding and abetting Father Dickenson in saying mass by serving him. In this case the judge openly offered him his life if he would only once attend the new services, and acknowledge the queen's supremacy in spirituals. But he firmly declined. And when the offer was repeated to him in prison, the day before he suffered, he still refused it with scorn, but in very simple and respectful language. On the morning of his last day upon earth, when he was about to suffer a frightful and cruel death, his seven miserable children in tears were brought to him, in the hope that the sight of them, about to become orphans, might melt his constancy. But instead of yielding to the reasonable suggestions of Nature, he first embraced them affectionately, gave them each his last paternal blessing, urged them to a pious life after the old rules, and declared, in the hearing of the anxious and interested multitude around, that he could wish his sorrowing little ones no greater happiness than to shed their blood in defence of the true faith. The two sufferers died on the 7th of July 1591, by the accustomed cruelties, and after the disgusting legal barbarities had been duly perpetrated.

Seven maiden ladies were likewise condemned to death at the same assizes for having harboured Dickenson and heard mass, but for very shame's sake on the part of the judge were reprieved and imprisoned.

At the same time the persecution of the Brownists, Puritans, and anti-prelate agitators went on apace. They, too, suffered severely, and often bore their sufferings bravely and manfully. For example :—

Two men, John Greenwood a clergyman, and Henry Barrow a lawyer, were, in the spring of 1595, convicted of having written sundry seditious books, tending to the slander of the queen and state. In these there were violent attacks on the Book of Common Prayer, and on the queen as sanctioning its use. Their publications had been sown broadcast, and being in strong and vigorous language, readily found readers. In the opinion of the judges such productions conclusively proved that their authors denied to the queen her rightful spiritual supremacy as bestowed upon her by Parliament. On the 31st of March they were taken to Tybourne, and temporarily reprieved, but were both cruelly executed there on the 6th of April.

Two months afterwards, Henry Penry, a native of Wales, was tried, under an Act passed in the twenty-third year of the queen's reign, for having uttered "seditious words and rumours against the queen." He had received his education at both Universities, and was a young man of considerable abilities and great power of invective. His writings, full of the keenest satires of the bishops, whom he described as "limbs of Antichrist," were directed forcibly against the then state of affairs, and more particularly against the queen as making, governing, and deposing the prelates. His indirect account of the state of affairs then existing in the Church is often graphic, entertaining, and startling. Comprehension[1] was certainly considerable, but what principle obtained save that of persecution it is not easy to determine. He is generally credited with having been the author of the Martin Marprelate Tracts, which were personally most distasteful to Her Majesty, and, of course, entirely subversive of her spiritual supremacy. For the preachers maintained their own official superiority in things spiritual to that of the queen. In Wales, where the old religion had been for some years slowly dying out, he preached and exhorted, in woods and fields, churchyards and village greens, with singular power and unusual boldness. On several occasions he defied the bishops, whom he covered with ridicule and satire, and challenged their officers to do their worst against him. Many people followed his lead, often applauding to the echo his daring statements, while his various publications, scattered profusely by faithful allies, became seriously damaging to the new religious establishment. He was seized at Stepney, charged, and condemned. He was found guilty, not from any statements in his publications, nor from admissions of his own, but from the contents and terms of certain manuscript *memoranda* found upon him, containing the heads of a petition to the queen. To strike directly at the bishops and

---

[1] A cathedral dignitary of research and candour, Mr. Prebendary Walcott, remarked in his Introduction to the *Canons of the Church of England* (Parker, 1874) that "comprehension without compromise of principle is the true policy of our Communion"—a state of affairs certainly not yet arrived at, after all these years; and no more likely to be attained by the corporation in question, apparently, than the "godly discipline of the Primitive Church,"—the absence of which is formally lamented by everybody on every recurring Ash-Wednesday, but which discipline nobody has the least intention of endeavouring to restore, or the least desire of restoring, or the smallest expectation of living to see restored. There is plenty of comprehension, abundance of compromise, and exceeding little principle.

their jurisdiction, however, was, as the judges laid down, to strike indirectly and wickedly at Her Majesty. For the queen had notoriously made the bishops by her supreme spiritual authority, all defects having been overcome, and all difficulties removed by a special Act of Parliament; if, therefore, ministers and people disparaged and contemned the bishops, they thus disparaged and contemned the queen and her spiritual supremacy. Hastily hurried from dinner, Penry was not allowed to secure a remission or mitigation of his sentence by a declaration of his faith, which he seemed ready to make, or by an exposition of his allegiance to the queen. A riot on the part of his adherents being anticipated, he was hurried off to St. Thomas of Waterings in the Kent Road, and there barbarously executed.[1] Thus, at the early age of thirty-four, he died for conscience' sake,—for being unable to accept the new reformed system, which he himself, with equal reason and authority, desired to reform anew. The judges, who condemned him, maintained that any attacks upon the Liturgy, which the queen had settled and appointed to be used, was a distinct denial of her supreme spiritual authority, as bestowed upon Her Majesty by Parliament, and consequently that such offence was treason.

During the last ten years of Elizabeth's reign very little real belief in the new religion existed. Even the opinions of experienced official people differed concerning its value. Of course those who had benefited by it in things temporal, as in duty bound, tried to prop it up morally. Parliamentary props, however, having thus early broken in the using, were found to be only of small value. Dr. William James,[2] then Dean of Durham, complained loudly to the Council of the utter indifference and lofty contempt with which he and his disputatious co-religionists in the North were treated; and gave a most miserable and depressing account of the state of morals[3] in those parts. The married clergy were still treated with great contumely, and continued to be the subject of much "mislike" and satire. Holgate, some years previously, had set a bad example.[4] On the other

---

[1] See Stowe's *Chronicle*, p. 765; Strype's *Annals*, vol. iv. p. 176.

[2] Dr. William James had been Master of University College in 1572, Dean of Christ Church, Oxford, in 1584, Dean of Durham in 1596. Eventually he became Bishop of Durham.

[3] *State Papers, Domestic, Elizabeth*, vol. cclxii. 25, cclxiii. 55 (A.D. 1597). See also "Considerations in favour of Erecting a College at Ripon. *The people in a manner are all ignorant in religion, having been for above thirty years untaught.*"—*State Papers, Domestic, Elizabeth*, vol. cccxxxiv. 35.

[4] As a sound English Churchman so forcibly remarked: "What a pitiful case was it to see old, doting, lecherous priests and bishops of sixty, seventy—

hand, the Dean of Durham went on to declare that "the number of recusants is great and increases;[1] and, as they are of good calling and wealth, and generally refuse to confer with any, or to join in prayer for Her Majesty, we suppose that many of them are reconciled." It was not to their "ignorance" that his very reverence so much objected, as to their firm faith and good resolutions. They avowedly preferred the religion of their fore-fathers, since St. Augustine's day, to any modern "gospel" which the dean, at the dictation of the queen and Parliament, might officially recommend to them. "They are," he continued, "almost all ignorant and obstinate, generally refuse all confer-ence, and not only do not come to church, but, when prayers are had before us, the Commissioners, for Her Majesty's safety and protection from all her enemies, the Pope and Spaniard, they have denied to say 'Amen'"—a plain dereliction of duty. These good people, who would not respond, evidently held that the faith was not a matter to squabble about, to confer concern-ing, or to mutilate and halve, but to accept heartily, to believe thoroughly, and to defend faithfully. Nor would they, as they so constantly declared, pray with those of a different religion. "Your religion is not mine, mine is not thine, as thou ofttimes avowest; how then, if we be not joined, may we pray together?" asked one. Another somewhat pointedly and powerfully put on record that "an aunciente body with a newe Head, must be a dead body—a meere corpse." Several prayed in secret, after the old manner, and observed the ancient rites, feast,[2] fast, and

yea, and of eighty, years of age, run a catterwawling; among whom [was] one Holgate, Archbishop of York, a man about fourscore years of age, which had been a religious man [i.e. a Gilbertine Prior] also, married a young girl of fourteen or fifteen years of age, and yet for three causes she never was his wife: the one for that he had been a religious man and had solemnly vowed chastity; the second for that he was a priest; and the third for that she was betrothed to another man, and by very force kept from him."—*The Pretended Divorce between Henry VIII. and Queen Katherine*, by Nicholas Harpsfield, LL.D., edited by N. Pocock, pp. 275-276. London, 1878.

[1] A remarkable and acute theologian, as well as an able ecclesiastical states-man, thus confirms the Dean's impression as to the increase of "recusants": —"I see on every side cause of hope and fear. In these days the ports are so strictly closed that few escape of those who come to us, or go from us to England. Ten who were coming over to these parts have been seized in the very port and sent back, or rather dragged *vi et armis* before the Privy Council. *The number of Catholics daily increases in a wonderful manner.* Our brethren are animated with such zeal amidst these dangers that it is diffi-cult to restrain them."—Letter of Dr. Richard Barrett, of Rheims, dated December 28, 1583. Translated from the original in the Archives of Westminster.

[2] A remembrance of the Catholic festivals took some time to die out, as the following extract from the *Parochial Registers of Chearsly, Bucks*, shows:

U

solemnity, as best they could.   Migratory priests of the old rites
came round occasionally to aid, and minister to, trusted families.
" Many of them," the Dean went on to inform Lord Burghley,
"are married, if not by seminaries and Jesuits, by old mass
priests,[1] and by the words of the Mass Book (?)[2]; their children
are not christened in the churches, neither do their wives go
there to return thanks for deliverance ; their education is in the
same way, not being [brought] up in common or good schools,
but at home and in secret ; and with their nurses' milk they suck
[in] dislike and disloyalty, and learn first to hate the truth "—by
which this grumbling worthy[3] evidently means his own form of
misbelief—" before they know it, which I wish was only a disease
in the North : " a very expressive and notable testimony of
universal failure everywhere on the part of the authorities in
State and Church, even with the aid of rack and gyves, spy and
false witness, fine, pillory, floggings, and expatriation, to secure
either regard or respect for their daring novelties and un-Catholic
innovations.

—" 1611 Domini anno, 23 day of May, Ihon Parker, otherwise called Iohn
Richardson, and Jane Woodebridge, were married together *die Corporis
Christi.*"

    [1] The race of "old mass priests"—those, that is, who had been ordained
under Queen Mary—were, in the current opinion of all English deans and
dignitaries, of quite a different order to those recently appointed.

    [2] In Elizabeth's time the Salisbury Manual was used for baptisms by the
clergy of the old faith ; and a convenient abbreviated edition of the Sarum
Missal, printed abroad—of which the Rev. W. J. Blew owns a rare copy—
was carried about by the old clergy.

    [3] The previous dean, Dr. Toby Matthews, who afterwards became Bishop
of Durham, is said to have preached no less than five hundred and fifty
sermons during twelve years—a remarkable homiletic feat in those days ; but
one which apparently had effected extremely little good, measured by the too
accurate gauge of his outspoken successor.

CHAPTER X.

Such executions as those just recorded,—they were still very numerous,—serve to place in a strong light both the personal bloodthirstiness of the queen (passed over by Protestant historians) and the stern, cruel, and intolerant spirit of the age in which she ruled. The former is perfectly apparent when the actual influence which Elizabeth insisted on exercising is duly remembered. At her Council-board she was no mere dummy in diadem and diamonds; but, having a will and power of her own, constantly exercised them with authority and decision. She was always interested in the work of "Seminary-hunting," as it was termed; she listened with engrossed attention to Burghley's accounts of what had happened in the work of dismembering and disembowelling her religious opponents. Of Topcliffe's secret dealings with the poor prisoners in his keeping—to whom the well-born wretch showed no mercy—she often ordered that all the intricate cruelties of the torture-chamber should be either recorded on paper, or recounted in person, for her satisfaction. She herself was on "the side of the Lord Jesus Christ" she asserted, and would maintain at any cost "the Blessed Faith of the Blessed Gospel." The men who were imprisoned, tortured, hung, and disembowelled, were "ministers of Satan's synagogue," "wily slaves of Antichrist"; consequently there could be "no communion betwixt Christ and Belial," between those of the old religion and those of the new.[1] Her new prelates had long ago

[1] In the *Tablet* of February 17th, 1877, "An English Catholic" objects to members of the Church of England using Father Faber's beautiful hymn, "Faith of Our Fathers," and makes the following reasonable and pertinent remarks:—"For three centuries and more, according to their opportunities and the progressive stages of opinion and civilisation, they [Anglicans] have burned and hanged us, ripped us up, confiscated our private property, seized our churches, universities, ecclesiastical titles and revenues, kept us out of Parliament, insulted our hierarchy, and in all possible ways made the exercise of the Christian faith difficult. Now, when the more refined part of these enjoyments is withdrawn from them they turn round, but without penitence or satisfaction, and take the fruits of our long centuries of desolation and endurance . . . Which 'Faith' do the Protestant singers mean? Do

proved from Scripture, as they maintained, that torture was reasonable, and that all mass-mongers, being idolaters, should be killed. Special tortures, as in Archbishop Heath's case, the queen herself had sometimes recommended or personally enjoined ; she was greatly irritated and disappointed that those who suffered because of Babington's plot could not have their death-sufferings made crueller and considerably prolonged ; while, when clever and distinguished adherents of the old religion were the subjects of them, she frequently signed death-warrants with an expression of satisfaction from her lips or a twinkle of demoniacal delight in her eye. The cruel, whether women or men, are ever cowardly. And all the while Elizabeth was a pitiful coward. While dreading pain herself, and greatly fearing death, she frequently exhibited the most contemptible delight at the mental and physical sufferings of her victims. Occasionally, as in the case of Thomas Pormorte, who was executed on February 20th, 1592, she displayed the grossest and most cruel levity when affixing her sign-manual to the death-warrant,—an exhibition which disgusted some who were present, as the Duchess of Feria (one of the Oxfordshire Dormers) put on record.

On some occasions, the queen was informed that her enemies were seeking her life [1] and plotting to poison or assassinate her. Sometimes the Court authorities artfully made use of these pieces of gossip, or random rumours, or bragging utterances of excited fanatics,[2] in order to induce her to be less wayward and uncertain, both in her home and foreign policy, and to act on some particular occasion with decision. What often appeared to authenti-

they mean the Faith as professed before Cranmer, or as professed after him and after Parker? If after, they associate themselves with the pretended ' Martyrs ' of Foxe, and to the statements of Cranmer, Jewel, Parker, and the rest of that company. If, however, they mean the Faith professed in the ancient Church of England, and retained by suffering Catholics ever since to this day, then the reply of the Church of Jesus Christ is—*Nescio vos.*"

[1] On one occasion Father Robert Parsons carefully and strongly dissuaded certain persons from even entertaining such a notion. No one can at all wonder at the idea entering the minds of the poor, down-trodden, shamefully persecuted Catholics ; but, to one man who seems to have actually gone a hundred miles on his way to attempt the queen's life, Father Parsons reasoned with him because " the English Catholiques themselves desired not to be delyvered from their miseries by any such attempt," and convinced him of the inexpediency of such a policy.

[2] On October 28th, 1583, divers persons were examined before John D'Oyley concerning John Somerfield's [ville] speeches against Her Majesty, having maintained that he intended to shoot her through with his dagg, and hoped to see her head set on a pole ; for that she was a serpent and a viper. —*State Papers, Domestic, Elizabeth,* vol. clxiii. Nos. 23, 53, 54, 55.

cate such reports were the tattling letters of spies, foreign and home appointed, who in order to prove their intense interest in Her Majesty's tortuous policy, their devotion to her person, and to show that they had themselves merited the rewards and favours bestowed upon them, were less scrupulous than they might have been in the rumours they so artfully dressed up, or in the circumstantial accounts they had deliberately invented.[1] A spy who spied nothing worth noting was both a poor and an expensive tool. A disguised agent abroad who did nothing was a still poorer. A falsehood-monger who circulated no falsehoods was like a goldsmith without any gold—of small repute and less value. The agents, therefore, were obliged to be at once imaginative and inventive, so as to entrap the unwary, excite the enthusiastic, and betray the innocent; the spies, furthermore, were often as daring, bold and lying as their degraded office compelled them to be. They were, in fact, occasionally, quite worthy of the woman who officially employed them, and of the ministers who gave them approbation and rewards.

At home all classes of people were constantly suspected of "working conjurations" to Her Majesty's evil and loss. The suspicions and superstitions which Dr. Dee had long ago fostered had taken a deep root in the queen's mind. Amongst others, Lord Paget, Sir George Hastings, and Sir Thomas Hanmer, were each believed to have thus plotted Her Majesty serious harm, and to have gone the round of the popular conjurers so as to work her some great personal mischief. The superstitions then existing on these subjects were, of course, degrading and disgusting; though no doubt they were founded on very solid facts. For witchcraft is as certainly a reality as it is a sin, and evil spirits, both active and potent, were most probably on the side of those who went about from place to place, invoking them and seeking their active aid. The devil and his angels are evidently quite ready to render their powerful and practical assistance to mankind, if it be only sought after with system, earnestness, and proper subservience and devotion. Protestantism, from Luther's time downwards,[2] seems to have received it abundantly. "Old Birtles, the great devell, Darnally the

---

[1] "To satisfy their employers they were often compelled to transmit false and alarming intelligence ; sometimes they actually formed conspiracies that they might have the merit of detecting them ; and not unfrequently meeting associates as abandoned as themselves, they perished in the very snares which they had laid for others."— *The History of England*, by John Lingard, D.D., vol. vi. p. 270. Dublin, 1874.
[2] See Bossuet's *History of the Variations of the Protestant Religion*, Book IV. chap. xvii.

sorcerer, Maude Twogood enchantresse, the oulde Witch of Ramsbury, several other ould witches,"—as the record exactly describes them—well known and popular in their arts [1]—were all looked upon as the queen's personal enemies; and it was feared that their greatly-dreaded services had been formerly secured and paid for by her influential enemies.

When five out of the seven Catholic sacraments had been abolished, for henceforth two only were allowed in the New Church,—two of three abolished, viz., Unction at Confirmation, with its divine grace, and the Last Anointing for the sick and suffering, were more especially and most sorely missed by thousands. Baptism had, of course, made all those who had received it, true and undoubted heirs of other sacraments. When some of these were thus arbitrarily abolished, the faithful were by consequence deliberately robbed of their rightful inheritance. Many of the "recusants" examined in the North had long ago openly complained that poor Christian people had been thus defrauded of their rights. Some who "waxed bold" amid shouts of "No greasing!" had in open Court expostulated with Archbishop Sandys for having consented to abolish extreme unction. Dr. Thomas Vavasour was one of these. But His Grace in reply only characterised that sacrament as "a vain and filthy oiling by the Pope's crew," and enjoined upon the persons complaining to "shut their mouths without delay."

Wherever the Catholic religion once known has been deliberately abolished,[2] there some form of superstition or another has almost invariably become current and popular. Astrology, witchcraft, necromancy, and spirit-seeking, were, under Queen Elizabeth, largely patronised. They exactly fitted into the new system where the gaps were large, and the spiritual wants numerous. And reasonably so. For man either looks upward or downward—to the Light of the World, and the unfallen spirits of His beautiful creation; or to the lost and unquiet spirits of darkness, malignant and merciless, ruled by the prince of the powers of the air. The Court authorities set the fashion in these practices, and others followed them. The queen had frequently consulted Dr. Dee, since the occasion on which he fixed a lucky day for her coronation at Westminster; and, though they had had some misunderstandings, it seems perfectly clear that he had been promised a bishopric [3] in reward

---

[1] *State Papers, Domestic, Elizabeth*, vol. clxxv. 90.

[2] See *Origines Protestanticæ: or, Suggestions for an Historical Inquiry into the Origin of the Protestant Religion.* London, Longhurst.

[3] The Lord Treasurer told him on Dec. 23, 1591, and he recorded it in

for his conjurations, ambiguous promises, flatteries, and pre-
dictions.

In 1590, one Ann Frank, Dee's nurse, as his Diary records,
was certainly "possessed." On August 22nd he writes in his
Diary that she "had long byn tempted by a wycked spirit, but
this day it was evident now she was *possessed* of him." . . .
Later on, that is upon August 26th, as he quaintly puts on
record, "I anoynted (in the Name of Jesus) Ann Frank her
brest with the holy oyle. Augst. 30th in the morning, she
required to be anoynted [again], and I did very devowtly prepare myself and pray for virtue and powr and Christ His blessing
of the oyle to the expulsion of the wycked; and then twyce
anoynted [her]. The wickyd one did resest a while." But on
Michaelmas-day, notwithstanding all his profane conjurations,
consecrations, and invocations, the poor creature committed
suicide by cutting her own throat.

Dee by no means stood alone in his practice of these irregular
and unlawful performances; on the contrary, in remote parsonage
or secluded rectory-house, quite a race of similar conjurers rose
up to fill the aching void which Protestantism had made in the
human heart by turning people's attention to the dark side of the
unseen world. Many of these were ministers. They practised
in secret, mumbling their invocations of the devil or his angels,
drawing the mystic circle according to old rules, and plaintively
asking the practical aid of some familiar spirit in their unhallowed
and forbidden researches; and were generally left alone by the
State authorities, unless they made use of these their occult arts
for political objects—sometimes the case. When this was
believed, they were tracked out,[1] discovered, and punished, on
the ground that to thus labour for the overthrow of their
political opponents—to borrow a contemporary phrase—was
"to stab them in the dark with the sword of an unseen spirit."
Most of the new bishops in their Visitation Articles, and subsequently in a Canon,[2] faithfully endeavoured to put down such

his Diary that "the Quene would have me have something at this promotion of bishops at hand."

[1] In one of the *State Papers* is provided "Information touching certain
men taken up in the parish of Edmonton for practising the art of witchcraft
and conjuring; mystic articles found in their possession, with powders and
ratsbane, which the parties that fled strewed in the way, disappointing the
bloodhound thereby."—*State Papers, Domestic, Elizabeth*, vol. ccxxxiii., n.
72.

[2] See the seventy-second canon of those passed in 1603 as also *The
Question of Witchcraft Debated*, by John Wagstaffe. London 1669;
2nd edition, 1671.

black arts, which men of renown, like Sir Nicholas Bacon, and Blackstone the lawyer, believed to be undoubted realities.

In all great social changes and grave revolutions amongst the nations, the influence of the unseen world is far more potent and direct than shallow sceptics and frivolous critics allow to be possible.   Believing only in what they can see and handle—the material things of the present life—the vision of such people is often as narrow and confused as the nonsensical jargon of which they are the purveyors, and not infrequently as distorted, perverse, and diabolical.

In the year 1593, Roderigo Lopez, a clever Portuguese Jew, who had been made a prisoner in one of the ships of the Armada, and had subsequently practised medicine in London; and who, because of his great and remarkable success, had been some time previously sworn Physician of the queen, was accused of privately meditating the death of Her Majesty, having offered to poison her, as it was asserted, for the sum of fifty thousand crowns. The copies of the letters preserved in the indictments are all most enigmatically worded, and in no way prove what the upholders of the charges endeavoured to maintain.   The accusers, "intelligencers," and witnesses employed in the case were mostly unprincipled adventurers, persons of infamous character, and men whose arts of lying and dissimulation had long been patent and notorious—well-tested by their employers. Lopez himself admitted that he had occasionally received presents from the Spanish Court, at one time a jewel worth one hundred pounds; but denied that he had either said or done, or meant to do or say, anything prejudicial to the interests or person of the queen.   It was asserted likewise that he had pledged himself to burn the English fleet.   He was put on his trial with two others, Ferreira and Louis, both Portuguese— whose confessions made upon the rack were of small moral value,—and Lopez and the others were all found guilty, but judgment was respited for three months.   It was hoped that full information of the design, or supposed design, of the Spaniards might be obtained from them.   Torture was used in the Tower, threats of worse tortures were uttered, mild starvation attempted. Their small allowance of food in prison—they appear to have been denied any drink for some days—might have broken the spirits and destroyed the resolution of any one, even the bravest. In consequence of their having declined to say what was not true, or unjustly to inculpate the innocent, they were treated more cruelly than usual when the sentence was carried out; for the whole summer's day, June 7th, was spent in their execution.

Brought from the Tower to London Bridge on foot, they were then taken in a barge to Westminster, where, though called upon as a matter of form to say what they might and could in their own defence, they were very soon brow-beaten and silenced. Their mispronunication of the English language was caricatured and laughed at. The populace, instructed by the authorities, howled and yelled at them whenever they appeared; so that, as one writer remarks, " the voices were like the barking of hunting-hounds at their fullest cry." At Westminster they were delivered to the Marshall of the Queen's Bench, who took them by water to Southwark Stairs, and so to the Marshalsea. At the southern foot of London Bridge they were given over to the Sheriffs of London, who had them placed on hurdles, and conveyed them to Leaden Hall (the residence of Lopez). Thence they were taken to Tybourne, followed by the accustomed rabble. There they were hanged for a very short time, but intentionally cut down alive. One of them, after this process, with the rope yet round his neck, in great pain because of the twist and jerk he had received, recovering his feet, struggled for some time for his life. He struck out at the executioner boldly, and was applauded by the populace, who pressed forward through the guard of pikemen to see the encounter. Being a powerful man, the officer of death could neither remove his dress nor secure him efficiently. Two burly assistants, however, hastened forward to the executioner's aid. But the poor half-strangled wretch, gathering up all his strength in defence of the natural right to live, felled one of them to the ground with a single stroke, and it was some time before the condemned man could be secured. He was first stunned by a blow on the head and thrown on to the straw; his clothes being hastily pulled off. Then followed the accustomed barbarous mutilation—a bloody business indeed—and the frightful act of disembowelling a still breathing mortal. But the legal butchers, with knife and hatchet and bared arms, closed in upon their suffering victims, whose blood flowed before the sun went down, and whose lives then soon ebbed away. So, after lingering over the horrors of the spot, the grinning rabble dispersed towards sunset. Thus the supposed enemies of the queen were efficiently removed.

In the latter part of this reign, John Wolton was Bishop of Exeter from 1579 to 1594; Hugh Bellot was first made Bishop of Bangor in 1586, but was subsequently removed to Chester in 1595, where he died in less than a year; Thomas Bickley was Bishop of Chichester from 1586 to 1596; John Still first filled the see of Bath in 1593; Anthony Watson was Bishop of

Chichester in 1596.   But these names and others on the vellum registers are mere Christian and surnames, and nothing more. They proclaim nothing, they illustrate nothing.   In fact they convey no idea of any sort or kind to nine persons out of ten; possibly not to one in a hundred.   The exalted people who bore them, no doubt walked in the footsteps of Dr. Parker and his company, were appointed ministers, married, made themselves comfortable, preached Calvinism, carefully and confidently numbered themselves and their families amongst "the elect," flattered the Queen, and duly fleeced the sheep; grew old in the profitable process, and then in due course departed this mortal life.

Dr. John Whitgift, who had been appointed Bishop of Worcester as early as the year 1577, as we have seen, became the most prominent and able of the prelates of this period, possibly the only truly remarkable one of his day.   Sprung from a respectable middle-class family of the West Riding of Yorkshire, his father Henry, a merchant of Grimsby, having married a Lincolnshire lady named Anne Dynewell, had six sons, of whom the future archbishop was the eldest.   His uncle Robert, his father's only brother, had been Abbot of Wellowe near Grimsby, but seems at an early period to have openly taken the side of the innovators, for he renounced his religious life, received a pension, and lived in the world.   John Whitgift in due course went to Cambridge, where he had Jewell and Grindal for his tutors, who, of course, influenced him considerably.   Having taken his M.A. degree in 1556, he was made Margaret Professor of Divinity ten years afterwards.   In 1567 he was created D.D., having maintained in his public thesis for that honour—*Papa est ille Antichristus*,—a tolerably clear indication of his mental delusions and of the novel and ridiculous character of his theology.   He was, by his own admission, an Erastian,[1] as all were in his day.   In July of 1567, he was made Master of Trinity College, Cambridge, where he opposed Cartwright and the more fanatical Puritans, and in 1577 was appointed to succeed Bullingham in the See of Worcester.   As filling that position he has already been referred to.

It ought ever to be remembered to his credit, however, that

[1] " If by 'the Head' you understand an external ruler and governor of any particular nation and church (in which signification head is generally taken) then I do not perceive why the magistrate may not as well be called the Head of the Church, that is the chief governor of it in the external policy, as he is called the head of the people and the Commonwealth."—*Defence of the Answer to the Admonition*, p. 85.   *Whitgift's Works*, vol. ii., *Parker Society's Works*, 1852.

| he protested in the strongest and plainest terms to the queen against the alienation of Church property. An absolute power had been recently given by Act of Parliament to the Crown, and the queen had made Lord Leicester sole Commissioner. His lordship, like certain other of the peers of that period, owned somewhat inexact ideas of the difference between *meum* and *tuum*. But, when criticised, he sheltered himself under the terms of his appointment. Whitgift, however, by his boldness, stemmed the tide of robbery with success, and of course made Lord Leicester his deadly enemy.

His Grace thus addressed the queen :—

" Though you and myself were born in an age of frailties, when the primitive piety and the care of the Church's lands and immunities are much decayed; yet, Madam, let me beg that you would first consider that there are such sins as profaneness and sacrilege "—two shocking forms of transgression, the existence of which the queen had apparently quite forgotten,—"and that if there were not, they could not have names in 'Holy Writ, and particularly in the New Testament."

" I beg posterity," he went on to remark, "to take notice of what is already become visible in many families, that Church land added to an ancient and just inheritance, hath proved like a moth fretting a garment, and secretly consumed both ; or like the eagle that stole a coal from the altar and thereby set her nest on fire, which consumed both her young eagles and herself that stole it. And though I shall forbear to speak reproachfully of your father, yet I beg you to take notice that a part of the Church's rights, added to the vast treasure left him by his father, hath been conceived to bring an unavoidable consumption upon both, notwithstanding all his diligence to preserve them. And consider that after the violation of those laws, to which he had sworn, in *Magna Charta*, God did so far deny him His restraining grace, that as King Saul after he was forsaken of God fell from one sin to another, so he ; till at last he fell into greater sins than I am willing to mention."

Archbishop Whitgift likewise endeavoured to stir up the indolent, passive, and common-place prelates under his jurisdiction to do their duty. The alarming Calvinism of some tended to exclude practically any, even a theoretical, consideration of the importance of good works—an unfortunate feature. It is evident from his own words that no one more accurately realised the frightful state of degradation into which, during the previous forty years, the national religion had sunk than the Archbishop himself. The evil he beheld too clearly, and has most forcibly described.   But how to remedy it was a perplexing and puzzling problem.

Many of the bishops were notoriously over-engrossed in things temporal, farming the property of their Sees for their own personal advantage, or entering into private arrangements with the queen's favourites to secure privileges and readier profits. In 1594 Dr. John Coldwell, Bishop of Salisbury, wrote to a friend at Court,[1] complaining of Sir Walter Raleigh's treatment of him.   It seems that these two worthies, according to custom, had been together quietly making the most of the Church lands between themselves, and had quarrelled violently during the process.   Twenty marks due to the bishop had been seized by Raleigh, and yet he desired to have three more manors, Burton, Holmes, and Upcorne, but without paying any rent for them. The bishop, who was not dull or indifferent to his own interests, could hardly have approved of such a proposition.

On the one hundred and eighty-first folio of His Grace's Register at Lambeth, is preserved a letter which was addressed by Archbishop Whitgift to the bishops of his province, enjoining them to see that children were catechised, taught and confirmed. The picture which this document indirectly draws is melancholy to contemplate.   It harmonises completely and perfectly with the records of neglect and apathy already referred to.   From its perusal, the existence of the greatest and almost universal neglect of the rite of confirmation is apparent.   "I am very sorry to hear," are His Grace's exact words, "that my brethren, the bishops of my province of Canterbury do so generally begin to neglect to confirm children."[2]

Whitgift's complexion, to note a personal characteristic, was very dark.   The queen admired him because he was self-denying, given to hospitality, and had remained a celibate.   She notoriously preferred this state for the clergy, and "honoured him with the familiar name of 'her Black husband.'"[3]   Although she was naturally nettled by his letter concerning the proposal for the confiscation of Church lands, yet, on reflection, she evidently admired his boldness, and regarded his most creditable expostulation with favour.

The bishops in His Grace's day appear to have had a hard

---

[1] *Burghley State Papers*, ed. W. Murdin, pp. 675, 676.   "John Sarum to Mr. Henry Brook."   London, 1759.

[2] *Whitgift's Register*, folio 181, letter dated "From Croydon, the . . . of Sept. 1591."

[3] Preface to *A Godlie Sermon*, etc. by Doctor Whitgift, republished by John Wyat at the Rose in St. Paul's Churchyard, 1714.

lot sometimes. They were commonly called ".limbs of Anti-christ," and the "Bishops of the Devil," by the ultra-Puritan party, while Whitgift himself was politely styled the "Beelzebub of Canterbury,"[1] "an ambitious wretch, sitting upon his cogging-stool which may be truly called the chair of pestilence." Though strongly tinctured with Erastianism he was, however, a learned prelate, who had not only read much, but had well digested what he had read, and used it discreetly for his dialectical purposes. As regards episcopacy, and disputes concerning it, though much in advance of his contemporaries, most of whom in principle were rank and bitter Puritans, he maintained,—not that the order of episcopacy was of divine origin and institution, but that originally the Church no doubt had the right of determining how it should be governed; and argued that as it had determined to be governed by bishops, and not otherwise, such government ought to be maintained, consistently, however, with two independent conditions: first, the absolute and inherent rights of the Christian magistrate; and, secondly, due soundness of doctrine,—though who was to be judge of this last (except himself) will not be discovered in his painful and laborious writings. Nor was it clear who, in his judgment, was to determine the nature and extent of the powers and rights of the Civil Magistrate.

However difficult for one whose official position cut him off from all relations with a higher ecclesiastical authority, it may have been to have enjoined duties *more antiquo* upon his inferior officers—for, of course, he appeared like a rebel preaching obedience; yet his intention was evidently less faulty than his logic, and no doubt he sincerely meant to do his duty. He it was—and all honour to him for it—who, with many short-comings, first managed systematically to stem wilder and more outrageous innovations, and in some measure to turn the Puritan tide.

In the year 1595, amongst others, two priests suffered for treason, both of them being members of ancient or knightly Norfolk families. The first was Robert Southwell, the second Henry Walpole. Of each some brief account must be given.

1. Robert Southwell was the grandson of Sir Richard South-well of Woodrising, who had lived in Henry VIII.'s reign, and had been one of the Visitors of the Norfolk monasteries, Master of the Ordnance, Steward of the Duchy of Lancaster, and one of the executors of Henry's will. His father was Richard

---

[1] "A Dialogue, wherein is playnly laide open the Tyrannical Dealing of L. Bishopps against God's children."—No place nor date.

Southwell of Spixworth, and his mother, Alice, daughter of Sir Thomas Cornwallis. He was born at the Priory of Horsham St. Faith. He was educated first at Douay, then at Paris, where he came under the influence of Archdeacon Darbyshire,—one of the earliest English members of the Society of Jesus. Into this order young Southwell was admitted at the age of seventeen, on the 17th of October 1578. Six years afterwards he was ordained priest at Rome, and soon afterwards, in the summer of 1586,[1] came to England, where he found a home in the mansion of Philip, Earl of Arundel's lady. For six years, with great piety and discretion, winning admiration from many, he laboured in his Master's cause. His refinement and tenderness made him a great authority with many of exalted rank, and he was most successful in winning back a considerable number to the ancient faith. At the end of the period mentioned, having been betrayed by an unhappy woman named Ann Bellamy, at her own father's house,[2] he soon found himself in the safe keeping of Topcliffe, who, with his officers and servants, had surrounded the place and arrested the father.

He was tortured in the private torture-cell of this infamous persecutor, as both law and custom enjoined, no less than ten times, or, as Lord Burghley admitted, thirteen times; and this with such pitiless severity, that he openly declared to the judges that death would have been again and again far preferable. The account of his fearful agonies is on record still, and to turn over the printed pages of it makes the eye dim and the heart sick. Anything more utterly revolting and merciless could scarcely be conceived. Its perusal makes one blush for the honour of humanity.

Others suffered with him. His account, in his own handwriting of what took place in another London prison, still exists, from which the following graphic extracts are taken :—

"A little while ago they apprehended two priests, who have suffered such cruel usages in the prison of Bridewell, as can scarce be believed. What was given them to eat was so little in quantity, and withal so filthy and nauseous, that the very sight of it was enough to turn their stomachs. The labours to which they obliged them were continual and immoderate, and no less in sickness than in health; for, with hard blows and stripes, they forced them to accomplish their task, how weak

---

[1] Some affirm that he came two years earlier; but for the date in the text there seems to be direct authority.

[2] See the London and Middlesex Archæological Society's *Transactions*, vol. i. pp. 293-294.

soever they were. Their beds were dirty straw, and their prison most filthy.

"Some are there hung up, for whole days, by the hands, in such a manner that they can but just touch the ground with the tips of their toes. In fine, they that are kept in that prison, truly live *in lacu miseriæ et in luto fæcis*, Psalm xxxix. This purgatory we are looking for every hour, in which Topcliffe and Young, the two executioners of the Catholics, exercise all kinds of torments. But come what pleaseth God, we hope we shall be able to bear all *in Him that strengthens us.*"

The cell in the Tower where Southwell himself was confined, was situated far below the ordinary water-mark of the Thames, and was consequently damp and musty. Sometimes it was a full foot deep in water. The only light admitted was through a narrow window high up above. He lay on rank and corrupt straw, in which vermin abounded : and was kept on very small allowances of food. The cell had only a stone seat in the wall, and there was no ventilation. He was not permitted to have any books, and no intercourse with the outer world.

When he had been confined there for some time, his father presented a petition to the queen, asking "that if his son had committed anything for which by the laws he had deserved death, he might suffer death ; if not, as he was a gentleman, he hoped Her Majesty would be pleased to order that he should be treated as a gentleman, and not be confined any longer to that filthy hole."

The queen, to a certain extent, granted the prayer of this petition. He was consequently removed from the " filthy hole " to a better lodging. His father at the same time received permission to supply him with common necessaries. He had asked only for two books, a copy of the Holy Scriptures, and the works of St. Bernard. These he was permitted to receive.

After three long weary years of imprisonment, thus punished before he was convicted, he was brought to trial on his own special application. Lord Burghley, to whom he had written, somewhat brutally remarked that "if he was in such great haste to be hanged. he should speedily have his desire." And so he had. For he was tried on one day and martyred[1] the next.

---

[1] " I care not to dwell any longer on this judicial murder. I pronounce it to be such ; and it is the sorrow and shame of our common human nature and Christianity that both sides have like blood-wet pages. I must regard our worthy as a martyr in the deepest and grandest sense—a good man full of the Holy Ghost."—*The Complete Poems of Robert Southwell,* edited by Rev. A. B. Grosart. Memorial Introduction, p. lxv. Privately printed, 1872.

The indictment which clearly enough sets forth the true nature of the so-called offence, ran thus :—

"The jury present, on the part of our Sovereign Lady the Queen: that Robert Southwell, late of London, clerk, born within this kingdom of England ; to wit, since the Feast of St. John the Baptist, in the first year of the reign of Her Majesty and before the first day of May, in the thirty-second year of the reign of Our Lady the Queen aforesaid, made and ordained priest by authority derived and pretended from the See of Rome, not having the fear of God before his eyes, and slighting the laws and statutes of this realm of England, without any regard to the penalty therein contained, on the 20th day of June, the thirty-fourth year of the reign of Our Lady the Queen, at Uxenden, in the county of Middlesex, traitorously, and as a false traitor to our said lady the queen, was and remained contrary to the form of the statute in such a case set forth and provided, and contrary to the peace of our said lady the queen, her crown and dignities."

A true bill having been found, Southwell appeared at the bar, and pleaded " Not guilty."

" I confess," he admitted, " that I was born in England.   I admit that I am a subject of the queen.   I allow that by authority derived from God, and no State authority, I have been promoted to the Christian priesthood, for which I ever thank and bless His divine majesty and goodness.   I confess that I was at Uxenden, that I was betrayed and apprehended ; but I emphatically deny that, either by word or deed, I ever entertained or plotted any plan or design against the queen or her kingdom. In returning to my old home and country I had but one aim—to minister the sacraments to those who desired them according to the ancient rites."

He was not allowed to say more, and was soon brought in guilty.

He then begged God to have mercy on all who had been, or should be, accessory to his death.

Judge Popham pronounced the horrible sentence, which need not be again set forth in detail, in the usual terms.

Then Southwell was taken to Newgate, from whence, early on the morrow morning, February 21st, 1595, he was dragged on a hurdle to Tybourne.

As he was being drawn from Newgate to the place of execution, he bade farewell to a kinswoman who had come to greet him.   The day was cold and wet, the sky leaden, and for some time a drizzling rain drove from the north-east.   Yet here and there crowds had gathered to witness the "drawing," and a motley mass followed on either side and behind, as the sufferer, jolted, bruised, and shaken, lay with his face turned heavenwards in mental prayer.

On reaching Tybourne, and being unbound, Southwell wiped his face and mouth with a handkerchief, which he then threw to a member of his own society in the crowd, whom he had recognised.

Knife and rope, caldron and hatchet, had been all duly prepared. He was then placed in the cart under the gallows, round which lay a litter of straw and a newly kindled fire. Having received permission to speak, he mildly maintained that he had never done, meant, nor intended any harm to Her Majesty; and expressed a hope regarding her that both body and soul might be saved by the mercy of the Most Highest.

Here he commended to God his poor afflicted country, which had been robbed of all the sacraments, except baptism and matrimony, praying that it might be led back again to a perfect insight into and understanding of God's truth, and so be blessed once more in the spiritual order, and restored once again to unity.

He acknowledged himself to be a Catholic priest and a member of the Society of Jesus, and thanked Almighty God for these high favours.

The hangman then stripped him to his shirt, fastened the halter round his neck, and secured it afresh to the horizontal bar of the gibbet.

Hereupon a person, who turned out to be a minister, addressed him—"Mr. Southwell, explain yourself further. If your meaning be according to the Council of Trent, it is false and damnable."

"Good master minister," he replied, with great humility, "for God's sake leave me alone in this my extremity. I want no controversy now. I do not argue, I will not criticise. I believe. Note you that I die a Catholic, putting my whole trust and confidence in the Passion and Death of my Saviour. I desire no controversy."

He then asked the prayers of those near,—pressing forward to hear his words,—who were awed into silence and attention by his sweet words and most modest manner. His face, as some remarked and afterwards recorded, was as the face of an angel.

"*Sancta Maria, Mater Dei, et omnes Sancti Dei, orate et intercedite pro me,*" he ejaculated. "God be merciful to me a sinner. Lord, into Thy hands I commend my spirit!" and he then made the sacred sign on his breast several times.

Here the cart was drawn away. At this act the knot of the rope slipped round to the back of his neck, and, as an eye-witness[1] records, "he remained hanging a good while, knocking his breast and making divers times the sign of the cross, turning his eyes up and down wide open."

One of the hangman's officers wished to have him cut down alive; but the people intensely excited, cried out so furiously against the proposal, that Lord Mountjoy forbade it. On the other hand, a humane person, holding on to his legs, this sudden weight ended his sufferings. He thus yielded up his soul to God.

The sanguinary details which followed, already described, took place as usual. When, however, the dissevered head was lifted up by the hangman, no one cried "Traitor," nor did any voice say "Amen" to the accustomed form.

Some of the preachers were intensely impressed by what they had witnessed; while one nobleman exclaimed, "When I die, God grant that my soul may go where his soul has gone"; for the poor sufferer had died in the holiest of causes—a defence of the unchangeable truth of God. He met death without fear, he was not only perfectly resigned, but suffered with joy. During his lifetime he had long truly measured the world's vanities, and duly apprehended the crimes and follies of men. The ever-fresh consolations of the faith, the majestic glories of the one Universal Church, the loving mercy of God his Saviour, and the peace promised to those who endure, had often been the themes of his sweet and melodious verse. Grace had evidently descended like dew in his death-agony; and so he soon found the longed-for calm after the storm, and reached the haven where he would be.

Has it never occurred to the reader, when asking God to "remember not our offences nor the offences of our forefathers," that such atrocities as these—for which there were precedents under Nero and Caligula—cried, and perhaps still cry, to heaven for vengeance; and that our miserable divisions, our sorrows, heart-sicknesses, and the evils of the present day, may be a part of our nation's well-deserved punishment?

2. Henry Walpole was the eldest son of Christopher Walpole of Docking and Hammer Hall in Norfolk, by Margaret, daughter of Richard Beckham of Narford. He was born in the last year

[1] Concerning Southwell, see *State Papers, Domestic, Elizabeth,* vol. cxcv. 114; also the volume for 1586, 755; Harl. MSS., Brit. Museum, No. 6998, folio 21; Lansdowne MSS. vols. lxxii. 39, and lxxiii. vols. 47; *State Papers, Domestic, Elizabeth,* vol. ccxxxv. 8.

of Queen Mary's reign. After receiving a good education, he proceeded to study the law, but witnessing the religious and political confusion which had been intensified by the change of religion, and after studying some of the current controversies, embraced the religion of his forefathers. In 1582 he went to Rheims, where in the register-book of the college he is described as " *Vir discretus, gravis et pius.*" After some study he proceeded to Rome, and in 1584 entered the Society of Jesus. Subsequently, three of his younger brothers, Richard, Christopher, and Michael, followed his example. Having been ordained to the minor orders by Goldweil, Bishop of St. Asaph, in 1583, he was eventually made priest in Paris in 1588. For some time he had been in Spain, helping in the work of the two English colleges of Seville and Valladolid. He was always earnest, zealous, and brave, ever displaying a calm enthusiasm. In this respect he was not unlike others who had already suffered for conscience' sake. Of Walpole it is on record that he was "an English gentleman of birth and fortune, a man of exceptionally high culture, of great intellectual gifts, of deep and fervent enthusiasm, who had sacrificed everything that most men hold dearest for what he believed to be Divine truth."

He came to England with the sole intention of labouring in defence of that truth, on December 4th, 1593. Within twenty-four hours he was apprehended, examined by the Earl of Huntingdon, Lord President of the North, and then by order of the Privy Council sent up to London. He was at once committed to the Tower, where he remained for a year. What there took place is set forth in the following record :—

He "met in the Tower of London with the greatest misery and poverty, so that the lieutenant himself, though otherwise a hard-hearted and barbarous man, was moved to inquire after some of the father's relations; and told them that he was in great and extraordinary want, without bed, without clothes, without anything to cover him, and that at a season when the cold was most sharp and piercing; so that himself, though an enemy, out of pure compassion, had given him a little straw to sleep on.

" Besides this, the father himself, in public court, upon occasion of answering some question that was put to him, declared *that he had been tortured fourteen times*, and it is very well known how cruel any one of those tortures is which are now in use. For it is a common thing to hang them up in the air six or seven hours by the hands, and, by means of certain irons, which hold their hands fast, and cut them, they shed much blood in the torture. The force of this torment may be gathered from what happened last Lent to a laic, called James Atkinson, whom they most cruelly tortured in this manner, to oblige him to accuse his own master, and other Catholics and priests; and kept him so long in torture, that he was at length taken away for dead after many hours' suffering, and, in effect, died within two hours. Some time after they carried the father back to York, to be there tried at the Midlent assizes.

"In all the journey he never went into bed, or even laid down upon a bed to rest himself after the fatigue of the day, but his sleep was upon the bare ground. When he came to York he was put into prison, where he waited many days for the judges' coming. In the prison he had nothing but one poor mat three feet long, on which he made his prayer upon his knees for a great part of the night; and when he slept it was upon the ground, leaning upon the same mat."[1]

Henry Walpole[2] was accused of three offences. Firstly, that he was a priest, ordained by the authority of the See of Rome; secondly, that he was a member of the Society of Jesus; and, thirdly, that he had returned to England to exercise the ordinary acts of these two callings, viz., to gain souls to God. Sergeant Saville was the prosecutor. The accused was tried by a jury before two judges, Francis Beamont and Matthew Ewens, with whom sat Lord Huntingdon, and Hillyard the Recorder of York; and made a spirited, forcible, and faithful defence. At times he was most opportune in his remarks, finding his education at Gray's Inn, of much advantage, and was often brilliant in his comments; moreover, he compelled one of the Judges to admit that his sole offence was his refusal to acknowledge the queen to be "supreme in things spiritual." He maintained that no earthly law, not in harmony with the law of God, could bind any Christian man's conscience; and that the due and proper submission to be paid to earthly princes must always be subordinate to that submission which the baptized directly owe to the great King of heaven and earth. His own confessions obtained on the rack were read by the Clerk of the Court. But his own spoken words were not lost upon the spectators.

He was offered his discharge if he would make his submission,

[1] Letter translated from the Bishop of Tarrasona's *History*, pp. 695, 696, dated 23rd of October 1595.

[2] For a most interesting and valuable life of Henry Walpole, the reader is referred to Dr. Jessopp's *One Generation of a Norfolk House*, 2nd edition, London, 1879, in which much research and singular impartiality are manifest throughout. It is a volume which is as interesting to the archæologian and genealogist as it is to the historian and divine; and could not be studied by any reader without both benefit and profit.

acknowledge the queen's usurped authority, and comply with the terms of the recent statutes. But to this offer he turned a deaf ear. It was impossible. It could not be done.

The jury, having been consequently directed to find him guilty of the indictment did so with very little consideration or consultation amongst themselves. This took place on April 3rd, 1595; he was sentenced to death on the 5th, and he suffered on Monday the 7th. With him was drawn another priest, Alexander Rawlins, who had been tried and condemned on the 5th of the same month, a Worcestershire gentleman's son, who had been educated at Oxford, ordained priest at Soissons, and had laboured in England with much success for nearly five years.

On the Sunday these two men were subjected to the spite and annoyance of certain ministers and others, who persisted in plaguing them with Protestant controversy. Sir Edwin Sandys, a lay-prebendary of York, not a minister, and Dr. George Higgens, Prebendary of Southwell, were the chief disputants. Sandys, who took up the "Gospel doctrine of justification," and "the supposed dignity of Peter's chair," preached for an hour and a quarter. The other man dealt with the subject of Elizabeth's supremacy. Walpole, who readily apprehended their sophistries, condescended to answer both, for many spectators had gathered for the encounter. On these his speech made a great impression.

On the following morning Rawlins suffered first, most bravely, without quailing or flinching—Walpole being a witness of all the sanguinary cruelties. Walpole's turn soon came. And he was prepared for it. He, too, died calmly, with the *Paternoster* and *Ave Maria* on his lips, and thus his righteous soul passed into the keeping of God,—a noble member of the Society of Jesus.

The Benedictines, as we know, had originally converted our country in Saxon times, while the impress of their glorious order is even now almost indelibly stamped on the sacred but desolated fanes of the land. Under Henry VIII. the devoted and saintly sons of St. Francis were found bold in their protest against sacrilege, and faithful even unto death. But persecution having done its work, and confiscation having wrought out so much ruin, it was reserved for the devoted sons of St. Ignatius (who had himself written to Cardinal Pole[1] of his desire to serve the souls in England), like Southwell and Walpole, to whose sufferings reference has just been made, to stand in the breach, to be

[1] *Epist. Card. Poli.* v. 119.

self-sacrificing and devoted, even to court the confessor's sufferings and to gain the martyr's crown.

A few other facts are worthy of note.   In 1595 Whitgift had attempted to impose what are known as the "Lambeth Articles,"[1] on the two provinces.   They were approved by many of the bishops and ministers; for being thoroughly Calvinistic, and Calvinism being in the ascendant, the proposed formularies were certainly popular.   At that time any other kind of theology was scarcely known.   But the queen, whose duty it was to govern the Church, as she well knew and often remarked, having consulted some shrewd and worldly-wise laymen and lawyers— whom the Calvinists had troubled,—would not allow these Articles to be accepted.

Two years afterwards the queen's general pardon[2] was granted for "all offences committed or done against the ecclesiastical state or government established in this realm, or any heresy or schism whatsoever."   The strong comments made abroad possibly led to this. . For of all the horrors which had been perpetrated for religion and conscience' sake, foreigners had received a true and plain-spoken account from the publications of exiled Catholics.   This pardon, like others, was to be "construed most beneficially for the subjects"; but the list of special cases and exceptions was so considerable that scarcely any offender, or supposed offender, could by any possibility have profited by it.

Sir John Harington, a most observant onlooker and a graphic writer, thus describes a dinner-party which was held towards the close of the queen's reign.   It is, for several reasons, so interesting, that it is here given without omission or amendment:—

"I was hourede at dinner with the Archbishoppe & several of the Churche pastors, where I did finde more corporeal than spiritual refreshmente; and though oure ill state at cowrte maie, in some sorte, overcaste the countenance of these apostolical messengers; yet were some of them well anointed with the oyl of gladnesse of Tuesdaie paste.   Hereof thou shalt in some sorte partake.   My Lorde of Salisburie had seizen his tenantes corne and haye, with sundrie husbandrie matters, for matters of money due to his lordshippe's estate : hereat the aggrievede manne made suite to the bishoppe and requestede longer time and restitution of his goodes :—'Go, go (saithe the bishoppe) I heare

---

[1] They were afterwards brought forward at the Hampton Court Conference, but rejected.   The Protestant Church in Ireland accepted them in 1615.
[2] 40 Elizabeth, c. xxviii.

ill reporte of thie livinge, and thou canst not crave mercie ; thou comeste not to Churche service, and haste not receivede confirmation; I commande thee to attend my ordinance and be confirmed in thy faithe at Easter nexte cominge.' 'I crave your lordshippes forgivenesse (quothe the manne), in goode soothe I durste not come there, for as youre lordshippe hath laine your hande on all my goodes, I thinke it full meete to take care of my heade!' Suche was parte of our discourse at dinner. So . . . although the bishoppes hande was heavy, oure pesantes head was not weake, and his lordshippe said he woude forego his payment."[1]

Some personal account of the queen, in order that the character of one who left so marked an impress on the Established Church, may be apprehended, must now be given. There are those who look upon her as a great political light, others as a " bright occidental star " in the orbit of religion ; while some might hesitate to bestow such praise as many partisan historians have so unstintedly rendered, and yet own an exceedingly inadequate idea of her varied characteristics and true character. From no single aspect could a just and impartial judgment be passed. ⌠It is necessary, therefore, to take more than a single standing-point in judging her fairly.

Queen Elizabeth was learned both in sacred and profane literature, and this learning was recognised and acknowledged by competent judges both at home and abroad. She wrote a firm and beautiful hand ; was skilful in composition, and frequently expressed herself in her mother tongue with as much grace as vigour. The foreign ambassadors were often struck by a display of her cultivated powers, as well as by her tact in action and her undoubted charm of conversation. She could reply in Latin to a formal address, and was often extremely happy in her apt quotations from classical authors. Like her father, of great natural abilities, she was proud of her theological acumen, and sometimes thought fit to set right her astonished prelates and divines by quoting some patristic aphorism or cleverly-selected text of Scripture ; or by perceiving a weak place in their ponderous homiletic arguments, into which, with no mercy, she pointedly and promptly thrust a sharp dialectical dart. With a Calvinistic bishop Her Highness was strongly anti-Calvinistic; with any one who had a tendency to favour the " old learning," she became for the nonce both destructive and revolutionary, or even rigidly Calvinistic, in her logical conclusions. An easy-going, obedient, and good-tempered man,

[1] Sir John Harington's *Letters*, p. 323.

like her godson, Henry Cotton,[1] however, was sure to be favoured, if he never crossed her wishes nor thwarted her will.

The language of flattery used by her favourites and attendants was so fantastic and extravagant, that it became almost always absurd and gross — so that maids-of-honour smiled sometimes in the background, or listless and yawning male idlers grinned or giggled. But nothing could be too gross for Her Highness's greedy acceptance. The greater the extravagance of the compliment, the more favourably it was received. Those at Court who were incapable of paying compliments and originating high-sounding and laudatory phrases, remained in the background, without either smiles, favours, or promotion.

Her unbounded vanity, in truth, often rendered her the laughing-stock of the more acute courtiers, who ridiculed her heartily because of it. Nothing pleased her better, or won her favour more surely, than profuse admiration of her person, and verbosely elaborate laudation of her natural graces; — both of which it was found positively necessary to use with unstinted generosity, by those ambitious adventurers who so anxiously sought to rise to power and influence in the State. When the graces of youth and middle age were steadily fading away, when the lines of her face were deepening and natural feebleness supervened, when her dressers had to truss her with care, and support her jewel-bedecked body with artificial appliances, she was more exacting of her admirers of the other sex than she had ever been before; while the least tokens of wavering on their part in their accustomed phrases of admiration, both merited and secured her certain and severest displeasure. To question her perfect grace and beauty, even as an old woman, when her bust had shrunk, and her neck had become sinewy and yellow, was an unpardonable sin.

She was likewise singularly irresolute. On subjects of great as well as of small moment, matters of state as well as of personal fancy, she could never make up her mind. From all sources, high as well as low, influential as well as the reverse, from maids-in-waiting as well as from ministers, she was accustomed to ask advice and counsel, but was altogether unable and unwilling to take it when offered. Ever deliberating, balancing

---

[1] Of this prelate, who was made Bishop of Salisbury, Sir John Harington thus wrote :—"She had blessed many of her godsons, but now this godson should bless her. Whether she were the better for his blessing, I know not ; but I am sure he was the better for hers. He married, very young, a woman whose name was Patience, and she brought him no less than nineteen children."—*Brief View of the State of the Church*, pp. 95, 96. London, 1653.

this consideration with the other, and delighting in so doing, she found it most difficult to come to a conclusion and decision on any subject, trivial or important; so much so that this habitual irresolution caused the greatest trouble and vexation to her ministers, as Cecil often cautiously noted in his written record of events. The queen's mind, as Sir Thomas Smith remarked in a letter to the Lord Treasurer, was "sometimes so, sometimes no; and in all times uncertain and ready to stays and revocation." "It makes me weary of my life," he went on to declare most piteously,—"I can neither get the other letters signed, nor the letters already signed permitted to be sent away; but, day by day, and hour by hour, deferred till anon, soon, and to-morrow." [1] The same, too, was more especially the case with Lord Burghley later on,[2] who wished his body had been made of iron or steel, so worried was he when he grew old.

At times her language was so coarse and unchaste[3] that foreign attendants and ambassadors, who sometimes accidentally heard it, were paralysed with astonishment. She rated both Houses of Parliament in such terms as a slave-driver might use to his slaves; she was often insolent to, and domineering over, her obsequious spiritual officers the bishops; abusing them with unwomanly violence, or silencing them with a vigorous and sometimes a frightful oath.[4] "Hedge-priest" was the scornful term she frequently applied to the obsequious but astonished new ministers. Their elaborate and painful preaching she characterised as "noisome babbling," occasionally telling the more stupid, or the prosy, or the over-fanatical, to come down from the pulpit and to "cease that useless noise." "Babble no longer, Master Dean," she once called out to Nowell, the chief officer of St. Paul's Cathedral, who was preaching. Though, on one occasion, she had condescended to be entertained at

---

[1] See "Sir Thomas Smith to Lord Burghley," the 6th of March 1574, in Strype's *Life of Sir T. Smith*, p. 139.

[2] Lord Burghley, writing to Walsingham, asked if he should attend at Court morning or evening, according to the tide. He wishes his body were of iron or steel, for with flesh and blood he cannot long endure.—*State Papers, Domestic, Elizabeth*, vol. cxc. 37.

[3] In a MS. "Memoria Mortuorum" which Cecil had made, the following questionable entry occurs:—"1558. 17 Nov. Maria Regina Angl. obiit, cui successit Eliz: *semper Virgo.*"—*State Papers*, Murdin, p. 745. London, 1759.

[4] Her usual oaths, varied a little in form, were, "By the death of God," "By God's Passion," "By God's blood," or "By God's wounds." When she was unusually excited, such formed the opening or close of almost every incoherent sentence.

Lambeth Palace, and to accept Archbishop Parker's munificent hospitality and valuable presents, she pointedly insulted his wife in her husband's domain and presence, with unnecessary sentences of epigrammatic spite ;[1] while Her Highness, on another occasion, irritated by his wit, was not above chastising an offending courtier by giving him a sharp box on the ear.

If her courtiers and flatterers spoke the truth, which is by no means certain was always the case, their mistress was a paragon of virtue, piety, and beauty. Though certainly not beautiful, her complexion was undoubtedly fair, her nose aquiline, her hair fine and yellow. Her teeth, too, were of the same colour. To judge from the numerous portraits existing, her arched eyebrows, like her lips, were thin and pale, her neck was long and scraggy; but, until she passed the age of fifty, her figure was tall and her general bearing stately. Her hands were thin, delicate, and white. So well-formed and graceful did she regard her own calf and ankle, that, coyly lifting her kirtle, she occasionally condescended to exhibit her royal legs for the admiration of her favourite courtiers or the most exalted representatives of foreign monarchs.[2] For such favours she expected in return a cluster of admiring adjectives in a set speech or an impromptu epigram on the perfect form of the limbs in question; or else an embellished compliment upon her remarkable grace of motion and her acknowledged capacities for dancing with agility. Furthermore, she had such an excellent idea of the unflecked brilliancy of her complexion, that she would never allow Nicholas Hilliard, the royal miniaturist, to make any, even the faintest, shadows whatsoever, in her portraits.[3] Contrasts to

[1] " You, Madam," she exclaimed, " who and what are you? *Madam* I may not call you; *Mistress* I am ashamed to call you; ' *Lady* ' I will not call you; but whatever you be, or think yourself to be, I thank you for your hospitality." See also Strype's *Life of Matthew Parker, in loco.* On another occasion, "When one of her chaplains, Mr. Alexander Nowell, Dean of St. Paul's, had spoke less reverently, in a sermon preached before her, of the sign of the cross, she called aloud to him from her closet window, commanding him to retire from that ungodly digression and return unto the text."—Dr. Peter Heylyn's *History of the Reformation*, p. 124.

[2] "The Duke of Nevers was honourably entertained by Her Majesty; she danced with him and courted him in the best manner; he, on the other side, using may compliments, as kissing her hand, yea and foot, when she showed him her leg."—*Von Raumer*, vol. ii. p. 180.

[3] This may be abundantly seen from an inspection of several miniatures belonging to the Duke of Buccleuch, K.G., which were exhibited at the Royal Academy in the spring of 1879, *e.g.* Case F., Nos. 4, 6, 7, 8, 19, 23, and 24—all representing Queen Elizabeth—with the exception of No. 8, each being from the pencil of Nicholas Hilliard. Some of the other miniatures of this successful artist,—notably his own and his wife's portraits, as

bring out the obvious projection of the nose, or the natural·
rotundity of the chin and cheeks, were strictly forbidden by
royal command.   Her complexion, in Her Highness's judgment,
was so pure and good that only white paint could represent it.
Hence the existing portraits of her are invariably as flat and
colourless as Chinese paintings, and very often as uninteresting
and unattractive.

Even the bloody statute of Elizabeth's twenty-seventh year,
after it had been in operation for eighteen long and weary years,
at the close of her life, could not utterly root out the ancient
faith.   The maintainers of this, though hated of all men for
Christ's sake, endured nobly even unto the end.   Such, at least,
was the case with many.   Avoiding the old churches, rifled and
bare, which they looked upon as desecrated and degraded anew
by the Calvinistic rites and homiletic orgies performed in them ;
regarding the new bishops as State superintendents — "the
queen's wedded superintendents," as they were termed — and
looking upon the successors of the ancient priests as mere
ministers, they sought none of their aid, but passed them by
with contumely and scorn.   Into some of the benefices tailors
and tinkers, who had heartily adopted Calvinism as a religion,
had long been previously thrust by Protestant patrons and duly
inducted by the bishops.[1]   Whether such persons were ordained
by any visible act seems exceedingly doubtful.   For with such
sectaries "the outpouring of the Spirit" manifested in wild
reasoning and tortuous talk, was the only needful ordination ;
while, as to the receipt and possession of this self-selected gift,
the preachers themselves regarded their own convictions and
testimony on this point as far superior to any ".greasing or
patting of pates," as some amongst them so profanely phrased
it.   The fonts, where of old the people's ancestors had received
the washing of regeneration, were unfilled and unconsecrated ;
and so baptism was consequently sought in secret and solitary
places, the glade or the moor, away from human habitation ;
where by appointment true priests met them to shed the grace

well as that of Lady Arabella Stuart,—are less flat and more artistic.   A large
oil-painting at Dytchley, Oxon., which the queen herself gave to Sir Henry
Lee, shows that other and more ambitious portrait-painters were likewise
obliged to avoid the making of shadows on representations of her royal face.

[1] " Many of those who were presented to the livings in private patronage
were mere laymen ; and there is room, therefore, for us to believe that what
have been thought insults done to the Blessed Sacrament, were really only
the trampling under foot of that which really was what these fanatics believed
it to be—mere bread and wine."— *The Reformation and the Prayer Book*, by
Nicholas Pocock, M.A., p. 38.   London, 1875.

of regeneration, or unite the faithful in the marriage bond. In Yorkshire,[1] for example, Squire Cholmley, of Branderby, and a daughter of the knightly house of Hungate of Saxton, in the presence of four trusty witnesses, as the existing record narrates, "were married by a Popish priest in a fell." The mansions of each family had, no doubt, long been carefully watched by spy and pursuivant. So the company in question went out with some trusted priest, at the risk of his liberty and life, to some secluded spot on the wild moorlands, and there under the canopy of heaven the sacrament was ministered and God's blessing asked on the happy union.

In the northern counties, it is certain from existing MSS.—"Lists" of so-called "Recusants"—that from ten to fifty persons in every village openly stood apart from the new religion, while hundreds secretly disliked and despised it. Though disputes were popular in that restless period, and controversy all the rage, yet a sturdy and honourable number of all classes were thoroughly true to the faith of their fathers. Bribes could not win them to error, nor persecution daunt their unshaken resolution to maintain the cause of truth.

Early in January 1601, Orsini, Duke of Graciano, arrived in London upon a courtly mission. He was a young and handsome nobleman, and the Italian merchants received and feasted him sumptuously. A certain Alderman Radcliffe housed and entertained him. The poor queen, trembling and wrinkled, who had then passed her sixty-seventh year,—and who went into a paroxysm of fury if any one even indirectly hinted at mortal sickness, death, or the grave,—was carefully and painfully prepared by her dressers and maids-in-waiting, for the work of receiving the duke; upon whom she evidently desired to make a deep impression, which no doubt she did. A stomacher set with pearls, diamonds, and gold embroidery, was brought out of her well-stocked wardrobe-house,[2] and in this, over a laced chemise, the infirm body of Her Highness was carefully encased. Her petticoat, rich with open pomegranates embroidered in gold

---

[1] A list of the Roman Catholics in the county of York in 1604. Tran scribed from the original MS. in the Bodleian, and edited by Edward Peacock, F.S.A., p. 121. London, 1872.

[2] "One Sunday (April last) my lorde of London [Aylmer] preachede to the Queene's Majestie, and semede to touch on the vanitie of deckinge the bodie too finely. Her Majestie tolde the ladies that 'if the bishope held more discorse on suche matters, she wolde fit him for heaven, but he shoulde walke thither without a staffe, and leave his mantle behind him.' Perchance the bishope hath never soughte Her Highnesse wardrobe, or he woulde have chosen another texte."—Sir John Harington's *Nugæ Antiquæ*, vol. i. p. 170.

thread, was at once stiff and gorgeous. She wore a pair of the
newest, and then still rare, pink silk stockings; a huge frill,
studded with pearls and made to stand up and stick out by
means of gold wire, was placed round her long neck. Jewels
in profusion, pendent and fastened, emeralds, diamonds, and
sapphires, were everywhere displayed upon her person; and,
after having been carefully painted, trussed, and scented, and
then allowed to repose for awhile (as well as might be, in such
a fatiguing costume), she announced herself as ready to receive
the duke. This was done with exceptional state and dignity,
Her Highness supporting herself when she rose from her chair
of state with an ivory walking-stick, inlaid with gold and orna-
mented with rubies and brilliants.

"The queen," as may be read in an original letter, "hath been
pleased to have many pleasant discourses with him, and to dance
before him; and he, as a well-experienced courtier, knew [how]
to make show of admiring herself as most excellent, and her
actions as incomparable."[1] But by this time amusement began
to pall upon her, and she was losing her appetite.[2]

To show the duke that she had not cut herself entirely off from
the Christian religion, the queen "invited him to go with her to
the closet over the chapel, having before given order that the communion-table should be adorned with basin and ewer of gold and
evening tapers and other ornaments, some say also with a crucifix,
and that all the ministry should be in rich copes. The Duke [out]
of curiosity, accompanied her, and she was very pleasant thereat,
saying she would write to the Pope, not to chide him for that fact."

At the close of her life, a close now slowly drawing on, survey-
ing the religious devastation which had been created at home,
and the frightful divisions which had resulted from "the reforms"
effected;—knowing, too, the misery and dissatisfaction which
existed amongst the poor,—the queen was anxious to show to
this foreign nobleman that she was not so bad as she had been
painted by certain foreign enemies; and that the new National

---

[1] Author's Original MSS. and Excerpts.

[2] "Her Majestie enquirede of some matters I had written; and as she was
pleasede to note my fancifulle braine, I was not unheedfull to feed her
humoure, and reade some verses, whereat she smilede once, and was pleasede
to saie, "When thou doste feele creepinge tyme at thye gate, these fooleries
will please thee lesse; I am paste my relish for such matters: thou seeste my
bodilie meate doth not suite me well; I have tasted but one ill tastede cake
since yesternighte." She rated me most grievouslie, at noone, at some who
minded not to bring uppe certaine matters of accounte. Several menne hath
been sente to, and when readie at hande, Her Highnesse hath dismissed in
anger; but who, dearest Mall, shall saye "Your Highnesse hath forgotten."'"
—*Harington's Letters*, vol. i. p. 323.

Church which had been set up, as regards the taste and wishes of its supreme governess,[1] owned certain external features in common with the Church of the Nicene Creed, born on the first Pentecost, that is with the Church of the living God.

The weakness and paralysis of old age were in Her Majesty now more marked than ever, while sometimes rheumatic pains in her left arm and left side were so trying and unbearable, that she was obliged for very suffering to call in the aid of some "cunning bone-setter or surgeon."[2]   The most distant hint from such an

[1] The best defence of this office in the Christian Church, or perhaps in a National Church, which the author has lighted upon is the following from the pen of Dr. Heylyn.   But bad is the best :—"For that an abbess may be capable of all and all manner of ecclesiastical jurisdiction, even to the denouncing of that dreadful sentence of excommunication ; and that they may lawfully exercise the same upon all such as live within the verge of their authority, is commonly acknowledged by their greatest canonists.   First for Suspension ; it is affirmed by their Glosse that an abbess may suspend such clerks as are subject to her, both from their benefice and office.   And, questionless, either to suspend a clerk or to bring his church under the sentence of an interdict, is one of the chief parts of ecclesiastical and spiritual censures.   Nor have they this authority only by way of delegation from the Pope in some certain cases, as is affirmed by Aquinas, Durandus, Sylvester, Dominicus Soto, and many other of their schoolmen, but in an ordinary way as properly and personally invested them, which is the general opinion of their greatest canonists.   Next for the sacraments ; it is sufficiently known that the ministration of baptism is performed by midwives, and many other women, as of common course ; not only as a thing connived at in extreme necessity, but as a necessary duty, in which they are to be instructed against all emergencies by their parish priests ; for which we have the testimony of the late Lord Legate in the articles published by him for his visitation.   And finally for excommunication : it is affirmed by Palladanus and Navarre (none of the meanest in the pack) that the Pope may grant that power to a woman also : higher than which there can be none exercised in the Church by the sons of men.   And if a Pope may grant these powers unto a woman, as to a prioress or abbess, or to any other, there can be, then, no incapacity in the sex for exercising any part of that jurisdiction which was restored unto the Crown by this Act of Parliament."—*The History of Queen Elizabeth*, by Peter Heylyn, p. 109.   London, 1671.

[2] "The Court hath been at Richmond these twelve days, but the queen in many humours to have removed to Greenwich, by reason of an ache in one of her arms, expecting more ease by change of air.   A cunning bone-setter or surgeon had lately a sight hereof ; he said it was a wind with a cold rheumatic humour settled there, and to be removed by rubbing and applying of wet oils and ointments.   Her Majesty told him he was mistaken, for that her blood and constitution were of its nature very hot.   He replied that neither flesh nor blood in that part made any show thereof, but much more the contrary ; whereat she was exceedingly displeased, commanding him from her presence, she being most impatient to hear of any decay in herself, and thereupon will admit no help of physic or surgery, fretting and storming when she feeleth any little pain, and sometimes retiring herself from all access for three or four hours together."—*State Papers, Domestic, Elizabeth*, vol. cclxxxvii. 50.

one as to natural decay or reasonable infirmity being the direct cause of her increasing ailments, insured Her Highness's sore displeasure. Storming and fretting, as was her wont, she ordered a physician out of her presence, merely because he had ventured to imply that an old lady of nearly seventy years of age could not expect to be as hale and nimble as a girl of eighteen.

For now her cheeks were shrivelled and had fallen in; but when she appeared in public she managed somehow to have them filled inside with pads or folds of linen cloth,[1] so that they might appear to the sightseers unshrunken and full; while pink and white paint was artfully laid upon her face and breast in several coats and layers.[2] But all to no purpose or effect. Neither paint, nor fine clothes, nor false flattery, nor rich jewels, could stave off the advent of the last enemy. The inevitable end was drawing on, her "frolicksomeness" was artificial and strained; when over-frolicksome she stumbled sometimes, or fell heavily upon a couch, wounded in hip-bone or elbow-joint, and was unable to get up again; while physical weakness was steadily increasing. The evening of life was surely nearing and closing in; the day of retribution was at length about to dawn.

It is not an uncommon belief, that when old people approach their latter end—no matter how dulled their hearing may have become or how imperfect their sight—they not only realise again all the details of the past (like a drowning person), but sometimes begin to see glimpses of the world beyond the grave, with a vividness which mere words all too inadequately depict. Judging by the testimony of astonished onlookers, such was the case with this perturbed and wretched woman in her latest days. The past was dark indeed. Gazing, but not seeing, she sat for hours with glazing eyes, staring into vacancy. Occasionally she drew a long sigh and shuddered visibly. The least sound annoyed her. Her irritability was excessive and most disquieting to all those who were in attendance.

The poor creature, as her end drew nearer, became more and

---

[1] "The ache of the queen's arm is fallen into her side, but she is still, thanks to God, frolicky and merry. Only her face showeth some decay, which to conceal when she cometh in public, she putteth many fine cloths into her mouth to bear out her cheeks; and sometimes as she is walking she will put off her petticoat, as seeming too hot, when others shake with cold."—From Anthony Rivers, dated 17th of March 1602, from Venice, and signed "Giacomo Creleto."—*State Papers, Domestic, Elizabeth*, vol. cclxxxvii.

[2] "It was commonly observed this Christmas (A.D. 160⅔) that Her Majesty when she came to be seen, was continually painted, not only all over her face, but her very neck and breast also, and that the same was in some places near half an inch thick."—Anthony Rivers to Robert Parsons, dated, London, 13th of January 160⅔. Stonyhurst MSS., Anglia, vol. iii.

more disturbed—as her now drawn and wizen features too truly
demonstrated.   She had long suspected every one near her, and
did not hesitate to declare, in deep bitterness of spirit, that all
her former friends were turning their eyes from the setting to the
rising sun.   It was no wonder that they did so.   For the spectacle they might have witnessed in an oak-panelled chamber of
Richmond Palace was certainly distressing and terrible to contemplate.   The thread of her existence was being gradually
attenuated.   Sleep had fled from her.   Throughout the long
winter nights her sighs and groans had been painful to listen to.
She turned from side to side constantly.   Sometimes the flicker-
ing of a lamp or the flaring fire-light made strange shadows on
the arras; or the smouldering logs fell suddenly on to the
hearth from the brazen dog-irons with a. noise, and then she.
started up in bed harassed and terrified anew as if by the presence of unquiet spirits.   When the wind sighed round the
palace eaves, or made the loose-fitting lattices rattle, her
disturbed imagination drew dark and dreadful pictures.

Her friend, the Countess of Nottingham, had recently died,
and this greatly troubled the queen.   It carried her in thought
to the very edge of an open grave—which she hated and feared
more than any other object.

In March of the year 1603, the symptoms of declining powers
were more than ever evident.   Her physicians saw that the end
could not be far off, and by their words implied as much.

From this time the Lord Admiral, the Lord Keeper, Sir
Robert Cecil, and one of the Secretaries, remained constantly
at Richmond, and were duly informed of her state.

On one occasion, for two days and three nights she sat
huddled up on a stool, partly dressed,, and propped up by
pillows, and no one could persuade her either to move or to go
to bed.   Whitgift proposed to "read a Scripture and to pray," but
she ordered him to desist and make no disturbance.   What a
spectacle it was!   When the artificial hair and the paint and the
puffs and the paddings were absent, she seemed but a shrivelled
and yellow old woman, possessed by some demon of obstinacy.
Her lank forefinger was often placed for hours upon her thin
lips, her eyes resting on the ground.   A shudder now and then
passed through her wrecked frame.   Her toothless gums spas-
modically chattered.   She refused all food and often declined to
open her pursed-up and parched lips at all.

From Lord Howard she once consented to receive a basin of
broth, of which she took a portion.   But, when he urged her to
return to bed, she replied that if he himself had seen what she

had beheld as she lay there, he would never have made such a request.

When, however, possibly to humour her fancies, Sir Robert Cecil, Burghley's son, asked her with some earnest anxiety whether she had not seen spirits gliding by, she replied that his question was idle, and quite beneath her notice. " Perhaps she had, perhaps she had not."

When, in company with others, he, implored her to take rest, saying, "Your Majesty must go to bed to satisfy your loving subjects," she stared with astonishment.

" Must !" she exclaimed in feeble and broken accents, but with effort,—"is 'must' a word to be addressed to princes? By God, little man, if your father had been alive he durst not have used such a word to Us. But ye have all grown daringly presumptuous, because you know that I shall die. Away with ye, each one. Be off."

They retired, all but Lord Nottingham, whom she begged to stay, and who induced her to take to her bed at last, where she lay for a fortnight. (" My lord," she once said, "I am tied with an iron collar round my neck. I have none whom I can trust. I am forsaken by all and left alone. I have no hope. All my affairs are changed.")

Such indeed and in truth was the fact, and in that final plight, lapsing into insensibility and so remaining for several days, her spirit passed away. On the 24th of March 1603 she died[1] at two o'clock in the morning.

In the world's judgment, a judgment sometimes reversed, she was the greatest and most renowned of the rulers of England. Her temporal successes, her victorious wars, and her determined policy had made this country more potent than heretofore. Posterity, it is assumed, has ratified the judgment of the World.

We may well ask ourselves calmly, some centuries after her day, in what this woman's so-called "glory" and "glorious reign" had consisted? Numerous treaties and solemn compacts with other sovereigns were notoriously broken, to the scandal of diplomacy and the shame of her diplomatists. Some of her naval officers were little better than pirates and adventurers. She was frequently found assisting the rebellious subjects of neighbouring kings, by money, arms, and moral influence—thus, at her advisers' suggestion, committing the kingdom and the helpless people who comprised it to an acceptance of anti-

---

[1] " It is not known that in all this sickness she said 'God, help me !' or any prayer or aspiration calling on God or asking His mercy."—*Life of Jane Dormer, Duchess of Feria*, A.D. 1616, p. 100. London, 1887.

Christian principles.   These still energise; while many of the
nation's greatest and most pressing social evils and political
dangers obviously date from Elizabeth's reign.   From that day
to this confusion has never been absent, and discord has never
been banished.   While, after all the reforms and changes
continually effected, change is still desired and fresh reforms are
being constantly planned.

It has now been shown in the present historical sketch by
what method the changes of Queen Elizabeth's reign were
brought about. (Force constantly triumphed over conscience
and right.) How the faithful were robbed of their spiritual
privileges and graces—privileges, rights, and graces bequeathed
at His Ascension by our Divine Lord to all the baptized of
every subsequent age,—how, from the ranks of those who
systematically resisted change, a crowd of martyrs [1] were sent up
to their well-won rest and glory,—is here faithfully sketched and
recorded. (Nothing has been set down in malice.   For charity
ever forbids the raking-up of needless scandals, and therefore
none which were needless to be known *have* been raked up in
these pages.   Some, unearthed from their obscurity, have been
allowed to rest again unnoticed.) Only those have been lightly
touched upon, however, which seemed necessary to enable
historical truths to be rightly apprehended, and the true position
of the Established Church under Elizabeth to be realised.

What it is, and where it stands now, we all know too well.   Its
position, in regard to the domination of the State or public
opinion, is far more abject· than that of the contemporary
Established community in Scotland, which notoriously owns
much greater freedom and independence.

Where is the statesman, for instance, who does not maintain
the absolute right of Parliament—wholly independent of the

---

[1] The author of an article on "The Elizabethan Martyrs," in the *Church
Quarterly Review* for April 1879 (pp. 98–125), asserts most confidently that
"it is well and just to remember that the Church of England, as a Church,
had no complicity with Elizabeth and the Privy Council in this miserable
business" of hanging and quartering priests.   The author of it is evidently
unacquainted with the doings of Pilkington, Sandys, Chaderton, Aylmer,
Cowper, and others—all of whom were cruel and tormenting persecutors.
The expression "as a Church" is ambiguous : it is quite true, of course, that
no synodical action enjoined the use of torture or sanctioned the cruelties
practised, but some of the rulers of the new institution were members of the
Council, and others were certainly active in punishing its conscientious
opponents who clung to the ancient faith ; and in almost every diocese the
bishops led the way in these cruelties.   Moreover, no prelate ever protested
against them. ·

spirituality—to regulate the affairs of the Church of England equally with the internal arrangements and actual working of the Post Office or the School Board? Where is the bishop who actually and practically adopts, or dreams of adopting, any other principle than that embodied in the precedented and venerable Oath of Homage? Where, then, can be found the reasonably-instructed person who, if not an Erastian, does not, as a consequence of realising this fact, feel keenly the moral degradation involved in accepting such a position? According to one great authority,[1] however, Englishmen can no more escape the royal supremacy than they can shun the air they breathe,—an assertion, it may be, somewhat too sweeping and bold. For a system which has come to be despised, and which appears to have made such demands and strains on the solemn oaths of the judges to enable them to uphold it at any cost, and by any method ready to hand, is not very likely to enjoy a prolonged life. Possibly future, and not very remote, events may point a way for such an escape. Possibly even the existing ecclesiastical newspapers may chronicle its painless decease. Like Hindoo women who are sacrificed at their husbands' funeral-pyre, however, other deaths may occur, and other feebler institutions soon die, when this has taken place. So be it. Time will show.

But the one Church of Pentecost, the Ark of Salvation, not national but universal, in the nations, but not dominated by their secular rulers, can alone bring order out of our disorder—harmony and unity out of chaos. It depends not for success on the will of sovereigns, nor on the babble of senates, nor upon the changeable fancies of the multitude. It has a message to deliver, clear, concise, consistent; and this message, whether men hear or whether they forbear, it delivers with unfaltering

[1] The Editor of the *Guardian* (June 18th, 1879) specially called the attention of two clergymen to the exact question at issue, thus:—"Canon Carter and Mr. Berdmore Compton, if they think the matter out, will find that they *can no more escape the royal supremacy than they can shun the air they breathe*. Religious societies which are established have their tribunals for determination of differences constituted by State law, or, at least, recognised and authorised by State law. Religious societies which are not established no doubt set up their own tribunals with 'consensual jurisdiction'; but these are always liable to have their decisions reviewed on actions for breaches of contract and appeals *comme d'abus*. Cool-headed and thoughtful men deem the interests of truth (?) more stable and more safe, on the whole, under the former system than under the latter. But there is nothing to prevent Mr. Carter and his friends proposing such a Court of Appeal as they can submit to with a good conscience. The difficulty will be that any court that would satisfy them would be rejected by a large majority, as we believe, of lay Churchmen; and so would have slender chance of obtaining the necessary legal authority."

utterance and unfailing boldness.   When it is proposed to halve
or compromise God's Truth, entrusted to man for man, the only
answer is, or can be, "*Non possumus.*" Its terms and definitions,
instead of being obscure and ambiguous, as some profess to
maintain, are only too clear; and, though many deny this, the
fact is again and again the more apparent as the years pass by.

The Reformation, commenced under Henry VIII. and completed under Elizabeth, was justifiable, in truth, on one principle,
and one principle only—that which for half a century was
enunciated and proclaimed by supreme authority, set forth by
all the archbishops and bishops, read four times a year by the
ministers, and accepted by their allies; but which all reasonably-
informed members of the Church of England now repudiate as
historically false and inherently ridiculous, viz. "*that laity and
clergy, learned and unlearned, all ages, sects, and degrees of men,
women, and children of whole Christendom (an horrible and most
dreadful thing to think) have been at once drowned in abominable
idolatry, of all other vices most detested of God and most damnable
to man, and that by the space of eight hundred years and more.*"[1]

On this astonishing statement of principle, which obviously
guided all the Reformers of Elizabeth's reign, the changes, works
of destruction, and various frightful cruelties then perpetrated,
and already recorded, might, in some respects, have had some
shadow of justification, but not otherwise.

Those, consequently, who believe this awful statement of the
"Homilies" to be true (a few persons still cling to a now
exploded tradition) are perfectly justified in labouring to
maintain[2] the state of confusion, disorder, neglect,[3] contradic-

---

[1] "Homilies Appointed to be Read in Churches."   Third Part of the *Homily
against Peril of Idolatry*, p. 201.   Oxford, 1816.

[2] "It was the Papists who, as we all know, reared the-e abbey-churches,
where they offered mass continually, but some four centuries ago the
buildings were taken away from them, and wholly or in part destroyed.
That this was really done with the approval of the Most High, no matter
what instruments were employed, we cannot doubt—the principle being the
same as that which obtained in the case of the idolatrous Canaanites who,
when 'their iniquity had come to the full,' were driven out of their land,
which fell forthwith into the hands of the Israelites.   Now *it is only on this
principle that the Reformation can be defended.*   The Papists were idolaters,
and when *their* 'iniquity had come to the full'—like the heathen nations of
Palestine and for the self-same cause—they, too, were despoiled of their
possessions.   But they may justly claim the right of re-entry if their
Protestant successors do the same things for which they themselves were
driven out."—*The Rock*, a Church of England family newspaper, September
26th, 1879.

[3] Some recent statistics given to the world by the bishops themselves (A.D.
1879) afford some idea of the degraded and disgraceful state of the country.

tion, and conflict, which threatens our beloved country with the destruction of all belief in any revelation from God Almighty of any sort or kind; and which has its poisonous root in the daring principle of reform already referred to.

A recent Bishop of Winchester[1] recently put the following exact and incisive question concerning that series of events which has been partly recorded here—"Was it not clearly," he asked concerning the Reformation, "either a dire necessity or a most dreadful crime?"

For himself—fearing neither horn of this defined dilemma—the author is free to confess that, though he never altogether liked the account of those events, as dressed up and exhibited by cunning writers, like Burnet, Hume, and the late Professor Blunt, whom as a youth he read; yet he had not the faintest conception of the true nature of the proceedings of the Reformers and their patrons, until he began to study systematically and closely their actual sayings and doings in historical records and contemporary publications. He now sees what they were. He now knows something of their principles. He has at length discovered who was their Master, and by whom they must have been instigated to the work they so artfully accomplished. No doubt they were inspired. The result of their successful labours (which conclusively show it) is before our very eyes in unity broken, in authority,[2] civil as well as ecclesiastical, almost destroyed; in schism of every sort completely justified; in heresy at once fostered, strengthened, and sheltered. This is a distressing discovery—a startling acknowledgment—a most painful confession. Would to God it were false or a mere phantasy! But alas, alas! notwithstanding what some of our highest officers in the State continue to assert[3]—it is only too true.

For example, in the diocese of Norwich there are exactly one thousand and fifty churches—in seven hundred and forty-six of which there is only a monthly communion; while in more than two hundred it is only administered quarterly. In the diocese of Hereford, containing four hundred and thirty-six churches, monthly communion is the rule in nearly three hundred. In the diocese of Bath and Wells, where the churches number five hundred and forty-six, there is no weekly communion in four hundred and nine. The state of the Welsh dioceses, of which less is known, is even more deplorable.

[1] Bishop E. Harold Browne.

[2] At all events, the only true Christian basis on which Authority should rest. All power belongs to our Lord. Authority comes from above, not from below; from God, not from the rabble, as Mr. J. R. Green has maintained.

[3] "The immense majority of the clergy and laity of the Church of England believe the Reformation to have been under the guidance of God's Providence, a return to the doctrine, and a nearer approach to the worship, of the earliest ages of the Church of Christ."—Bishop of London's Charge, November 1879.

The National Church, however, after all, is a great and important as well as a very useful and valuable institution, and is the
source of immense advantage to the people of England.   It
teaches them, as they acknowledge, a reasonable religion, which
satisfies and pleases them,—a religion of sobriety, compromise,
and moderation.   This was made expressly for them, with some
art and greater tact, under the Tudor monarchs; and has been
frequently modified and wisely mended, from time to time, in
order to suit the variable dispositions and wishes of majorities of
the people under varying circumstances and during silent revolutions.   The politician who proposed to destroy it would certainly
incur a most grave and serious responsibility.   For at present
there is obviously nothing sufficiently organised to take its place.
It has perhaps lost half the population,—though this seems
doubtful, as the Nonconformists, though bragging loudly, have
long feared the results of an official Census,—and it undoubtedly
owns considerable mundane vigour.   Perhaps the present
activity of the various conflicting religions within its pale is its
greatest and most pressing danger.   A community founded on
the principle of reform, however, is of course ever liable to reform.
The Church of England, consequently, is always being reformed
by the active, by self-seekers, and by the prescient amongst its
masters and pastors.   There is no rest because of the labours of
such; while, after all, internal dissensions are certainly neither
less frequent, less extended, nor less bitter than they were of old.
To be a clerical reformer—more especially to reform, and cast a
slur upon, what little of the Christian Faith remains—is sometimes to win the blue riband of worldly honours and Authority,
and to merit the nation's ungrudging applause.   Such Reformers
by consequence flourish and abound.
• Notwithstanding all such drawbacks, however, the Church of
England—with perhaps a clear majority of the nation, even if
the indifferent be subtracted—seems to a certain extent rooted
in their affections, having been marvellously bound up with the
customs and institutions of the country for some centuries ; and
still exercises an obvious influence beyond its own immediate
limits.   It has partially forgotten the hideous heresies, the wickedness, and the confusion under Elizabeth.   It has survived
the horrors and persecution of the Civil War and Cromwell's
sanguinary atrocities.   It has lived through the legal expulsion of
the Nonconformists, the intrusion of William the Dutchman, and
the bold breach made by the Nonjurors—long ago extinct.   The
mischievous influence of Deism, Latitudinarianism, and the
Hanoverian Erastians, though chilling and deadly, was partially

cast out.   Then Joseph Butler wrote, a master and a guide.
Wesley and Whitfield preached to the dry bones in our very dry
valley; while, later on, Keble, learning the Catholic faith concerning the Eucharist and Our Lady in middle life, sang so
beautifully[1] that Englishmen listened and learnt; and thus their
sentiments now happily are neither so ambiguous and inexact as
heretofore regarding the faith of their fathers, nor are their
prejudices either so grotesque or so deep as once they were.
Foxe, the so-called "martyrologist" has been found out; while
the historical artifices and arts of Gilbert Burnet, the Scotchman,
are now more truly and properly appraised.   For all this, no
Christian Englishman can be too heartily grateful.

As regards "Our Church" and country, we have lived to see
great changes both abroad and at home, in our colonies and
dependencies as well as in England.   Even greater seem likely
to ensue.   The seeds of Paganism, strange to note, are springing
up on Christian soil. Of old, for example, the resolution and
might of the Turks often alarmed Europe in bygone ages ; now
their social decay and abject weakness actively stimulate its
jealousies.   At the "Reformation" at home, abbeys and churches
were destroyed by thousands ; now they are being restored and
rebuilt.   Ugliness and baldness were then popular; now Art has
once more become the proper handmaid of religion.   Then,
again, some kind of spiritual independence has already been
secured in Canada, South Africa, and elsewhere ; while "Bishops
by Letters Patent" seem likely to become an extinct race.
Anciently the prejudices of our own people were intense even to
absurdity, as regards the faith of their forefathers and the Primate
of Christendom, both of which they feared as well as hated; now
the modern principle of civil and religious liberty, commended
even by a Roman Catholic historian,[2] but perhaps even now a
little run to seed, has done something towards blunting the
weapons of professional controversialists, and securing a fair field
and no favour even for those who have so consistently maintained
the value and importance of Authority, existing on a Christian
basis.

For our manifold religious evils there is but one true and efficient remedy—corporate reunion with the rest of the Christian

---

[1] The enormous sale of "The Christian Year," beyond that of any other
contemporary poetry, and the unparalleled success of "Hymns Ancient and
Modern," proves what an influence poetry and verse may exercise on all
classes of a nation.

[2] *The History of England*, by John Lingard, D.D., vol. vi. p. 324.
Dublin, 1874.

family; not to be attained by the presence or act of compromise nor by the sacrifice of truth, nor by the rejection of Authority nor by flattering the rabble that Authority of right belongs to them—the ignoble work even of certain of the clergy. If there be a union or compact for united action amongst the enemies of Christianity to maim and destroy and overturn; surely, on the other hand, there should be active co-operation and harmony amongst the servants of the Crucified, to repair, to restore, and to build up again anew. Some are beginning to see this,[1] and to adopt a wise and far-sighted policy of peace and co-operation. For "union is strength."[2] No scheme of union founded on self-seeking or self-pleasing can be lasting. Its only sure foundation is Christian Authority—based on the Rock of Divine Truth.

To effect this, men must be patient and enduring. The insults of the Erastians (who have been put into places of trust and high office because they *are* Erastians) are sometimes difficult to bear;[3] the studied contumely which some in ecclesiastical

[1] At a meeting of those interested in the reunion of Christendom, held at the Westminster Palace Hotel, on July 8th, 1879, the chair being taken by the Earl Nelson, the following resolutions were proposed and carried unanimously :—(1) "That the movement of 1833 can only attain its proper and adequate completion in the corporate reunion of Christendom;" (2) "That 'the religious difficulty' in Christian countries, and the failure of missionary enterprise to affect sensibly the vast masses of heathendom, are at once a record and a warning of the fatal consequences of disunion;" (3) "That there is much in the present attitude both of the religious and the irreligious world, as well to encourage the hopes as to deepen the zeal of those who are labouring for the restoration of visible unity."

[2] See the various interesting documents on this important subject given in Appendix No. II.

[3] The Erastian principle appears to be steadily making way abroad, under the Archbishop's patronage and authority. For example, the *Barbadoes Agricultural Reporter* of June 27th, 1879, has the following remarkable paragraph in its leading columns :—"The impulsive and indiscreet Bishop of the diocese (Dr. Mitchinson) has again, as usual, been using his best endeavours to earn himself what is now technically expressed by the stereotyped phrase, 'unenviable notoriety,' this time in gratuitously mutilating our beautiful marriage service by *omitting the names of the Second and Third Persons of the Blessed Trinity, while reading the Service, in order to pander to the religious views of a scion of the Hebrew race in this community, lately united in wedlock at the Cathedral to a Protestant lady by his lordship, who undertook to perform the Service when no other clergyman could be found to do so.* The most profound sensation has been erected by this unseemly, indecorous, unepiscopal, unprotestant, and unprecedented little illegal *faux pas* of his lordship; and it is the opinion of many that he can and ought to be brought to book for presuming to do, in Barbadoes, what the Archbishop of Canterbury would not dare attempt to do in England." Another *protégé* of Dr. Tait, the Bishop of Gibraltar, in his last Pastoral Letter, writes as follows concerning a school at Tunis, which he visited, supported by English money :—"The boys' school had on its books one hundred and forty, the girls'

authority deliberately throw upon the Catholic movement is often irritating to those who have to endure it.   But to be irritated is neither wise nor Christian, and, in the long run, promotes no cause.   When once, therefore,—in the light both of Reformation-revelations and recent events[1]—the true character of the Establishment is apprehended and taken in; when the windows of the mind have been cleaned; when foolish ideals of actual facts have fallen down like Dagon, and dusty cobwebs of some antiquity have been carefully brushed away: when the individual sight is clearer—other people's green spectacles being put away —and the actual light is stronger, many more will be able to see that, in its chief phase, the National Church of England is indeed "of the earth earthy," and that the official utterances and action of its rulers constantly proclaim that fact.   With some persons, ere they can realise this, patience and research are needed.   As an expressive Arab proverb declares for those who are over-impulsive or too zealously random—"He has all things who waits."   Let us wait, therefore, in faith and in confidence, but at the same time let us work with discretion, charity, and zeal.

school two hundred and sixty members.   Though they are taught the doctrines of the Christian religion, and repeated to me long passages of Holy Scripture, *none are baptized Christians; they are deterred from taking this step, as I am informed, by fear of persecution.*"—"A Pastoral Letter," by C. W. Sandford, D.D., p. 28.   London, 1879.

[1] A new crisis has arisen . . . It is found to the sorrow and shame of many that the spiritual freedom of the Church, together with the actual jurisdiction of its episcopate, is practically extinct.   And, having been forced by the invasion and active powers of these evils to investigate more closely the whole history and condition of the Established Church since the Tudor changes, certain other defects and abuses have become evident to the Founders of this Order which urgently call for remedy."—"Statement concerning the Order of Corporate Reunion, A.D. 1877."   See Appendix, No. II.

APPENDIX I.

———

A LIST OF MARTYRS WHO SUFFERED UNDER QUEEN ELIZABETH.

"What Christian can be found who after reading the well-substantiated narratives of their pitiful sufferings, their ardent zeal for the souls of others, their joyous endurance of excruciating trials, and their fortitude in approaching a death of peculiar agony, could dare to deny their genuine title to the martyr's crown? Through much tribulation we must enter into the kingdom of God; and well will it be for us, if we have marched as far as that noble army on the royal way of the holy Cross."—*The Church Quarterly Review*, vol. viii. pp. 124, 125. London, 1879.

———

Cuthbert Maine, priest, born at Yarlston, near Barnstaple, Devonshire. Student of St. John's College, Oxford, and, after his conversion, of Douay College. Apprehended at Volveden, near Truro, tried at Launceston, and condemned for high treason; hung, drawn, and quartered at Launceston, November 29, 1577.

John Nelson, priest, son of Sir N. Nelson, Knt., born at Shelton, near York. Student at Douay. Taken prisoner in London, condemned for denying the queen's supremacy, and executed in the usual manner as a traitor at Tybourne, February 3, 157⅞.

Thomas Sherwood, scholar, born in London; educated at Douay. Apprehended, tried, and condemned in London for denying the queen's supremacy; executed at Tybourne, being cut down while yet alive, dismembered, disembowelled, and quartered on February 7, 157⅞.

Everard Hanse, priest, was born in Northamptonshire; educated at Cambridge, and ordained a clergyman of the Church of England. A convert, studied at Rheims, and was ordained a Roman Catholic priest on March 25, 1581. He was apprehended while visiting prisoners in the Marshalsea prison, and cast into Newgate amongst thieves, and loaded with irons. He was condemned for high treason and sentenced to be hung, drawn, and quartered. He suffered at Tybourne on July 31, 1581.

Edmund Campion, priest, S.J., was born in London; educated first at Christchurch Hospital; student of St. John's College, Oxford; ordained deacon of the Church of England.   After his conversion he studied at Douay, was admitted into the Society of Jesus at Rome, in 1573.   Coming to England in 1580, he laboured in his vocation for thirteen months, and was taken at the house of Mr. Yates of Lyford.   He was brought to London, and after being cruelly racked and tortured, was arraigned and condemned for high treason, but offered life and one hundred pounds a year if he would change his religion.   He suffered in the usual manner, being hung, disembowelled, and quartered at Tybourne, December 1, 1581, aged forty-two.

Ralphe Sherwine, priest.   He was born at Rodesley, near Langford, Derbyshire.   Student and Fellow of Exeter College, Oxford.   A convert in 1575, and studied at Douay until he was made priest in 1577.   On his return to England he was soon after taken in London, in November 1580.   After being twice cruelly racked and imprisoned for seven months, he was arraigned and condemned for high treason.   Six months afterwards he was martyred by being hung, drawn, and quartered at Tybourne on December 1, 1581.

Alexander Brian, priest, S.J., was born in Dorsetshire, and studied at Hart Hall, Oxford ; a convert, and afterwards a student of Douay, A.D. 1576 ; returned to England a priest in 1579, and apprehended in London 28th April 1581.   After cruel racking and torturing, he was condemned and sentenced as a traitor to be hung, disembowelled, and quartered, which sentence was executed upon him at Tybourne, December 1, 1581.   Before his death he was admitted into the Society of Jesus.

John Paine, priest, born in Northamptonshire.   Admitted into the English College at Douay in 1575 ; ordained priest the following year, and sent upon the English mission.   He resided chiefly at the house of Lady Petre in Essex, was apprehended in 1581, and brought to the Tower of London, where he was cruelly racked.   He was tried at Chelmsford in Essex, and condemned to suffer for high treason in the usual manner, but offered life if he would go to church.   The sentence was carried out on April 2, 1582.

Thomas Forde, priest, was born in Devonshire ; graduated at Trinity College, Oxford ; took his degree of Master of Arts in 1567, and admitted Fellow of that college soon afterwards.   Became a Roman Catholic and entered the seminary at Douay in 1571 ; ordained priest in 1573.   He returned to England and laboured for some years upon the mission, and was taken, together with Father Campion, in the house of Mr. Yates at Lyford in Berkshire.   He was tried and received sentence of death in London on November 21, 1581, but was not executed until May 28, 1582.

John Shert, priest, was born in Cheshire ; educated at Brazenose College, Oxford, where he took a B.A. degree in 1566.   He became a convert, and studied at Douay, from whence he was sent to Rome, when he was made priest, and thence proceeded to the College at Rheims.   From thence he came to England, in 1579, and laboured in his vocation until he was taken prisoner on July 14, 1581.   He was tried and condemned to suffer as a traitor, which sentence was put into execution at Tybourne on May 28, 1582.

Robert Johnson, priest, was born in Shropshire ; educated at Douay ; was made priest and sent upon the English mission in 1576.   On December 5, 1580, having been previously in some other prison, he was sent to the Tower, and there, at three different times, cruelly racked.   In November following, he was arraigned and condemned, as being a traitor, to be hung, drawn, and quartered, but was not executed until the 28th May 1582.

William Filbie, priest, was a native of Oxford, and educated there at Lincoln College. He became a convert, and went over to Douay or Rheims, where he was made priest in 1581. Returning to England, he was apprehended at the house of Mr. Yates of Lyford at the same time with Father Campion and his companions ; committed to the Tower on July 22, arraigned and condemned the following November 20. For six months he remained in prison, cruelly pinioned with heavy iron manacles, and suffered at Tybourne the usual death of a traitor on May 30, 1582, aged twenty-seven.

Luke Kirby, priest, was born in Yorkshire, either at Durham or Richmond. He was Master of Arts at one of the English Universities, but after his conversion went to Douay, and was made a priest there in 1577. He returned to England, after having been at the English College at Rome for some time, in 1580, and was soon after apprehended and committed to the Tower. There he endured the torture of "the scavenger's daughter." He was sentenced to death at the same time and for the same cause with Father Campion and others, but was not executed until May 28, 1582.

Laurence Richardson, *alias* Johnson, priest, was born in Lancashire ; educated at Brazenose College, Oxford, of which he was a Fellow, but on his conversion went over to the Douay College in 1573, where he was made priest in 1577. He laboured in his native county, Lancashire, until his apprehension in 1581. On November 21 of that year he was condemned to die the death of a traitor, and executed on the 30th of May 1582, being hung, drawn, and quartered at Tybourne.

Thomas Cottam, priest, was born in Lancashire, and educated at Brazenose College, Oxford, where he took his B.A. degree in 1568. For some time afterwards he was a schoolmaster in London, but becoming a Roman Catholic he went over to Douay. From thence he went to Rome and entered the Society of Jesus. He returned to England in 1580, and was taken and tried at Westminster with Father Campion and others. On the 30th of May following (1582), he was executed at Tybourne in the usual manner.

William Lacy, priest, was born at Hanton in Yorkshire, in which county he for some time held a place of trust under Queen Elizabeth. His house was ever open to the seminary priests from abroad, to whom he rendered every assistance in his power. On his wife's death, though now advanced in years, he resolved on dedicating the remainder of his life to God's service as a priest. He went over to Rheims, where he studied divinity, and from thence went to Pont-a-musson in Lorraine, and afterwards to Rome, where he was made priest. Returning to England in 1580, he laboured in his own county of Yorkshire, with great fruit, for about two years. He was apprehended at York on July 22, 1582, and committed to the castle there, and loaded with irons. He was sentenced to die for high treason, and executed at York on August 22, 1582.

Richard Kirkeman, priest, was born at Adingham, in Yorkshire, of a good family. He studied at Douay, and was made priest and sent upon the mission in 1578. He laboured in the northern provinces, where he was stopped upon a journey, near Wakefield, and sent to prison. He was tried at York, where he was condemned for high treason—"First, for being a priest of Douay ;

secondly, for persuading the queen's subjects to the Catholic religion." He was executed in the usual manner at York on August 22, 1582.

James Thompson, priest, was a native of Yorkshire, in the western part near York. He went over to the college at Rheims, was made priest there, and sent on the mission to England in 1581. He was apprehended at York on the 11th of August 1582, and on November 25 was brought to trial and condemned. He received his sentence of death with great joy, and was hung, drawn, and quartered at York on November 28, 1582.

William Hart, priest, was born at Wells in Somersetshire ; educated at Lincoln College, Oxford, where he greatly distinguished himself. From thence he passed over to Douay, and removed with the rest of the students to Rheims in 1578. Afterwards he studied at the English College at Rome, where he was made priest, and sent upon the mission. He laboured chiefly about York, visiting the Catholic prisoners and edifying the faithful by his exceeding charity, zeal, and devotion. He was apprehended with others after assisting at mass at York Castle, but then escaped. He was, however, again taken six months afterwards and imprisoned at York Castle, where he was heavily ironed. He was tried and condemned for high treason, and suffered at York on March 15, 158⅘.

Richard Thirkill, or Thirkeld, priest, was born at Cunsley in the Bishopric of Durham. His early history is uncertain, but it seems that he was advanced in age when he went abroad to Douay and Rheims, and was then made priest in the year 1579. His mission was chiefly in and about York, where he was apprehended on suspicion of being a priest, while visiting a Catholic prisoner. He was confined at Kilcote prison, but removed to York Castle, and from thence to trial and execution. He suffered in the usual manner for high treason on May 29, 1583.

John Slade was born in Dorsetshire, and after his education at home became a student at Douay. Returning to England, and, on account of his religion, being unable to exercise his talent as a lawyer, he became a schoolmaster. He was apprehended for zealously maintaining the Old Religion and denying the queen's supremacy, and tried and condemned at Winchester. He was hung, drawn, and quartered at that city, October 30, 1583.

John Body, M.A., was born at Wells in Somersetshire ; educated at New College, Oxford, where he took his degree, but, disliking the Established religion, went over to Douay in May 1577. He was apprehended at the same time as Mr. Slade, with whom he is commonly associated, and tried and condemned with him at Winchester for the same cause. He suffered the traitor's death, with great constancy, at Andover on November 2, 1583.

George Haydock, priest, was son of Evan William Haydock, Esq., of Cottam Hall, near Preston, Lancashire. He was educated at Douay, and afterwards studied at Rome and Rheims, where he was made priest. He returned to England in 158⅓, and had scarcely arrived in London when he was betrayed and apprehended (February 6). He was offered his liberty if he would renounce the Pope. Refusing to do this, he was examined by Popham the Attorney-General, and afterwards by Cecil, and then sent to the Tower. Here he remained for two years, closely confined and watched, and deprived of all human comfort and assistance. He was tried at Westminster on February 6, two years after his apprehension, and condemned for high treason. His execution took place at Tybourne on February 12, 1584.

James Fenn, priest, was born at Montacute in Somersetshire, and educated first at New College, Oxford, and afterwards at Corpus Christi. Being unable to take the Oath of Supremacy tendered him when about to be made a Fellow of his college, he was expelled, and became first a tutor, and afterwards steward to Sir Nicholas Poyntz. He quitted this worldly employment to become a priest, and after studying at Rheims, was ordained there, 1580, and sent upon the English mission. He laboured in Somersetshire for a short time, and was apprehended and sent to Ilchester gaol. From thence he was conveyed to London and imprisoned in the Marshalsea for two years. He was tried and condemned for high treason, and suffered at Tybourne in the usual manner, February 12, 1584.

Thomas Hemerford, or Emerford, was born in Dorsetshire, and educated at Oxford, but being dissatisfied with the Established religion, went to Rheims, and from thence to Rome, where he was ordained a priest, about 1581. Returning to England, he was taken prisoner and tried, and executed at the same time and manner as Mr. Haydock and Mr. Fenn, February 12, 158¾.

John Nutter, priest, was born at Burnley in Lancashire, and educated at the University of Oxford, where he was admitted Bachelor of Divinity, June 13, 1575. Afterwards, on his conversion, he went abroad to Rheims, was made priest in 1582, and sent upon the mission. He was apprehended immediately upon landing in England, and committed to the Marshalsea. After being confined there about a year, he was tried and condemned at Westminster for being a Catholic priest and denying the queen's supremacy. His execution took place at Tybourne, with four other priests, on February 12, 158¾.

John Munden, or Mundyn, priest, was born at Maperton, Dorsetshire; educated at New College, Oxford, where he was admitted Fellow in 1562. He was deprived of his Fellowship for being a Catholic, in 1566, and after many years went abroad, where he was made priest, either at Rheims or Rome, in 1582. He returned to England, and was apprehended for being a priest, about the end of February 158⅔, and was committed to the Tower, where he remained a prisoner for about a year before being brought to trial. On the 6th and 7th of February 158¾, he was tried and condemned, at the same time, and for the same cause, as the other four last treated of. He received his sentence with great joy and cheerfulness, and was executed with his companions at Tybourne on February 12.

William Carter, a printer, was hanged, drawn, and quartered at Tybourne on January 11, 158¾, for printing a "Treatise on Schism" against Catholics attending the Protestant services.

James Bell, priest, was born at Warrington in Lancashire, brought up at Oxford, and ordained in Queen Mary's days. He conformed to the New Religion upon Queen Elizabeth's accession, but was reclaimed in 1581. In 158¾ he was apprehended by a pursuivant, committed to Manchester gaol, and afterwards tried at Lancaster for the supremacy, together with three others. He suffered the usual traitor's death on April 20, 1584, with great joy and constancy, being then sixty years old.

John Finch was born at Eccleston in Lancashire, and brought up a Protestant. He became a zealous and fervent convert, and assisted the clergy in their labours in every possible way. At length he was apprehended, and when neither by threats nor promises they could induce him to "go to church," he was shamefully maltreated, being violently dragged through the streets, his head beating all the way upon the stones.   He was then thrust into a dark, stinking dungeon, with nothing to lie on but the bare wet floor.   Here they kept him for whole weeks together, sometimes for months, not to speak of innumerable other sufferings which he endured for many years.   He was brought to trial at Lancaster for asserting the Pope's supremacy, found guilty of high treason, and executed on the following day, April 20, 1584, together with Mr. Bell.

Richard White, born at Llangdllos, Montgomeryshire, was educated at Cambridge.   He was for some time a schoolmaster, first at Wrexham, and then at Orton, in Flintshire.   He was reconciled to the Catholic Church, and soon afterwards apprehended and committed to Ruthin gaol, where he lay three months loaded with chains.   Being brought to trial, he was offered pardon if he would once go to church, but refusing, was again returned to prison.   The following year he was carried by force to church, and then put in the stocks and suffered many indignities.   He afterwards was cruelly tortured at Bewdley, and finally suffered death for denying the queen's supremacy, at Wrexham in Denbighshire, October 17, 1584, being cut down alive, and butchered in a most cruel manner.

Thomas Alfield, priest, was born in Gloucestershire; studied at Rheims, where he was made priest in 1581.   He came over to England, and was a prisoner in 1582.   He was cruelly tortured in prison for dispersing, with the help of one Thomas Webley, a dyer, copies of Cardinal Allen's " Modest Answer to the English Persecutors," and being brought to trial, together with Webley, they both were condemned and executed at Tybourne on July 5, 1585.   Both were offered life if they would renounce the Pope and acknowledge the queen's spiritual supremacy.

Hugh Taylor, priest, was born at Durham; studied at Rheims, where he was made priest in 1584, and then sent upon the English mission.   He was apprehended in the following year, and tried and condemned at York for being a priest and denying the queen's supremacy.   He was drawn, hanged, and quartered at York, November 26, 1585.

Marmaduke Bowes, a married gentleman, of Angram Grange, near Appleton, in Cleveland, was executed at the same time with Mr. Taylor, for having entertained the latter at his house.

Thomas Crowther, priest, was born in Herefordshire; educated and ordained at Douay in 1575.   He died in the Marshalsea, after about two years' imprisonment.

Edward Poole, priest, sent from Rheims in 1580, was apprehended and cast into prison the same year.

Laurence Vaux, formerly warden of Manchester, sometime convictor of the College of Douay or Rheims, afterwards a canon regular, was cast into the Gatehouse prison, together with N. Tichbourne, Esq., by Aylmer, Bishop of London, in 1580, and died there the same year.

Edward Strancham, whom Stow in his *Annals* calls Edmund Barber, by which name he disguised himself upon the mission, was born at Oxford, and educated at St. John's College, where he took his B.A. degree in 157$\frac{8}{9}$. Soon after he went over to Douay and afterwards to Rheims, where he was ordained priest and sent to England in June 1581. He suffered at Tybourne, January 21, 158$\frac{5}{6}$, for being a priest.

Nicholas Woodfen, *alias* Wheeler, priest, was a native of Leominster in Herefordshire, and studied at Douay and Rheims, where he was made priest and sent upon the mission at the same time with the above Edward Strancham. He was apprehended, tried, and executed at the same time and place (January 21, 158$\frac{5}{6}$) for being a priest.

William Thompson, *alias* Blackburn, made priest at Rheims, was con demned and executed at Tybourne, for remaining in England, on April 20, 158$\frac{5}{6}$.

Richard Lee, *alias* Long, made priest at Lyons, was, together with the above, drawn, hung, and quartered on April 20, 158$\frac{5}{6}$.

Richard Sergeant, *alias* Long, was born in Gloucestershire, and was an alumnus and priest of the college at Rheims. He was apprehended, tried, and condemned simply for being a priest and remaining in the kingdom, and suffered at Tybourne on April 20, 1586.

William Thompson, *alias* Blackburn, priest, born at Blackburn, Lancashire, suffered at the same time and for the same cause as the above.

Robert Anderton, born of an honourable family in Lancaster, and

William Marsden, born in the parish of Goosenor, in the same county, studied together at Rheims. Being made priests, they were sent on the English mission, and were immediately apprehended and soon after found guilty of being priests, and sentenced to die as traitors. They were executed together in the Isle of Wight, on April 25, 1585.

Francis Ingolby, priest, was son of Sir William Ingolby, Knt., born at Ripley, Yorkshire, ordained at Rheims, and sent to England in 1584. He suffered at York on June 3, 1586.

John Finglow, or Fingley, was born at Barmby, in Yorkshire; educated and made priest at Rheims, on March 25, 1581. He was sent upon the English mission in the April following, and apprehended and committed to York gaol. He suffered at York, August 8, 1586.

John Sandys was born at Chester, made priest at Rheims, and sent to England in 1584. He was apprehended, tried, and condemned for being a priest, and executed at Gloucester on August 11 or 12, 1586.

John Lowe, born in London, was for some time a minister of the Established Church, but being converted went to Douay College, and afterwards to Rome, where he was made priest and sent upon the English mission. He was apprehended, tried, and condemned for his priestly character and functions, and executed at Tybourne, October 8, 1586.

John Adams, born at Martin's Town in Dorsetshire, was ordained at Rheims and sent to England in 1581. He was banished in 1585, but returned and was again apprehended.   He was condemned solely for being a priest, and was executed at Tybourne, October 8, 1586.

Richard Dibdale, priest, born in Worcestershire, alumnus and priest of the college at Rheims ; sent on the English mission in 1585 ; apprehended, tried, condemned, and executed for his priestly character and functions at Tybourne, October 8, 1586.

Mrs. Margaret Clitheroe, gentlewoman, was pressed to death at York, for harbouring and relieving priests, on March 26 (or 25), either in 1586 or the foregoing year.

Robert Bickerdike, gentleman, born at Low Hall in Yorkshire, was executed at York for refusing to go to the Protestant Church, in October or July 1586, or the foregoing year.

Richard Langley, Esq., born at Grinthorp in Yorkshire, was executed at York, for harbouring and assisting priests, on December 1, 1586.

Thomas Pilchard, priest, born at Battle in Sussex ; educated at Douay, made priest, and sent upon the mission in 1583.   He was committed to prison and banished in 1585, but returned, and was again apprehended, tried, and condemned for being a priest.   He was executed at Dorchester, March 21, 1587.

Edmund Sykes, priest, born at Leeds in Yorkshire ; educated at Rheims, made priest, and sent to England in 1581.   He was banished the same year, but returning was taken again, and arraigned and condemned for high treason, and executed at York, March 23, 1587.

Robert Sutton, priest, born at Burton-upon-Trent ; studied at Oxford and afterwards at Douay, where he was made priest and sent upon the mission, 157¾.   He was apprehended, and suffered death, for being a priest, at Stafford, July 27, 1587.

Stephen Rowsham, priest, was born in Oxfordshire and brought up at Oxford, where he was for some time minister of the Church of St. Mary.   On his conversion he went to Rheims, was made priest, and sent upon the mission in 1582.   He was taken and imprisoned in the Tower in the dungeon called "Little Ease" for eighteen months, and afterwards banished in 1585. Returning to England, he was again apprehended, and sentenced to die for high treason.   He suffered with wonderful constancy, at Gloucester, either in March or July 1587.

John Hambley, priest, born at Exeter, alumnus and priest of Douay, and sent upon the mission 1585.   He was apprehended, tried, and sentenced to die for being a priest, but was offered his life and a good living if he would conform to the Established religion.   He suffered with great constancy, at York, September 9, 1587.

George Douglas, priest, a Scotchman, suffered at York with the above, on the same day and for the same cause.

Alexander Crowe,[1] priest, was born in Yorkshire, made priest at Rheims,

---

[1] See *Historical Sketches of the Reformation*, pp. 385-397.   London, 1879.

and sent to England in 1584. He was condemned for his priestly character and functions, hanged, drawn, and quartered at York, November 30, 1586.

Nicholas Garlick, priest, was born at Vinting in Glossopdale, Derbyshire; studied and made priest at Rheims; suffered for his religion and character at Derby, July 24, 1588.

Robert Ludlam, priest, was born near Sheffield; studied and made priest at Rheims; and was apprehended, tried and condemned at the same time and for the same cause as Mr. Garlick, July 24, 1588.

Richard Simpson (sometime a minister), priest,[1] executed at the same time at Derby, in 1588.

William Dean, priest, executed at Mile End, London, August 28, 1588.

William Gunter, priest, executed on the same day.

Robert Morton, priest, executed in Lincoln's Inn Fields on the same day.

Thomas Halford, son of a minister, ordained priest at Rheims; executed on the same day at Clerkenwell.

James Claxton, ordained priest at Rheims; executed near Hounslow on the same day.

Robert Leigh, priest, executed at Tybourne with five Catholic laymen and Mistress Margaret Ward, on August 30, 1588.

William Way, a Cornishman and a priest, was executed at Kingston-on-Thames in Surrey, October 1, 1588.

Robert Wilcox, Edward Campion, and Christopher Buxton, priests, were likewise executed.

Robert Widmerpool of Widmerpool, Nottinghamshire, gentleman, tutor to the Earl of Northumberland, about the same time.

Ralph Crocket and Edward James, priests, at Chichester, October 1, 1588.

John Robinson, priest.

William Hartley, priest, executed October 5, 1588, in his mother's presence, near Bankside.

John Weldon, priest, executed the same day.

Richard Williams, priest.

Robert Sutton, schoolmaster, executed at Clerkenwell.

Edward Burden and John Hewitt, priests, executed at York, October 5, 1588.

William Lamplough, layman, suffered at Gloucester in 1588.

Robert Dalby and John Amias, priests, on March 16, 1598, suffered at York.

Richard Yaxley of Lincolnshire, and George Nichols of Oxford, priests, executed at Oxford, July 5, 1589.

Thomas Belson of Brill, Bucks, gentleman, executed at Oxford, July 5, 1589.

Humphrey Pritchard, layman, executed at Oxford, a servant to Belson, suffered on the same day.

William Spencer, priest, executed at York, September 24, 1589.

Robert Hardesty, layman, at York, at the same time.

Christopher Bayles, priest, executed at Fleet Street, London, March 4, 1590.

Nicholas Horner, layman, executed at Smithfield, March 4, 1590.

[1] It should be noted that all the priests in this list were drawn, hung, dismembered, beheaded, and quartered.

Alexander Blake, layman, executed at Gray's Inn Lane, March 4, 1590.

Miles Gerard and Francis Dickenson, priests, suffered at Rochester on April 30, 1590.

Edward Johnes, priest, executed at Fleet Street, London, May 6, 1590.

Anthony Middleton, priest, executed at Clerkenwell, May 6, 1590.

Edmund Duke, priest, suffered at Durham, May 27, 1590.

John Hogg, priest, suffered at Durham, May 27, 1590.

Richard Holliday, priest, suffered at Durham, May 27, 1590.

Richard Hill, priest, suffered at Durham, May 27, 1590.

Robert Thorp, priest, hung, drawn, and quartered at York, May 31, 1591.

Thomas Watkinson, yeoman, hanged at York at the same time.

Mountford Scott and George Beesley, priests, executed at Fleet Street, London.

Robert Dickenson, priest, executed at Winchester, July 7, 1591.

Ralph Milner, layman of Winchester, suffered at the same time and place.

William Pikes, layman of Dorchester, suffered there for denying the queen's supremacy.

Edmund Jennings,[1] priest, suffered at Gray's Inn Fields, December 10, 1591.

Swithin Wells, gentleman, suffered at the same place.

Eustachius White, priest, suffered at Tybourne, on December 10, 1591.

Polydore Plasden, priest, suffered at Tybourne, on December 10, 1591.

Bryan Lacey, layman, suffered at Tybourne, on December 10, 1591.

John Mason, layman, suffered at Tybourne, on December 10, 1591.

Sydney Hodgson, layman, suffered at Tybourne, on December 10, 1591.

William Paterson, priest, at Tybourne, January 22, 1592.

Thomas Pormorte, St. Paul's Churchyard, London, February 8, 1592.

Robert Ashton, gentleman, suffered at Tybourne, June 23, 1592.

Edward Waterson, priest, suffered at Newcastle, January 7, 1593.

James Bird, gentleman, suffered at Winchester, Ladyday, 1593.

Anthony Page, priest, was hung, drawn, and quartered at York, April 20, 1593.

Joseph Lampton, priest, at Newcastle, July 27, 1593.

William Davies, priest, at Beaumaris, July 21, 1593.

John Speed, layman, at Durham, February 4, 1594.

William Harington, priest, at Tybourne, February 18, 1594.

John Cornelius, priest,[2] at Dorchester, July 4, 1594.

Thomas Bosgrave, gentleman, at Dorchester, July 4, 1594.

Terence Carey, layman, at Dorchester, July 4, 1594.

Patrick Salmon, at Dorchester, July 4, 1594.

John Bost, priest, suffered at Durham, July 19, 1594.

John Ingram, priest, suffered at Newcastle, July 25, 1594.

George Swallowell, sometime a minister, executed at Darlington in 1594.

Edward Osbaldeston, priest, executed at York in 1594.

Robert Southwell, priest, at Tybourne (see pp. 317–322) in 1595.

Alexander Rawlins, priest, at York in 1595.

Henry Walpole, priest, at York (see pp. 322–325) in 1595.

James Atkinson, layman, in 1595.

William Freeman, priest, at Warwick in 1595.

George Errington, gentleman, suffered at York in 1596.

William Knight, yeoman, suffered at York in 1596.

---

[1] See *Historical Sketches of the Reformation*, pp. 361–382. London, 1879.

[2] To the case of Father Cornelius, and to that of several others in this list, special reference has been made in the body of this book.

William Gibson, yeoman, suffered at York in 1596.
Henry Abbott, yeoman, suffered at York in 1596.
William Andleby, priest, suffered at York in 1597.
Thomas Warcopp, gentleman, suffered at York in 1597.
Edward Fullthorpe, gentleman, suffered at York in 1597.
John Britton, gentleman, suffered at York in 1598.
Peter Snow, priest, suffered at York in 1598.
Ralph Grimstone, gentleman, suffered at York in 1598.
John Jones, priest, suffered at St. Thomas' Watering in 1598.
Christopher Robinson, priest, at Carlisle in the same year.
Richard Horner, priest, at York in 1598.
Matthias Harrison, priest, at York in 1599.
John Lyon, yeoman, at Oakham in 1599.
James Dowdall, merchant, at Exeter in the same year.

In the year 1600 the following priests were executed :—
Christopher Wharton, at York.
Thomas Sprott, at Lincoln.
Thomas Hunt, at Lincoln.
Robert Nutter, at Lancaster.
Edward Thwing, at Lancaster.
Thomas Pallasor, at Durham.

And the following laymen :—
John Rigby, at St. Thomas' Watering.
John Norton, at Durham.
John Talbot, at Durham.

In the year 1601 the following priests were executed :—
John Pybush, at St. Thomas' Watering.
Mark Barkworth, at Tybourne.
Roger Filcock, at Tybourne.
Thurston Hunt, at Lancaster.
Robert Middleton, at Lancaster.

And the following laity :—
Ann Line, gentlewoman, at Tybourne.
Nicholas Tichbourne, at Tybourne.
Thomas Hackshott, at Tybourne.

In 1602 four priests were executed, viz. :—
James Harrison, at York.
Thomas Tichbourne, at Tybourne.
Robert Watkinson, at Tybourne.
Francis Page, at Tybourne.

And the following laymen :—
Anthony Batty, gentleman, at York.
James Duckett, bookseller, at Tybourne.

And in 1603, one priest, William Richards, was drawn, hung, dismembered, disembowelled, and quartered at Tybourne.

APPENDIX II.

SOCIETIES RELATING TO REUNION.

No. I.—ASSOCIATION FOR THE PROMOTION OF THE UNITY OF CHRISTENDOM.

(ESTABLISHED SEPTEMBER 8TH, 1857, FEAST OF THE NATIVITY OF THE BLESSED VIRGIN MARY.)

AN Association has been formed under the above title, to unite in a bond of intercessory prayer members both of the clergy and laity of the Roman Catholic, Greek, and Anglican Communions. It is hoped and believed that many, however widely separated at present in their religious convictions, who deplore the grievous scandal to unbelievers, and the hindrance to the promotion of the truth and holiness among Christians, caused by the unhappy divisions existing amongst those who profess to have "One Lord, One Faith, One Baptism," will recognise the consequent duty of joining their intercession to the Redeemer's dying prayer, "That they all may be One, as Thou, Father, art in Me, and I in Thee, that they also may be One in Us, that the world may believe that Thou hast sent Me." To all, then, who, while they lament the divisions among Christians, look forward for their healing mainly to a corporate reunion of those three great bodies which claim for themselves the inheritance of the priesthood and the name of Catholic, an appeal is made. They are not asked to compromise any principles which they rightly or wrongly hold dear. They are simply asked to unite for the promotion of a high and holy end, in reliance on the promise of our Divine Lord, that "whatsoever ye shall ask in prayer, believing, ye shall receive"; and that "if two of you agree on earth as touching anything that they shall ask, it shall be done for them of My Father Who is in heaven." The daily use of a short form of prayer, together with one "Our Father"—for the intention of the Association—is the only obligation incurred by those who join it; to which is added, in the case of priests, the offering, at least once in three months, of the Holy Sacrifice, for the same intention.

FORM OF PRAYER.

O Lord Jesus Christ, Who saidst unto Thine Apostles, Peace I leave with you, My peace I give unto you; regard not my sins, but the faith of Thy Church; and grant Her that Peace and Unity which is agreeable to Thy Will, Who livest and reignest God for ever and ever, Amen. Our Father, etc.

Note.—In joining the Association, no one is understood as thereby expressing an opinion on any matter which may be deemed a point of controversy,
or on any religious question except that the object of the Association is
desirable.

Those who are desirous of joining the Association are requested to *sign* the
following Declaration printed in italics, *adding the date and their place of
residence in full*, and return it to the Secretary of the A.P.U.C.

DECLARATION :—

"*I willingly join the Association for the Promotion of the Unity of
Christendom, and undertake* [*to offer the Holy Sacrifice once in three months
and* ¹] *to recite daily the above prayers for the intention of the same.*"

Signature_____

Address_____

Date_____

N.B.—The names of members will not be made public.
All baptized persons are eligible to become members of the Association.

No. II.—THE HOME REUNION SOCIETY.

OFFICE—DEANS' YARD, WESTMINSTER, S.W.

"That they all may be One."—*S. John* xvii. 21.

RULES AND CONSTITUTION.

I. This Society shall be called "The Home Reunion Society."

II. The purpose of this Society shall be to present the Church of England
in a conciliatory attitude towards those who regard themselves as outside her
pale, so as to lead towards the Corporate Reunion of all Christians holding
the doctrines of the Ever-Blessed Trinity and the Incarnation and Atonement
of our Lord Jesus Christ. The Society, though it cannot support any scheme
of comprehension compromising the three Creeds, or the Episcopal constitution
of the Church, will be prepared to advocate all reasonable liberty in matters
not contravening the Church's Faith, Order, or Discipline.

III. The action of the Society will comprehend—

1. Special private prayer for Unity as the first duty of all who desire
Reunion.
2. Special public services with Sermons on Christian Unity, and the
frequent use of the " Prayer for Unity" from the Office for the
Accession in the Prayer-Book.
3. The removal of all defects and abuses in the practical working of the
Church's system which may justly give offence to Nonconformists.

¹ Lay persons will erase the words in brackets.

4. Lectures on the history, doctrines, and formularies of the Church of England, and the circulation of books and papers likely to advance the purpose of the Society.

5. The promotion of freer social intercourse between Churchmen and Nonconformists.

6. The appointment of Committees to arrange for Conferences with . Nonconformists, in furtherance of the purpose of the Society.

No. III.—STATEMENT CONCERNING THE ORDER OF CORPORATE REUNION.

(FOUNDED SEPTEMBER 8TH, A.D. 1877.)

"That they all may be One."

IT has long been felt that there is need of united action for the purpose of supplying certain defects, opposing certain abuses, and carrying out certain objects in the Church of England; and this feeling has led to the formation of various Societies, more or less numerous and influential. Such are—The Society for the Propagation of the Gospel; the Church Missionary Society; the English Church Union; the Guild of St. Alban; the Home Reunion Society; the Confraternity of the Blessed Sacrament; the Society for the Maintenance of the Faith, and the Association for the Promotion of the Unity of Christendom, all of which extend their operations as far as possible over the entire Anglican Church.

But a new crisis has arisen with which these Societies are powerless to deal; for now it is found, to the sorrow and shame of many, that the spiritual freedom of the Church, together with the actual jurisdiction of its episcopate, is practically extinct. And, having been forced by the invasion and active power of these evils to investigate more closely the whole history and condition of the Established Church since the Tudor changes, certain other defects and abuses have become evident to the Founders of this Order, which urgently call for remedy. The attention of Catholic Churchmen, therefore, is especially invited to the ensuing brief statement of its object and the method by which it desires to work.

The evils deplored, and which have to be contended with, are these :—

1. Extreme confusion in organisation and discipline.
2. Grave diversity of doctrinal teaching.
3. Lapse of spiritual jurisdiction.
4. Loss of the spiritual freedom of the Church.
5. Uncertainty of sacramental status, arising from the long-continued prevalence of shameful neglect and carelessness in the administration of Baptism, contrary to the directions contained in the Book of Common Prayer.
6. Want of an unquestioned Episcopal Succession.

All these defects and evils have been carefully examined into; and, after long and prayerful deliberation, adequate remedies have, by the help of God, been secured. The Rulers of this Order are in a position to satisfy every person who may desire further information, that nothing which is needed for a sound dogmatic basis—actual power of jurisdiction for the Rulers of the Order, spiritual freedom to worship and serve God Almighty as did our fore-fathers, and certain integrity of all sacraments—is wanting to the same.

Not only have the Rulers succeeded in obtaining all these things, but they have carefully done so without adding to the existing confusion, without infringing upon the lawful rights of any, and without hastening that disin-tegrating and destructive process which is rapidly going on around, and which they so unfeignedly deplore.

They therefore affectionately invite all faithful Catholics in the Church of England to examine and study the principles of action of the Order. This can be done by perusal of their Pastoral Letter, and by personal application to their duly-appointed officers. That the work of the Order should be conducted in accordance with the methods laid down, it is necessary that those only should be made acquainted with the details who may be practically concerned in them. As it is desired to interfere with no one who is not willing to co-operate, so it is the strong and solemn determination of the Rulers of the Order not to allow any one not concerned to interfere with them in any way. If this great work be of God, as it is believed to be, then by His help it will prosper. If not, it will soon enough come to nought without the intervention, opposition, or contrivance of man.

Finally, attention is called to the fact that certain defects and misunder-standings which have hitherto beset the path of Churchmen have constituted very serious obstacles and hindrances to the attainment of corporate reunion with other portions of the One Family of God. These defects and misunder-standings are now, thanks be to the Blessed and Adorable Trinity !- entirely obviated in the persons of all who enter this Order. For twenty years, thousands of faithful Christians have been unceasingly praying for the restoration of corporate reunion to the Churches of Christ ; so that many cannot but regard the formal foundation and successful institution of this Order as a direct answer to these prayers.

Ad majorem Dei gloriam.

No. IV.—ASSOCIATION OF PRAYERS FOR THE RETURN OF THE SEPARATED PORTIONS OF CHRISTENDOM TO CATHOLIC UNITY.

(FOUNDED, A.D. 1877.)

OFFICE—ST. ETHELREDA'S CHURCH, ELY PLACE, HOLBORN, W.C.

THE establishment of an Association of Prayers for the return of the separated Churches of the East, especially of the Greco-Russian Church, to Catholic Unity, was the dying legacy to the Barnabite Order of the late saintly Father Schouvaloff, himself a Barnabite and a Russian convert.

In introducing this Association into England, it is proposed to include in its intention all the separated portions of Christendom, particularly the Anglican and other Christian bodies of this country.

With a view to this the following petition was laid before Our Holy Father, to which His Holiness was graciously pleased to give a favourable reply :—

" MOST HOLY FATHER,—Prostrate at the feet of your Holiness, Father

Tondini of the Barnabite Order, at present resident in England, desires humbly to state that the 'ASSOCIATION OF PRAYERS FOR THE RETURN OF THE NON-UNITED CHURCHES OF THE EAST, AND ESPECIALLY OF THE GRECO-RUSSIAN CHURCH, TO CATHOLIC UNITY,' as expressly sanctioned and enriched with indulgences by your Holiness, and warmly recommended by many of the bishops, is already under their protection widely spread, having been established in many of the Dioceses of France, Italy, Spain, Belgium, and Austria, especially in her Sclavonic provinces.

"Your humble petitioner, considering that if our Lord, in His mercy, moved by many prayers, should vouchsafe to restore England to Catholic Unity ; owing to her influence and dominion over so many and such vast regions of the world ; she might become a powerful instrument of Divine Providence in the fulfilment of the words of our Redeemer, 'THERE SHALL BE ONE FOLD AND ONE SHEPHERD ;' and seeing the happy effects which have been produced, not only on Catholics but on non-Catholics as well, by the high praise and hopes which your Holiness has lately expressed in regard of England ; asks once more a special Benediction from your Holiness on the above ASSOCIATION OF PRAYERS, earnestly requesting your approval, that this work, already recommended by many of the Catholic Bishops of the United Kingdom, and especially by His Eminence the Archbishop of Westminster, may be extended so as to include in its intention, not only the non-Catholics of the East, but also all Christians now separated from the CENTRE OF UNITY, and more especially the Anglicans and others of these Kingdoms.

"BENEDICAT ET EXAUDIAT VOS DEUS.

"13 MAII., 1877.   "PIUS. P. P. IX."

A Mass, together with prayers for this intention, as given below, is said every Saturday at 10 o'clock in the Church of St. Ethelreda, Ely Place, Holborn ; where communications may be addressed to the Rev. F. Tondini of the Barnabite Order, chief promoter of the Association, or to the Rev. F. Lockhart of the Order of Charity.

In the night before His Passion our Divine Redeemer prayed, saying : "*Holy Father, keep them in Thy Name whom Thou hast given Me, that they who believe in Me may be One in Us ; that the world may believe that Thou hast sent Me.*"   All are hereby invited to unite daily in this intention of the Divine Head of the Church.

PRAYER FOR THE RESTORATION OF ENGLAND, SCOT-LAND, AND WALES, AND OF THE NON-CATHOLICS OF IRELAND, TO CATHOLIC UNITY.

O merciful God, let the glorious intercession of Thy Saints assist us ; particularly the most Blessed Virgin Mary, Mother of Thy only begotten Son, and Thy Holy Apostles, Peter and Paul, to whose patronage we humbly recommend our country.   Be mindful of our fathers, Eleutherius, Celestine, and Gregory, Bishops of the Holy City ; of Patrick and Palladius, Augustine, Columba, and Aidan, who delivered to us inviolate the faith of the holy Roman Church.   Remember our holy martyrs, who shed their blood for Christ ; especially our first martyr, St. Alban, and Thy most glorious Bishop, St. Thomas of Canterbury.   Remember all those holy confessors, bishops, and kings, all those holy monks and hermits, all those holy virgins and widows, who made this once an Island of Saints illustrious by their glorious merits and virtues. Let not their memory perish from before Thee, O Lord, but let their supplication enter daily into Thy sight ; and do Thou, Who didst so often spare Thy sinful people for the sake of Abraham, Isaac, and Jacob, now also, moved by the prayers of our fathers reigning with Thee, have mercy upon us, save Thy people, and bless Thine inheritance : and suffer not those souls to perish, which Thy Son hath redeemed with IIis most precious blood. Who liveth and reigneth with Thee, world without end. Amen.

WESTMINSTER, *May* 22, 1877.

We hereby approve and sanction for this Diocese the "Association of Prayers for the Return of the Separated Portions of Christendom to Catholic Unity" ; and we pray that the Holy Spirit of God may gather them once more into the only true fold.

HENRY EDWARD,
Cardinal Archbishop of Westminster.

APPENDIX III.

HAVING made inquiries concerning the remarkable cures which took place in London in the spring of 1879, I am favoured with permission—for which I am truly obliged — to publish the following letter from Lady Gertrude Douglas :—

ST. VINCENT'S HOME, HARROW ROAD, W.,
November 15, 1879.

DEAR DR. LEE,— John McCarthy, aged 13, was completely cured of paralysis of the spine and legs, on the 25th of March 1879, at the end of a Novena to Our Lady of Lourdes, having drunk of the water and been sprinkled with it for nine days. The occasion of the laying of the foundation-stone of the Church dedicated to the Immaculate Conception, under the title of Our Lady of Lourdes. The ceremony took place on the afternoon of the 24th, and the Novena ended on the 25th, when at 5 A.M., suddenly, and without any intermediate convalescence, John McCarthy, for a year previously a helpless cripple, got up and dressed himself and appeared to us all completely cured. He has never suffered the least relapse, and can walk and jump and play as well as any child in the school. On the same day, at about 8.30 A.M., James Dwyer, aged 10, recovered also suddenly from paralysis of the sciatica nerves, which had rendered him a cripple for three weeks. He was carried to church, made his first Communion in front of the Altar of Our Lady of Lourdes, and after the Holy Communion had been given him, and that he had received the water of Lourdes, he got up from his chair and knelt by himself before the altar. He was also completely and instantaneously cured, and has never suffered the least relapse.

These are the facts, dear Dr. Lee, which I send you according to your request. For any further explanation or references you might require, I can only refer you to His Eminence the Cardinal Archbishop.—Believe me, Yours truly,

GERTRUDE DOUGLAS.

INDEX.

E

F

MORRISON AND GIBB, PRINTERS, EDINBURGH.

www.ingramcontent.com/pod-product-compliance
Lightning Source LLC
Chambersburg PA
CBHW030814110726
47900CB00006B/1615